The Pure Food, Drink,
and Drug Crusaders, 1879–1914

The Pure Food, Drink, and Drug Crusaders, 1879–1914

by
LORINE SWAINSTON GOODWIN

McFarland & Company, Inc., Publishers
Jefferson, North Carolina, and London

Library of Congress Cataloguing-in-Publication Data

Goodwin, Lorine Swainston, 1925–
    The pure food, drink, and drug crusaders, 1879–1914 / by Lorine
  Swainston Goodwin.
       p.   cm.
    Includes bibliographical references and index.
    ISBN 0-7864-0618-6 (library binding : 50# alkaline paper) ∞
    1. Food adulteration and inspection — United States — History.
2. Consumer protection — United States — History.   3. Women social
reformers — United States — History. 4. Food adulteration and
inspection — Law and legislation — United States — History.   5. Food
law and legislation — United States — History. 6. Beverages — Law and
legislation — United States — History. 7. Drugs — Law and legislation —
United States — History. 8. United States. Food and Drugs Act —
History.   I. Title
HD9000.9.U5G66 1999
363.19'0973 — dc21

                                             99-28286
                                                CIP

British Library Cataloguing-in-Publication data are available

Manufactured in the United States of America

McFarland & Company, Inc., Publishers
  Box 611, Jefferson, North Carolina 28640
    www.mcfarlandpub.com

To Ray

Contents

Preface

The subject of pure food, drink, and drugs carries particular pertinence for a society obsessed with the quality of its food supply and frustrated by its attempts to stem substance abuse. Our health and well-being are in jeopardy, the moral infrastructure of our society is being compromised, and our existing institutions are inadequate to cope with the problems related to the food we eat, the beverages we drink, and the drugs we use.

If historians are correct in asserting that we can learn from the past, perhaps we can derive ideas or at least draw inspiration from others who faced a similar situation. In the closing decades of the nineteenth century no effective government agency existed to protect the consumer. Contamination, adulteration, and fraud were so prevalent that the American people could not determine which food, drinks, and drugs were safe to use. This condition was undermining the physical, mental, and moral health of the nation and no one seemed able or willing to do anything constructive about it. With a dedication that has rarely been equaled, the women of America organized against intolerable conditions under seemingly intractable opposition to remedy the situation. The focus of this book is their fight to control the quality of their food, drink, and drug supply, and their fight to stamp out drug abuse. Perhaps the faith and hope of these crusaders, their energy and innovation, their altruism and determination are what is lacking today.

This study of their experiences is a product of ten years of extensive research, careful consideration, and conscientious writing. It has required searching numerous local, state, and national archives, examining hundreds of obscure manuscripts, surveying the primary evidence used by other historians, and developing a viable framework within which to understand the meaning of the data.

1

Much of the evidence was gleaned from the records the crusaders generated themselves — from the journals of women's organizations, women's magazines, letters, official documents, newspapers, and numerous other manuscripts. The interpretations are my own, but they coincide fairly closely with the evaluations that the crusaders themselves made of their own activities. Because such evaluations challenge accepted historical opinion, they may attract controversy. I accept responsibility for them and welcome sincere criticism.

An introduction to the book defines the scope and direction of the study, gives a brief review of the available pure food, drink, and drug literature, and explains some of the terms the crusaders used. From this point the book is divided into three main parts. Part One investigates the roots of pure food, drink, and drug activism in the last quarter of the nineteenth century, when women were organizing into local and state societies to improve the quality of their food, drink, and drug supply. It argues that the crusade was not a mere impulse of the opening decade of the twentieth century, but the response of American women to a situation they found intolerable. Part Two discusses the breadth and nature of women's involvement in the national crusade. It explores the extent to which women were willing to cooperate across lines of affluence, religion, occupation, ethnic origin, and region to protect their homes and communities against adulteration, addiction, and fraud. Part Three explains how the crusaders overcame the industrial and political opposition they encountered, the ways in which they were able to push federal food, drink, and drug regulation through the national Congress, and the processes through which they continued their fight after the law became operative. Following Part Three, a conclusion provides a brief commentary on the significance of their experience.

Gathering information for a work of this scope required the help of personnel in numerous archives and libraries across the country. Librarians in the National Archives, various regional archives, and the Library of Congress were particularly helpful in helping me locate and identify sources. I owe debts of gratitude to the staffs of state historical societies in Missouri, Kansas, Alabama, and Idaho; special collections at the Universities of Georgia, Colorado, Mississippi, Idaho, and Washington State; the Denver Public Library, the Wichita City Library, and various other libraries; the archivists in Western Historical Manuscripts at the University of Missouri in Columbia, Missouri, and Brigham Young University in Provo, Utah; Al Epstein at the Frances Willard Memorial Library in

Evanston, Illinois; and Anne Edwards, the interlibrary loan librarian at Ellis Library, University of Missouri.

Professor Eli Zaretsky guided me in evaluation and organization, and Professor David P. Thelen provided much of the intellectual inspiration for the study. Also, I wish to thank Professors Robert Collins, Steve Watts, and particularly John Bullion for constructive criticism and suggestions for revision. To Louanna Furbee for helping me understand the traditional patterns of women's behavior in bonding, groups, and networks, I express my appreciation. Financially, I was assisted by Louis Atherton Travel Grants from the University of Missouri.

My husband, Ray, has been a constant source of support. He has freed up my time for study and writing, has accompanied me on research tours, and has assisted me in countless ways. I owe him my deepest appreciation. Last, I thank my cheering section: my children, grandchildren, sisters, and friends, who encouraged me to complete this project.

Introduction

U nder a likeness of Theodore Roosevelt in the Library of Congress, a plaque lists the Pure Food, Drink, and Drug Act of 1906 as one of the three landmark achievements of his administration. Few authorities disagree. Designed to ensure the safety, accurate labeling, and purity of foods, drinks, and drugs, this law marked the beginning of social legislation to promote the welfare of the general public in the United States. Controversy surrounds the identity and motives of its promoters, the strengths and weaknesses of the bill, and its ultimate effectiveness, but most textbooks rank the legislation high in their list of Progressive Era accomplishments.[1]

This book is about the crusaders who fought to secure and enforce this and related laws. The study focuses primarily on the activities of women because it was among women's groups that I discovered the enthusiasm, energy, persistence, organization, and cohesion that some historians have found lacking in this and other Progressive Era reforms. In addition to examining the origins, campaigns, and continuity of their crusade, the study also explores the struggle for pure food, drink, and drugs. Further, the study examines this struggle in the context of certain issues of identity, social conditions, attitudes, and activity relating to Progressive reform and participatory democracy that have provided fuel for decades of historical debate.

Considering the importance of pure food, drink, and drug legislation, and despite the historical controversies surrounding it, surprisingly little in-depth scholarship is available concerning the subject. Still less has been written on the participation of women in securing the laws. Several historical studies of the 1980s, one by Peter Temin and another by Paul Starr, deal explicitly, but briefly, with the drug regulation aspect only. Temin's study attributes the federal pure food, drink, and drug laws in the

Progressive Era to a combination of three factors: the response to Upton Sinclair's exposure of meat contamination at packinghouses in *The Jungle*, the pressure from interested business groups, and the reorganizational needs of Harvey W. Wiley and the United States Division of Chemistry. Paul Starr's imaginative and comprehensive study of the social transformation of medicine from Colonial times to the present categorizes food and drug regulation as a part of the American Medical Association's successful attempt to dominate all medical-provider services.[2]

Robert Crunden and Arthur and Lila Weinberg have written chapters dealing with the contributions of investigative journalists in alerting the public to the dangers of food adulteration and fraud. Both of these studies address interesting facets of the crusade, but neither traces the origins of pure food, drink, and drug activism, nor considers the role of the consumer.[3]

Accounts which devote more space to pure food, drink, and drugs deal superficially with public involvement. Harvey Washington Wiley's three books — *Harvey W. Wiley: An Autobiography*, *The History of a Crime Against the Food Law*, and *Foods and Their Adulteration* — detail the colorful government chemist's fight against the "special interests" for pure food, drink, and drugs, but his accounts are notably egocentric, providing few clues to Wiley's dependence on consumer groups to influence legislation. In *The Toadstool Millionaires* and its sequel, *The Medical Messiahs*, James Harvey Young presents vivid accounts of proprietary medicine and quackery in America, detailing the involvement of Wiley, other bureaucrats, and a number of federal legislators, including Senators Weldon B. Heyburn (Idaho) and Porter J. McCumber (North Dakota), and Representatives James R. Mann (Illinois) and William P. Hepburn (Iowa). Young mentions collaboration between women-consumer groups and Wiley. He also notes that Wiley gave credit to women's clubs on one occasion, and asserts that women's organizations were "the most important and steadfast of consumers' champions," but, having mentioned their participation, he leaves the women anonymous. The focus of Young's works are in other directions — toward the origin and development of proprietary medicines and quackery in the United States, and in evaluating the concurrent government attempts to regulate those industries.[4]

Perhaps Oscar Anderson's *The Health of a Nation* provides the best portrayal of women's activities. Primarily a biography of Harvey W. Wiley, Anderson's book recognizes that "women's organizations proved surprisingly effective in agitating the question and keeping a constant pressure on legislation." It mentions Alice Lakey, Helen R. Guthrie McNab Miller, and other consumer advocates in several places, but devotes only a few paragraphs to their activities.[5]

Each of these accounts introduce intriguing aspects of pure food and drug history. In addition to contributing valuable data regarding food and drug adulteration and regulation, they detail some of the fears accompanying industrialization, outline the political maneuvering attending legislative attempts, and expose the means through which bureaucratic expertise invaded law enforcement. For these reasons, chapters in this book give attention, in appropriate places, to the positions they advance.

Most of the extant literature builds on prevailing historical opinion which casts the fight for pure food, drink, and drugs as a prototype of democratic reform perverted — as a fragmented, uncoordinated product of status anxiety and a search for order. This body of literature also suggests a conspiracy among large corporations to use the state to suppress competition. Closely related and often combined, such interpretations reflect a pessimistic view of the possibility for real reform. After all, they argue, what did the pure food, drink, and drug law actually accomplish? What remedies remain? In one form or another, are not most, if not all, of the problems still with us today? Relying on bureaucrat-generated documents and accepting statements of involved politicians and businessmen at face value, these interpretations find little evidence of significant public concern before the turn of the century, and that concern expressed only as a limited and short-lived apprehension triggered by muckraking publicity.

Proponents of the status-anxiety thesis maintain that the goals of Progressive Era food, drink, and drug reformers were not to enact laws to protect the public and to restore government to the people. Quite the reverse, in their opinion, federal pure food, drink, and drug legislation was an attempt to serve the interests of a well-educated group of professionals who desired to establish their hegemony in the medical field and of bureaucrats who wanted to validate their legitimacy by conducting government on a business-like basis. Richard Hofstadter considered status anxiety the prime motive in Progressive reform. George E. Mowry saw progressivism as a movement by the middle class to restore its leadership, and Samuel P. Hays felt that progressivism reflected the desire of a select group of urban professionals to make government more efficient. Although neither Hofstadter, Mowry, nor Hays directly addressed food and drug regulation in any detail, their general views have been applied to almost every successive evaluation of food and drug reform.[6]

Robert Wiebe attacked the subject more specifically. He argued that food and drug reform was part of a search for order to serve the interests of a growing number of urban professionals who desired to dominate the medical field, of high-level bureaucrats who tried to rationalize government under their own departments of expertise, and of big businessmen who wanted to protect themselves against the encroachment of small business and regulation from agencies within individual states.[7]

Gabriel Kolko, who saw progressivism as a regrettable triumph of conservatism over liberalism, cited the Meat Inspection Act of 1906 (meat amendment to the Agricultural Appropriation Act) as the "crowning example" of big business initiating and supporting government regulation for the purpose of eliminating competition, and the Pure Food, Drink, and Drug Act as little better. Kolko found that the major meatpackers wanted to extend already considerable government regulation to eliminate "their smaller competitors" and to protect the industry's access to foreign markets. Further they equated the interests of society with the interests of their businesses, and that the leaders of the packing industry eventually headed government agencies in charge of regulating their own firms. Reasoning that through this process "federal regulation of business became federal regulation for business," Kolko dismissed evidence of business opposition to the law as insignificant and consumer pressure as irrelevant. He suggested that similar criteria be applied to the federal Pure Food, Drink, and Drug Act and other Progressive legislation. As a whole, he saw the Progressive Era dominated by political capitalism which "redirected the radical potential of mass grievances and aspirations" away from real reform and toward establishing the primacy of big business.[8]

Despite their usefulness in helping us understand the variety of tangents trailing the crusade for pure food, drink, and drugs, such interpretations leave much that is unexplained. Status anxiety ignores the wide participation of less affluent people and fails to explain the remarkable extent to which people were willing to work together across lines that separated them in the past. A search for order credits professionals and bureaucrats with more influence, unity, and dedication than they were able to muster at the time. Regulation for the benefit of big business does not explain why most of the largest industries who were tagged for regulation fought tooth and nail to shelve, defeat, amend, and circumvent pure food and drug legislation.

This study is unique in approaching the fight for pure food, drink, and drugs from the viewpoint of the general public and in addressing questions pertaining to the mechanisms of popular participation in democratic processes. What social conditions created public demand for pure food and drug legislation? Who were the crusaders? What were their goals? Why the predominance of activity in women's organizations over that in men's organizations? What was the extent of participation? What were the modes of operation? How did innovation, attitudes, rhetoric, organization, membership, momentum, expediencies, coalitions, and opposition affect the course of the crusade? How did the crusaders relate to other Progressive Era reforms and how did the crusade affect the lives of the reformers?

The concern is not so much with social status, success, or failure, as with what triggers mass movements, the extent to which diverse groups of varying backgrounds cooperate to achieve common goals, and how public concern translates into political action. The study deals with the mainstream forces that held the crusade together, insured its continuity, and secured legislation. Presenting new evidence and reevaluating that already used provides a more complete portrayal. It elevates the perception of the crusade from that of a fragmented and poorly organized impulse generated by the elite to an organized crusade of the people.

This study suggests that cooperative effort did make a difference; that public opinion was not uncaring, stupid, or impotent; that the natural response to exploitation was not to accommodate, but to remedy. Participatory democracy was not futile, and a handful of influential men did not dominate reform. In short, the evidence reflects hopefulness, energy, and innovation generated by the crusaders themselves.

This does not imply that I discount either class divisions or achievement. The tendency of industrialization to separate society into classes was a major difficulty that the crusaders worked to overcome. Indeed, organized women felt that bridging class distinctions was a by-product of working together in a common cause, such as the pure food, drink, and drug crusade. Regarding achievement, if the crusaders had left no legacy, their experience would have little lasting interest. This study intends to illuminate a considerable body of accomplishment that we might well consider building upon today.

The study does not approach the pure food, drink, and drug crusade as an aberration. Pure food and drug reform was not an isolated concern, but part and parcel of an entire body of difficulties that American people confronted to make their democratic values operate for the public good. Closely associated and sometimes combined with other Progressive Era reforms, it was a component of a complex mass movement. This movement

gained support from a troubled society where the intrusion of industrialization and commercialization had so disrupted the acceptable norms of
human living and behavior that not merely isolated groups of elites motivated by status anxiety, not simply professional classes trying to assert
dominance, not only business interests trying to control or eliminate competition, but, more significantly, the entire society became involved in trying to cope with the new problems created by technological, industrial,
fiscal, and social change.

I see the crusade as both a powerful magnifier which revealed the
pathogens in American life and a strong magnet which drew participants
into its force field. I do not believe the maladies it exposed and the remedies it attempted have been obscured over time. Its significance for us
today lies in its dynamics and in the standard it projected for meeting the
needs of the consuming public.

This approach draws its inspiration from a strong belief in human
capacity and a faith in the potential of democracy. We hope it will contribute to a growing tradition of exploration into the significance of public participation, altruism, and community effort. Mary Beard's account
of women's reform in municipalities exemplifies this tradition. David Thelen's analyses of Wisconsin and Missouri Progressives, men and women,
who allied as consumer-reformers to maintain their values and dignity in
an industrial society are a landmark study in this area. Anne Firor Scott's
studies illuminate feminist activism among Southern women. Karen Blair's
examination of how women's clubs provided a core of unity and intellec-
tualism that drew their members into reform stands as a vital contribution. Paula Baker's investigation of the domestication of American politics
adds other components.[9]

The Pure Food, Drink, and Drug Crusaders differs from most other
recent feminist analyses in placing its main focus on the value of women's
cooperative efforts, rather than on "first-wave" feminism. The issue addressed
in this study is not the struggle of women to achieve equality, but rather
the struggle of women to protect themselves, their families, and their communities against the undesirable encroachments of the market system.

Although the fight for pure food, drink, and drugs was closely inter-
twined with other Progressive reforms and cannot, and should not, be isolated, I try to limit the discussion to issues addressed in the pure food,
drink, and drug bills — adulterated meat and processed foods; adulterated
milk, juices, soft drinks, liquors, wines, and beer; as well as proprietary
medicines, narcotics, stimulants, and other drugs. I exclude, as outside

the bounds of this study, the home economics, prohibition, and anti-tobacco crusades, except when they contributed directly or interrelated closely to the pure food, drink, and drug crusade.

Sometimes separating the issues is difficult. The Woman's Christian Temperance Union crusaders were among the most avid pure food, drink, and drug advocates, but they focused their primary emphasis on prohibition. They worked for pure food, drink, and drug laws and for prohibition laws at the same time. Often they did not isolate pure food, drink, and drug issues in their own minds, in their rhetoric, or in their activities. To them, the crusade against adulterated food and dangerous drugs was an integral part of temperance. In the same vein, many clubwomen considered the fight for pure food, drink, and drugs as part of their domestic science program. In selecting the evidence pertaining to pure food, drink, and drugs, I consider the context of the issues women were addressing at the time and the activities in which they were engaged.

The terms "crusade," "movement," "agitation," "pure food," and "patent medicine," as used by the crusaders, require explanation. "Crusade" referred to the collective activities of reformers for a specific cause. Besides the "pure food, drink, and drug crusade," reformers spoke of the "criminal justice crusade," the "civil service crusade," the "conservation crusade," the "social purity crusade," the "city beautiful crusade," or the "save the birds crusade." When applied to the fight for pure food, drink, and drugs, crusade was an appropriate designation. Progressive reformers often spoke of their cause in terms of righteousness and pursued it with religious zeal.

The term "movement" might seem synonymous with "crusade," but it usually implied a more comprehensive and, perhaps, a more evolutionary, mode of activity. Reformers joined and supported the "women's movement," the "temperance movement," the "political reform movement," the "social justice movement," and clumped them together under the "Progressive movement" designation.

"Agitation" designated reform activities, including lobbying, trying to influence voters, distributing propaganda, obtaining newspaper space for articles, conducting demonstrations, circulating petitions, exhibiting displays at fairs, or any means intended to advance their cause. Rather than stirring up trouble, agitation meant soliciting and organizing public support. Stepping up agitation referred to redoubling efforts and promoting reform.

From the beginning of the crusade, "pure food" was an abbreviation for pure food, drink, and drugs. Women's groups, magazine and newspaper articles, and legislators often referred to the issue as "pure food," when drinks and drugs were intended to be included. The Pure Food, Drink, and Drug Act was commonly known as the Pure Food Act and was recorded as such in the margins of the *United States Statutes at Large*, although its official title was "An Act for preventing the manufacture, sale or transportation of adulterated or misbranded or poisonous or deleterious foods, drugs, medicines, and liquors, for regulating traffic therein, and for other purposes."[10]

As various groups and leaders pointed out, "patent medicine" was a commonly used misnomer. The term "patent medicine" survived from the time when rulers granted permits, or "patents," to monopolies for manufacturing secret medical compounds. Such preparations were secret concoctions and their formulas carefully guarded. To patent a preparation in the United States required disclosing the contents, something few manufacturers were willing to do. Some drug companies copyrighted their labels or the name of their product, but most of them found the measure ineffective because the copyright laws were seldom enforced. A more accurate designation for these remedies was "proprietary medicines," or in a negative context, "nostrums." Proprietary, in this context, applied to a product intended for medicinal use and which was produced and marketed under a trade name by a business establishment, or by an individual, either of whom were referred to as "proprietaries."

Changing attitudes toward identifying with the words, "lady," "female," and "woman" also require explanation. In the last decades of the nineteenth century many organized women began to object to the designation of any organization, institution, or undertaking planned or executed by or for women as a "ladies'" or "female" organization. To them, the appellation "ladies" denoted isolation, elitism, the cult of domesticity, the subjection of women, and uselessness outside the home. The term "female" pertained to the entire animal kingdom and designated only gender. Applied to women, it had a vague and negative connotation, implying inferiority. Use of the corresponding adjective, "male," pertaining to men's activities and institutions, had become already obsolete and organized women felt that the same criteria should apply to the adjective "female." A club or union member preferred to be called a "woman." Woman was specific to humans, had come to mean more than gender, and expressed the highest type of the animal kingdom. The word carried the suggestion of an uplifting moral and spiritual force, working for the benefit of society.[11]

This study attempts to preserve the integrity of the crusaders' endeavors. Their opinions deserve respect; their activism, consideration. Whenever practical, the crusaders speak for themselves and relate their own experiences. Their accounts are revealing and colorful, consistently reflecting the thought of their time, occasionally revealing the intensity of their feeling, but, more often than not, understating the value of their contributions. If appraised objectively, their logic makes sense and their assessments are verified by a preponderance of evidence. This is their story.

PART I:
ORIGINS

"Material results are but the tardy sign of invisible activities.
The bullet has started long before the report reaches us."
—*Club Notes*, June 1907

One of the primary considerations in understanding the pure food, drink, and drug crusade is to realize that it did not materialize overnight from nowhere. Dating the beginning of the fight for pure food and drugs after the turn of the twentieth century is clearly too late. Politicians, bureaucrats, and journalists of the early 1900s often wrote of food and drug adulteration as if it was their exclusive discovery. They also saw the pure food, drink, and drug law as the recent fruit of their influence with the legislature and their own efforts in alerting a hitherto disinterested public to the extent of adulteration and fraud. The reverse is nearer the truth. The law was passed by Congress following a long and bitter consumer struggle that politicians and journalists took up only after organized women had laid the infrastructure. A preponderance of the evidence reveals that the demand to improve the quality of food, drink, and drugs gained momentum during the three preceding decades.

Next, we need to realize that the crusade broke loose on multiple fronts simultaneously. Pure food, drink, and drug advocates organized first on local and state levels to cope with problems which affected their community. Although various groups encountered similar situations initially, they responded as individual groups, showing considerable innovation in the methods they employed.

Another element that requires emphasis is the breadth and extent of participation in pure food, drink, and drug activism. Because adulteration and drug dependence were rampant in every part of the country, crusaders in considerable numbers throughout the nation found food, drink, and drug reform necessary to protect themselves, their families, and their neighbors. The crusaders came from a variety of ethnic, social, economic, and geographic backgrounds; they subscribed to diverse religious and political philosophies; they harbored different hopes and aspirations, and they applied various remedies to solve their common problem.

1
The Vanguard

"...the diviner womanhood that shall ere bring in the era of sweeter manners, purer laws."[1]

New York City. December 9, 1884. Fifteen Beekman Hill women officially declared war on the major source of their meat supply. Armed with a state charter designating their organization as The Ladies' Health Protective Association, they targeted a neighboring region extending along First Avenue from Forty-third to Forty-seventh Street—New York City's slaughterhouse district—which they described as a tangle of 55 "rickety, tumbled-down, wooden" sheds, "reeking with filth" from accumulations of refuse and blood of slaughtered animals.[2]

Earlier that year, members of the Association had initiated the first phase of their campaign by demanding removal of manure piles adjacent to the slaughterhouses. For almost a decade, a fertilizer dealer had ripened excrement and offal from the slaughterhouses on flat-bottom scows docked along the East River and in an adjoining 20,000-ton manure pile, measuring 30 feet in height and 200 feet in length. The accumulation generated flies, dust, and drainage that contaminated slaughtered carcasses, created odors so "foul" that residents could not open their windows "even in the dead of summer," and "posed a perpetual threat to the health and comfort" of their homes and their community.[3]

An Association investigation identified the owner as a "brother-in-law of a senator at Albany," who had been able to "defy law and decency" through political connections. The owner explained to representatives of the Association that he could not afford to remove the accumulation because it was of greater value when sold for fertilizer in a rotted state and that on-site aging in piles and scows near the stockyards saved money and facilitated delivery.[4]

When the Association contacted their city health agencies to take action against the fertilizer dealer, delegates found officials at first indifferent and then hostile. Members of the board of health not only refused to order the hazards removed, but they resented any insinuation that they were not performing their duty and attempted to persuade the women against further action. The reaction of these officials reflected their history of noninterference with business operations dating back to shortly after enactment of an 1866 ordinance granting virtual autonomy to the health department.[5]

The New York City Health Department had replaced a corrupt corps of health wardens who functioned as local political bosses within Boss Tweed's Tammany Hall spoils system. It was created through the efforts of a citizen's committee to protect the public against fraud and exploitation, and against courts sympathetic to commercial interests. Stephen Smith, the chairman of the citizen's committee and public health enthusiast, became the board's first president.[6]

By the time The Ladies' Health Protective Association organized in 1884, Tweed no longer controlled the city and Smith had left the board of health to become president of the American Public Health Association. In its support of unhampered economic progress, the Council of Political Reform, which had taken control from Tweed's regime, had distanced itself from public need and pressures that interfered with the free operation of business. Conforming to the Council's policy, the health board refrained from vigorous enforcement of its health protective prerogatives. When he was confronted by representatives of the Health Protective Association, the president of the health board admitted that he had neither visited nor had a report, from the slaughterhouse district for six years.[7]

The Association women were energized to take legal action almost as much by the attitude of the city bureaucrats as by the need to protect their families and the neighborhood from the scows, manure piles, and slaughterhouses. If the designated agency had been willing to order the scows and manure piles removed and had agreed to clean up the slaughterhouse district, the ladies might have been content to return to their "afternoon tea-cup visitations," as one of the health board members suggested, but unable to work through the board of health, the Beekman Hill women found a judge willing to hear the case in the Court of Oyer and Terminer. After a four-day hearing, the court found the scow owner guilty of maintaining a public nuisance and gave him 30 days to remove the accumulation. The owner ignored the court injunction in the same way he had "tossed off" others "holding over him," confident that city enforcement agencies would disregard the new injunction, as they had others in the past. The Beekman Hill women pursued execution of the penalty, forced the owner to comply with the decision, and maintained "constant vigilance" to keep animal waste from building up again in the slaughterhouse district.[8]

The verdict against the fertilizer dealer came as a surprise to the board of health. One member warned the ladies not to "build on their victory." The situation was very unusual, he admonished, they had "better go home" and "not meddle any more in matters that did not concern them." It was then that the Health Protective Association incorporated under state charter and directed their attention toward the rest of the slaughterhouse complex.[9]

The horrors of their designated "jungle" rivaled conditions in the Chicago stockyards portrayed 22 years later by Upton Sinclair. Much of New York City's meat supply, like that of many other cities, reached the stockyards afoot through labyrinths of residential streets, strewing manure and trailing clouds of dust and flies. The remainder came from diseased cows fed on distillery swill in the city's notoriously filthy dairies. Slaughterhouses crowded the animals into cellars, "the air of which was so stifling and fetid that the poor creatures" clambered over each other "in frantic efforts to reach up to the grate for a breath of fresh air." Children "reveled and played" downstream in ditches which drained the slaughterhouses, and, to the horror of the Beekman Hill women, watched the slaughtering processes from outside the doors and pens, becoming so "utterly demoralized that the sight of blood was not more to them than so much running water."[10]

An Association inspection found the pens and slaughtering areas unbelievably filthy. Large suppurating sores covered the hides of cows brought in by the dairies. Excrement and blood plastered the walls and tables. Workers shoveled out manure only when the accumulation prevented movement. Carcasses mingled with filth on the floors until workers hung them to cure on hooks above the curbstones, where the meat collected street dirt and attracted flies. The adjoining rendering works were equally filthy. Delivery men collected waste material, fat, and bones from retail butchers on their rounds, throwing bones and rotting material on the fresh meat, and depositing them at slaughterhouses where they befouled the surroundings.[11]

Neighboring residential regions, including both the slums surrounding the slaughterhouses and the exclusive Beekman Hill area, shared the dust, flies, stench, and disease generated by the slaughterhouses. Wealthy and poor alike ate diseased and contaminated meat processed under these conditions.[12]

Proprietors of the slaughterhouses told the Association that they saw no need for improvement. They were perfectly satisfied with their establishments and had no intention to change. Again, the Association appealed to the board of health and this time persuaded it to send its report to the state legislature. Under constant pressure, the legislature, in June 1885, passed an amendment that restricted slaughterhouses to an area bounded by the Hudson River and Eleventh Avenue between Thirty-ninth and Fortieth Streets. The health department noted some improvement, but complained that universal noncompliance required constant inspection.[13]

Cleaning up the slaughterhouses took years of effort. During the prolonged campaign, new members flocked to the Association. The organization replaced its designation "Ladies'" with "Woman's" to project a more active image and formed specialized legislative and publicity departments designed to combat the slaughterhouse evils. Under the "energetic" administration of its president, Mary E. Trautman, the New York City Woman's Health Protective Association continued to sponsor a succession of bills intended to regulate slaughterhouse procedures. Business interests defeated each bill in the state legislature, but the Association persisted. Eventually, in 1890, it was able to secure the appointment of Charles G. Wilson as president of the New York City health board. Wilson was a successful businessman and a conscientious reformer, described as working hard himself and demanding the same from his inspectors. Unlike previous health board members, he and his inspectors aided the Woman's Health Protective Association, worked beside the women in agitating for legislation, inspired confidence in their undertaking, and released regular reports of the board's activities to the press.[14]

A combination of Wilson's injunctions, the cost of defeating legislation, and adverse publicity wore the opposition down. Addressing his colleagues at an annual convention, the Butchers' Association president advised, "Gentlemen, if we have to pay out all this money we may as well put it into what the women want ... it is the thing that ought to be done." A joint meeting of the executive board of the Woman's Health Protective Association with the executive board of the Butchers' Association agreed that the Protective Association would take no further legislative action if the butchers implemented a list of reforms that the women had prepared. The demands were so great that the slaughterhouse interests decided to tear down the existing facilities and construct a "system of magnificent abattoirs," equipped with all of the machinery "known to modern science," including fertilizer factories, connected with the abattoirs, which daily converted refuse, offal, and bones into fertilizer, and chilling vaults which kept aging meat fresh and clean.[15]

Conditions analogous to those which the Beekman Street women encountered in New York City motivated the formation of neighborhood health protection associations in other locations. With the growth of American cities, the meatpacking industry had centralized in large metropolitan centers where it slaughtered, processed, and distributed fresh, smoked, and canned meat, lard, and commercial grease, converted bones into glue, and sold manure for fertilizer.[16]

In the past, consumers in smaller communities had relied on social constraints to control the quality of their meat. The local butcher bought his cattle, hogs, and poultry from local farmers, slaughtered the animals in local facilities, and cut the meat in his shop. He took pride in his trade. The consumer could observe the processing of his product. As Mark Sullivan, an investigative journalist, wrote, the financial success and the social standing of a "one-man-and-a-helper operation" depended on its reputation for cleanliness and reliability. The butcher "looked across his counter into the eyes of the customers who knew him, who had known his father before him, whose children went to school with his children."[17]

Moving the meat industry from small communities removed the traditional safeguards. Separated from the direct observation of consumers, slaughterhouses and packinghouses had no social pressure to maintain cleanliness. Their main concern was to produce profits, often at the expense of the health and safety of the consumer. Throughout the industry, sanitary conditions were poor and few packinghouses were adequately equipped to treat offal, tallow, and blood. Packers heaped up by-products in cutting rooms and yards where they rotted before processing. Carcasses were not separated from the debris, employees were not furnished sanitary facilities, and meat from diseased animals was marketed along with the rest.[18]

To combat this situation, aroused citizens in eastern and midwestern cities organized against the most offensive and dangerous conditions. In her 1898 *The History of the Women's Club Movement in America,* Jane Croly mentioned 11 city health protective associations growing out of the need to clean up stockyards, some of them, to varying degrees, inspired by the organization in New York. Brooklyn women formed their own health protective association from which three branches emerged to protect different sections of the city. Philadelphia women banded into a health protective association to clean up the slaughterhouses in their city. The civic clubs of Chicago, organized under settlement-house worker Mary E. McDowell, "angel of the stockyards," petitioned, complained, and campaigned against health hazards created by the rotting refuse, filth, and stench in the Chicago stockyard district and Bubbly Creek.[19]

During the next two decades, unsung residents in many towns and cities, each employing appropriate methods to fit their local situations, organized to combat food contamination and to create local government agencies sensitive to consumer needs. The large health protective organizations in New York City, Brooklyn, Philadelphia, and Chicago may have attracted more media attention, but others, such as the Village Improvement Association of Green Cove Springs, Florida, organized in 1879, and the Village Improvement Association of Cranford, New Jersey (whose best-known participant was Alice Lakey, later prominent in the national crusade), pursued their goals with equal energy and less publicity. A woman's club in Big Rapids, Michigan, tackled a local problem with meat adulteration in their city with drastic action. When the health officials and the owners of the abattoir failed to act satisfactorily on their requests to improve conditions, the women went into the slaughter pen and cleaned it up themselves. One of the participants, the Reverend Caroline Bartlett Crane, told a General Federation of Women's Clubs convention that the Big Rapids clubwomen made the place "clean enough for a pink tea," but she admitted that she had never regained her appetite for meat after she took an interest in putting the place in a more hygienic condition. Mrs. Richard Bloor of Taylorville, Louisiana, took individual action. Accompanied by her husband, she visited a packinghouse where she found all sanitary measures lacking. When her suggestions to improve the sanitation were ignored, she sent a description of the conditions to Upton Sinclair to use in his exposés of the meat industry.[20]

In many respects, the experiences of both large and small local organizations paralleled the New York City Protective Association's fight to clean up the slaughterhouses near Beekman Hill. These groups found that organizing was necessary in order to remedy dangers created by uncontrolled businesses that were indifferent to the health and safety of the community. They discovered that existing government agencies were averse to or unable to correct the problem. These dedicated volunteers were willing to sacrifice time and energy to accomplish their goals. They sponsored statutes and created local government agencies to carry out their wishes. When they

did not achieve their goals at first, they persisted, sometimes for decades. But even after statutes were on the books, at times these organizations found it necessary to aid in the enforcement.

ঽ▲

Leominster, Massachusetts. Easter Sunday Evening, 1879. The people of Leominster packed the town hall to consider Mary Hannah Hanchett Hunt's proposal to protect their community against substance abuse. They attended out of concern over the health and moral problems created by the escalating use of habit-forming drugs and alcohol in postbellum American society. Hardly a home or a community was free from addiction induced by medical prescriptions, proprietary medications, or the pressures of social life. The Leominster meeting was noteworthy because it marked the beginning of a nationwide drug prevention program in the public schools.[21]

The lecturer did not fit stereotypes of the robust, hatchet-wielding women of the Temperance Crusade, or the firebrands of abolition, neither was she a prominent philanthropist, nor a great beauty. Rather, this pioneer in the pure food, drink, and drug crusade was a quiet and unassuming retired schoolteacher; middle-aged, motherly, and tastefully attired. She lived in nearby Hyde Park, Massachusetts. Her husband, Leander H. Hunt, was a steel agent and her son a metallurgical chemist and industrial engineer.[22]

A deep religious experience had prompted Mary Hunt to develop her plan to prevent substance abuse. At one point in time, her Hyde Park pastor had told her that she was fitted for "a wider Christian service" in life. Later, while recovering from a serious illness, she prayed to know the nature of this Christian service and promised that if she recovered, she would do whatever God wanted her to do. At that time she thought the answer might be to discover a new pupil for her Bible class, or find a poor family she could help. However, she found the "real answer" in recognizing a need to alert the "whole people" to the "dangerous character and evil effects" of stimulants and narcotics.[23]

Hunt was a different kind of temperance woman. She defined temperance in a broader sense than most of her contemporaries and she approached habituation from a stance of prevention, instead of reform. To her temperance meant avoiding the use of opium, morphine, chloral hydrate, and all other dangerous and habit-forming substances, whether used separately or as ingredients in proprietary medications, as well as abstaining from alcoholic beverages. She felt that substance abuse was a response to the stresses of industrializing society, that users were the victims of false advertising, medical avarice, and commercial greed, and that prevention was better than rehabilitation.[24]

Her plan involved preventing habituation through introducing the study of physiology and hygiene, with a special emphasis on substance abuse, in the public school systems. Hunt suggested that the only effective protection against substance abuse was to educate children against the dangers of stimulants and narcotics. Schools should reinforce parental admonitions with instruction in physiology and hygiene with particular attention to the nature and dangers of addictive drugs, whether packaged individually or hidden from public detection among the secret ingredients of proprietary medications. Justified or not, she felt that teaching the dangers would immunize children against the use of harmful substances throughout their lives.[25]

Still frail from a recent illness and uneasy when speaking to large audiences, Hunt's voice quavered occasionally, yet she projected her plan with conviction and enthusiasm. She drew her illustrations from the concerns of the communities, sharing their alarm for the future of a race poisoning itself, body and soul, with stimulants and narcotics. She warned them that substance abuse was more than an individual or family concern. In her opinion, the use of stimulants and narcotics could very well contribute to the demise of the great American society that their New England forebears, not so many generations removed, had established and fought to preserve. She asserted that the American form of government, based as it was on the integrity of individual citizens, could not function if the causes of vice and crime continued to be tolerated and protected by law. Unabated legal traffic in stimulants and narcotics threatened the nation's children who were in danger of becoming chemical victims of the stresses, uncertainties, and advertising practices of industrializing America.[26]

She compared their mutual situation with the evils of chattel slavery, still an ulcer in recent memory. The chains of chemical slavery destroyed the individual, brought hardship and shame to the family, and stultified their society in much the way that black slavery had afflicted the nation before abolition.[27]

Part of the problem was that the majority of consumers had no way, except through personal observation, to determine the exact nature of stimulant and narcotic damage to the human body, mind, and morals.

Statistics were not available. Medical schools extolled the value of opium alkaloids, and physicians used them indiscriminately. Almost every newspaper and magazine advertised "patent medicines" guaranteed to cure, and people dosed themselves to alleviate pain and distress. Most people knew that dangers, sickness, death, spouse and child abuse, neglect, and poverty attended overdose and overuse of some of the substances, but they did not know how stimulants and narcotics affected human organs, nor were they aware of the wide extent and full implications of drug abuse and adulteration. Hunt addressed this aspect, expounding on the potential damage to the digestive system, brain, and the ability to make sound moral judgments. She condemned proprietary soothing syrups, tonics, and sedatives, pointing out that because only the manufacturer knew what they contained, no one could judge what dangers might attend their use.[28]

Hunt placed much of the blame on schools for not teaching the dangers of substance abuse. Teaching physiology, in itself an anomaly in most public schools, and tutoring her son had given her ample opportunity to discover the inadequacies of the educational system. It was evident to her, as it was to many parents of school-age children, that both elementary and higher institutions of learning had not kept pace with the requirements of children who were facing the problems of an industrializing society. Studying mythology and memorizing Latin and Greek to the exclusion of modern science fell short of teaching students how to develop healthy bodies, innovative minds, strength of character, and a sense of moral responsibility. She felt the classics should supplement more practical studies — those branches of knowledge that addressed the problems children would encounter in real life, which improved their society, and promoted domestic happiness. Children planning to become manufacturers, farmers, mechanics, miners, weavers, teachers, housewives, and merchants would be better equipped for a more healthy and purposeful existence by learning community improvement, home economics, horticulture, physiology, hygiene, and moral behavior along with their Three Rs. To advance democratic society, teachers should encourage students to care for their own health, to take responsibility for their behavior, to understand the latest discoveries, to innovate and invent, and to provide a rich legacy for the future. Students should learn the nature of the air they breathed, the water they drank, and the plants and animals that nourished their bodies. Children had a fundamental right to good health and to know the latest advances in science. Instruction should come early enough to forestall superstition, here-say, and the dangers of the streets. Children were "the legal heirs to every truth of science that warns against the use of alcohol and other narcotic poisons." To deprive them of such knowledge was "an unpardonable sin, not only against the children, but also against the nation soon to be governed by them."[29]

Whereas Hunt articulated deepening universal concerns that had resisted solution, her remedy seemed fresh, logical, inspired, and in accord with the ideals of her audience. Scientific education in public schools seemed a conservative and practical step toward protecting their young people. Unlike hammering down saloon doors, legislating prohibition, campaigning in favor of the ballot for women, or measures that entailed political issues and identified women with law-breaking and interference in party politics, scientific education looked only toward educating children. It was a measure that seemed so reasonable and sensible, so free from controversy and political entanglements that a wide range of individuals — prohibitionist and anti-prohibitionist, woman suffragist and anti-woman suffragist, Democrat and Republican, male and female — could support the cause without being considered extreme.[30]

Hunt billed her "vision of hope" as easy to put into practice, imposing no undue hardship on any one group, and requiring no constitutional change. It involved only a simple procedure of introducing the new discipline of Scientific Instruction, with "special reference" to the effects of alcohol, tobacco, opium and its congeners, chloral hydrate, and other harmful narcotics and stimulants, into public and private school curriculums. Hunt felt sure that such teaching could direct future generations away from destructive habits and toward health and moral-building life-patterns. Making the teaching mandatory would insure that every school child in the community would receive adequate instruction.[31]

Hunt's suggestions appealed to her audience. In less than six months she was barnstorming Massachusetts, speaking on the same subject three and four times a week, frequently under the auspices of churches or local temperance unions. In most of the places she spoke, unions and parents' groups organized to persuade school boards to add scientific instruction to their local school curriculums.[32]

Perhaps the greatest significance of Hunt's message was its wide appeal. Clearly, the popularity of her message indicated the magnitude of anxiety attending substance abuse and the desire to do something about it. There is no other way to explain the approval she won in so short a time. In the summer of 1879, her activities attracted the attention of the National Woman's Christian Temperance Union (N.W.C.T.U.), which adopted

Scientific Instruction as a one of its departments and installed Mary Hunt as superintendent.[33]

&

Battle Creek, Michigan. The last week in January, 1884. A group of Michigan W.C.T.U. women launched another spearhead in the fight for pure food, drink, and drugs. Adopting the form of summer normal institutes to update teachers in new methods, the Michigan women developed a "Health and Heredity Normal Institute" which taught the fundamentals of pure food, drink, and drug activism to W.C.T.U. delegates from 30 Michigan communities. Designed under the leadership of Ella Eaton Kellogg and Mrs. "Dr." Mechem of Battle Creek, the institute lasted five days and addressed the difficulties pure food, drink, and drug advocates encountered while trying to organize campaigns against substance abuse: lack of literature, scarcity of personnel well enough acquainted with the subjects to feel confident in teaching, and methods of presenting lectures. The Michigan "Normal" was significant to the crusade because it served as a pilot program for a nationwide adult education campaign to rid American homes of dangerous and adulterated food, drink, and drugs.[34]

Building upon a growing W.C.T.U. concept that all branches of health and hygiene were closely related to temperance, selected health instructors presented interrelated classes in physiology, adulterated foods, and dangerous drugs, along with "the hygiene of the air and ventilation," exercise, sensible clothing, household hygiene, and nutrition. In the evenings, Mrs. Kellogg followed up the classes with lectures relating each subject to alcohol and drug abuse.[35]

Ella Kellogg was a hygienist and nutritionist. She was one of the editors of *Good Health* magazine that advocated total abstinence from all narcotics. She supervised a large experimental kitchen, taught cooking classes, wrote several series of articles for the *Union Signal*, and served as superintendent of the national and state W.C.T.U. Departments of Hygiene. Since her marriage in 1879, she had worked closely with her husband in his medical practice and business ventures in Battle Creek, and he supported her W.C.T.U. activities. Thus, each reinforced the advancement and career of the other. Dr. John Harvey Kellogg was one of the few physicians who opposed the medical use of alcohol and proprietary medicines. At the instigation of Mrs. Kellogg, he lectured at regional and national W.C.T.U. conventions, where, frequently, presiding officers introduced him as an "honorary member of the W.C.T.U." or a "W.C.T.U. brother-in-law."[36]

Ella Kellogg's concern over a rapid increase of substance abuse among American women had led her to search for possible causes. Although she could draw upon no reliable statistics, personal observation had convinced her that drug abuse was creating problems for many of her acquaintances. Her research revealed that the "highway" to substance abuse was "reached by many cross-roads and by-paths." She did not discount popular concepts, reminiscent of Tocqueville's observations one-half century earlier, that the American climate, form of government, diverse population, "numberless racial crossings," exciting political activities, and strenuous business life into which people were "drawn as into a maelstrom," all created a "peculiar and complex people" who were especially susceptible to all forms of narcotics. She did not doubt that "night entertainments with their excitement and unseasonable refreshments, their loss of sleep and morning headaches" made chloral hydrate "as common as soap upon the toilet table" of society women. Kellogg found that both the national characteristics and the lifestyle of socialites contributed to the substance abuse problem, but she identified poor health and defective nutrition as the most proximate and plausible contributors.[37]

The delegates agreed with Kellogg. Their own observations had shown them that whatever impaired "natural strength and vigor" created a demand for "artificial strength," and whatever impaired health became an incentive to use narcotics and stimulants. The "untold numbers of feeble, nervous, or invalid" women who became dependent on widely advertised tonics, cordials, and bitters, which left the sufferers susceptible to greater and more chronic distress, convinced them that poor health, whether physical illness or neurasthenia, was foremost among the causes of substance abuse.[38]

Kellogg felt that all American women should be taught that poor nutrition contributed to substance abuse. Using adulterated or diseased food, too much meat and fat, refined sugar, bleached flour, and artificial foods deprived the body of nutrients and led to the use of stimulants and narcotics. Condiments, such as pepper, mustard, and pungent sauces, by overstimulating the digestive organs, made them lose their natural tone and unable to perform their functions without the aid of artificial excitants. Too many pastries, desserts, and sauces created "mischief" in the "laboratory of the stomach" by hindering the digestion of wholesome foods with which they mingled. Minor stimulants, such as coffee and tea, produced a desire for "a still stronger degree of artificial stimulation."[39]

Kellogg suggested teaching women that minor and major illnesses responded better to preventive and "natural" measures. Women, particularly, should be aware that "feminine afflictions" responded better to sensible eating, fresh air, exercise, adequate rest, less restrictive clothing, and eating unadulterated and uncontaminated food, than to Lydia Pinkham's Vegetable Compound, Wine of Cardui, or dozens of other highly advertised emmenagogues.[40]

Colic in infants responded better to a warm water bath, judicious feeding, and more attention, than to opium-containing soothing syrups. Frail children needed sunlight, mild exercise, good nutrition, rather than fraudulent "pure Norwegian" cod-liver oils, which contained sugar, alcohol, glycerin, and sometimes opium, but no hint of oil and "no connection to a fish."[41]

Kellogg pointed out that despite extravagant marketing claims, proprietary medications lacked curative powers. She believed that nature alone had the power to heal. If judiciously used, a very few drugs might assist nature. For example, quinine, the natural alkaloid of cinchona bark, could overcome malaria, but most medications only masked symptoms and weakened the body's immune system.[42]

In connection with teaching women how to avoid substance abuse, Mrs. Kellogg advocated a great national housecleaning to rid American homes of dangerous and harmful food and medications. Delegates should advise mothers to "Burn in the kitchen stove" that which should not be consumed; condemn "patent medicines, especially alcohol preparations and soothing syrups;" and prepare to "instruct and assist" children "in the formation of such habits as insure health."[43]

After all, she declared, "the home is woman's citadel; it is here disease most often threatens; and who shall meet the foe at the threshold if not she?" She requested that delegates work to insure that a "thorough, theoretical and practical knowledge of the science of health," including "awareness of contamination and adulteration," was an "imperative requisite" of every homemaker's education.[44]

The heredity portion of the Normal focused on methods that delegates could use to teach women how to avoid the congenital dangers of substance abuse. Working from a premise that acquired, as well as genetic, characteristics were passed from generation to generation, the Normal developed a eugenic "law of heredity" intended to add fuel to the reasons why people should abstain from the use of habit-forming substances. According to the law's creed, parents transferred disease, character traits, mental dysfunctions, and moral incapabilities to their children in the same way as physical characteristics — facial expressions, the color of the hair and eyes, the complexion, the texture of the skin, gait, and stature. Rheumatic parents produced rheumatic children, consumptive parents produced consumptive children, and syphilitic parents transferred the disease to their children. Addicted parents transmitted "tainted blood," and "depraved" parents passed down immoral tendencies to their progeny. Relating a biblical admonition that "the sins of the fathers are visited upon the children to the fourth generation" to the use of "habit-forming poisons," heredity lecturers prophesied degeneration of the entire society if recent increases in "narcotic and stimulant" use were not checked. They claimed that children of alcohol or drug dependent parents were often untruthful, unscrupulous, and indifferent to the rights of others. These people, they argued, were lacking in an appreciation of right and justice, and liable to indulge in predatory business practices or criminal behavior. Lecturers felt that dosing and dissipation provided roots for much of the cruelty, crime, and corruption of the "gilded age." No one but the "All-seeing One" could know the horrors that plagued countless victims of substance-abuse heredity. Because alcoholism was more common among men, fathers were more likely than women to pass alcohol related illnesses to their children. Because women resorted more to using opium, chloral hydrate, or patent medicines to relieve "the viscidities of life," mothers were more apt to transmit the majority of drug related illnesses. When both parents were either alcohol or drug dependent, the risks were greater.[45]

A redeeming message of the Normal was that the ravages of heredity might be alleviated. Stress free environments, drug and alcohol free homes, proper education, and uncompromising temperance living might "starve out" the "morbid" tendencies. "Untainted blood" on the mother's side could counteract "bad blood" on the father's.[46]

The Michigan Normal Institute contributed to the emerging pure food, drink, and drug crusade in several substantial ways. It provided for its own continuity by deciding to hold state normal institutes once a year "to further the interests of these branches of W.C.T.U. work." It served as a model for similar institutes in other locations. It propagated a number of health and heredity papers which, among other things, warned against adulterated food, drink, and drugs, proprietary medicines, drug abuse, and offered alternatives. These papers provided study material for local unions, supplied the *Union Signal* with several series of articles, provided propaganda to circulate among interested persons, and propagated ideas that appeared in newspapers, school textbooks, and influenced American thought. The Normal also trained a corps of enthusiastic delegates determined to "gird on the whole armour" for aggressive pure food, drink, and drug campaigns. These efforts were intended to work in conjunction with health and heredity departments in local unions, and, wherever practical, in health clubs among the general populace, arming them with new methods of presentation, including the use of experiments, manikins, blackboard outlines, and "stereopticon views."[47]

ஃ

Frances Willard's Western Tour. Summer, 1883. In Denver, Colorado, another group of W.C.T.U. women injected the aspect of federal drug regulation into the crusade by convincing Frances Willard, President of the N.W.C.T.U., that drug abuse was becoming a serious threat to the American home. During what Willard described as "four of the pleasantest days" of her 1883 journey among "old and long cherished friends," Mrs. Telford, editor of the Colorado W.C.T.U. journal entitled the *Challenge*, apprised Willard of the drug problems facing their state. Governor Evans, "the second Chief Executive Colorado ever had, as well as the best," in Willard's opinion, told her of the personal misery and difficulties related to the use of "loco weed" among people of Indian and Mexican descent. Dr. Kate Bushnell, Colorado W.C.T.U. superintendent of Hygiene, punctuated her hospitality to Willard with tales of her recent visit to China and her subsequent work with Chinese immigrants in Denver. Among her description of the "wonders of the Orient," Bushnell recounted the extent of opium smoking among the Chinese, revealed the existence of "opium dens" brought by Chinese immigrants to Denver and other major cities in the United States, and called attention to the growing misuse of narcotics among American women. Each of her hosts encouraged Willard to consider ways to expand the N.W.C.T.U. programs to encompass drug regulation.[48]

In San Francisco, Willard received a similar reception. Mrs. H. N. Harris and other temperance women plied the N.W.C.T.U. president with additional evidence of growing drug problems and accompanied her to opium dens in Chinatown to show her, first hand, the "degradation resulting from a poison habit which curses the victim more, but his home less" than the "frenzy of the alcohol dream." They wanted Willard to confirm for herself the authenticity of sensational newspaper accounts describing the "sickening sight" in Chinese brothels of young American women from 16 to 20 years of age lying, along with Chinese slave girls, even younger, "half undressed on the floor or couches," smoking opium with their Chinese "lovers."[49]

Willard was appalled. The opium dens struck a chord etched in her memory from previous experiences with victims of drug abuse. In the recent past, she had encountered a young woman in the Chicago Harrison Street Police Station. Crouched on the floor, with her head in her hands, the young woman was waiting to be arraigned on prostitution charges. When Willard approached her with outstretched hand and the standard W.C.T.U. inquiry, "My sister, may I help you?" the girl told a melodramatic story. She was a teacher, came from a well-connected Southern family, and arrived at her "unenviable state" through the necessity of supporting her addiction, induced by a tonic prescribed by her family physician. The Chinatown visits also brought to Willard's mind facsimiles of women of her own acquaintance and background, "not few in number," who habitually dosed themselves and their families with opium and cocaine based proprietary medications, or who became addicted to morphine injected by physicians.[50]

Pieces of the entire "horrendous" substance-abuse puzzle began to fall into position for her. The British had perpetuated their opium invasion of China; opium and hashish dens plagued major cities. There were reports of working women using opium to combat fatigue. In the Southwest "loco weed" smoking was increasing. Shipping companies supplied coca leaves to increase the endurance and loyalty of stevedores on the New Orleans docks. Druggists doped soft drinks to attract customers. Manufacturers of proprietary medicines filled their products with hidden addictive ingredients. Tobacco companies added opium to cigarettes. There was a connection between the spread of venereal disease and drug abuse, and a disturbing relationship between adulterated food and alcoholism. The recreational abuse of laudanum among artists, socialites, and young southern men was equally alarming, as was the growing incidence of morphine addiction. All these horrors were in the same category as alcohol abuse and all indicated an exploding "enslaving substances" problem.[51]

Willard described how the semi-tropical climate of California, "the true Garden of the Gods," quickened her awareness to both the "pulsation of the newest America" and the need for international alcohol and narcotic reform. On the Pacific coast she felt the "breezy breath of a new Japan, flowering" in "magic transformation" accompanying its willingness to adopt Western customs, and "trembled" with the women of California at the consequent danger of Western vices "becoming domesticated" in Asia. She looked into the "mystic face of the Orient" to see China burdened by "opium bondage," imposed by British Empire trade policies that mandated opium importation from India into China for the purposes of "enriching English pocketbooks" and sedating the Chinese populace.[52]

The seed of W.C.T.U. expansion into the international sphere, already planted by a growing interest among European and Asian reformers in American W.C.T.U. activities, sprouted in Denver and took shape in San Francisco as a part of the remedy. With the W.C.T.U. women in the West, Willard began to lay out a plan to attack the "poison problem," in its entirety, through broader and more intensive programs and a worldwide organization. In comparison to women in the eastern states, Willard found Colorado, California, and other Western women "better informed," harboring a more "international spirit," and ready to work toward a new and "most catholic endeavor"— the formation of a World Woman's Christian Temperance Union that would "belt the globe and join the East and West in an organized attack upon the poison habits in both hemispheres." From the inception of the plan, its founders anticipated strong support at home and the "hearty cooperation," at the least from "British Cousins across the line and across the sea," the leading pastors of Paris, and English speaking populations in India, China, and Japan.[53]

That fall, Willard arrived at the annual W.C.T.U. convention with her vastly expanded vision of the dimensions of temperance, a sharpened appreciation of the responsibilities of American women, the "inspired" plan, and a sense of expediency. To extend the work, Willard recommended that the W.C.T.U. immediately join with temperance organizations in Europe to organize a World's W.C.T.U. and to adopt a polyglot pledge that included a commitment to abstain from the use of opium in all its forms and to employ all proper means to discourage the use of and traffic in opium, as well as alcohol. She also recommended supporting Mary Clemitt Leavitt on a temperance mission to the Orient at W.C.T.U. expense. Leavitt was to contact Protestant missions and organize English speaking women first, and then "native" women, into unions to combat opium smoking among Orientals. At the same time, temperance women in America and Europe would launch a campaign against importing opium to China.[54]

Most of Willard's recommendations were approved. Mary Leavitt left for Hawaii (then the Sandwich Islands) with $35 in her pocket and the W.C.T.U. promise of a "dime a member" subscription to support her activities. Delegates from various countries formed a World W.C.T.U. and elected Frances Willard president. The World W.C.T.U. adopted the polyglot pledge, but the national organization did not. Opposition among some temperance women in the United States toward broadening the program too far prevented all-out support for "opium temperance."[55]

At home, Willard and her associates initiated an attack against the "parallel" danger of American women using "enslaving substances." To combat widespread opium and other drug abuse among American women, they reorganized the Department of Tobacco to form the Department of Narcotics, which emphasized activism against opium and other narcotics and stimulants, as well as tobacco. Mrs. Harris was installed as the new chairman, and Mrs. Havens as a full-time lecturer. Their investigations confirmed Willard's observations that addiction was more widespread than was generally supposed, opium use was on the rise, drug abuse was more common among women than men, and habituation was initiated most frequently by medical use. Laudanum, paregoric, soothing syrups, crude opium rolled into pills, morphine injections, and patent medicines of every description were the most commonly abused medications.[56]

ᶻ▲

Thus, popular demand for pure food, drink, and drugs arose in the villages, the towns, and the cities, in different places, at different times. The demand also appeared in different forms, as the need became urgent and people devised ways and means to combat the threat of adulteration and substance abuse in their homes and communities. They centered their activities around protecting the public health from contaminated meat, teaching children the dangers of using dangerous drugs and eating adulterated food. Adults were alerted to the prevalence of adulteration and fraud in their food, drink and drug supply, and to work for local government intervention when industrialists refused to discontinue dangerous practices. Health improvement associations incorporated under state charters and utilized local court action. Scientific instruction enthusiasts organized to introduce physiology and hygiene in schools. Health and heredity normals generated and circulated oral and written propaganda that related pure and healthful food and drugs to personal and community well-being. Temperance unions initiated campaigns for government drug regulation. They approached the problems through firsthand investigations and expected their existing institutions to correct the situations.

Before the early 1880s their attempts had not reached crusade proportions. They still addressed local problems and issues, yet these local activists set the tone, established the patterns, and introduced standards for the rapid momentum which followed.

Pure food, drink, and drug reform gained impetus as social pressure and local statutes failed to correct intolerable conditions. Grassroots groups of urban and rural women belonging to a great number and variety of other independent organizations incorporated the fight into their discussion and reform agendas. Moving beyond church auxiliaries, hatchet-wielding prohibition forays, and bloomer-girl suffragette marches, these women had formed less flamboyant and less restricted women's groups. They had formed independent literary clubs, village improvement societies, women's granges, mother's circles, and a wide assortment of other groups dedicated to self-improvement and to the well-being of their families and neighbors. The altruistic nature, conservative facade, and vitality of the new organizations appealed to a wide cross-section of discreet women who saw the need to improve and protect their society by employing prudent means, such as circulating petitions, and using personal influence, exposé, and court action to achieve effective methods of controlling food, drink, and drugs. The formation of these women's organizations forsaged the end to male supervision of formal women's alliances and projects, and opened the door for a great diversity in association, experimentation with fresh ideas, and participation in almost all aspects of Progressive Movement reform.

Temperance women began to associate adulterated food and drug abuse with alcohol abuse. Incorporating these issues into their agendas broadened activities beyond the original scope of the W.C.T.U. and attracted a great number of women who recognized the need to address the tangle of abuse that was consuming American communities.

Club women laid the foundation for their pure food, drink, and drug campaigns in the early 1880s, while their activities centered around study, self-improvement, and philanthropy. Louisa Poppenheim, editor of the Charleston, South Carolina, *The Keystone*, described this initial phase as a seed time during which club women accumulated force for the future "laying deep foundations so elastic that they adapted themselves to the growing needs of the community." By providing an atmosphere of sisterhood where each member felt comfortable and wanted, it became a training ground for activism.[57]

Women who had organized originally to study literature, art, or history widened their interests into correcting social problems. Critiquing Shakespeare, Browning, Ibsen, Paine, Rousseau, Mills, Eliot, Spencer, and Ruskin led to identifying the ideas they studied with their own situation and translating their concerns into reform. Poppenheim described the

transition as a "Great Awakening" of the real woman to her potential —
an accumulating force for developing responsibility and opportunity.

In the beginning, their object in organizing was self-advancement.
The lines of study were confined mainly to literature and history. Creating a social atmosphere of equality where each member felt comfortable
and wanted, free to express her convictions, and encouraged to contribute
was the first step in binding the sisterhood together. Sharing their opinions with others gave them breadth of outlook, sympathy, growth, and
confidence. Personal participation developed the communication and leadership skills they used later to improve their society.[58]

Many literary, history, art and philanthropic clubs began to set aside
time for unstructured discussion of current affairs. Subjects varied, but it
is surprising how frequently the issues of pure food, drink, and drugs came
up. The conversation of women who had to pass stockyard waste on their
way to listen to a lecture on Dante or attend a "delightful Browning program," who were considering where they were going to be able to buy
wholesome food on the way home, or worrying about the contents of medications they were taking, naturally turned to what they could do to allay
their anxieties.[59]

The Shakespeare Club of Clinton, Missouri, was one of the clubs
that extended its interests to include works of the Brownings, other
authors, history, and "timely topics." On December 18, 1901, after a lesson on *Henry VIII*, they discussed the news of the day. In October 1902,
they met with the Civic Club to improve public health. By February 1904,
they were lobbying for pure food laws.[60]

Paula Baker, Karen Blair, Anne Firor Scott and other scholars of
women's history have traced the development of numerous women's clubs
from their literary phase to activism. Scott observed that thousands of
women's clubs followed the pattern of broadening interests. By applying their energies to the problems of their communities, these women
built the infrastructure to deal with the social maladies of the Progressive
Era.[61]

Some local groups organized spontaneously and independently, drawing strength from their own convictions and ideals, choosing leaders from
the rank and file, and implementing their own plans without outside support. They entered food and drug reform without collective experience to
prepare them for political activism. They had no role models to follow and
they developed their ideas and methods as they went along. Others patterned their activism after campaigns waged in similar circumstances, or

functioned under the aegis of national organizations from which they drew strength and direction.[62]

Sometimes, like the temperance union in Columbia, Missouri, they worked behind the scenes, circulating petitions among registered voters, instead of signing themselves so that their requests would be taken seriously by legislators who might otherwise think that the only persons interested in food, drink, and drug reform were "women and ministers." At other times, groups such as women's clubs in Massachusetts were very much in the limelight, forming leagues with male reformers to create local agencies to eradicate the dangers.[63]

Throughout their campaigns they stressed progress, equality, altruism, and persistence. They were future-oriented. They did not accept, as inevitable, conditions threatening themselves and their community. They resisted threats to their well-being by analyzing, organizing, and agitating for change. More than exposing problems, they exhibited endless innovation in offering solutions, both instructive and legislative. Despite, and because of, their diversity, a common pattern of problems, opposition, and purpose brought food and drug reformers into a remarkable unity of thought and activity.

In combating current problems, they were building for the future. In the words of Frances Willard:

> Beloved, we have given hostages, not to fortune, but to humanity. We are building better than we know. We stand for ... the diviner womanhood that shall ere long bring in the era of sweeter manners, purer laws.... We are the prophets of a time when the fashionable frivolities of women and the money worship of men shall find themselves confronted by God's higher law of a complete humanity.[64]

2
The Pure Food, Drink, and Drug Dilemma: Social Causes for Activism

Historical interpretations that attribute the participation of women in progressive reform to a desire to occupy free time with which new inventions and urbanization had provided them, to impose middle-class Protestant values on a reluctant public, or to assert their equality with men do not supply adequate explanations for pure food, drink, and drug activism. Each makes untenable assumptions.

The first of these suppositions assumes that the majority of reformers had access to washing machines and other new innovations, which was not the case with poor and rural crusaders. It further assumes that the new inventions actually saved a great deal of time and energy, which any woman who has coped with the idiosyncrasies of a turn-of-the-century washing machine questions. Finally, it does not take into account that urbanization had created additional burdens upon housewives and mothers.[1]

The second interpretation leans on a premise that leaders of reform movements belonged to an urban Protestant middle class. Adherents to this viewpoint argue that class-conflict as well as gender-conflict motivated women — that middle-class women organized to combat the emerging values of a rapidly growing immigrant working class. The problem with this explanation is that it focuses on the rhetoric of a small minority of leaders to the exclusion of assessing the participation of women across lines of ethnic background, religion and class — women of all kinds and occupations, in cities, towns, and rural areas throughout the country.[2]

The third argument portrays their activism as motivated by "the growing, if frequently unconscious, need of women everywhere to assert themselves."[3] This perspective is attractive in light of later twentieth century feminist struggles. Undoubtedly feminism entered the equation, but too much attention on the feminist aspect of activism during the nineteenth-century can be misleading. At that time, most reformers did not conduct their activities in a gender-conflict context, resented accusations that they were trying to step out of their traditional roles as wives and mothers, and opposed the vote for women until well into the twentieth century.

The overwhelming preponderance of evidence indicates that the pure food, drink, and drug advocates organized out of a sense of necessity and responsibility. Nineteenth century women required no restless impulse to relieve boredom, visions of dominance, or desire to protect their status to convince them that they needed to take action to improve the quality of their food, drink, and drug supply. Urgency and altruism prompted them to act. Women organized when meat contamination in slaughterhouse districts exceeded their tolerance level. Women flocked to scientific instruction to protect their children from substance abuse. Health and heredity advocates were willing to devote their time and energy to improve health and well-being. Women expanded their W.C.T.U. activities to include all stimulants and narcotics because they perceived danger in opium and proprietary medicine use. Each group mobilized out of a pressing need to protect their families, their society, and their continuity against immediate and accelerating health threats. They acted out of a growing apprehension that no one else was doing anything constructive to remedy an intolerable situation, and from the sense of human responsibility residing in their collective folk memory.

In 1885, a Jacksonville, Illinois, Congregational church pastor, identified only as Dr. Butler, insisted that the women of his church organized to combat a "desperate danger," that left the voices of men "mute or muffled," hands of men "prone by the side," and the hearts of men faint. According to Butler, when men refused to act, women decided that they would have to save the home. If men were led by party politics and business "necessities," women would follow a higher authority. If men did not have the time, women would find it. If men were too weak or confused to lead, they would have to follow. The women in his congregation did not organize out of a love of notoriety, nor for the sake of invading a sphere occupied by someone else, but out of necessity. The work which men should have been doing was not being done, and women were trying to fill the need. Their activities were a "necessary consequence" of seeing their families and community threatened without anyone rising to remedy the condition. They acted out of a conviction of their responsibility to protect their families and community.[4]

Despite a decidedly patronizing tone, Butler defined the reasons why women organized in much the same terms as they did themselves. Sarah Platt Decker asserted that club women did not unite "for fame, for notoriety, for discontent," but had "joined hands to work for better homes" and "for better care of children." Mary Sherman decided to join the crusade on a hot summer day as she watched small children enjoying ice cream sandwiches bought from street vendors "with a feeling of trepidation" concerning "how many germs and how much dirt" they swallowed with each "mouthful of cool pink cream." Mrs. F. Merrick, a W.C.T.U. leader in Louisiana, claimed that it was the "true mother instinct to protect her young from danger" and the "God spirit that yearns for utterance on behalf of poor weak human nature, not the anticipation of office, or the love of fame that allured" her to work for scientific instruction laws. Clara Hoffman said that "passionate love for home, husband and children was the motive power" that "nerved the heart and strengthened the arm" of Missouri women. Judith Ellen Foster wrote, "the garnered teachings of science, the pleadings of philanthropy, the commands of faith," all prompted Christian workers to "go forward." One Detroit woman felt that the Lord had raised up women "to do what some men do not want, and others do not dare to do." Clubwoman Mary I. Wood asserted that "the desire to be of service, whenever, wherever and however needed" was an overarching principle that bonded women of the "North, South, East and West, both in America and abroad, regardless of religion or condition of life," into "one great body of workers."[5]

It was not that nineteenth century crusaders were the first to face the adulterated food, drink, and drug problem. From the advent of written records, women found precedence for protesting against adulteration. The author of Ecclesiastes complained that "Dead flies cause the ointment of the apothecary to send forth a stinking savor," and ancient Greek and Roman physicians protested that fillers were added to bread, wine was diluted, and drugs were adulterated. From the Middle Ages through the nineteenth century, medics bemoaned the increasing sophistication of adulteration among herbalists, dealers, wholesalers, and retailers accompanying the expansion of trade and competition in drugs, spices, bread, wine, and beer.[6]

Similarly, reformers were aware that drug habituation had existed since "time immemorial." Jennie Stevens Elder, M.D., observed that anything which caused a "morbid craving for brain stimulation" was "as old as the human race." Throughout the ages, people had invented every conceivable method of manufacturing drugs and intoxicants. They infused teas, percolated plants, fermented "grains, roots, fruits, juices, and sap," chewed "various leaves," and smoked "herbs and gums." The propensity for substance abuse was so general, that "Brain exciters"— something that quickens the nervous system — had "always been found with all classes and conditions of people." Elder's research convinced her that once drug habituation took possession of people, no amount of moral suasion was effective and laws "only held it slightly in check." Her overwhelming fear was that Americans would suffer the same difficulty in overcoming "this evil" as civilizations in the past.[7]

The Need

The problem that women faced in the last quarter of the nineteenth century was not one of kind, but of magnitude, intensity, urgency, and lack of alternative. From about 1871 American consumers saw an unusually rapid deterioration in the quality of readily available food, drink, and drugs. Processing plants had become increasingly filthy, preserving and coloring their products with new and more dangerous chemicals. Disease-and-chemical contaminated milk and water were spreading disease and killing babies. Proprietary medicines, considerably more dangerous with the introduction of new alkaloids, were marketed as safe and effective cures, when few were either safe or capable of cure.

Clubwoman Ella Hoes Neville spoke of an enemy becoming "so insidious" that it often brought death or impaired health. She charged, "The adulteration of food is a sinful dealing, worse than short weight or dishonest fabric. Give us short measure and we lose; give us adulterated food and we die."[8]

Reliable morbidity and mortality statistics were not available. The few existing estimates lacked documentation and were probably exaggerated or biased. One physician, David Paulson, reported that one-half of the infants he delivered died from preventable causes before age five and a large number of those who survived "soon drifted into a life of miserable invalidism." He alleged that insanity was increasing three times more rapidly than the population and that tuberculosis, comparatively rare among the previous generation, was "weeding out" one-third of the adult population.[9]

Despite lack of documentation, many consumers found his and other equally dismal estimates well within the range of their own observation and opinion. One clubwoman felt herself "part of a great procession marching toward premature graves, debilitation, and moral decay." A W.C.T.U. official lamented the number of members unable to attend a meeting because of a "long list of miserable ailments with which humanity expects to be afflicted."[10]

The incidence of drug dependence was equally difficult to assess. If judged by the proliferation of establishments advertising morphine, cocaine, and other cures in newspapers and magazines, habituation was common enough to support a number of sanitariums in every city and at least one in most towns. Conservative appraisals estimated 60,000 "morphine fiends" in Chicago alone, and at least 1,000,000 addicts to various kinds of drugs in the United States.[11]

At first, reformers thought the threat fell almost entirely on the uneducated poor, who, in order to survive, were forced to buy food that had been cheapened by adulteration. The poor, it was further thought, could not afford a physician. In itself, this was reason for concern. Danger to part of the population weakened the entire society through lower productivity, contagion, discontent, and crime. People reasoned that because the more affluent and better educated could be more selective, they were less subject to food, drink, and drug adulteration, and because they could afford a physician, they were safe from addiction.[12]

This rationale broke down as consumer-instigated investigations and analyses conducted by the Massachusetts Board of Health and the New York Medical Society, with the aid of newly developed chemical technology, began to show that adulteration extended to almost every item of food on the American dinner table; regardless of cost, beverage adulteration was more insidious than commonly suspected, and no commercial medication could be considered safe. Samples from well known reputable brands, as well as those more obscure, revealed blatant misrepresentation and dangerous adulteration in every segment of the food, drink, and drug industries.[13]

Assays conducted by the Department of Agriculture and other agencies confirmed that food adulteration had reached disastrous proportions. Samples of flour contained ground rice, plaster of paris, grit, and sand. In addition to being made with adulterated flour, bread contained copper sulfate as a preservative and ashes from cooking ovens. Butter contained copper, excess water and salt, lard, vegetable fats, starch, and curd. Cheese contained mercury salts. Lard contained caustic lime, alum, starch, cottonseed oil, and water. Canned foods were adulterated with copper, tin, chemical preservatives, and excess water.[14]

Federal and state chemists indicated that spices and condiments of various kinds contained flour, starches, and other fillers. Cayenne pepper was adulterated with red lead, rice flour, salt, Indian meal, and iron oxide; ginger with turmeric, cayenne, and mustard; mustard with lead chromate, lime sulfate, flour, turmeric, and pepper; pepper with flour, mustard, linseed meal, pepper hulls, and nut shells. Horseradish was adulterated with turnips. Pickles contained alum, apples, and flour. Vinegar contained sulfuric, hydrochloric, and pyroligneous acids, burnt sugar, and water.[15]

Citizen investigations disclosed that sanitation and quality control in most meat processing plants were at an all-time low. At the gigantic Chicago stockyards, meat was "shoveled from filthy wooden floors and piled on tables." Without being washed, "it was pushed from room to room in rotten box carts, all the while collecting dirt, splinters, floor filth, and the expectoration of tubercular and other diseased workers." Meat scraps, "dry, leathery, unfit to be eaten," were ground up along with pieces of pigskin, rope strands, and other rubbish to make potted ham. An alarming number of canned meat samples contained spoiled and parasite-infested products.[16]

The common practice of substituting pork and lamb in canned meats for more expensive poultry products led the New York *Evening Post* to parody a popular nursery rhyme:

> Mary had a little lamb,
> And when she saw it sicken,
> She shipped it off to Packingtown,
> And now it's labeled chicken.[17]

Consumer groups and dairy officials found that doctored beverages contributed equally to the problem. Milk was watered to increase the volume, flavored with burnt sugar, and colored with yellow annatto and analine dyes to hide the dilution. It was preserved with formaldehyde, boric acid, borax, and nitrates, and carelessly contaminated with dirt, sand, manure, urine, and pathogens. Coffee was adulterated with chicory, peas, beans, acorns, shells, and burnt sugar. Cocoa and chocolate contained iron oxide, animal fats, coloring matter, starch, and flour. Fruit juices were diluted, flavored with artificial agents, and preserved with salicylic acid. Soft drinks, notably Coca-Cola, contained varying amounts of cocaine and a medical dose (about five grains per eight ounces) of caffeine due to its derivation from the kola nut. Reportedly, drug store soda fountains laced other soft drinks with opium or cocaine to habituate young people to their establishments. One parent warned his children against buying drinks, "not even soda water or lemonade," at drug stores, confectioneries, or other retail outlets. On holidays and special occasions he gave them money to buy "all of the lemons and sugar they wanted" to make lemonade at home.[18]

Although brewers insisted that their beers were made from malt, hops, and pure water, Jacob Spahn, the director of a Rochester, New York, brewery discovered their claims to be false. He sold his stock and exposed the brewery's practices in the Sunday issue of the Rochester *Democrat and Chronicle*, where he pointed out that salicylic acid, quassia wood, tannin, glycerine, and grape sugar were added to the product during its processing. Bicarbonate of soda "which was fashioned forth in molded morsels shaped each like a candy lozenge" was added to each barrel to make it froth, after which the product had to be strained through isinglass to render it translucent. He described the brewery office as more like a chemist's laboratory than a place to supervise brewing and stated that head brewers recommended the use of substitutes when the price of hops and malt rose.[19]

The editor of the *Union Signal* quoted various authorities to show that *Cocculus indicus*, a poisonous plant, along with aloes were used to give beer a bitter taste and to substitute for the more expensive hop extract. Tannic acid was used as a preservative. Glycerine and glycolic acid, composed of refuse fat from lard rendering, was used to speed up fermentation. Valerian, a sedative and antispasmodic, was added to "stupefy" the drinker and prevent vomiting.[20]

Fermented wines were adulterated before they reached the market. Physician J. S. P. Lord told consumers in southern California that wines were "manipulated and doctored and drugged and nursed." He did not know exactly which drugs were used because "wine doctors," differed "in their methods of treatment like horse and dog doctors, or for that matter all sorts of doctors, and none but themselves" knew how "poisonous their decoctions" were. He alleged that the greatest percentage of brandies were made by distilling wines that had gone sour in fermentation. He pointed out that wine producers guarded their recipes with "sleepless vigilance," and employees who developed secret recipes of their own could demand fabulous prices for their services.[21]

A pharmaceutical salesman reported that he did not know where he could obtain five gallons of unadulterated brandy in the entire city of New York. C. B. Cotton, a retired liquor manufacturer, told a New York City *Tribune* reporter, "A man stands about as good a chance of being struck by lightning" as of buying pure brandy in New York.[22]

Only about five percent of the whiskey manufactured in the United States was "pure" distilled spirits. The rest was blended or rectified. Blended whiskey was a mixture of two or more straight whiskeys. Rectified whiskey was pure whiskey adulterated with neutral spirits and other agents. Any brand might contain fusel oil from storage in treated wood vats or, much more dangerous, menthol alcohol, as a product of careless distilling or handling.[23]

Reportedly, national brand tobacco companies mixed opium with their products to make them more addictive, and the makers of less expensive brands added various kinds of animal and plant refuse. A revenue agent who inspected millions of cigarettes stated that he had given up a confirmed cigarette habit when he observed tobacco and cigar butts picked up from the streets, barks of certain kinds of trees, tobacco stems, and refuse "heaped together in one filthy pile and saturated with opium" on the floor in a leading Chicago cigarette firm. The Elmira, New York, *Advertiser* reported a similar account from an interview with a local chemist whose analysis of twelve brands of the "most prominent and high priced cigarettes," revealed addictive doses of opium in each. The "poorer brands" were "devoid of anything so expensive" as opium, but adulterated with "various vile drugs" mixed with refuse of the "most unwholesome sort."[24]

If anything, adulterated and mislabeled medications, mainly proprietary medicines, presented a more dangerous and immediate threat. The nineteenth century was a heyday for the makers of soothing syrups, tonics, sarsaparillas, celeries (a class of vegetable drinks), and preparations designed to "clean out the system," to relieve complaints "peculiar to women," or to restore "lost manhood." The 1900 United States Federal Census revealed the annual retail sales of proprietary medicines to be above $100 million, $1.25 for each man, woman, and child in the country.[25]

Although intense competition and high advertising costs limited profits, except for the most successful manufactures, consumers regarded the proprietary medicine industry a multimillion-dollar threat. They viewed the Proprietary Medicine Manufacturing and Dealers Association, which the proprietary companies formed in 1881 to protect pharmaceutical interests, as a giant and sinister drug cartel.[26]

Organized women objected to proprietaries primarily because of the danger to society, and secondarily, because of fraud. Nostrums caused addiction, poor health, and sometimes death. The industry preyed especially upon women and the poor. They acquired testimonials by fraud, secured agreements with newspapers to conceal dangers to life and health, kept the ingredients of their preparations secret, and frequently substituted impure or adulterated drugs for pure drugs. The successful operation of a proprietary medicine firm required no scientific knowledge, medical expertise, or code of ethics. Patent medicine companies claimed medical skill, diagnosed by mail, ignored dangerous conditions, and recommended their preparations knowing that they might be worthless or dangerous. They falsified the curative power of their preparations, and claimed universal applicability for their products. In addition to taking advantage of the public by fraudulent advertising, they formed a strong central organization among themselves and joined in an alliance with the liquor interests to protect their industry against hostile legislation and to block the drive for the female franchise, which they feared would end up regulating their products.[27]

As previously indicated, the extent of drug addiction cannot be measured accurately. Recent studies indicate that "real addiction," treated by institutional care, was about 4.5 patients in one thousand, that the patients were over 65 percent female and 95 percent white, and that most of those who sought treatment had become addicted by a physician. Addiction was more common among women in the South than women in the North. Of course, institutional case studies are misleading because they cover only a small percent of actual addiction.[28]

The prevalence of habituation to proprietaries was thought to be very common. Concepts of drug dependence were poorly understood in nineteenth century medicine. Physical and psychological symptoms of withdrawal were confused with a return of the symptoms of the disease for which the proprietary was used in the beginning. A person taking a proprietary for a cough or diarrhea over several weeks time probably identified the recurrence of symptoms of the malady when the medication was discontinued, rather than with habituation, especially if the individual was unaware that the preparation contained opium, morphine, or other habituating drugs.[29]

In 1918, summarizing fifty years of investigation of drug dependence, Charles B. Pearson found that all classes of people were affected, with what he referred to as "the better class of native American stock" being the most susceptible to morphine addiction. Other studies support Pearson's view. In 1889, Dr. Benjamin H. Hartwell surveyed Massachusetts pharmacists and physicians concerning which classes of people in their communities were habituated to opium or its preparations. Of the 446 pharmacists in a sample group, 22 percent answered all classes; 22 percent, middle classes; 7 percent, upper classes; 11 percent said that they did not know anyone who used opium; and the rest evaded the question. The response among physicians was 30 percent, all classes; 22 percent, upper classes; 12 percent, upper-middle classes; 8 percent, middle class; and 8 percent said that they did not know. Exclusion of proprietary preparations in the study probably skewed results toward people who could afford a physician. The rate of addiction was highest among women associated with medical professions — midwives, nurses, and physician's wives.[30]

Specific instances at the time indicate that drug dependence was no respecter of prominence. Harriet Beecher Stowe's daughter, Georgiana, became addicted to morphine following a nervous breakdown. Harriet Robinson's daughter, Hattie, became so dependent on her daily morphine injections from Dr. Richard Kennedy, a former affiliate of Lydia Pinkham, that she could not accompany her husband when he moved from Boston to Maine. Correspondence between Jefferson Davis' female relatives indicated routine use of opium preparations for all kinds of illnesses and depression in the South. Reportedly, socialites and debutantes downed bottles of laudanum or paregoric to steady their nerves and increase endurance.[31]

Preparations containing opium, its derivatives, and cocaine were used to treat a wide range of problems from suppressing pain and inducing sleep to countering aberrant behavior. The preparations were also used to alleviate coughs, check diarrhea, cure rheumatism, soothe babies, treat asthma, relieve anxieties, and treat communicable diseases, including malaria, smallpox, syphilis, and tuberculosis. Drug dependence increased steadily until after the turn of the century.[32]

Reformers saw the separation of manufacture from consumer, the advance of technology, and an uncontrolled market system as underlying reasons for the remarkable decline of the quality of their food, drink, and drug supply. Before 1870, consumers had felt little need for outside protection. In a predominately agricultural society, people raised much of their own food, bought most of the rest from local merchants, and depended on simple and tried remedies to treat their maladies. Consumers could observe conditions under which their food and medical supplies were produced, handled, and

marketed, and a tradesman's social and business future depended on his reputation for cleanliness and honesty. Towns and cities felt capable of controlling business practices by statute if social mores did not.[33]

Industrial growth and more rapid transport following the Civil War
had removed control of food, drink, and drugs from the community and
created a growing dependence of people upon outside manufacturers and
distributors. Responding to an increasingly centralized need for preserved
foods and packaged medications, packing and packaging firms competed
to fill the demand. Railroad systems transported the product to outlying
areas, replacing small businesses and removing the person-to-person control of acceptable norms of merchandising.

Alice Lakey observed, "Practically all the industries have now been
taken from the home. The brewing, the baking, the canning, the preserving are now all done outside." With these industries gone from the home,
the average woman had paid little attention to food processing, until "a
rude awakening convinced her that what she was feeding her family did
not meet the standards of human decency."[34]

Carl L. Alsberg, a food and drug chemist, claimed:

> The first factor was the gradual change of the manufacture of
> food from the home to the factory. Before 1871, except for a few
> staples like flour, much of the food consumed on American
> tables was either made in the home or purchased from neigh-
> bors, so that the conditions under which the food was produced
> and the materials from which it was made were well known to
> the consumers. Gradually, however, more and more food was
> produced in factories and shipped for longer and longer dis-
> tances, until ... city consumers purchased all of their food and
> others an increasingly larger portion of the food, after it had
> been transported for long distances, the consumers being unac-
> quainted with the sources of the food, with the processes it had
> gone through, by whom it was produced or handled and, in
> many instances, with its composition.[35]

Mark Sullivan, an investigative reporter, characterized the industrialization of the food and drug industries as a process through which substituting the corporation for the individual and distancing the producer
from the consumer had removed the traditional person-to-person control
of acceptable methods of merchandising. Under the new system, no con-
trols compelled manufacturers to use wholesome products, prepare them
with "a decent regard for the health of the Public," or inform consumers

of the contents. Potent chemicals, shipped from every part of the world, replaced the traditional supply of home-gathered herbs — boneset, pennyroyal, St. John's wort — perhaps supplemented with a package of dried senna, a few lumps of alum and camphor, and perhaps a bottle of turpentine from the store.[36]

The development of bacteriological and chemical science contributed to the upsurge of food, drink, and drug adulteration. New techniques for isolating and identifying bacteria, molds, and yeasts led to the discovery of chemicals for preserving food and masking evidence of deterioration. Large firms began to employ industrial chemists to develop deodorants for rotten eggs and rancid butter, dyes to enhance color, agents to alter flavor, methods of softening turnips in jam, and ways to keep pickles crisp.[37]

Although a boon to manufacturers who warehoused and shipped their products to diverse localities and to those who wished to keep the prices of their products competitive, the pharmacology of these chemicals in humans was ignored. Food chemist Harvey Wiley accused commercial chemists of debasing their profession by developing harmful chemicals for fraudulent use. Mark Sullivan said that food chemists and bacteriologists were commissioned "to make an impossible bridge between nature and the new philosophy of bigness ... to cheat, deliberately and flagrantly" by "restoring foods already deteriorated" and substituting artificial chemicals for natural products.[38]

Chemists were developing new chemicals for medical use and extracting alkaloids from opium and other plants. Acetylsalicylic acid, although not altogether safe, was among the most useful of the chemicals. Acetanilid and bromides were among those with dangerous side effects. Morphine and other opium alkaloids, cocaine, and *Cannabis indicus* were effective, but required cautious use because small differences in quantity produced great changes in the human body and psyche, and because of their potential for abuse.

A third factor in food, drink, and drug adulteration was the uncontrolled market system with its proclivities toward human avarice, lack of concern for the individual, and fraud. Manufacturers and processors deliberately adulterated their products to make greater profits. Ella Kellogg spoke of the "iniquity of the businesses in their efforts to advance their personal pecuniary interests." Anna Wiley recalled, "industry-wide change in food and drug processing presupposed that the individual manufacturer owed responsibility only to his own conscience. Apparently, many food and drug manufacturers had no consciences. The public was at the mercy of every fraud known to human ingenuity." Others pointed out that some ingredients meant to reduce the cost of processing might not be harmful to health, but injured the body by reducing nutrition. Milk to which water was added was not harmful in itself, but the child, invalid, or other person who derived his chief source of food from milk might be deprived of adequate nourishment.[39]

Crusaders classified incidental adulteration as criminal negligence. Incidental adulteration occurred when zinc, copper, and other metals leached from containers in which foods were stored, or when pathogens contaminated food during careless food preparation or handling. Equally as dangerous as intentional adulteration, incidental adulteration indicated an arrogant, uncaring, profit-above-all attitude on the part of processors.[40]

Why did consumers buy adulterated products? Consumers purchased these products because they had no reliable means of determining what was eroding their health, except by trial and error. Unless they experienced immediate and acute symptoms, they had no way of knowing which products were adulterated. Finally, adulteration was so common consumers could not find pure products.

Lack of acceptable alternatives was one of the most frustrating parts of the consumer's situation. Consider the seemingly simple problem of selecting a leavening agent for bread. Consumers could choose between cream of tartar, phosphate, or alum baking powders. The problem was that each of the baking powders left a residue that hygienists and physicians considered harmful. Without any guidelines, consumers had to choose for themselves which was the least objectionable. Nutritionists recommended that people use more bread made with yeast and less rolls made with baking powder. Consumers took the utility and convenience of baking powder into account. Yeast bread took 10 to 24 hours to make, baking powder biscuits only a few minutes. In addition, yeast introduced the congeneric products of fermentation and alcohol, which some temperance women found unacceptable.[41]

Consumers used proprietary medicinals because they were readily available, extensively advertised as safe and effective, promised a cure, and because many people did not trust physicians. In 1882 few laws regulated the manufacture, merchandising, and purchase of drugs. Consumers could obtain drugs from a physician, a retail drug or general store, a medicine wagon, the manufacturer, or a mail-order house. Each presented a seductive image, but many American women did not feel entirely comfortable with medications from any of these sources. Chicanery flourished in each outlet to such an extent that one did not seem appreciably worse than the other.[42]

Often physicians were the choice of last resort. Medical doctors supplemented their income and enhanced their reputation by dispensing their own compounds or favorite preparations. Patients often found the physician's compound more expensive, less effective, and just as dangerous as preparations available from other sources. The advertising practices of physicians were so similar to proprietary medicine advertising that patients found little difference.[43]

Patients did not need to consult physicians for remedies. They could buy equivalent compounds from a retail outlet, usually a drug store, but often from a general store. With the exception of a few narcotics and poisons, no laws prevented them from buying whatever drugs they desired. Drug stores stocked a wide variety of drugs, proprietary and otherwise. For druggists, the division of medical providers was no better defined than it was for physicians. Despite medical licensing laws that restricted the practice of medicine to physicians, few druggists hesitated to diagnose their customers' ills, or felt either legal or ethical compunction against promoting the most profitable products they carried on their shelves or compounded themselves. People depended on druggists to recommend medications for common maladies. The druggist's reputation depended on his diagnostic and prescriptive ability. Consumers could buy the same drugs and combinations physicians prescribed, and many others, across the counter. Drug stores kept physicians' prescriptions that proved effective in an active file and dispensed them to sufferers with similar symptoms. When a particular remedy became popular, druggists often manufactured it in bulk and recommended it at every opportunity. They advertised the remedy in the newspapers as a cure-all, and marketed it as the local physician's miraculous remedy, sharing profits and credit with the physician or not, depending on the symbiosis between physician and druggist.

Consumers could also order remedies by mail, directly from the manufacturer, or through a mail-order house. Manufacturers advertised extensively in newspapers, magazines, and journals, on billboards and barns. They distributed pamphlets and samples through the mail, or delivered them on doorsteps. Patent medicine advertisements gave an address from where the product could be ordered and testimonials obtained regarding the product's efficacy. Lydia Pinkham and other proprietary concerns provided free medical advice. In their catalogues, mail-order companies (notably Sears, Roebuck) offered and promoted the most popular proprietaries, along with some of their own compounding.

A surprising number of consumers bought from peddlers or medicine-show wagons.[44]

No One Else Was Doing Anything

Dangerous foods, drinks, and drugs posed recognized threats, yet no one seemed to be doing anything constructive to correct the situation. In every segment of society, women found those who ought to have "known how the burden should be carried ... shirking, dodging, or stumbling" over their responsibilities, then wondering what was "wrong with their world." Politicians, bureaucrats, ministers, journalists, physicians, businessmen, and voters did not "offer their shoulders to try the weight."[45]

As women discovered repeatedly, politicians seldom became interested in anything relating to reform legislation until public demand became embarrassing. On every local, state, and national level, women found the structure of party politics antithetical to reform. One Southern woman, who preferred to remain anonymous, protested that the evils of personal ambition and selfishness were "abroad in such force in high places" that new and unnecessary offices had been created for the "ebullition." She warned that "favoritism, partisanship, bribery in all of its forms, money, and promises" had linked forces "to confuse and dispel the honest convictions of men." The ballot box was "no longer a register of patriotic sentiments," the senate "chamber creaked" with the "stealthy tread of the avaricious," and the courts no longer heard "all men alike." Cries of reform often "cheered the hopes of the faithful and true-hearted," but political "promises of reform so far" had only guaranteed that the public would be "called upon for additional finances to be squandered in the public offices, and suffer a graver disappointment in the fidelity of their representatives." The editor of the *Union Signal* wrote that the "times" were "out of joint." Good men had "withdrawn from politics and as a natural consequence machine methods and bossism" prevailed. She decried the vacuum of "great philanthropic ideas" and "living issues" to promote "human betterment."[46]

Women considered churchmen derelict in their duties. Although a number of pastors and their governing boards were sympathetic to the cause, few felt that the church should sponsor reforms to protect the community. Instead, they tended to shy away from controversies that might split their congregations, offend affluent parishioners, or take time and energy away from traditional church functions. A presiding elder of one

Methodist congregation represented the view of most churchmen. In his reply to a request for help from scientific instruction advocates in his congregation, he wrote, "Pastors are a very busy lot of men, and I doubt if they would feel stimulated by a request ... to spend their time in circulating a petition." It seemed to him that women were more suited for the task than preachers. Such attitudes convinced women that churchmen seemed "disposed to throw" all of the work, fighting, and financial burden on the women.[47]

The difference in opinion regarding the role of the church in community welfare led women to realize the "sorry fact" that the average church not only failed to satisfy their intellectual and spiritual longings, but that it also fell short of their ethical standards. To fill the void, they turned to women's organizations where they could find active expression for their "indisputable belief" that "Jerusalem was in the home" and "the vital interests of the home" took precedence above "many of the worthy activities of the church further down the street." A Detroit resident warned that if ministers did not lead reform, their congregations would lead them. She attributed much of the "less than usual rate of increase in church membership" to the refusal of the churches "to take up the work of making a better environment and to unify in moral reform."[48]

The late nineteenth century medical community was too riddled by internal dissent to mobilize a united front. We cannot equate the struggling nineteenth century organization of physicians with the powerful medical association of the mid–twentieth century. Then, the benefits from drug regulation was far from universal. A number of influential members, such as Ray Vaughn Pierce, his son, V. Mott Pierce, and James C. Ayer, who marketed proprietary medicines, resented government or professional interference.[49]

Pharmacists exhibited ambivalence toward drug regulation. With the lighter foot tentatively in the professional camp and the heavier foot in commerce, many pharmacists sided more with the Proprietary Association's *Bulletin*, which promoted the interests of proprietaries, than with the *Druggist's Circular*, which maintained an "active and uncompromising opposition to fraud and sham in the drug business." Critical of an escalating tendency to "push commercialism to the front" and "let professionalism take care of itself," druggist Henry P. Hynson referred to pharmacy as "a double-faced thing," both "learned in the sciences and trained in its special art," and a trade ready to supply whatever the market supported. Another pharmacist, William C. Alpers, thought that although the

pharmacist should regard his goods from a higher standpoint than a tradesman, the commercial side of the question carried more weight than the
ethical. He asserted that "any idea that druggists studied pharmacy and
conducted business for the sole purpose of advancing science or gratifying"
a "desire for higher education" was an "absurdity." They were "in business
for the sake of profit." In practice the commercial aspect of pharmacy won
out. Income from the sale of nostrums salved the scientific conscience of
the retail druggist. He could always point out that if he did not stock proprietaries for a "gullible public," grocers would take away his business.[50]

An aborted attempt to enact Missouri state labeling laws for dangerous drugs illustrates the influence of the Proprietary Association. When
Missouri consumers proposed a state drug law to require labeling medications containing arsenic, cocaine, chloral, or opium with the "full and
complete formula of the entire contents," druggists from every part of the
state sent petitions to Jefferson City to block the legislation. Preprinted
petitions alleged that provisions of the bill were "uncalled for and unjust,"
and would take too much trouble and expense for retailers "without any
corresponding benefit to the public." Letterheads indicated that the petitions were circulated by the Chamberlain Medical Company of St. Louis,
whose president, James C. Ayer, represented the National Proprietary
Association. The number of petitions and the intensity of proprietary lobbying persuaded legislators to vote against the bill.[51]

Selective groups of pharmacists supported truth in labeling. Pharmacist Charles H. La Wall of Missouri felt an urgent need for pharmacy
and medicine to throw off the burden of "artistic mysticism," "fanciful
names," and "ridiculous claims" under which the professions and the
public "had been staggering for years." For La Wall, the "nostrum evil"
constituted "a veritable ogre Frankenstein, whose crimes" were "no less
atrocious than those of its mythical prototype, but whose form" had
become so familiar to pharmacists and physicians that they defended "the
system of charlatanism and fraud" within which their professions
"enveloped" themselves.[52]

Regardless of scattered support for pure food, drink, and drug legislation, self-regulation was the kind of control most medical practitioners
had in mind. They felt that free trade and professional education would
foster ethical practice. Unlike the sociopolitical tradition of Continental
Europe, where people expected arbitrary government regulation, the spirit
of free enterprise in America led medical professionals to view government intervention as oppressive.

Division also affected other segments of business. Involved organizations divided on food, drink, and drug issues according to how specific provisions helped or hindered their industry, and shifted position when it suited their advantage. The National Association of Retail Grocers endorsed a pure food proposal in 1900, opposed bills in 1901 and 1902, and withdrew their opposition in 1905. Initially and basically, closely affected business alliances — the national retail druggists, wholesale druggists, and distillers associations — opposed pure food and drug legislation until public pressure became so great that they feared opposition might affect sales and restrictive bills would follow. Only then did they register public support for regulation, while at the same time using every political, legal, and monetary means at their disposal to modulate legislation or to turn it to their advantage.[53]

Newspapers and magazines did not attack the food, drink, and drug problem because of their business and political affiliations. Proprietary medicine makers were by far their largest advertisers. Alcoholic beverage and food processing ads came in second. One has only to examine the pages of the average newspaper or magazine of the time to realize the magnitude of that advertising. The W.C.T.U. discovered that the proprietary drug companies reinforced their hold over newspapers by inserting a "red clause" in their contracts which invalidated their agreement if the state enacted any law restricting or prohibiting the manufacture or sale of proprietaries. When Maine enacted regulatory legislation, the drug companies canceled contracts with all of the state's newspapers. Even the official organs of women's clubs and temperance unions depended on drug ads.[54]

There were notable exceptions. William Allen White's *Emporia Gazette*, the *Chicago Tribune*, *Scientific American*, *Outlook*, and a few others, deleted drug advertising from their columns and maintained a policy of publishing instances of drug related deaths.[55]

Investigative journalists did not attack food and drug adulteration until about 1902. Their assaults came well after the problem became a national issue among consumers and in Congress. In actuality, muckrakers borrowed their material from the W.C.T.U. and achieved their success from building on what women's organizations had already accomplished. Muckrakers did not create public outrage, but reinforced and publicized concern that already existed.

The question remains, Why did not men's organizations initiate the crusade? Actually, scattered groups of men were interested. A few, notably dairy and health commissioners, participated in civic and health leagues working for local, state, and national legislation. Individually, some husbands of the crusaders, such as Judge W. H. Goodale of Louisiana, supported the pure food, drink, and drug activities of their wives with funds and political influence.[56]

A far greater number of women became involved. Women were the vocal, passionate activists. The leadership and ranks came from women's groups. Women suggested a number of reasons why this was so.

One explanation was that men did not have time. By the opening of the twentieth century, most of them, whether employee or businessman, worked 12 hours a day. Ordinary labor often required prolonged physical exertion. Serious businessmen spent most of their time conducting or promoting business. Tradition dictated that men were entitled to relax after work.[57]

A popular misconception held that women had more free time than men. In actuality, most housewives worked at least as many hours as their husbands. Many women contributed to the family income by engaging in cottage industries or working in factories. It is true that some of the women may have enjoyed greater flexibility in their hours. By efficient planning, housewives could create time for reform activities, and some of the women who worked outside the home managed to squeeze in reform planning during their lunch breaks.

Some speculated that because women were more tied to the home, they were the first to recognize and respond to threats. Others proposed that the female species was programmed to protect its young and, by nature, the most ferocious in defending them against harm.

Women felt that the activities of men were too closely controlled by political affiliations to engage in reform. As voters, many men clung to the dominating party in their section of the country. They left legislative matters to the existing political process and maintained an opinion that legislation should originate from the top because elected representatives were more qualified than they to decide what issues were suitable and important enough for government to pursue.

Many women believed that party leaders had structured the political process to curtail the voter's ability to influence legislation. The editor of the *Union Signal*, Mary B. Willard, observed that elections might address official wrongs "if they were free, and if every man's vote was controlled by his judgment," which was far from being the case. She felt that party was more powerful than public need. The few who made management their business controlled the party while the "mass of voters" discharged their government duties during caucuses, conventions, and elections only "after the course of things" was "conclusively fixed by self-elected rulers." The objective of the "entire political camp" was to bypass the voter by selecting candidates from its own organized group. The slate of officers in each community was made out by "the political expert of that community," who was "in constant communication with the political boss of that part of the state, and so on, to the party political bosses of the nation itself." The editor charged that the individual voter in the United States was as powerless as a serf in Russia. His candidate was "selected, his platform written," and he went "to the polls to register the previous decision of those political manipulators" who were "in secret league with corporations" that were "perpetually seeking the job of locating water works, gas works, street cars, telephone lines, and other public conveniences in every locality," and who made "so large a margin on their investments" that they had "money left over with which to buy up such political favors."[58]

As nonvoters, women owed less loyalty to political parties and preferred to identify with consumer causes. Political bosses seldom took women's activities seriously, countering attempts at reform with easygoing patronization, ridicule, and caricature.

Another concept, which may have had greater popularity than validity, was that men and women were socialized differently. Psychologically, career-oriented men often found it difficult to place the interests of others ahead of their pursuit of individual success. Women were programmed to think of helping others, whether it was their immediate family or the sick and unfortunate in their community. The difference in orientation led men to ignore reform and women to correct societal abuses.

In stereotype, as women saw them, and to a sizable degree in actuality, men's clubs differed diametrically from women's clubs. A writer for *Keystone* observed that men usually established clubs for sport, pleasure, informal business links, or political connections; women formed their clubs for study, charitable work, industrial purposes, or reform. For men, the club was the most relaxed part of their lives; for women, club life was the busiest. No doubt, the article exaggerated the differences, but the contrasts illustrate the unsuitability of men's clubs as agents for reform.[59]

One of the most plausible explanations was that participation in consumer reform was antithetical with men's role as producers. Because men were more closely integrated into the industrial system, they were more subject to threats to their roles as providers for the family, and because most women were excluded from that system they had less to lose. A businessman might suffer significant damage to his reputation if he participated in reforms like working for pure food, drink, and drug legislation that threatened powerful industries with which he was directly or indirectly associated. If workers affiliated with reform causes that jeopardized free trade, they might incur the displeasure of employers, suffer ridicule, find themselves looking for other employment, or worse, be blackballed from their industry.

A Traditional Sense of Responsibility

Traditional attitudes toward their responsibilities influenced women to work for pure food, drink, and drugs. No one questioned the feminine role to nurture, to nurse, and to guard the family's well-being. By custom and necessity, women were entrusted with these aspects of family care and preservation. Responsibility for the family health, along with care of the sick and aging, resided primarily in the domain of the mother, who supplemented her task with a support network of female family and community members.[60]

In every instance cleanliness may not have the most observable hallmark of her successful motherhood and she may not have known or even heard of the germ theory of disease, but she knew enough to strain milk before she cooled it in the spring house, along with meat and butter. And she knew enough to cover her baked goods against flies. She considered herself a poor housewife if she could not make pickles without alum, and use pure fruit in her preserves to insure natural color and texture without the addition of aniline dyes or fillers.

The mother diagnosed, nursed, and dosed. She used medications that she found effective from personal and family experience. She gathered, cultivated, preserved, and prepared herbs. Occasionally she purchased them. In either case she was familiar with the drugs she worked with; she knew how to use, prepare, and control them. Her folk memory and religious orientation told her, accurately or not, that God had caused specific medicinal plants to grow where the diseases they cured were likely to occur.[61]

When she needed advice, she called on networks of female kin, consulting with women more experienced than she in treating disease. She called for a physician, if one were available, only when she and her support network could not handle the problem. If the family member died, it was God's will and she knew she had done everything in her power to save the life of the patient.[62]

Catherine Beecher has described the use of home remedies in New England for everything from colds, menstrual pain, and the universal menace of constipation, to consumption and cancer. Catherine Clinton revealed the burden of Southern plantation mistresses in caring for the illnesses of their families and ailing slaves. Some women became prominent as lay practitioners. According to Joseph Kett, medical practice belonged mostly to women in New Jersey as late as 1818.[63]

Women migrating to the West took their knowledge and often their networks with them. In Missouri, they encountered Creole mothers from whom they acquired "cherished and healthful remedies" from carefully gathered and stored herbs. In Indiana and other states, they learned the properties of herbs from their contacts with Indian women. Their medicine chests contained recipes for preparing medications and a cherished doctor book, handed down from generation to generation, perhaps resembling William Buchan's *Domestic Medicine*, which explained the causes and prevention of disease, the symptoms and treatment of specific maladies, and advised mothers that "physicians should be consulted when needed, but they should be needed rarely."[64]

Women inured to the practice of domestic medicine approached activism for pure food, drink, and drugs not from the standpoint of stepping out of conventional roles, but as a natural and necessary extension of their historic function as creators and protectors of life. In the context of traditional motherhood, promoting and pursuing food and drug legislation did not breach social mores.

In the crowded, secular, and industrializing climate after the Civil War that took men out of the home during the day and placed greater responsibility for the family upon the mother, such functions as overseeing health, nutrition, and education became more crucial than it had been. A great many mothers found they could not discharge their responsibility for the home and children unless the outside influences, with which their family came into daily contact, were pure and wholesome. Noting that custom had "bestowed upon woman the especial care of the home," and conditions had placed almost the entire charge of rearing and training the family upon the mother, Sophie F. Grubb, of Jacksonville, Illinois, wrote that women were obligated to take an interest in everything that threatened the safety of the home. Mothers must be as "interested in the basic principles of government as those who secured them" and concern themselves with every activity that ensured good health. Mothers could not isolate families "within the four walls of the house." Children had to attend school, perform all kinds of duties, and play with other children. Like many other reformers, Grubb felt that a woman's mission to build character, to teach self-discipline, to promote health, cleanliness, purity, sobriety, and all virtues which made up "the sum of noble manhood and sweet and gracious womanhood," was effective only to the extent that children found "corresponding virtues" in the community. God intended the human family to mingle and depend on each other. He had ordered people's lives so that unless they cared for their neighbors the neglect reacted upon their own beloved and forced them to recognize the necessity of caring. Women's role as protectors of the home demanded expanding their activities into the community — into town councils, school boards, and health improvement associations.[65]

The family could not be healthy unless the primary purchaser for the family was able to find wholesome food and unadulterated medications. Unwholesome substitutions, particularly if they were hidden and she was unaware of them, eroded her traditional ability to care for her family properly.

Jane Addams was among those who articulated the opinion that women could not discharge primary duties that belonged "to even the most conservative women," unless they joined "the more general movement looking toward social amelioration through legal enactment." By her own efforts an urban woman could no longer perform the obligations of keeping her house "clean and wholesome," feeding her children properly, or obtaining "untainted meat for her household."[66]

Anna E. Dickinson wrote, "A woman can only do her duty to her home ... her duty to her children, her duty to her own soul, by going into the world, not to strive in unwomanly fashion for place, and name, and authority, and rights; but, in womanly fashion, to do the work that no man is doing, the work that men are doing ill, the work that men are actually forbidding to be done."[67]

This attitude did not stop at the Mason-Dixon line. Many Southern women expressed the same opinion. In 1883 Mrs. C. S. Burnett wrote from Tullahoma, Tennessee, that woman's work could not end with her duties in the home. Women were "not only justified," but exhibited "the most exalted virtue when they" stepped "for a time ... beyond the domestic circle," and entered "upon the concerns of their country, of humanity, and of God." Many women would "much rather sit quietly" at home and watch the "good work go on;" but if men would not do "this work, women must." Burnett said she would rejoice if the work could be accomplished without women's suffrage. If their vote was necessary, women would "take up this new duty in the fear of God." Women should not think or say that they were "already overburdened with work." They had "only to lay aside some of the more trivial matters" and "substitute the paper for the novel," to become informed and to find time for reform activities.[68]

3

The State Crusaders

Before long the pure food, drink, and drug activists realized that local ordinances scratched only the edges of their problem. Despite concerted local attempts to control the quality of food, drink, and drugs, manufacturers continued to deceive the public and circumvent ordinances. Perceiving that the extent of adulteration and the dangers of habituation required wider participation and more stringent regulation, groups of consumers began to organize at state levels to demand state legislation, and stronger provisions for enforcement. The activities of crusaders at the state level reveal that the drive for pure food, drink, and drugs was not confined to any one geographic section of the United States. Consumers in every state expressed concern and attempted to improve the quality of what they consumed. In the process, these crusaders assembled a vocabulary to express their concern and describe their activities. They also developed a set of methods to advance their cause. Although they met with varying degrees of success, by the end of the century, most crusaders realized that state regulation also had its limitations.

Massachusetts

The experience of crusaders in Massachusetts illustrates a nearly complete composite of state pure food, drink, and drug activity across the country and provides a basis for comparison with the activities in other states. By 1898, Massachusetts stood as a model for what pure food advocates hoped to achieve. Working together, coalitions of consumers, health providers, and public health officials were able to secure fairly comprehensive pure food laws, update and supplement them as needs arose, and claim, with some justification, that Massachusetts led the nation in enforcing the food laws on its books. Its laws were clearly defined, placing the burden of compliance upon the retailer, providing for chemists and inspectors, and specifying seizures, fines, and closures for violations. With the active support of the governor, a board of health administered the laws, except those under the jurisdiction of the Dairy Commission. Both agencies collaborated with local medical societies, the state W.C.T.U., and the Massachusetts Federation of Women's Clubs.[1]

Provisions for drug regulation in Massachusetts were not as adequate as those for food regulation. The Massachusetts drug law required labeling of pharmaceutical mixtures and proprietary medications with a legible list of contents and exact percent of each ingredient. It allowed harmless coloring and preservatives if the label indicated their presence. Fines were specified for failing to comply with the law, but, beyond furnishing copies of the statute to retailers, manufacturers, and health professionals, the state provided few facilities for its enforcement.[2]

Physician Bessie Cushman claimed that a Massachusetts woman originated the idea of health boards and that states established health departments "in pursuance" to her plan. Cushman cited the *Medical Record* as her source, but did not identify the woman. Massachusetts founded the State Board of Health in 1866 as a research and reference agency to determine the causes of disease and distribute its findings. With a staff of chemists, physicians, and public health officials, it probed into problems of popular concern, such as the causes of infant mortality; the effects of alcohol, poor ventilation, and inadequate housing upon human health; the means by which smallpox, typhoid, and other diseases spread; and the relationship of sanitation to public health. Its studies on water purification and sewage attracted worldwide acclaim. Other than recommending laws, however, the Board remained aloof from active reform until the 1880s, when health improvement associations, citizen committees, and temperance unions persuaded the legislature to designate the Board of Health as the agency to detect food adulteration, determine the contents of nostrums, inspect food establishments, and prosecute those who violated state health laws.[3]

Aware that inspectors could not be everywhere at the same time, the Massachusetts W.C.T.U., in collaboration with women's clubs, organized vigilante groups to alert merchants to violations, collect samples of suspect foods, and report to the State Board of Health or the Dairy Commission, any infractions of state food laws that they (the women) could not resolve by discussing the offense with the merchants involved. Women felt an obligation to insure compliance to the law that protected them, their families, and their communities. Clubwoman Elizabeth Foster wrote, "We are not working for ourselves alone. When any violation of the State law comes under notice, … it should be reported to the Board of Health." For Foster, food adulteration was no "trivial matter." The lives of "countless babies and invalids" depended on a pure food supply. She urged all women to give serious interest to the matter, and told them, "What we get in this world depends largely on what we demand, and if we demand pure and wholesome food … we shall get it." In cooperation, women's organizations and health officials enforced the law more consistently than in states where agents worked less closely with consumers.[4]

The January 1906 list of convictions revealed the nature of the adulterations they discovered. It included nine convictions for unsanitary or adulterated milk; one for coloring milk to make it appear richer; one conviction each for adulterated ale, catsup, and lard, one for renovating butter, two for adulterating olive oil; six for adulterating "hamburg steak," and two for filling "frankfurts."[5]

Pursuant to consumer request, Massachusetts health agencies fortified their laws by publishing the results of their investigations in a monthly bulletin, listing the names, addresses, and violations of offenders and, also, of merchants who complied with the law. In addition, the Dairy Commission published a "white list" of dairies who met sanitation standards. They gave copies of these bulletins to the public and published them in the press, supplying consumers with guides of where to buy, where not to buy, and providing advertising incentives to businesses which upheld food standards.[6]

The close interaction of consumer groups with the health department fostered confidence in both. As retailers began to refuse to order adulterated products and demanded guarantees of purity from manufacturers and handlers, such measures were effective in improving the quality and safety of at least part of the food supply.[7]

State women's organizations provided undeviating nuclei for pure food, drink, and drug education and research, as well as for legislation and enforcement. The Massachusetts W.C.T.U. sponsored lectures and debates featuring public officials, physicians, and lawyers to spread the gospel of pure food and drugs. It encouraged a wide variety of research projects, such as a compilation of statistics and case studies of inmates in the Hampton jail to determine the relationship of substance abuse to crime. And it distributed an immense number of pure food and drug leaflets.[8]

Massachusetts was home ground to Mary Hunt. Through her

connections with educational institutions, clergy, and medical people, she was able to amass a vast collection of evidence that supported the pure food, drink and drug cause. On several occasions, she turned to the Board of Health to assay proprietaries she suspected of containing alcohol and other narcotics. In 1888 the Board of Health chemists found dangerous amounts of opium and alcohol in samples of children's medications — in Mrs. Winslow's Soothing Syrup, advertised for years in church and secular papers as "invaluable for children," Ayer's Cherry Pectoral, Dr. Bull's Cough Syrup, Jane's Expectorant, Hooker's Cough and Croup Syrup, Moore's Essence of Life, Mother Bailey's Quieting Syrup, and others too numerous to mention — and recommended that the sale of all soothing syrups be prohibited.[9]

In 1896 S. P. Sharples, state assayer, examined 50 proprietary medicines and 21 brands of liquid foods for alcohol content. The percentage of alcohol in some of the most popular proprietary medications, whose labels recommended doses varying from one to four times a day and "increased as needed," exceeded that in ordinary wine, beer, or cider. Most of these preparations also contained opium, opium derivatives, or cocaine. Temperance unions and women's clubs used these statistics to alert consumers and to "agitate" for legislation to control proprietary medications.[10]

In 1897 and again in 1902, state chemists assayed a large group of food supplements widely "recommended for people in feeble health," for the W.C.T.U. Department of Non-Alcoholic Medicine. The published assay reported percentages of alcohol ranging from 3 to 23 percent and low nutritive contents. The recommended daily intake of Liquid Peptonoids (23.03 percent alcohol) contained less than one ounce of nutriment and the equivalent of 3.5 ounces of whiskey. The dose of Mulford's Predigested Beef (19.72 percent alcohol) supplied 1.5 ounces of nutriment and the alcoholic equivalent of about 6 ounces whiskey. Dr. Charles Harrington presented this data at a meeting of the Boston Society of Medical Sciences held in November 1896 with the comment that the Board of Health "found in no one the slightest diastatic power." All were alcoholic, "some stronger than beer, ale or even porter." A number of specimens contained salicylic acid and other drugs. The W.C.T.U. circulated the entire list, along with assays of popular proprietary medications, in a leaflet, entitled "Patent Medicines."[11]

The state W.C.T.U. crusaders organized unions and mothers' groups to select and vote for school superintendents sympathetic to teaching physiology and hygiene with a special emphasis on the dangers of using stimulants and narcotics. They recruited teachers into their ranks to encourage them to teach health and physiology, suggested methods that would appeal to the students, and supplied them with visual aids. Thirty-six school committees introduced the subject in 1883 into all of the public schools in their towns. Wareham, Massachusetts, offered scientific instruction in its high schools, from where one of the teachers, Miss Guernsey, reported that the students were "very enthusiastic over the study of physiology and hygiene." The Lawrence union donated physiology textbooks to nearby Methuen school. The school board of Holbrook supplied texts to be used by teachers in oral instruction. W.C.T.U. women established loan libraries equipped with the "best scientific works" as aids to teachers and often provided physiology and hygiene manuals. In 1890, the W.C.T.U. led associations of civic groups and mothers' clubs in monitoring schools in each of the 23 towns in Hampshire county to insure that physiology and hygiene were taught. It conducted similar surveys in other counties.[12]

Despite united efforts, by the early 1900s Massachusetts consumers, health agencies, and health providers, concluding that their united measures were inadequate, began to demand federal regulation. Retailers found difficulty in determining which products were adulterated. Litigation was slow and costly. State officials had no jurisdiction over encroachment by manufacturers from other states who took advantage of consumers, retailers, and small firms who tried to comply with the law. Both Dr. Charles Harrington, secretary of the Board of Health, and Carlton D. Richardson, chairman of the Dairy Commission, reported that although Massachusetts was recognized as the leading state in the enforcement of pure food laws, they needed a national law to stem the flow of adulterated products from other states.[13]

Since its incorporation in 1893, the Massachusetts Federation of Women's Clubs had promoted pure food, drink, and drugs. In 1905 it took on the crusade for federal regulation in earnest, forming a separate Pure Food Committee to accelerate pure food and drug activism. The chairman, Elizabeth Foster, requested that every club in the state discuss the "food supply question" in at least one public forum before the end of the year, stressing both economic and public health points of view, but subordinating the aspect of fraud to the problems affecting health. As an agenda for these meetings, Foster outlined methods to expose common forms of food adulteration, commercial fraud, substitution of less expensive ingredients, and injurious preservatives and dyes used to mask deterioration.[14]

Each of the 22 forums that complied to Foster's request drafted a petition to their United States senators, Henry Cabot Lodge and W. M. Crane, urging that a federal pure food bill, regulating traffic in adulterated and misbranded food and drugs be enacted with all speed. In October, the State Federation sent a similar petition, requesting that the Massachusetts senators use "their best endeavor to further the passage" of the bill in the upcoming session of Congress. In sending the petition to Lodge, they were aware that he was one of the most influential lawmakers opposing pure food, drink, and drug legislation. Lodge had been successful in blocking the bill in the previous session, and Massachusetts club women chose the petition as one way of expressing their displeasure.[15]

When the law did not come to the Senate floor in 1905, Massachusetts women did not give up. In early 1906 women's clubs in Massachusetts distributed over 500 pamphlets and held 42 pure food and drug meetings, nineteen of which were open to the public. Each of these meetings forwarded resolutions endorsing a national food and drug law to their senators and representatives in Washington.[16]

Other States

Massachusetts may have led the nation in food regulation, but consumers in other states also sustained widespread and intense campaigns for pure food, drink, and drugs. Since the early 1800s states had enacted food laws pertaining to specific products and supplemented these early laws to address new problems as they arose. For example, the state of Missouri granted charters to most cities and towns that gave citizens the authority to pass specific ordinances to "establish and regulate markets" and to "secure the public health." The people of St. Louis were able to extend these provisions to allow inspection of butter and lard, and to establish standards of weight and quality for bread. Updates granted additional authority.[17]

Although the initial purpose of some of the early food and drink laws was to protect local industries against competition, the element of consumer safety and protection against fraud was a consistent consideration. For example, most frequently, it was the dairy industry that introduced laws governing butter imitations and adulteration to protect itself against competition from oleomargarine and slaughterhouse simulations. However, one of the dairy interest's main arguments in favor of regulation was the danger to public health. Danger to health from adulteration was the issue that aroused public opinion and brought consumers, public health officials, and medical groups together to fight for the enactment of state laws.[18]

In 1874 Illinois passed one of the earliest state laws applying to foods in general and in 1879 attached a supplement relating specifically to dairy products. New York passed a general pure food and drug law in 1881. Michigan and New Jersey enacted more limited food laws in the same year. In 1883 Maine, Nebraska, and Ohio passed general laws. Pennsylvania followed suit in 1885; Virginia in 1887; Iowa and Vermont in 1888; Connecticut, Kansas, and Wisconsin in 1889; and Maryland, New Hampshire, Colorado, California, Georgia, Indiana, North Carolina, North Dakota, Washington, and other states between 1890 and 1895. Each of these states renovated their laws periodically, but few provided adequate enforcement agencies.[19]

Laws and methods of enforcement varied significantly from state to state. After an extensive commissioned review of state laws relating to the adulteration, labeling, and marketing of food, drink, and drugs, Professor J. H. Beale reported to the second annual convention of the National Pure Food and Drug Congress in 1899 a great disparity between both the products that state statutes covered and the methods of control. In some states the laws were "few in number and meager in proportion," in others they were "voluminous, covering almost every conceivable variety of adulteration, misbranding and sophistication." Separate surveys by the federal Bureau of Chemistry and by the National Consumers' League confirmed Beale's findings.[20]

The extent of participation in pure food, drink, and drug activism was remarkable. Examples taken from the Consumers' League survey, W.C.T.U. reports, and women's club magazines illustrate the diversity, focus, depth, and breadth of cooperation between state crusaders and state agencies.

In Connecticut, where women's clubs and temperance unions "on the side of the consumer," agitated continuously for laws and enforcement "throughout the state," the pure food and drug laws were considered better than average. The Dairy Commissioner enforced part of the laws, and the state Experimental Station examined the samples. E. H. Jenkins, food commissioner, observed a positive "moral effect" of the Connecticut law. Certain grossly adulterated brands had been driven out of the state. Occasionally when prosecutions were needed, every court action resulted in conviction. Because defendants pleaded guilty without contest, no fines were imposed. Like Massachusetts, Connecticut published the results of its inspections.[21]

In nearby New Hampshire, officials furnished copies of their food and drug provisions directly to dealers and solicited cooperation at the same time. The officials felt direct contact and cooperation with dealers produced better compliance than if they used prosecution. Not convinced, New Hampshire women tried to offset the defects of state arbitrations by circulating literature to the public and to physicians, by agitating for compliance in lectures and conventions, and by monitoring retail outlets.[22]

Citizens in New York were successful in securing a general food and drug law in 1881. The law prohibited selling misbranded or adulterated food products and required labeling "to show the character of constituents" so that the purchasing public could be aware of the contents of the "commodities" they were "putting in their stomachs." In 1902, W.C.T.U. unions in 50 counties lined up to fight against proprietary medications, demanding truth in labeling and adequate law enforcement. Chemung County marshaled the resources of its eleven unions, generated seven original papers, held two conventions, and issued appeals to all local physicians. Steuben County sent pamphlets, accompanied by a personal letter, to 91 physicians. All unions "agitated" for truth in labeling and adequate law enforcement.[23]

New Jersey had a general food law, but focused its efforts on insuring the quality of its milk, shellfish, and meat supply. In 1904 and 1905, public outrage led to prosecuting dairies when an increase in infant mortality accompanied the "boldness and cupidity of certain unscrupulous milk dealers" who ignored the law.[24]

Ohio maintained active and effective pure food and drug enforcement agencies. In one three-month period in 1905 they obtained 189 convictions and collected $8,194.40 in fines. Sixty-one county and 144 local women's temperance unions sustained active campaigns to alert the public to dangerous drugs. In Athens, superintendents devoted the first ten minutes at two meetings each month to the subject and distributed the pamphlet, "safe remedies," to every member. In Marietta the union attracted large audiences and recruited a sizable "increase of membership," including the mayor, by devoting one meeting each month to the subject, scheduling a Dr. Beardsley to speak on the "evil of indiscriminate use of patent medicines," providing articles to the press, and distributing literature.[25]

A. C. Bird, State Dairy and Food Commissioner for Michigan, considered the laws of his state effective when they were properly administered.

Michigan had eight regular inspectors and seven special investigators constantly at work. His department supplemented the law by cooperating with honest manufacturers and jobbers, so that the markets were "more thoroughly rid of adulterated food products than ever before." This plan included monthly educational scoring contests to which every creamery, cheese factory, and private producer of butter in the state was invited to contribute, and that grew in popularity and provided a convenient way of scoring a great number of samples every month. In Ella Kellogg's home state, temperance unions and health clubs were engrossed with pure food. Ninety-six unions, in addition to district and county unions, maintained active departments of health in 1886 that generated numerous lectures and original papers, and distributed sets of pure food, drink, and drug literature. A Mrs. Barnes, of Manistree, wrote a series of essays issued by the unions in collaboration with the State Board of Health. Two women served as health officers. Their crusade was still alive and growing in 1902 when Sophronia M. Bowerman of Opechee won recognition for distributing more health leaflets than any person in the nation.[26]

In 1887 the high incidence of opium habituation prompted the Indiana Medical Association and other influential bodies to press for regulation, but the state legislature did not pass laws restricting the sale of opium and providing care for opium addicts until later. During subsequent sessions, the state furnished crusaders with postage, stationery, and blank petitions. By 1905 Indiana had a general food and drug law, covering sanitation of all food-producing establishments, alcoholic beverages, candy, dairy products, meat, vinegar, water, food, and drugs. State statutes provided for a state chemist and authorized the board of health to prepare rules and ordinances regulating minimum standards for food and drugs, defined specific adulterations, and empowered the board to adopt "such measures as may be necessary to facilitate enforcement of food and drug laws." The general food laws were adequate, but State Food Commissioner J. N. Hurty of Indianapolis reported that Indiana had "never attempted to enforce her pure food laws except by occasionally calling the attention of the dealers to the fact that laws exist."[27]

Pure food and drug crusaders were active in the territory before North Dakota became a state. By general consensus, their representatives placed general food, drink, and drug laws in the original state statutes and provided for a state chemist. Their laws were administered with exceptional energy by Edwin Fremont Ladd, food commissioner of North Dakota, through the Agricultural Experimental Station, and the assistant dairy commissioner under the direction of the Commissioner of Agriculture. North Dakota required and enforced strict truth in labeling and maintained one hygienic school. The W.C.T.U. was surprisingly active for such a sparsely populated area. In 1887, twenty-two local unions and four county unions had operational departments of health that held regular meetings, sponsored six lectures, and generated and circulated ten original pamphlets. Dr. Annie C. Hall wrote 360 letters, submitted a series of plain health talks for the state W.C.T.U. paper, wrote regular columns for local newspapers, and circulated several thousand leaflets, all the while caring for an invalid husband. In 1902, Nellie Mott, superintendent of the Department of Non-Alcoholic Medicine, sent out 15,600 pages of literature, including "Patent Medicine," and "Safe Remedies."[28]

In Colorado, where women had secured the right to vote, both women's clubs and temperance unions were active in promoting pure food and drugs. As early as 1883, women's groups organized to expose opium dens and proprietary medications. In 1887 women's clubs included pure food activism in their schedules and followed up by introducing state legislation. In 1887 Mary Shields, president of the state W.C.T.U., and Mrs. James Havens, superintendent of the W.C.T.U. Department of Narcotics, presented a petition to the state legislature for a law prohibiting the sale of narcotics without a physician's prescription, and promised the members, "If we do not succeed this winter we will try next, and the next, until our faith is swallowed up by victory."[29]

In 1890 the State Federation of Women's Clubs, led by Martha A. B. Conine of Denver, in cooperation with the state W.C.T.U., introduced a pure food law into the legislature. The bill failed that session, but Conine continued working for pure food after she was elected to the state congress, and women's clubs and unions continued "agitating" and lobbying for effective pure food bills. In 1904 a law prohibiting the adulteration of all foods and a law prohibiting the publication of objectionable and fraudulent medical advertisements remained two of their primary objectives. By then, Colorado had a general food law and statutes regulating the quality of alcoholic beverages, dairy products, honey, and meat. However, State Dairy Commissioner Mary Wright reported that other than enforcing laws relating to butter and cheese, the state had made no provisions for enforcing the food and drug laws. When a bill requiring stronger enforcement failed to pass in 1905, Isabell Churchill, president of the State Federation of Women's Clubs, advised local associations to remain "thoroughly awake to the need" for pure food legislation and to keep pure food committees ready for "concerted action" as soon as the bills came up for consideration in the next session.[30]

The great majority of crusaders in western and southern states, like Missouri State Dairy Commissioner Robert Washburn, regardless of the kinds of food and drug statutes on their books, reported that they had no effective comprehensive pure food and drug laws, nor any means of enforcing the few laws on the books, except in isolated cases, relating to dairy foods. Kentucky had a good general law, but was able to use only the "lever of publicity" to enforce it. Kansas relied on the publication of offending products in the local newspapers, with the only "visible results" being the "quickening of public conscience." Alabama accorded the Commissioner of Agriculture and the board of health limited powers. Ineffective laws in Georgia led clubwoman Mrs. O. A. Granger to suggest a sin tax on the makers of nostrums to support public schools. Arkansas, California, Delaware, and Florida had food laws but no provisions for enforcement.[31]

In 1905 fourteen states introduced legislation to make public the contents of patent medicines containing narcotic drugs or large quantities of alcohol. North Dakota alone succeeded. For most of the crusaders this was a dismal defeat. The Maine W.C.T.U. president pointed out that in no other country were "quacks given so free an opportunity to deceive the people with their nostrums," some of which were "not even patented, simply trade marked [sic]." Much to her delight, when Maine passed a law banning drug adulteration, some of the proprietary companies canceled their contracts with Maine newspapers and suspended shipments of their products into Maine. Other crusaders found the bills requiring proper labeling "productive of much good because of the enlightenment which came through the discussion before the Legislative Committees and elsewhere, and through numerous press reports." They predicted renewed efforts to obtain the desired legislation and greater support from those interested in the public welfare, but realized that securing their objectives would not be easy under the bombardment of "multiple forces."[32]

Language

In the process of campaigning for pure food, drink, and drugs in their states, the crusaders assembled a language of words and images to give concrete expression to their concepts. They referred to adulterated food, drink, and drugs as poisonous, enslaving, stupefying, tainted, contaminated, and a societal curse. They regarded the use of such products as unnatural, disease-producing, bondage, slavery, addiction, and the poison habit. They characterized manufacturers and marketers of adulterated substances as purveyors of poison and dealers in death who were guilty of fraud, murder, vice, greed, sin, crime, boodle, and quackery. They portrayed their own activities in terms of concern, self-defense, altruism, patience, mutualism, cooperation, fellowship, equality, democracy, progress, and enterprise. Those who did not support the cause were timid, selfish, do-nothings, conservative, or ambiguous. When those who opposed food, drink, and drug regulation accused the crusaders of being fanatics, radicals, socialists, cranks, fools, or lunatics, the crusaders tried to turn the criticism into a positive image.

Examples of their rhetoric is rich and colorful. Ella Kellogg spoke of adulterated food as "unnatural" and creating "abnormal cravings." Harriet N. K. Goff, of Brooklyn, spoke of "seductive substitutes" for "brain food." The Frankfort Businessmen's Club petitioned Congress to pass a pure food bill that would protect the people of Kentucky from "such fraud in food and drink as is now being imposed upon them through the operation of interstate commerce."[33]

At the Senate Hearing of 1904 one witness called adulterated food "fraud," and those who mislabeled their products "robbers." He spoke of people all over the country who were "poisoned" or "falling dead" from "deleteriously adulterated" products for sale in the "average corner grocery" manufactured by "unscrupulous dealers in human life." He asserted that it was "demoralizing" for these "miscreants to get rich in such revolting traffic in ill health, pain, and death," and to buy their way out of "infamy" by holding out a few "ducats" to enter into the "respectability of good company." "What an example is that for our youth!" he exclaimed. "Is it any wonder that our nation is full of scamps in office as well as in the penitentiary." He claimed that "Nine times in ten, first-class barrooms" sold an "adulterated article" for beer or whiskey. That was the reason so many people died of Bright's disease. When he was a boy "whisky would make a man drunk if he took too much of it, but it did not kill him." He hoped that the "pure-food bill" would give the country "pure licker."[34]

The California W.C.T.U. reported that the Secretary of the Pasadena Union was a physician who did not "dose" her patients with "liquid perdition and call it medicine." Mrs. O. A. Granger, of Georgia, spoke of proprietaries as "decoctions" and "insidious mixtures" that injured men, women, and children. F. Emory Lyon, of Chicago, spoke of articles of diet and drink that were stimulating many a "sister sober" who was a "slave to the daily dose of alcohol" in proprietary medicines. The *Union Signal* wrote of the sale of adulterated candy as the "slaughter of the innocents."[35]

Frances Willard equated the "poison gathered from poppies" with "poison distilled from fruits and grains." She warned of the "insidious" nature of "habit-forming poisons" in proprietaries which seemed to do little harm at first, if taken in small quantities, by people with strong "constitutions" who were able to "bear up under their curse" for considerable periods of time. They were "poisons" and the "law of poisons" dictated that the "tendency of yesterday becomes the habit of today, and the bondage of tomorrow."[36]

In a "Band of Hope" lesson in the *Union Signal*, Russell Land Carpenter drew an analogy between criminal poisoning and adulteration, asking, "What is a poison?" He explained that the word "poison" derived from the Latin verb *potare*, meaning "to drink." Originally the term *poison* meant something to drink, particularly a medicinal draught, but soon came to apply to anything ingested, breathed, or touched that produced toxic symptoms or death. People stood in "horror" of poisons. "Secrecy" was their "especial danger." "Treacherous murderers" and "cowards," who were afraid to try force, used them. Whether "masked" in food, drink, medicine, or purchased as "pleasure poisons," governments did not provide the same safeguards against the sale of "pleasure poisons" that killed the soul, destroyed the brain, crippled the "moral nature," and threatened "myriads of lives" as it did against arsenic and strychnine.[37]

Both deliberately and subconsciously, Martha Meir Allen also chose metaphors of sin, death, and slavery to make the dangers of drugs vivid and the indignities imposed on the public tangible. She referred to proprietary medicines as "concoctions" and "toxic" drugs that had a "great hold" on the population, to "poisonous drugs" that the system had to "throw off," and to medications "inherently vicious" that were sold "indiscriminately to the laity." She wrote of cocaine as an "enslaving drug," the most "insidious of all drugs yet known," and warned that those who became "enslaved" to it were unable to discontinue its use. Most of those "addicted" to cocaine began its use "unwittingly" through "catarrh snuffs, asthma cures, and other proprietary preparations, the composition of which was secret."[38]

She spoke of the "fraud nature" of drug marketing and newspaper advertising. Newspapers were "easy to buy up" and "conscienceless as to the robbery of the unfortunate sick." She described manufacturer guarantees as not "truthful" and designed to "dupe," providing numerous illustrations of advertisers, such as the makers of Waterbury's Metabolized Cod Liver Oil and Lydia Pinkham's, who resorted to "wholesale fraud." Their advertising agents played "mean tricks" on "distinguished Christian workers" and notable persons by publishing "false" testimonials in newspapers and magazines. She claimed that large numbers of newspaper publishers were sharing the "ill-gotten gains" of "medical fakirs." She spoke of "missionary fraud," whereby proprietaries claimed that missionaries, ministers, and W.C.T.U. leaders endorsed their product, and "South America frauds" in which "unscrupulous quacks" claimed to have discovered new cure-alls in the jungles of the Amazon. She condemned the "patent-medicine" industry that thrived, "with all of its horrors of deception, fraud" and dangerous ingredients.[39]

The W.C.T.U. *Messenger* of Colorado called the proprietary industry the "Great Fraud," and referred to the meat industry as the "Beef Trust" that plundered the American people to the tune of a quarter of a billion dollars annually. Dr. Nathan Davis, dean of Northwestern University Medical School, Chicago, referred to phenacetin and antipyrine as "poisonous agents."[40]

In its October 1898 and February 1899 issues, a W.C.T.U. publication entitled *The Banner of Gold* printed articles upon the dangers of drug abuse and fraud. The author wrote that the United States seemed "to be rapidly becoming a nation of cocaine fiends," with "an insatiable craving" for artificial stimulation, and victims "in the lowest depths of an inferno." Few manufacturers were "honest enough" to label "dangerously seductive, narcotic" drugs. Pharmacists "relapsed into evil ways through coquetting with sin," and physicians were "careless, selfish, unprincipled, or unobservant" of the effects of the "various medicines" they prescribed. Drug manufacturers and merchants exhibited "will-paresis" and "moral paralysis," becoming "habitués" of untruthfulness and "low cunning," luring unsuspecting mothers with their "commercial nostrums" to condemn their "offspring" to a life of "toxic-slavery" and the "curse of baneful appetite"[41]

The Department of Public Charities published a "Report on the Use of So-called Proprietary Medicines as Therapeutic Agents" reporting a fraud against Bellevue Hospital whereby manufacturers sent samples of "secret nostrums" to the hospital and to members of the staff for trial, and subsequently published advertisements asserting that the preparations were used by the hospital with approval of its medical board. The report defined a secret nostrum as "a preparation, the origin or composition of which is kept secret, the therapeutic claims for which are unreasonable or unscientific, or which is not intended for a legitimate purpose." They gave as examples, soothing syrups, female regulators, and blood purifiers.[42]

Crusaders quoted various physicians who opposed the use of proprietary drugs. Dr. N. Roe Bradner of the Pennsylvania Hospital for the Insane, in speaking of the "marvelous cures" advertised in connection with use of these mixtures, called them "volumes of gilded falsehood, designed for an innocent, unsuspecting public." Dr. A. Emil Hiss asserted that "A secret compound" was "presumptively a fraud. Why a secret if not to permit extravagant, or fraudulent claims as to therapeutic merit? ... The ruling motive of the secret being essentially false and dishonest." A Dr. Frederic Coley compared using cocaine to relieve exhaustion with "casting out devils by Beelzebub, with a vengeance," and particularly dangerous because cocaine hid "Nature's danger signals" and ensnared "victims" by masking the symptoms of overwork and malnutrition. Dr. Walter N. Edwards wrote, "The proprietors have no particular regard for the welfare to the people; their business is to make a profit, and many of them gain enormous fortunes. By skillful and lavish advertisements, occult methods, and by carefully worded testimonials, they appeal to the credulity of the public, and often deceive even those who regard themselves as belonging to the thinking classes."[43]

In the *Monitor of Health*, Dr. J. H. Kellogg asserted, "The average manufacture of patent medicines regularly employs a person of some literary attainment whose duty it is to invent vigorous testimonials of sufferings relieved by Dr. Charlatan's universal panacea. In many instances persons are hired to give testimonials, and answer letters of inquiry in such a way as to encourage business. The shameless dishonesty and ingenious villainy exhibited are beyond description." In the April 1899 *Bulletin of the American Medical Temperance Association*, he referred to "a large family of intoxicating drugs, each of which is capable of producing specific functional and organic mischief, besides the vital deterioration common to the use of so-called felicity-producing drugs." He asserted that "every proprietary was necessarily mischievous in its tendencies" and its use was "intemperance, whether its name be alcohol, tobacco, opium, cocaine, coca, kola, hashish, Siberian mushroom, caffeine, betel-nuts, maté or another of the score of enslaving drugs known to pharmacology."[44]

Harvey Wiley described headache powders as "powerful" and in some cases "deadly." They produced nervous system depression, disturbed the digestion, interfered with natural sleep, and overworked the kidneys. To be effective, they required "increasingly larger quantities as the system" became "accustomed to their use," and they created a "habit of gaining relief" which became "an obsession and incapable of being resisted." Edwin Fremont Ladd, food commissioner of North Dakota, emphasized that at least 50 percent of proprietary medicines were preparations intended to "defraud" the public.

One critic of the pure food, drink, and drug crusaders described the language of alcohol, narcotic, and stimulant reform as particularly intemperate and those who advocated pure food, drink, and drugs legislation as fanatics. In answer, H. W. Hardy of Lincoln, Nebraska, replied that being labeled a fanatic or a radical was not necessarily uncomplimentary. Although some might call them "radicals," politicians call them "fanatics," and narcotic dealers call them "cranks," reformers should not be offended. Fanatic meant "excessively in earnest." It did not mean "earnestness of a hireling, or paid attorney, but the earnestness of heart and soul, ... moved to earnest effort." After all, it was the fanatics in the world that accomplished the most.[45]

Hardy asserted that "radical" was a term of honor. Crusaders should be as proud to be radicals as they were to be "Yankees." When some patriots, called radicals, attacked slavery as inconsistent with democracy and "a curse to the nation, to the slave, and to the slaveholder," and proposed to cut out "the institution by the root," they were called root cutters or "radicals." There was "not a single element of compromise" or "branch pruning," in the "make-up of the term." In the same way, radicals proposed to cut out dangerous drugs at the root. Radicals were those who accomplished reform.[46]

In Hardy's reasoning, "crank" was not as uncomplimentary as it sounded. A crank was the part that turned a machine. Attached to the main shaft, it was "all on one side" and had "no swivel" or "weathercock tendency." The person who was "solid on one side of any question" was the kind of person "to tie to." The "shilly shally" people, "riding the wave, dead or alive" were never missed. He preferred the "kind of flesh" that stood "full bigness for or against, on one side or the other of every question."[47]

The editor of the *Union Signal* wrote, "They call us fanatics, let them. Reformers of all ages were fanatics. They accuse us of being one-idead cranks. Very good; if we have one idea we are infinitely superior to the many who have none." Belle Mappin bemoaned the reluctance of some American women to join the band of "terrible fanatics" who were so "unladylike as to raise their voices" against "fashionable sin." Ellen Foster condemned the "conservative in society" as one of the greatest hindrances to effective reform.[48] Other food, drink, and drug reformers preferred moderate language and a conservative image. Louisa Poppenheim warned clubwomen that statements "lost weight by their very violence," and that "calm, exact, dispassionate" speech convinced more people than "brilliant word painting" based on emotion rather than evidence. Exaggeration reduced credibility, prevented accurate evaluation, and lessened their influence in the community.[49]

The language of pure food, drink, and drug reform reflected the attitude of cohesion — cooperation rather than competition. Phillip Graham Taylor wrote that among organized women, the Christian word "mutualism" was replacing the competitive word "independence." He felt that women's organizations provided a "broad general fulcrum" for the "special lever" of social "salvation" for all. Together reformers could "pool" their efforts to alleviate conditions in the "hard-pan city civilization" that was forced upon them, "not from books, theory, or lectures, but from the hard cares" of their fellow men and women.[50]

The editor of *Keystone* pointed out that it was the "spirit of cooperation" that "united" clubwomen of diverse taste in a "grand humanitarian effort" to spread an "altruism" that opposed selfishness and individualism — creating instead an "elevation of citizenship"; and the "raising of higher ideals."[51]

At the same time the crusaders developed a language of activism. E. W. A. Fisk, of Colorado Springs, Colorado, reminded her associates they should remember that "those who try to do something and fail are infinitely better than those who try to do nothing and succeed." Lizzie H. Sampson, a member of the Colorado W.C.T.U., warned, "We are living in a progressive age, and unless we keep up with it we shall find ourselves back numbers." The *Keystone* advised clubwomen, "Never be afraid of giving the world too many ideas; there are so many people who have no ideas at all," and "Be firm in your purpose; stand up for your ideas and champion your own convictions." Esther T. Housh said, "The labor is yours." Adding to the "good work of man," it brought "beauty and harmony where crudeness and discord prevailed." The heroes were those who knew the truth and were "not afraid to speak it"; they who knew the right and were "not afraid to do it."[52]

Methods

Despite the diversity of state laws and of consumer activities, crusaders developed a pattern of methods to attack their pure food, drink, and drug problems. Although flexible enough for innovation, their usual strategy followed a progressive configuration of investigation, planning, organization, agitation, perseverance, legislation, enforcement, and augmentation. This pattern of operation was important because it provided guidelines for the kind of activism that crusaders hoped would bring lasting results.[53]

Ordinarily, they approached food, drink, and drug reform cautiously, considering study the primary step of intelligent reform. Before they were willing to invest years of energy into the project, they insisted on equipping themselves with accurate evidence and becoming familiar with every aspect and every point of view. Approximate knowledge was of little use. In 1882 Sarah Hunt advised crusaders to beware of zeal without knowledge, because "guesses at science" brought a cause into disrepute. Two decades later, the editor of *Club Notes* still confirmed the necessity of investigation. She observed that "the firm basis of an accurate investigation, deliberation, and consultation," along with the determination and energy "to accomplish results," inevitably preceded entering "new and unworked fields." Committees tried to determine the viability of reform: the nature of the problem, how it could be attacked, what they hoped to accomplish, the resources and personnel required, and what support or opposition they could expect from community leaders.[54]

Once they decided to attack the problem, crusaders laid out blueprints, defining objectives and outlining procedures step-by-step. Advocates of non-alcoholic medicine developed an eight-point program that included exposing dangerous proprietary medicines and liquid foods, working for legislation, and persuading newspapers to drop fraudulent medical advertising. Scientific instruction enthusiasts constructed a twelve-step plan. Other crusaders outlined their agendas in similar fashion before they started their campaigns.[55]

Close organization was essential. Reformers organized into consumer groups to accomplish their educational and political goals. Realizing she needed the support of numbers, Mary Hunt decide to use the vast resources of her state W.C.T.U. In proposing drug education, Mrs. Judge Merrick asked delegates to the Louisiana W.C.T.U. to "join hands in a united, honest endeavor ... withholding nothing and doing everything." In every state women grouped together into departments and federations to attack the food and drug problem from varying vantage points.[56]

Exposing the problem followed investigation, planning, and organizing. Joseph Pulitzer once said that exposing plots and secret activities defused the power of manufacturing combinations. There was not a "crime," a "dodge," a "trick," a "swindle," or a "vice" that did not "live by secrecy." Get these "out in the open," he said, "describe them, attack them, ridicule them ... and sooner or later public opinion" would "drive them away." According to Pulitzer, exposé might not be the only necessary measure, but it was "the one thing without which all other agencies" would fail.[57]

Pulitzer's statement replicated the opinion of food and drug crusaders. They felt that if they publicized the dangers through word of mouth, lectures, conventions, pamphlets, articles, essay contests, and education, the public would demand pure products and legislation to control manufacturers. Mrs. Merrick counseled women to "urge and agitate" the question in "parishes where the majority of the voters of the state resided, for ... the education of the people" was an antidote for substance abuse. Crusaders could not "expect legislators to write laws" that "public sentiment" did not support. Elizabeth Foster advised women, after familiarizing themselves with every aspect of the problem, to interest others, "the voters in their families and among their friends."[58]

The crusaders considered exposing social problems part of their civic responsibility. The constitutional right of free speech was an essential of self-government. The voice of the people, "at liberty to arraign the wrong doer at the bar of public opinion" checked abuses, punished offenders, alerted public officials, prepared voters for intelligent exercise of their duty at the polls, and inflicted social censure. Those who made use of this liberty to enlighten their fellow citizens on public affairs were exercising a function of government. If they did not, they neglected a public duty that was imposed upon them by virtue of living in a free state.[59]

Crusaders realized that they must persevere. They did not expect immediate improvement. Lasting results required passive patience to endure and active patience to accomplish. To reach their goal required plodding, persistent "conquest of trifles; content with progress, no matter how slight, how trivial, how slow; the conservation of every ray of mental energy; working, watching, waiting, moving ahead."[60]

Unenfranchised women used the same techniques to influence legislatures that unenfranchised colonists had used to influence Parliament before the American Revolution. Crusaders studied Colonial history, compared their situation with that of the American colonists, and utilized the tactics that the colonists had found effective. When persuasion failed, women attempted to influence government by publishing, distributing pamphlets, petitioning, lobbying, and overt political coercion. They were successful only when the weight of numbers created adequate pressure on legislative, executive, and, eventually, judicial branches of the government.

Legislation was useless without enforcement. Usually women shied away from bringing court action, preferring to report violations to the authorities. Ellen Foster noted that it was "rarely wise for Unions, as Unions, to become prosecutors," but they could point out violations to the appropriate state officials and "set into motion those agencies: which could remedy the situation." Because she found enforcement "most irksome" and felt that women could use their time, strength, and money "in other channels of effort," Foster did not recommend that they "go forth with warrants and witnesses, with fines and penalties," until indirect enforcement failed.[61]

On the state level, organized women preferred to secure legal provisions and funding for enforcement agencies and officers. A few states, including Massachusetts, Ohio, and North Dakota, maintained fairly active enforcement agencies, but most states did not. Establishing enforcement facilities often required considerable time and effort. In Missouri from 1890 through 1906, the applications of pure food, drink, and drug advocates for a state chemist received little consideration from the General Assembly. When an 1899 arrangement with Dr. Frank Waters of the Agricultural Experimental Station at the University of Missouri to analyze samples of food for adulteration and to publish the results took too much of his time, members of the Missouri State Federation of Women's Clubs began to lobby for an act to provide for a full time state chemist whose "especial duties" included supervision of foods, "particularly as regards their adulteration." Eventually in 1905, the Federation was able to introduce a bill, intended to protect the consumer against "the adulteration, misbranding, and imitation of foods, beverages, candies, drugs, and condiments," and to provide funds and personnel for enforcement, but despite their intense statewide publicity campaign, the bill was shelved in committee.[62]

Crusaders in other states experienced similar difficulties and employed a variety of solutions. If state food and drug laws did not provide for full-time chemists, enforcement agencies often employed part-time chemists or contracted for specific sets of analyses with agricultural state experimental chemists who were associated with land grant colleges.

A number of state chemists attained prominence as pure food, drink, and drug crusaders. Some were physicians who had specialized in food and drug chemistry in German universities. Most were energetic public health defenders, who found women's groups their strongest advocates, and supported women's food and drug activities.

Harvey Washington Wiley, M.D., was the most notable of these chemists. He began his career as State Chemist of Indiana, did postgraduate studies in Germany, and soon moved to a position of Chief of the Bureau of Chemistry in the Federal Department of Agriculture, where eventually he became an avid supporter of pure food in the national arena and played a major role in helping to secure the federal Pure Food, Drink, and Drug Act of 1906.[63]

Another influential state chemist, Robert M. Allen, Kentucky State Food and Drug Administrator, through his political connections, had more or less free access to Theodore Roosevelt and eventually was appointed to the Department of Justice to aid in the prosecution of federal law. Edwin Fremont Ladd was a militant food administrator in North Dakota. James T. Shepard in South Dakota, A. C. Bird in Michigan, H. E. Bernard in Indiana, Julius Hortvet in Minnesota, W. M. Allen in North Carolina, and William Frear in Pennsylvania became outstanding consumer advocates in the crusade.[64]

State Support for a National Law

By 1905, few crusaders found state laws adequate to achieve their goals. Often consumers accepted less-than-comprehensive legislation over no legislation at all, in the hope that as soon as food statutes became operative, consumers could supplement the laws and reach out into related fields of activity. Milk and meat statutes needed to be strengthened, tuberculosis conquered, bakeries and canneries cleaned up, and dangerous drugs regulated.

Even in the states that implemented lively inspection and prosecution policies, enforcement was spotty and ineffective. Consumers remained at the mercy of "avaricious" manufacturers and dealers who were "constantly poisoning the springs of existence" by adulterating the food they ate, by selling "poisonous" products that killed, rather than nourished, and perpetrating seemingly endless forms of fraud to deceive the public. In a number of states, industries were so far-reaching in their political and economic influence that public officials refused to regulate them. Smaller concerns bribed state and local inspectors. Adulteration and fraud were so prevalent that none of the states could afford the expense of adequate personnel and equipment to deal with the problem.

Because state agents could not act extraterritorially, they could not regulate the importation of large quantities of tainted food, meats from diseased animals, adulterated beverages, misbranded food stuffs, and dangerous and addictive remedies into their state. Without federal regulation, no state was able to enforce statutes intended to protect the life and health of its citizens. The Ohio food and drug commissioner found that, as a general rule, local manufacturers complied with specific statutes and standards, but he advocated federal legislation to protect consumers against out-of-state manufacturers in the neighboring states of Kentucky and Indiana. Ohio's neighbor, Kentucky, complained of the same difficulty with Ohio and other nearby states. M. A. Scovell, Director of the Agricultural Experimental Station at Lexington, reported that Kentucky's state laws and the "lever of publicity" were raising standards of food supply, but "daily investigation illustrated the urgent need for a federal statute" to regulate "manufacturers and wholesalers in Illinois, Indiana, Ohio, Tennessee, West Virginia, and other states" who "imposed adulteration upon local dealers" and were "beyond the jurisdiction" of Kentucky courts. Robert M. Allen, secretary and treasurer of the National Association of State Dairy and Food Commissioners, wrote that food commissioners could not begin to address the magnitude of the problem. Food manufacturers in Cincinnati and Chicago shipped over 50,000 food products to approximately 8,000 stores in Kentucky. In order to enforce the law effectively, inspectors would have to accomplish the impossible task of inspecting each product in each store and when they detected violations, their only recourse was to prosecute the retailers instead of the manufacturer who adulterated the article. Food commissioners in Alabama, Arkansas, California, Colorado, Connecticut, Delaware, Florida, Georgia, Idaho, and other states registered similar complaints, advocating federal regulation to stop the shipment of adulterated and misbranded product from one state to another.[65]

By 1900 state temperance unions and women's clubs throughout the country were clamoring for an omnibus federal food, drink, and drug law in the consumer interest. State conventions and reform congresses passed resolutions to redouble their efforts. They distributed thousands of pamphlets, adopted the issue as a primary objective, wrote articles, sponsored numerous addresses, arranged for sermons, and held institutes.[66]

Commenting on the inability of states to deal with large interstate corporations, Elizabeth Foster said,

> For many years some of our States have been alive to the dangers involved in the high art of successful food adulteration, but their efforts to enforce their own laws have been terribly handicapped by the fact that certain other states cannot be induced to pass such laws. The reason is because the men who profit by this particular kind of infamy are able to prevent the passage of such laws by means best known to themselves, but which the public also understand fully.... The only remedy for this state of affairs is Federal legislation.[67]

PART II:
THE NATIONAL
CRUSADERS,
1882–1904

"To cure is the voice of the past, to prevent is the divine whisper of the day."
—*Union Signal*, April 6, 1899

Pure food, drink, and drug reformers began to organize on a national scale before regulation had an adequate trial in most states, and certainly before state politicians and bureaucrats were willing to concede that they could not handle their own food, drink, and drug problems. Although the national crusade operated concurrently with and supported state campaigns, it maintained a distinct identity and character of its own. More than responding to the inability of state crusaders to contain the food, drink and drug problem, the national crusaders recognized that a nationwide danger required national attention to insure that the nation's food drink, and drug supply contributed to, rather than detracted from, the public welfare. The majority of national crusaders organized into departments within the National Woman's Christian Temperance Union, and later, committees of the General Federation of Women's Clubs and the National Consumer's League. Working within these large women's organizations provided distinct advantages — immediate recognition as a legitimate force for needed reform, access to the resources and influence of already established institutions, and a vast army of supporters, whose combined numbers exceeded one million by the end of the century and whose influence extended to several times their official membership. Utilizing these resources enabled the crusaders to mobilize public opinion, disperse propaganda, and initiate legislation more effectively than if they had operated as an independent entity.

From these national organizations the crusaders were able to incorporate the ethic of "home protection," the ability to bridge diverse streams of sentiment, and cooperative bonding into their fight for pure food, drink, and drugs.

The idea of home protection was important to the crusade. The concept of mothers fighting to protect their children and their communities countered any criticism, from either within or without their ranks, that working for pure food, drink, and drugs breached traditional gender roles, or invaded political boundaries.

Women crusaders could argue that their homemaking skills were needed to clean up the public arena. Who had a better right to demand uncontaminated meat and safe drugs than she who prepared the family's meals and cared for the family's health? Who better to clean up the stockyards, sweep corruption out of the courthouse, mop the floors of legislatures, and wipe the dust off corporate conscience? What kind of villain could mock the W.C.T.U. banner, "for home, and God, and Native Land," when it was carried by concerned mothers, whose reputation for virtue was created in the cult of true womanhood, whose superior morality had become evident through volunteerism and philanthropy, and whose patriotism was sealed in the blood of their sons? Who could argue against "unity in diversity" when it was used to perpetuate the ideals of democracy? Eventually, there were critics enough, but in most cases opponents were careful to phrase unfavorable comments in terms that excluded the maternal image.

The crusaders were able to bridge opposing opinions. Sizable numbers of national crusaders thought that persuasion, education, and exposé were the best approaches to the problem. They reasoned that in the open market, consumers would refuse to purchase dangerous and fraudulent products once their dangers were identified. This in turn would force manufacturers to compete in producing the most healthful and desirable products. Others held out for regulation from the start. They argued that federal legislation was necessary because of the extent of adulteration and the power of business interests. Consumers had no way of determining the nature of every product that entered the market nor of evaluating false advertising. Only the federal government was large enough to support facilities to inspect and assay each product and powerful enough to control large interstate manufacturers and combinations. Consumers had the right to assume that any product on the market was safe and conformed to its labeling. As an agency of all of the people, the federal government owed an obligation to protect the public against the avarice of special interests. Crusaders were able to keep the free-market faction and the regulation advocates within their ranks from competing against each other by combining both forces within the W.C.T.U. through multiple and overlapping departments. Crusaders were able to achieve the same objective within the G.F.W.C. through a procedure of moving from education to reform, and, after 1900, within the National Consumers' League by bringing all of the interested forces together into one organization.

Through national female bonding, women created a coalition of consumers influential enough to challenge special interests. Working as a block of consensus within the national conscience, unenfranchised women were able to propel the pure food, drink, and drug crusade into the national political arena. Starting with self-improvement and the home, then extending their efforts into school curriculums, physician and pharmacist practice, domestic science, and political activism, the "homekeepers of the land" generated and perpetuated their gigantic fight along a number of organized national fronts to protect themselves and their fellow Americans against ingesting substances that not only threatened the well-being of individual homes, but weakened the infrastructure of their society.

In "A Bit of Retrospect," published in the December 20, 1883, issue of the *Union Signal*, Mary A. Livermore noted that the power of organization "floated women into a higher level of womanhood" and "lifted them out of a subject condition." It "translated them out of a domain of weak weeping, and idle wringing of hands," into "such a height of faith and prophesy that they joined hands with the Almighty." Unification gave them the moral courage, "force, firmness, and fiber" to "work intelligently, wisely adapting means to ends", gaining patience, tolerance, and the ability to disagree on minor matters while "standing as one" where principle was concerned.

4

The Banyan Tree and the Hydra: The National Woman's Christian Temperance Union Crusaders, I

> "The W.C.T.U. has often been likened to the banyan tree... Like the banyan tree, its branches are continually reaching and taking root in new places; like the Banyan tree, it grows in every direction and year by year it covers more ground; like the banyan tree it is many in one and the more it is divided, the stronger it becomes."[1]

Women crusaders working within the various and overlapping departments of the National Woman's Christian Temperance Union initiated, nourished, and promoted the national fight for pure food, drink, and drugs. They approached the issue from the standpoint of home protection and classified adulterated food and drinks, along with alcohol and dangerous drugs, as components of a worldwide substance-abuse threat. Their activities during the last decades of the nineteenth century reveal how the crusaders projected their concerns into the political arena. The numbers of those who participated, the focus of their objectives, the variety of their methods, and the intensity of their campaigns, measure the breadth, depth, and nature of public support for pure food drink, and drugs.

The N.W.C.T.U., as the name implies, was a coalition of religiously-activated women who organized initially for the purpose of abolishing alcohol abuse. At first they disavowed any intention of branching out into other reforms or of "soiling their skirts" in political involvement, but, under the leadership of their second president, the redoubtable Frances Willard, they broadened their focus toward correcting a variety of societal problems through political action to became one of the most influential woman's reform organizations in the nation.[2]

Barred from participating directly in government by the existing political process, these women developed alternative strategies based on the public good, rather than the party; maternalism, rather than materialism; consensus, rather than caucus; cooperation, rather than ambition; and equality, rather than patronage. Their politics, which mobilized troubled public opinion through inclusion, cooperation, and activation, directly contrasted with the politics of bureaucracy, which tried to impose reform on a supposedly indifferent public through expertise and exclusion.

Contrary to popular belief, it was consumers and reformers, not business combines, bureaucrats, politicians, or muckrakers, who fired the opening shots of the national pure food, drink, and drug crusade. The "special interest" concerns joined the crusade after women in W.C.T.U. departments and other organizations had already focused public opinion on solving the substance-abuse problem.[3]

Although the N.W.C.T.U. crusaders viewed the pure food, drink, and drug issue through a lens of temperance reform, the entire range of dangerous substances concerned them. They believed that adulterated food, drink, and drugs were both causative agents and an integral part of an expanded definition of intemperance. Adulterated food predisposed individuals to alcoholism and vice; doctored soft drinks and proprietary medications addicted individuals to alcohol and opium, and all addictive "narcotics and stimulants" — opium and its alkaloids, tobacco, chloral hydrate, cocaine, and cannabis — belonged in the same category with alcohol. This concept made sense to women already disturbed by their own observations of the dangers of substance abuse, and by a swell of reports that were being circulated by women's organizations, farmers, home economists, health workers, and state reformers proclaiming that much of the nation's food and drug supply was polluted, adulterated, or dangerous.[4]

Working for pure food, drink, and drugs within the N.W.C.T.U. contributed to and was congruent with the "do everything" vision of many W.C.T.U. members. In apposition to the "know nothing" reputation of mugwumpery, the "do everything" slogan encouraged women to lengthen their stride beyond the narrow confines of temperance into a wide spectrum of reforms that affected the welfare of women and children. This broadening policy evolved from the desires of local workers and was not dictated necessarily from the top. In 1881, when Frances Willard coined the term "do everything" in her presidential address, she did not mean to direct the W.C.T.U. toward an unlimited variety of reforms. Rather, she referred to utilizing multiple methods: moral suasion, distributing literature, lecturing, lobbying, and petitioning to accomplish their purpose. Most frequently, as demonstrated by the adoption of pure food, drink, and drug crusade, the widening impetus came from the membership. The executive committee approved new causes only as workers were able to establish their pertinence to temperance and prove their viability.[5]

Pure food, drink, and drug advocates began to depict the "whole problem" of temperance as a "hydra," which generated new heads as fast as reformers severed the originals, and the W.C.T.U. as a banyan tree that sent out shoots to protect the public from multiple evils. The editor of the Union Signal wrote that the "do everything" policy was the only course of action broad enough to meet the "hydra-headed" foe. Frances Willard spoke of alcohol, stimulants, and narcotics as heads of a "deadly foe conspiring to steal away the brain." Each head was so closely "related in structure and purpose" that, like Hercules, reformers could not immobilize one head without severing the rest. Mankind could be redeemed only by "going forth to war" against the "whole dragon of alcohol and narcotics." Lucinda H. Corr, an Illinois physician and tireless pure drug crusader, spoke of drug abuse as a "horrid phase of that hydra-headed monster, the liquor traffic."[6]

Before 1898, the Departments of Hygiene and Heredity, Scientific Instruction, and Narcotics were the most active N.W.C.T.U. auxiliaries to wage campaigns for pure food, drink, and drugs, but the entire W.C.T.U. organization — all of the other departments, including the Department of Legislation, the Union Signal, the official organ of the N.W.C.T.U., and the central committee, which Frances Willard compared to a "compact of magicians" who were working toward "miracles of reform" — endorsed and supported pure food, drink, and drug activism.[7] To a large extent these three departments conducted their activities independent of central supervision. The N.W.C.T.U. executive committee approved the general area of interest of each department, but assigned neither work nor limitations, vesting leadership in the national superintendent. The superintendent and her staff initiated, planned, and implemented their programs, made annual reports to the general secretary, provided articles for the *Union Signal*, furnished rhetoric for the President, and submitted annual recommendations to the national conventions.[8]

The superintendents depended on the rank-and-file members. After receiving input from local unions, the national superintendent and her staff designed the department's programs under a flexible form of organization, correlating local, district, and state activities with national dynamics. The national departments depended on individual members and local unions drew from the strength of national leadership. The national superintendent encouraged local unions to adopt national programs and to adapt them to their specific circumstances. At times she pressured local leaders to take specific action. Still, local units were not obliged to organize particular departments, or to support any branch of the reform unless they felt the need and had the resources to do so. When enough members became interested in a specific aspect of pure food, drink, and drug reform, they organized departments patterned after national departments and felt free to abandon any department when interest declined.

Effective central leadership depended on the dedication and tenacity of individual members, who, as workers in the field, remained the best judges of what to do under specific local circumstances. Because the life of their department depended on the popularity of their cause, national leaders promoted, goaded, advised, and pitched in to help when their services were requested, but they were not able to dictate local policies.[9]

In a complex analysis, Jonathan Zimmerman has argued that, in the case of the Department of Scientific Instruction, the loose relation between central and local unions created a democratic coalition that both imitated and contrasted with the rising bureaucracies of the Progressive Era. Even though the national department structure and autonomy resembled a government bureau, its dependence on the support of local units kept it democratic. Bureaus, as other historians have contended, owed their continuity to the central government and were not democratic. Although they claimed to protect the consumer, they took the power to decide away from the public by creating a buffer zone between the people and their elected representatives. The Department of Scientific Instruction achieved the efficiency of a bureau through its central leadership, but maintained an essentially democratic autonomy because regional chapters confirmed the superintendent's appointment and could veto her activities.[10]

Zimmerman's observation applies equally to the Departments of Hygiene, Heredity, and Narcotics. Local workers were not mere pawns of national leaders who wanted to impose their middle class values upon the nation, but participants in addressing a problem that affected themselves, regardless of their social or economic status. Flexibility to move independently, innovate, and decide for themselves attracted women to the departments, enhanced morale and motivation, and strengthened their cause.

Pure food, drink, and drugs coexisted with other issues in each of these departments. The primary objective of each was societal reform, each focused its programs on eradicating inebriation, and each classified adulterated food and dangerous drugs as "kindred" evils. Each tackled the problem through multiple programs. The Department of Hygiene dealt with various aspects of good health, sanitation, home economics, as well as pure food, drink, and drugs. The Department of Heredity fought against drug abuse, along with alcohol abuse, as a leading cause of genetic disorders. The purpose of the Department of Scientific Instruction was to prevent substance abuse by introducing the study of physiology and hygiene, with a special emphasis on alcohol, other depressants, and stimulants into public and private schools. The Department of Narcotics focused on trying to outlaw all dangerous and addictive substances.

Departments of Hygiene and Heredity

Within the national Department of Hygiene, pure food, drink, and drug advocates approached consumer protection through a combination of efficient leadership and voluntary participation. Following suggestions of the national superintendent and her staff, groups of W.C.T.U. members determined which products were eroding the health and morality of their families, began to rid their homes of the offending substances, brought in new recruits, and eventually became a major force in fighting for pure food, drink, and drug regulation.

Under the leadership of Ella Eaton Kellogg from Michigan, the national Department of Hygiene set a style of pure food, drink, and drug activity that continued into the twentieth century, encouraging unions to adapt national agendas to their local situations; to generate literature to supplement the pamphlets, articles, and reports circulated by the national department; to contribute articles to the *Union Signal*; to share new innovations with other departments; and to draw upon the national department for lecturers and support.[11]

Drawing from the activities of local unions that proved successful, the national department encouraged unions to devote every third or fourth session to hygiene, with an agenda of lectures, papers, and discussions to study local problems, to decide what they could accomplish, and to determine the best course of action. Kellogg suggested that local unions invite the most promising lecturers to present programs to the public and the most talented writers to submit articles to local newspapers. Local unions could organize and support health clubs, give public hygienic dinners, establish hygienic lunch stands and hygienic restaurants, and operate booths at fairs. Kellogg recommended that each union collect a library of health literature, establish reading rooms where pure food, drink, and drug literature was available to the public, and provide "rest rooms" where rural women could read and discuss current events while they relaxed from shopping, or waited for their husbands to finish business in town. With variations, the local crusaders, who had not already done so, implemented many of the suggestions and supplemented them with activities of their own.[12]

The National Union's Department of Hygiene designated institutes, patterned after the Michigan Normal, as a priority for the summer of 1884. A significant number of local and state departments complied. These normals trained local and state groups to teach and mobilize women to work for pure food, drink, and drugs.[13]

The institute in Washington, D.C., was notable because of the scientific legitimacy it contributed to the crusade. The organizers were able to draw lecturers from the A.M.A. convention, which was meeting nearby at the same time, to reinforce Dr. and Mrs. Kellogg's warnings against adulterated food and proprietaries. Addresses by such accepted authorities as Elliot Coues, professor of anatomy; Joseph Tabor Johnson, professor of obstetrics, from Columbia University; and Albert L. Gihon, medical director of the U. S. Navy and president of the American Public Health Association, confirmed the Department of Hygiene's research and strengthened its claims.[14]

A convocation at Lake Bluff, Illinois, offered an expanded version of the other institutes. In contrast to the Michigan and Washington, D.C., normal, which reached mostly delegates, the Illinois institute attracted thousands of interested participants. Located only 30 miles north of Chicago on the C. & N. W. Railroad, the 200-acre Christian summer resort accommodated a crowd of more than 5,000 people in the tabernacle alone, and set up tents and various structures for the overflow. A committee, headed by Dr. Sarah Hackett Stevenson, professor at the Medical College of Chicago, and Dr. Mary Weeks Burnett, administrator of the W.C.T.U. Hospital, screened lecturers from a slate of over 300 physicians and other authorities.[15] Under the auspices of the National Union, state unions in North Carolina, New Hampshire, Vermont, and New Jersey, and, on a smaller scale, local W.C.T.U. units began to hold similar institutes. The institute at Northfield, Vermont, featured a local physician, who lectured on the effects of stimulants and narcotics on the human mind, followed by discussions on health and heredity led by the Vermont State W.C.T.U. secretary. Hygiene and Heredity institutes met twice a month in Atlanta, and on a regular basis in some other cities.[16]

Matrons and mothers were not the only participants. Concurrent with the other normal institutes in 1884, four Washington, D.C., high school girls organized an ongoing health and heredity institute. They elected officers, held weekly meetings to which they invited lecturers from local medical schools, generated original papers, and collected dues to buy books for a health library that circulated literature among its members. Correspondence spread the idea of teen health institutes to localities throughout the country. Technically, most of these organizations were not affiliated with the W.C.T.U. Usually, they organized and operated independently, but ordered literature, enjoyed support, and secured lecturers through the W.C.T.U.[17]

The National Department of Hygiene encouraged the formation of adult health clubs to spread the gospel of pure food, drink, and drugs. By November 1885, the corresponding secretary reported that every housekeeper in the entire W.C.T.U. sisterhood was redoubling vigilance against outside influences that threatened to penetrate her "domain" and "contaminate" her children despite careful teaching and attention. As new chemical analyses uncovered the structure of patent medicines and the practices of food processors, women realized the dangers in many of their favorite remedies and foods.[18]

Gigantic housecleanings ensued. The Illinois W.C.T.U. reported that concerned women cleaned "up-stairs, down-stairs, and in my lady's chamber" to eliminate destructive influences. In the nursery, they threw out Mrs. Winslow's Soothing Syrup, laudanum purchased from the neighborhood drug store, and The Baby's Friend, all of which contained opiates. Mothers discontinued shoring up the health of frail sons with Wampole's Cod Liver Oil when they discovered that the remedy, bought in expectation of bringing robust health to delicate bodies, contained no oil from the cod fish, but instead depended on opium dissolved in 18 percent of alcohol for its popularity. They banished Lydia Pinkham's Vegetable Compound, containing opiates and 20.6 percent alcohol, and Wine of Cardui (The Southern Revenge), a similar product, from their daughters' medicine supply. They parted with their arthritis or prolapsed uterus medications once they discovered that the active ingredients included narcotics, and removed tonics and lost-manhood rebuilders from their husbands' medicine cabinets. In the kitchen they eliminated condiments that were adulterated and processed food that might be suspect.[19]

When Kellogg moved to the newly-formed National Department of Purity in 1886, her secretary Bessie Cushman, M.D., from Hannibal, Missouri, continued the Department of Hygiene program, focusing on introducing regulatory legislation, lobbying, and "agitating" for extension services in colleges and home economic departments in high schools where pure food, drink, and drug principles could be taught.[20]

The Department of Heredity found difficulty functioning on its own. Periodically, it combined with the Department of Hygiene. The two departments co-sponsored institutes in many localities, used many of the same lecturers, and shared research. Heredity issues did not attract enough women to organize separately in most localities. Women who organized under the Department of Heredity contributed to the pure food, drink, and drug crusade by relating the genetic data that they gathered to substance abuse. The leaders were outspoken against adulteration and addiction and lobbied for federal regulation. Perhaps the reason the departments of heredity did not attract many workers was that one of the objectives of its leaders appeared too extreme. Mary L. Griffith and Mary Weeks Burnett, M.D., hoped to contribute toward to a "higher type of manhood and womanhood," and to "lift the human race" through genetic engineering that would "hinder the production" of murderers, vagrants, and mentally retarded by selective sterilization. Sterilization did not appeal to the rank and file. Most W.C.T.U. members accepted genetic studies simply as another argument against using stimulants and narcotics and as a means of allying physicians to their cause. Frances Willard approached their objectives with caution, when she said that they aimed to "enlighten the members of the W.C.T.U. by wise and careful words concerning the relation of prenatal and natal inheritance" to substance abuse.[21]

Department of Scientific Instruction

The activism of consumer advocates within the Department of Scientific Instruction steered women into intense political activity. The popularity of physiology and hygiene in Massachusetts schools had led scientific instruction promoters to utilize the vast resources of the N.W.C.T.U. to recruit an enthusiastic "clientage of active loyal Christian women in every part of the country." In 1879 Mary Hunt presented their proposal to Frances Willard. Willard's initial response was that it was a "long shot at short range." An avid woman-suffrage advocate, Willard preferred to attack substance abuse by channeling the energies of the Union toward the female franchise as a means to reform, but, after consideration, she invited Hunt to present the plan at the fall N.W.C.T.U. Convention in Indianapolis. The proposal met immediate acceptance. The delegates formed a standing committee of scientific instruction, authorizing Hunt and her associates to originate, advise, and direct plans of work in all states and territories in the country.[22]

At its inception, the department was known as the Department of Scientific Instruction to reflect the goal of introducing physiology and hygiene into the schools with an equal emphasis on all types of substance abuse. Sometime during the first two years, the word "temperance" was added to the official title to be sure the department reflected a primary link to the temperance movement, but in introducing the program to legislators, its adherents referred to their proposal simply as scientific instruction. This was an attempt to relate the program more closely to education than to prohibition. A number of school board members and legislators objected to using the public schools to promote prohibition. In one instance, when school board members complained that a textbook was objectionable because the title implied school support for prohibition, the publishers changed the name from *Temperance Physiology* to *Hygiene for Young People.*[23]

The Department of Scientific Instruction moved deliberately before opposition had an opportunity to organize. Realizing that "no flights of oratory, no general and aimless agitation" could introduce the study of physiology and hygiene to "every pupil in every school in the land," they organized and actuated state and local unions to persuade school boards to introduce physiology and hygiene into their curriculums.

Disappointing first efforts confirmed Hunt's mistrust of the vote. In Massachusetts, Vermont, New York, and Michigan where women could vote for members of the school board, their ballots had made little difference in the outcome. Vermont reported that a "very small percentage of women qualified themselves" to vote. "Red tape and intimidation" kept them away from the polls. Instead of school boards being in "a state of siege at the hands of the mothers" as scientific instruction advocates envisioned, women encountered a bastion of educational expertise determined to maintain its integrity.[24]

Hunt turned from persuasion to coercion — to forcing school boards to adopt physiology and hygiene through state legislation. "Because no study goes universally into, or stays long in the public schools," and because normal schools would not train teachers to teach a new study unless required by law, the department concentrated its efforts on securing laws that would "place the study of the nature and effects of alcoholic drinks and other narcotics upon the human system, with other required studies … under state control."[25]

Universal scientific education required enacting separate laws in each of the 45 states, and in the national congress for schools in the District of Columbia, the territories, military and naval academies, and other schools under federal control — admittedly a gigantic task. Without pausing to give way to their misgivings that one lifetime might not be long enough to secure the legislation, that teachers might not comply, and that no textbooks were available, the department members charged ahead. Their watch cry was, "What ought to be done can be done by whoever has the faith and courage to undertake it and to persevere till it is accomplished."[26]

Scientific instruction drew adherents with phenomenal rapidity, swelling the ranks of temperance unions with legions of determined reformers who familiarized themselves with local laws, developed their plans, and convinced friends and neighbors of the merits of their cause. They distributed pamphlets and petitions, and arranged lectures and meetings according to the department's plan. The plan required intense cooperation. State unions directed the activities, local unions implemented the plan, and, as national superintendent and secretary, Mary Hunt and Mrs. C. C. Alford held themselves ready to advise, lecture, lobby, and make personal contacts wherever they were needed. The national executive committee focused the activities of the entire organization on specific areas at specific times.[27]

The crusaders realized that they could not expect legislators to enact laws without massive public support. Hunt recalled, "We took our cause to the people and the people demanded legislation. School law, like all law, is embodied sentiment." People, who were "the law-making power," had to "nurture" the sentiment in their hearts and minds before they asked legislatures to consider their proposals. "The people are the real source of power," she said. "They must be the lobby" and must gather together by "agitating through pulpit, platform, press, and prayer meeting" for election of legislators who were pledged to vote for scientific instruction.[28]

First, the national department targeted New York State, with its "five million and more people," and Pennsylvania, with "her four millions." Once those key states adopted their program, scientific instruction advocates expected the rest of the states to follow.[29]

Vermont passed the first scientific instruction law in November 1882. Within a few months, Michigan, New Hampshire, and Rhode Island passed similar laws. In each case, the law was a direct response to short, intense campaigns by state W.C.T.U. departments of scientific instruction in cooperation with the national organization and local members. In every instance, support for the law exceeded the most optimistic expectations. By April 1885, ten more states — Alabama, Kansas, Nebraska, Nevada, Maine, Wisconsin, Pennsylvania, Missouri, New York, and Massachusetts had enacted scientific instruction laws, and by 1902 every state in the Union had statutes requiring the teaching of physiology and hygiene in public schools. Pennsylvania's law exemplified the ideal. Missouri's law was disappointing.[30]

The Vermont law passed with little opposition. It was a popular measure because the legislators saw it as a conservative, uncomplicated way to bring the schools up to date without entailing appreciable financial outlay. It reflected an increased concern with the whole welfare of children, the necessity of preparing them, physically and morally to deal with a commercialized society, and a trend toward parent involvement in school policies. Although the law stipulated a more or less voluntary compliance by local school boards, Vermont women determined to see that their children enjoyed the full benefit of the statute by organizing mothers to oversee the program in every community.[31]

At its annual convention in 1882, the Michigan W.C.T.U. voted to make compulsory scientific instruction a leading line of work for the ensuing year. Under the direction of Mrs. M. J. C. Merritt, a committee planned, coordinated, and executed the campaign. Between the November elections and the opening of the legislature, local departments arranged meetings in which state and national lecturers explained the advantages of teaching physiology and hygiene and the need for a compulsory law. They drew large and enthusiastic audiences that signed petitions and organized into unions. The majority of the people, including educators, clergymen, and many local officials, supported them. When the bill came up for discussion at Lansing, Mary Hunt spoke to the combined houses. The Speaker commented that he could trace her "all over this State" by the petitions coming in and the comments of legislators who said that their constituents expected them to vote for the bill. The scientific instruction amendment passed the House on April 11, 1883, by a vote of 68 to 15, and the Senate on Friday, April 20, by 25 to 2.[32]

Hunt, Alford, and Elizabeth Ward Greenwood, the state W.C.T.U. superintendent, inaugurated the New York campaign in 1883, with "fear and misgiving." They did not know how people would receive them or react to the proposal. On the whole, they felt that country towns would favor the bill, but they anticipated a struggle in the large cities where the opposition forces were more powerful. They began by soliciting the support of existing local unions, then moved out into the field where women flocked to form unions with "great unanimity and enthusiasm." Early in 1883, Mary Hunt addressed large audiences at churches in Brooklyn and the other New York boroughs. In the months of November and December, she went "up and down" through the northern towns and the Adirondack Mountains, visiting legislators at their homes, lecturing, and gaining friends for the bill. In the central cities she worked steadily, speaking almost every night, until the whole region was "buzzing" with scientific instruction. In January 1884, the state committee, with Mrs. Hunt, went to Albany to find that the bill was "fairly launched on its perilous passage." Without pausing to lobby in Albany, they went back to the people. Mary Hunt spoke sixteen consecutive nights in a row. In February the bill passed the Senate; this alerted the opposition. From then on, as one New York observer wrote, "It was the brewers versus the children." Fear that the opposition might gain ground spurred the mothers to "fever heat." In the towns along the Hudson, Mrs. Hunt spoke to crowded houses. At Poughkeepsie an audience of more than 1,000, and at Auburn 1,500 people gave a unanimous rising vote when asked if they would instruct their legislators to vote for the bill. In a note home, Mrs. Hunt wrote, "Our bill goes on its final passage this week. We have more than enough votes promised to carry it. It may be decided before this letter reaches you."[33]

Despite a statute barring lobbyists from attending legislative sessions, Mary Hunt and her entourage passed the guards and observed from the balcony. When the bill did not pass as soon as they expected, W.C.T.U. lobbyists reminded legislators of their commitment to the bill, Hunt and her brigade resumed their lectures, while their coworkers in Massachusetts waited and prayed. For days the Massachusetts women received no news. Rumors spread that the bill lacked one vote. Finally, on Thursday, Mary Hunt telegraphed that the bill had passed the New York Assembly with "Only two adverse votes." W.C.T.U. members hailed their victory as an "affirmation of participatory democracy." A New Bedford writer marveled, "Even in New York the legislators obey the people's will."[34]

The bill was not all the W.C.T.U. hoped for. No penalty was attached for noncompliance, but state ordinances required the superintendent of education to remove any personnel who violated school law. Before the law went into effect on January 1, 1885, more than 250 towns, in addition to whole counties, such as St. Lawrence, Jefferson, Franklin, Clinton, and Ulster, introduced W.C.T.U.-approved texts into high schools and were waiting for the publication of books that Mary Hunt was helping to prepare before introducing the subject into the lower grades. In addition, the state normal schools ordered a series of stereoscopic plates to illustrate the physiological effects of narcotics upon the various organs of the human body.[35]

In Pennsylvania, the bill passed the Senate by 139 votes to 7, and the House, after a long filibuster, 131 to 39. The W.C.T.U. campaign followed the pattern set in other states. With Mrs. J. D. Weeks, the superintendent of the Department of Scientific Instruction, at the helm, lecturers went directly to the people. Concentrating on each lawmaker's hometown, they called a mass meeting to which they invited the legislator and sent a carriage to make sure that he attended. In every instance, they appealed to a large audience, took a standing vote that seldom failed to be unanimous in favor of scientific education, and, in the rush of enthusiasm, pledged the legislator to their cause.

Mary Hunt described an incident in one Pennsylvania locality where a "certain gentleman who was ... set up as a leader in the legislature" and had a reputation for being an "essentially good man except for being a bit 'slick'" was opposed to the legislation. The W.C.T.U. decided to deal with him by "pinning him to his constituents." Before attending a mass-meeting in his home district, the gentleman told the lecturer, "It's no use, don't you believe it. No, no, madam. Nothing this year whatsoever." The W.C.T.U. had convinced individual persons beforehand, and appealed to the audience to support legislation "to save their children." When the mistress of ceremonies asked the people who wanted the law to rise to their feet, the "wily, oily, smart man" sat with his back to the audience, but as he saw the audience getting up, he "came up in sections." After he faced his constituents and the people cheered, he addressed the chair, "Madam, my mind is changed. I think it is a reasonable thing; I don't understand it, but you certainly have my support." He had "heard from the people." Arriving at Harrisburg, the delegates found him among a "regular body-guard of friends" prepared to champion their cause.[36]

The Pennsylvania legislators assured W.C.T.U. leaders, "our people have asked us to help you." Hunt addressed several sessions, stressing the need, pleading in the name of the children, projecting the prospects for the legis-lation, and strengthening her argument by a "sub-strata of science and fact." Union members "bombarded" the legislators with petitions and letters — "letters admonitory and beseeching, letters solemn and warning, letters proper and patronizing, letters of all sorts, shapes, sizes and degrees of elo-quence." Representatives and senators followed their mandate. In one ses-sion, "almost before the amen to the opening prayer," scores of senators were on their feet to read petitions from their constituents. Hunt wrote home that there was not enough opposition to make the Senate sessions interesting.[37]

Unexpectedly a pocket of opposition organized. At the second read-ing in the House, one legislator accused the bill of being "the biggest book job that was ever heard of." The women "looked a little scared" as the oppo-sition gained scattered adherents who threatened to block the bill. The W.C.T.U. investigated. When the bill reported back from the committee, the women of Pennsylvania informed their legislators that the leader of the opposition was an attorney for the Brewers' and Malters' Association. They added, "We would like to call your attention to the fact that the petitions to the legislature on this bill have not emanated from the brewers, but from the people," and that it was "senseless" to accuse the people of being book dealers. Identifying the opposition as representatives of the "special inter-ests," had the intended impact. In the prospect of impending defeat, the opposition attempted to weaken the bill, saying it was a "good bill, a good thing, but needed polishing, striking out a word or a clause here and there," and that it should exempt "teaching physiology and hygiene to primary and intermediate school children, who were too young to understand." The women pointed out that exempting primary and intermediate grades would give the "special interests" 95 percent of the children and the peo-ple 5 percent. Their supporters stood firm, voting down every amendment. In a last ditch stand, 39 representatives staged a filibuster that lasted until the majority voted to sit in session until the final vote came in.[38]

In the interim, a Mr. George Morgan from Philadelphia, who "espe-cially declared in favor of the bill," could not resist a poetic diversion "from the roar of heavy artillery" in which the closing verses recognized the role of W.C.T.U. women in shaping the bill:

> Out from city, adown from the farm
> With many a grace and with many a charm,
> Ladies came trooping, numerically strong,
> Ah! who could resist a pressure so great,
> Combining the best of the church and the state,
> The good and wise, who come in their might,
> Determined, at last, to put mankind aright?
> And with justice to guide them, they go in to win,
> And they gather us in; aye, they gather us in.[39]

Long, continued applause greeted Morgan's rhyme. With the ice broken, and the opposition stymied, House Bill 206 became law after nearly 18 months of concentrated W.C.T.U. activism.[40]

Pennsylvania's law was stronger than those passed in any other state up until that time. It stipulated that physiology and hygiene be taught in all departments of all educational institutions supported wholly or in part by money from the commonwealth. It required that the study of the effects of stimulants and narcotics must follow the teaching of each division of physiology and hygiene, instead of being tacked on the end of the book. It also provided for the withholding of funds from any school board that did not enforce the law in its district.[41]

In Alabama, after a careful campaign, the law passed both the Senate and the House with large majorities. Their constituents had committed almost every legislator to support the bill. Representing the N.W.C.T.U., the corresponding secretary and Sally Chapin accompanied the State Superintendent of Education to Montgomery to insure favorable consideration of the bill. Ellen Clarkson Bryce, president of the Alabama W.C.T.U., and her associates met with the congressional committees to explain what they wanted. The bill passed the legislature without incident. The Maryland Union also took time to build firm support and was able to influence legislators to pass the kind of law for which it lobbied.[42]

Not all state scientific instruction campaigns brought the desired results. Missouri women "punished their corns and spoiled their best shoes" circulating petitions for scientific temperance. In 1883 and 1884, Hattie Worthington of Kirkwood, state superintendent of Scientific Instruction, sent out over 500 requests for unions to encourage teachers to support the

bill. To her surprise, she discovered that a number of teachers had introduced the subject on their own. By January 1885 nearly 3,000 clergymen
had been petitioned to preach and pray for the bill "to save the children."
The small resort town of El Dorado Springs, away from the railroad in
"rocky knolls and hills" where "magical springs of healing water" attracted
the infirm, initiated the program independent of national leadership. Ignoring the unusual severity of the 1884 winter, the members worked with
"unprecedented earnestness" in circulating scientific instruction petitions.
Clara Hoffman, the aggressive superintendent of the Missouri W.C.T.U., an
educator herself, marshaled the support of school boards and teachers. She
expected a law similar to that of Pennsylvania, but the General Assembly
tried to pacify the mothers by passing amended legislation that required
teaching physiology and hygiene to only those children whose parents
requested it. Missouri women accused the legislators of giving them a stone
when they had asked for bread, then set about to see that at least one mother
in every school required that her child be taught physiology and hygiene.
They reasoned that when one student was taught, all would listen because
it was the nature of "the descendants of mother Eve" to "acquire forbidden
knowledge" with "open ear and mouth." Missouri mothers intended to
make scientific instruction available to the children, when Missouri legislators had not. Doing this provided an incentive for activism among rural
women in remote areas, such as in Marion County, which had fifty small
schools and only two W.C.T.U. unions.[43]

By 1886 when they proposed a federal bill to require scientific instruction in the District of Columbia and other schools controlled by the national
government, the pure food, drink, and drug enthusiasts were veteran lobbyists. The national department drafted the bill, and every local W.C.T.U.
in all of the states and territories tried to commit their legislators. H. W.
Blair, of New Hampshire, in the Senate, and Byron Cutcheon of Michigan,
in the House, introduced the bill. Mary Hunt and others testified in committee and overcame opposition step-by-step, bringing pressure on the legislators through their constituents, breaking filibusters, manipulating
procedures, and taking advantage of Suspension Day in the Senate.[44]

By 1901 every state in the union, the District of Columbia, military
installations, and Indian reservations were teaching 20,000,000 children
the effects of narcotics and stimulants on the human system. These laws
were one of the entering wedges to drug regulation.[45]

Passing scientific instruction laws was only the first phase of the campaign. The Departments of Scientific Instruction had made teaching

physiology and hygiene fashionable, but they were not as prepared to insure that its program was implemented as they intended. When the campaign began, selecting suitable textbooks, training teachers, and the possibility of laws being rescinded were not immediate problems. However, in August 1884, when the laws of five states became effective — at the very moment when the continuity of the campaign depended on approved teaching material, trained teachers, and enforcement of the law — the W.C.T.U. could not recommend any textbooks without reservation. The vast majority of teachers were not trained to teach physiology and hygiene, unions were not organized in every outlying district to oversee school boards and teachers, and the opposing forces were organizing to rescind the law.[46]

A search for textbooks was unsuccessful. No book, including Steele's *Hygienic Physiology* and Julia Coleman's *Temperance Catechism*, both of which the unions used in Sunday School and Temperance Schools, was suitable for the public school program. Steele's *Physiology* fell short of the standards of abstinence by condoning small doses of stimulants and narcotics for medical conditions. Coleman's book came under criticism for sentimentality, subjectivity, and "extreme and untrustworthy" statements. Other physiology and hygiene books included temperance studies as an afterthought, or were too advanced for the students. The national department advised its unions to persuade school boards to wait for the preparation of texts which were suited to the age and interests of the students, were scientifically accurate, and were designed to warn students against the use of habituating substances.[47]

Mary Hunt and her staff, including a committee of physicians, educators, and ministers, flew into the task, directing the production of three graded texts under the name of *The Pathfinder Series*. For high schools and academies, they revised Steele's *Hygienic Physiology* to integrate teaching the nature of drugs and the consequences of substance abuse with anatomy, physiology, and hygiene. For intermediate classes, available shortly after school began, they produced *Temperance Physiology for Intermediate Classes in Graded and Common Schools*, which combined instruction in elementary physiology, anatomy, and hygiene, with their practical applications to the lives and habits of the students. For primary classes, Hunt directed preparation of the 17-chapter *Child's Health Primer* (35 cents clothbound) where she placed "the laws of life" (physiology) on equal footing with the laws of making money (arithmetic). Colored plates illustrated the effects of substance abuse on the human body.[48] Of course, school districts were free to choose the texts they considered best. In fact, the Department of Scientific Instruction recommended that states allow local districts to choose the texts for their own schools, thereby better expressing the wishes of the community. School districts usually adopted the book requested by the most vocal mothers and local union members made sure that they presented the majority of requests. Most of the books published in 1884 and after were more suitable than those available in the past. Local unions considered a few "really meritorious."[49]

Training teachers presented another challenge. Few normal schools were prepared to teach elementary physiology and hygiene, let alone teach the subject by W.C.T.U. standards. Pure food, drink, and drug advocates provided suggestions. Teaching abstinence from dangerous substances could be incorporated with scripture reading as the first lesson of the day. Reading and copybooks could address the subject. Pictures and diagrams could be hung on the walls. Lessons should be short, easily understood, and illustrated by examples.[50]

Mary Hunt opened a summer training school at Martha's Vineyard where she engaged a medical professor from the University of Michigan to teach the subject. Similar summer schools opened in the West. Hunt arranged lecture tours of colleges to train teachers. Frances Willard invited "gifted" speakers to deliver series of lectures at least annually to meet the demand of states that passed scientific instruction laws and to keep teachers apprised of new scientific discoveries. In various cities and towns, teachers organized their own preparatory classes, such as in the District of Columbia where the teachers organized four societies to train themselves.[51]

Almost immediately, various opposing interests began to pick at the laws. W.C.T.U. women identified the "liquor interests" as the primary opponents, but they encountered the most damaging opposition from educators and businessmen who argued that teaching hygiene and morality was the responsibility of the home, not of the schools. One local union determined that the New York State Brewers' and Malters' Association was behind a Rochester Board of Education decision to remove W.C.T.U.-approved texts from all of the schools of the state. Usually, the first tactic was to try to replace the W.C.T.U.-approved textbooks with texts that left out mention of liquor, tobacco, and patent medicines. If discrediting textbooks failed, the opposition tried to amend or annul the laws.

Countering deviations from the intent of the laws kept departments on the cutting edge of activism. Mary Hunt traveled thousands of miles annually and women in state unions fought some of the hardest battles of the crusade to strengthen and enforce the scientific instruction laws. In 1886 the New York State Teachers' Association denounced the scientific instruction laws in that state, followed in 1887 by the Massachusetts Board of Education. Although it failed to repeal the laws, this opposition alerted crusaders to the necessity of strengthening laws with penalties for non-compliance. The amendment of imperfect statutes was more difficult than enactment of a good law in the beginning. Certain legislators felt that the existing laws were the best that could be expected, and educators considered the request for stronger laws a reflection upon their integrity.[52]

In many ways, opposition strengthened the fight for pure food, drink, and drugs. It drew advocates to the cause and made mothers more determined to insure that all children were taught the essentials of good nutrition and the dangers of drug abuse. The textbook wars required careful study of facts concerning habit-forming substances. To obtain and evaluate data, the Department of Scientific Instruction set up a research headquarters that collected the scientific and medical literature as it emerged in every nation of the world. The department members placed their library at the service of textbook authors and used the evidence in public addresses, articles, and thousands of leaflets. Their exhibits of laws, methods, textbooks, and literature won medals and diplomas at the world expositions in Paris (1890), Chicago (1893), and St. Louis (1904).[53]

The Department of Narcotics

The Department of Narcotics grew out of concern over opium dens and the rapidly spreading habituation of American women to opium, its alkaloids, and proprietary drugs. The avowed purpose of the department was to study the extent of drug abuse; to alert the public to narcotic content in chewing gum, soothing syrups, headache powders, "patent" medicines, and tobacco; and to organize support for federal drug regulation. The first superintendent, Mary Byron Reese of Ohio, inaugurated a nationwide investigation to determine the extent and nature of drug abuse. The research indicated greater prevalence among both sexes and every age group than anticipated, with the highest risk factor among women, babies, and girls.[54]

Subsequent superintendents, Mrs. H. N. Harris, who had moved from California to Indiana, in 1885, and Mrs. James Havens of Colorado in 1886, continued the investigative processes and were able to organize departments of narcotics in most local unions. Both were strident in their attack against drugs. By what she called "some strange, incomprehensible impression of 'bounden duty' that no effort could erase from her mind," Havens became obsessed with the subject, making it her "special study" and full-time vocation. She found the nation "rapidly drifting into a general narcotic addiction" that threatened to "bring a heavier weight of woe, a deadlier load of sorrow" to the country than the use of alcohol. If allowed to approach the magnitude of opium abuse in China, she feared the "direst curse of the nation" could "surpass all computation."[55]

Havens warned that "danger attended the supposition" that only "the depraved and abandoned" became victims to the "deadly" opium habit. Havens encountered "white-souled women of exquisite culture and natural mental qualities who gradually fell victims to this fatal habit" until they "became mental and physical wrecks, lost to every sense of shame, of honor, of duty, and family ties." She found promising young women and men resorting to narcotics and stimulants "to assist them in their upward flight" until they "fainted by the wayside," eventually "dragged down, helpless and hopeless to the lowest, dankest depths of a narcotic hell." She saw "tiny babes, white-faced, ghastly and blue-veined," drawing "living death" from the "palsied breasts of mothers who had far better have died in the agonies of maternity than to have given birth to ... innocent victims of narcotic poisoning." Ministers of the gospel whose "pulpit eloquence entranced thousands of souls," were struggling with "the most despairing and hopeless energy to free themselves from the fatal entanglements" of opium. Physicians "daily and hourly" listened "to the song of the siren, knowing full well that every sylvan note" drew them nearer to their "impending doom." Addiction to opium and its alkaloids was the most common, cocaine abuse posed the most dangerous threat of all "enslaving habits," but "devotees of chloral, chloroform, and quinine" were "unwittingly drawn into the maelstrom" of the "fatal influence." "In the name of humanity," Havens sent out a call to the women of the nation to give lawmakers "no rest or peace" until the "great and overwhelming evil" was "restrained by rigid legislative enactment."[56]

Perhaps Havens' enthusiasm appeared too extreme. At that time, Indiana was the only state that responded to her appeal for a separate department to overthrow the opium habit. Likely, most agreed with Eliza B. Ingalls, superintendent of the Missouri Department of Anti-Tobacco, when she reported "It will be impossible for me to add opium to my Department, for I am overworked now."[57]

Regardless, Ingalls resumed leadership of the national Department of Narcotics in 1886, to serve for a longer continuous term than any other N.W.C.T.U. superintendent, except Mary Hunt. Initially, Ingalls gave first priority to outlawing the sale of tobacco products to minors. She had worked within the W.C.T.U. against the use of tobacco for many years and feared expanding the department to include other narcotics would diffuse the energies of already-operative workers. Because the use of tobacco was the most prevalent narcotic habit, she felt it required greater attention.[58]

Despite her earlier reservations, in 1887 she was ready to consider a national campaign against dangerous drugs. In her annual report for 1887, she argued that drug habits were a "home question," and that the drug issue had greater relevancy for women, personally, than either alcohol or tobacco because drugs appealed more to women than to men. Borrowing Mrs. Havens' rhetoric, she asserted that the opium habit was "almost incurable" and "worse than death." The first grain led to "more and more, until the victim" became a confirmed user.[59]

Extending the campaign to dangerous drugs on local, state, and national levels, required much more "machinery" and trained workers. Feeling the need too acute to wait for professionals to be recruited, she decided that unskilled workers would have to "study out plans and use the helps at hand," and prepare for an immediate attack.[60]

She advised unions to organize more effectively, write and circulate leaflets and books, train lecturers, hold meetings, and campaign for local and federal laws to restrict addictive and dangerous drugs to physicians' prescriptions. Short on funds, she urged members to hold fund-raising events and to solicit endowments for publishing costs.[61]

Interestingly, her survey of state-by-state activity indicated that a number of local and state W.C.T.U. departments of narcotics had activated drug campaigns already. Kate Loftin reported that the Indiana W.C.T.U. Department of Narcotics had held an essay contest, distributed a large number of pamphlets, written articles for the press, memorialized a number of influential bodies that passed resolutions to regulate poisons, and called the attention of the Indiana Medical Association to the dangers of opium. The department also presented a bill to the legislature to restrict the sale of opium and to provide for the care of habitual opium users. Pennsylvania, Colorado, Kentucky, and Mississippi reported similar activities. Ingalls seems to have been following a trend, integrating local methods already in operation into a national campaign for drug regulation.[62]

In 1889 Ingalls reported work in every state, with women lobbying for narcotic regulation in Arkansas, Alabama, Colorado, South Carolina, California, Missouri, Mississippi, Iowa, Kentucky, Vermont, Virginia, and Wisconsin.[63]

The Department of Legislation and the Union Signal

The Department of Legislation, one of the original departments of the W.C.T.U., was organized to sponsor legislation and aid other departments whenever they needed legal advice, or were working for legislation. The first superintendent of this department, attorney J. Ellen Foster, of Clinton, Iowa, and her staff were active in offering advice to other departments, supporting scientific instruction in all of the states, writing legislation, designing petitions, exploring legal alternatives when initial methods failed, and counteracting opposition. Defining the government as a tool of the people, Foster advocated intense political involvement.[64]

The *Union Signal* sent out conflicting signals. As the official organ for the W.C.T.U., it published pure food, drink, and drug articles in almost every issue. Ella Kellogg contributed a regular column. Mary Hunt and other department heads reported their progress and solicited support at least once a month. State and local unions wrote in to describe their activities. The editors wrote promotional material and reprinted articles advocating food, drink, and drug reform, but, like other periodicals of the time, the *Union Signal* found drug advertising necessary to remain solvent.[65]

Conclusion

One of the most striking aspects of the W.C.T.U. crusade for pure food, drink, and drugs from 1882 to the 1890s was the way in which American women mobilized their mutual concerns into a nationwide campaign. Attacking the problem from a scientific, as well as from a moralistic, point of view, attracted large numbers of women who were convinced they could relieve an intolerable situation through education and activism. The grassroots orientation of the W.C.T.U. encouraged innovation, participation, and determination. It also insured the continuity of the crusade into the twentieth century.

5

The National Woman's Christian Temperance Union Crusaders, II

Between 1895 and 1905 the National W.C.T.U. crusaders shifted the primary emphasis of their pure food, drink, and drug activities toward securing federal regulation. Combined with their belief that the federal government should protect consumers against industrial dangers, alarming rises in substance abuse and flagrant violation of state food statutes convinced the crusaders that stronger, more immediate measures were required. Working for federal legislation bolstered their political potential and the popularity of their cause by attracting hosts of new recruits. This effort fostered intradepartmental cooperation and formed alliances with women's clubs, journalists, bureaucrats, and other reform groups that also were becoming involved in pure food, drink, and drug activism.

At the same time, W.C.T.U. crusaders began to focus their pure food, drink, and drug activities more directly on alcohol abuse. Beginning in the mid–1890s, schisms within the national leadership led the executive committee to reexamine its "do everything" policy. From the genesis of the W.C.T.U., certain members had held reservations concerning what Frances Willard called the "broader vision" of societal reform. As the organization continued to branch out, ascending factions of the national leadership began to openly question the value of multiple and overlapping departments. The critics feared that extending the range of W.C.T.U. programs and becoming involved in politics had carried them too far afield from their original objective of eradicating inebriety. They found Willard's interests in trade unionism, party politics, socialism, woman suffrage, and the World W.C.T.U. particularly disquieting. In the 1894 and 1896 conventions, Willard was barely able to retain her leadership and salvage the broad spectrum of reform activities by combining some departments, deleting others that appeared tangential, disavowing partisan politics, and replacing as many dissenting officers and superintendents as possible with more loyal followers.[1]

A period of uncertainty and confusion followed Willard's death on September 17, 1898. Without her advocacy for broad societal reform, opposing factions attempted to gain control. The focus of the organization was not resolved for several years until the new president, Lillian M. N. Stevens, who was elected in November 1898, was able to effect a partial compromise between the two positions.[2]

The retrenchment process proved to be both a detriment and a stimulant to the pure food, drink, and drug cause. The process required advocates to establish a more direct tie to the temperance movement. Establishing the unequivocal connection to prohibition diverted time and energy away from trying to secure legislation, threatened to alter programs, and ultimately diminished both the crusader's credibility and their capabilities.

Conversely, particularly in the short term, pure food, drink, and drug activists were able to turn the N.W.C.T.U. retrenchment to their advantage. They used the interval of power struggles and realignment within the executive leadership to strengthen local influence and to attack their difficulties without interference from the executive committee. They also used the opportunity to devote renewed energy to their campaigns, and to establish independent liaisons with outside groups. In addition, the change to temperance fundamentalism worked to their advantage when the pure food, drink, and drug forces were able to reestablish the importance of their cause to straight-line temperance.

Although Lillian Stevens and her associates were far more conservative than Willard had been, they were also concerned with resuming their momentum and reuniting members. After she was able to establish her leadership, Stevens became a staunch supporter of the pure food, drink, and drug cause. She recommended expanding all aspects of pure food, drink, and drug activism, encouraged tireless efforts to secure state and national regulation, advocated aiding enforcement, proposed a boycott of publications that advertised proprietary medications, and encouraged members to convince local authorities to ban drug billboard advertising and displays in public places. Whereas prison reform, labor reform, and a host of other reforms that Willard had championed fell to the wayside, the departments that promoted pure food, drink, and drugs — the Departments of Health, Scientific Instruction, and Narcotics — remained intact and were reinforced by a newly reinstated National Union Department of Medical Temperance.[3]

The dichotomy between the broadening and restricting forces within the W.C.T.U. did not require abandoning the methods pure food, drink and drug forces found effective. The departments continued to generate and distribute pure food, drink, and drug literature, to sponsor normal institutes, food fairs, home science clubs, and mother's meetings, and to spread the gospel of pure food, drink, and drugs by whatever other means they could devise. The differences in their activities involved promoting each of these activities for the express purpose of securing federal regulation, cooperating more closely with other pure food, drink, and drug reformers, and declaring prohibition as their ultimate goal.

The Department of Health

Pure food, drink, and drug activism within the Department of Health (formerly the Department of Hygiene) between 1895 and 1906 provides a vivid illustration of the various processes that the pure food, drink, and drug crusaders used to maintain their integrity and introduce their cause into the United States Congress. In 1895, as part of the reorganization, Louise C. Purington, a physician in Dorcester, Massachusetts, transferred from the Department of Franchise to become the new superintendent of the Department of Health. She found pure food, drink, and drug advocates active in state and local unions, but in need of coordination. After Ella Kellogg's energetic send-off, local, state, and national W.C.T.U. departments of health had grown in numbers, size, and activity. Bessie Cushman, M.D., who succeeded Kellogg, maintained the original program for a few years, but the superintendents who served after Cushman remained in office for only short periods of time, rarely implemented new innovations, and steered clear of becoming involved in supporting legislation.

Purington revitalized the department. First, she strengthened the department's standing in the national organization by reminding the "few" who underestimated its significance to temperance that good health had always been a central component of the temperance creed. She argued that from the beginning, the organizers of the W.C.T.U. knew that "the way of temperance was the way of health," and that "the right to be well-born was elementary to victory in the conflicts of life." The early temperance women understood the relationship between health and temperance in their childhood. As they learned to read from the "Health Gospels" and family Bibles that lay side-by-side on the mantels of their family homes, they "drank in the truths" of both, and the "truths" of both mingled in "their blood." Physical well-being was "the tap-root" of temperance reform and the "health decalogue" was "as binding as the Ten Commandments."[4]

Purington continued to exploit the ideas that adulterated food and dangerous drugs led to inebriety, that people resorted to proprietary medications to counter the effects of poor nutrition and digestion, that proprietaries addicted the sufferers to alcohol and other dangerous substances, that addicted parents passed their affliction to succeeding generations, and that federal regulation was the best way to insure the quality of the food and drug supply.[5]

To boost the credibility of the department in the eyes of the scientific community, Purington elevated the element of professional proficiency. She made herself available as a physician-lecturer at local and state functions, chose physicians and home economists for her staff, and encouraged local and state unions to recruit as many practicing physicians and health educators as possible to serve as superintendents of W.C.T.U. departments of health.[6]

As her associate to lead the crusade for pure foods, Purington chose Marian A. McBride, a home economist from her home state of Massachusetts. McBride's position as Domestic Science and Sanitation instructor at the Mechanics' Institute in Boston provided her an ideal climate in which to spread the doctrine of pure food, drink, and drugs to hundreds of students and to link the W.C.T.U. department with extension agents and other nationally-known home economists, such as Ellen Richards, Mary Hinman Abell, and Fanny Merritt Farmer.[7]

A strong advocate for federal pure food, drink, and drug legislation, McBride, with the aid of local home economists, women's clubs, and the Massachusetts Board of Health, organized the October 1891 Boston food fair, which had become a Boston tradition. It was sponsored periodically by the Massachusetts Association of Retail Grocers to introduce new products and processes, to encourage higher standards for food products, and to "debunk fraud, remove abuses, and protect honest dealers." In the fair's booths, the country's leading food manufacturers exhibited their products and introduced their latest innovations. The 1891 fair attracted hundreds of participants and alerted thousands of visitors to the virtues of pure food and the dangers of adulteration. Managing the fair placed McBride into a working relationship with "honest" food manufacturers and established her reputation as a leading consumer advocate for pure food, drink, and drugs.[8]

In March 1898, she represented consumer interests at the first National Pure Food and Drug Congress held at Columbian University in Washington, D.C. McBride's participation in this congress was important because it provided the W.C.T.U. crusaders with a more intimate connection to other forces that were exploring the viability of federal food and drug legislation. Among these was the convening chairman, pure food enthusiast Alexander J. Wedderburn, editor of *National Farm and Fireside*, master of the Virginia State Grange, and the author of a Federal Bureau of Chemistry bulletin which was designed to appeal to the general public. Wedderburn had called the Congress to negotiate a consensus regarding food and drug legislation that would be acceptable to all of the involved parties. More than 150 delegates attended. They represented 24 states and territories, various departments of the federal government, and interested trade, manufacturing, agricultural, scientific, medical, and reform associations.[9]

Revising the pure food and drug bill, which Senator Marriott Brosius had introduced the previous year, and which had died in a House committee, was the main item on its agenda. To this end, the legislative committee assembled a group of trade representatives and considered their suggestions. Despite a break with Wedderburn during an interdepartmental power play in the Bureau of Chemistry, Harvey Washington Wiley, who the press later designated "the father of the pure food, drink, and drug law," served in an advisory capacity.[10]

McBride was disappointed with the outcome. In her estimation, the delegates gave away too many concessions to commercial interests. At the request of the *American Grocer*, the committee voted to exclude manufacturers from disclosing their trade formulas. It accepted the recommendation of the National Confectioners' Association, to narrow the definition of adulterated candy. Bowing to the wishes of the National Proprietary Medicine Association, it confined the definition of drugs solely to the cosmetics and medications that were recognized by the *United States Pharmacopoeia* and the *National Formulary*. Under the agreement, regulation of drugs no longer applied to proprietary medications and other dangerous preparations, and it provided for a cumbersome bureaucracy to establish standards that would require the Department of Agriculture to collaborate with a board of at least five physicians selected by the president of the United States, five chemists from the American Chemical Society, and an unspecified number of representatives from the involved industries. McBride felt that such a standards board would act too slowly and that including the manufacturers would be like turning a fox into the hen house.[11]

The advantage that McBride salvaged from attending the congress was to enable her to assess and evaluate the friends and enemies of effective legislation and to establish useful contacts with other delegates. As a result of their acquaintance, A. C. True of the Massachusetts Agricultural Experimental Station and Harvey W. Wiley, albeit with constant prodding, began to keep the Department of Health apprised of bureaucratic developments and to supply them with the latest Federal Department of Agriculture literature. Equally valuable, cooperation with the reliable manufacturers and food chemists she met at the congress, enabled McBride and her associates to compile a running list of "clean" foods authenticated by the "expert knowledge furnished by the United States Government" and "the constant aid of experts in food adulteration," for the use of women's groups and health departments throughout the country.[12]

Both Purington and McBride encouraged greater cooperation among women who were working for pure food, drink, and drugs within different departments at local, state, and national levels. This involved supporting the other departments' activities, as well as correlating programs. The National W.C.T.U. Department of Health set the example by endorsing and helping scientific instruction advocates, particularly in enforcement, and in encouraging the Department of Narcotics to spend more time promoting drug regulation. The sister departments responded in kind. By 1901 the New Jersey Department of Health reported that cooperation among W.C.T.U. departments was a "feature of their work," and a greater number of members were volunteering to participate in the pure food, drink, and drug activities of several departments. Superintendents in other states reported that reciprocal participation among pure food, drink, and drug activists in various departments was becoming the norm.[13]

The National Department of Health accelerated collaboration with agencies outside the W.C.T.U. McBride requested that local unions concentrate on enlisting the cooperation of other organizations of women in their vicinity and working with newspaper personnel. Members responded by initiating the formation of neighborhood health societies, home-science clubs, and schools of health that involved entire communities in pure food, drink, and drug activities. They invited newspaper people to their meetings and social functions and wrote articles for women's columns. Purington advised local unions to coordinate their activities with boards of health, with health protective associations, with "men and women of the 'new order' who were confronting questions of milk and water pollution," and with other groups who were trying to improve the quality of "the substances they ingested," fighting to control tuberculosis, or confronting the problem of drug abuse. She suggested that they encourage ministers to include "a new gospel of Health" and address the "great, grave theme of heredity" in their sermons.[14]

A decided upsurge in political activism for pure food, drink, and drugs accompanied the cooperative efforts of the various agencies. McBride reported almost universal consideration of the subject in the women's clubs and various organizations. W.C.T.U. lecturer, Helen D. Harford, along with other field workers, reported little opposition to expanding the program. They organized new departments of health and attracted new members to the W.C.T.U. wherever they went. Unions in Massachusetts and Pennsylvania reported a great upsurge in enacting specific health ordinances to improve the quality of milk, meat, and canned foods. They further reported that W.C.T.U. workers were organizing citizen groups to oversee the enforcement of the statutes and that most unions were "agitating" for federal regulation. In 1901, New Hampshire pure food, drink, and drug activities almost doubled over the previous year. The state union mailed bulletins to farmers, distributed thousands of pages of literature, and received encouraging replies to letters they sent out. In August, a state institute at Weiers adopted a resolution to champion omnibus federal pure food, drink, and drug legislation. During the same year, the W.C.T.U. Departments of Legislation and of Health collaborated with other reform groups to secure a state laboratory of hygiene, form a committee to consider a state sanitarium for consumptives, and enforce milk laws. In most states, W.C.T.U. workers were cooperating with boards of health, public health associations, social science reform groups, and women's clubs in a variety of pure food, drink, and drug promotions.[15]

In 1902 the N.W.C.T.U. Department of Health sent out a request for all local and state unions to throw the entire force of their organizations behind the drive for federal pure food, drink, and drug legislation. Most of the unions committed congressional candidates to vote for the bill, and sent petitions and resolutions to Washington, D.C., urging leaders to bring the bill out of committee so Congress could pass it that year. In 1903,

McBride reported that the General Federation of Women's Clubs had joined them in the fight.[16]

The Department of Scientific Instruction

Throughout the period of N.W.C.T.U. reorganization, the Department of Scientific Instruction remained intact. Although Mary Hunt was one of Willard's most outspoken critics, opposed woman suffrage, and feared that dabbling in partisan politics might threaten scientific instruction in the school systems, she was too well-known and powerful for Willard to displace.

By 1895 scientific instruction laws to require teaching the dangers of substance abuse in public schools were operative in every state in the Union except four. The less effective laws were strengthened by amendment, W.C.T.U.-approved textbooks were used by most school districts, and local W.C.T.U. representatives inspected the schools regularly to insure that scientific instruction was taught properly and regularly. Hunt took advantage of Willard's loss of influence and frequent absences from the country to construct an almost autonomous departmental empire with national headquarters and an extensive library at her home in Boston. She had expanded her staff to include an associate, Mary F. Lovell, four permanent secretaries, as many as eight part-time helpers when emergencies arose, and an advisory board of three clergymen, three educators, and three physicians. She had lobbied in person for scientific instruction laws in every state in the Union and had appeared before committees in Washington to instate the program in the District of Columbia, the territories, and the armed forces. She was a delegate and speaker at various educational, scientific, and medical conventions and was introducing scientific instruction programs into England, Germany, and other foreign counties.[17]

The most serious challenge to the department came in 1900 from a group of educators who opposed scientific temperance instruction on the grounds that it was "neither scientific, nor temperate, nor instructive." Among these, the presidents of Columbia, Cornell, Yale, Stanford, and Vassar colleges denounced the study as unprofessional. Teachers' associations in New York, Massachusetts, and Wisconsin declared the subject matter biased. A group of scholars, known as the Committee of Fifty, criticized the endorsed textbooks for representing theories as facts, telling half-truths, and expounding conclusions at odds with what they considered authoritative standards. Some state boards of education began to demand that scientific instruction laws be amended or rescinded.[18]

Opposition brought the department under attack from the media. Criticism in *Outlook, Popular Science Monthly, Science*, and the *Medical Record* accused the textbook publishers of exaggeration, and the W.C.T.U. of promoting prohibition under the pretense of teaching science. Publicly, the National W.C.T.U. stood by the Department of Scientific Instruction, but, under the barrage of criticism from educators and the press, the executive committee began to question Hunt concerning the accuracy of the textbooks.[19]

Besieged from within and without at the same time, officers of the Scientific Instruction department expanded their headquarters, staff, and advisors, and dissipated considerable time and energy in defending their program. Hunt countered the outside critics by accusing them of anti-temperance bias, challenging them to support their charges with specific instances of inaccuracy. Then, with the aid of the Temperance Committee of the State and National Association of Christian Churches, she assembled an independent investigative committee, consisting of two former A.M.A. presidents, a number of other eminent physicians, scientific experts, and clergymen, to prepare an objective opinion of the endorsed textbooks and school instruction. The investigative committee members found no evidence of inaccuracy or exaggeration. The department included the report, the testimonies of other medical and scientific authorities, and the endorsement of numerous Protestant churches and temperance organizations in a series of circulars that they sent to teachers' organizations, school boards, newspapers, periodicals, and local, state, and federal legislators and government officials. Hunt's "Reply to the Physiological Sub-Committee of the Committee of Fifty" became a Senate document in 1904. In it, Hunt asserted that the subcommittee had misrepresented the evidence, had examined only the oldest textbooks, had drawn its authorities from people who knew little or nothing about scientific instruction, and had not disproved the "poisonous nature" of dangerous substances.[20].

It seemed better to Hunt and her associates to sponsor new texts written by younger scientists who had "studied the question without prejudice" than to expend additional efforts in updating and defending the claims in older books. The staff directed its energies toward selecting and training professors from Harvard and Northwestern Universities to author a New Century Series that covered all grades from primary through high school and contained an oral lesson book for primary teachers, with enough lesson material, "worked out and illustrated," for three years instruction. By 1906 scores of old texts were replaced by more than forty new books.[21]

During the early years of the twentieth century, local department members spent most of their time introducing the new texts into school systems and working individually with teachers. They encountered fierce opposition from brewers, distillers, and professional educators. The intensity of the fight to defend their position attracted new members and made the veteran workers more determined. One state superintendent wrote that W.C.T.U. women in her area were "in love" with scientific instruction work. Their enthusiasm indicated more than "sentimental approval." It was "the working kind" of zeal that involved "perfecting the mechanism" of teaching, insuring compliance, enlisting new recruits, and promoting the pure, food, drink, and drug cause. It also entailed distributing six million pages of educational literature and using every means possible to secure a national pure food, drink, and drug law.[22]

Despite repeated praise from Stevens, in the late 1890s the department became alienated from the central W.C.T.U. leadership and began to operate almost entirely independent of National or World W.C.T.U. direction. Lack of support from the executive committee during the attacks against the scientific instruction program rankled Hunt, who became involved in several disputes with the national leaders over funding. By 1900, she and her associates were arranging financing from other sources. The department formed a Scientific Temperance Association to hold its contracts with publishers and to administer royalty funds accruing from their work on the textbooks. On its own, without N.W.C.T.U. sanction, it began to publish an independent educational journal entitled *School Physiology Journal* and to extend its program in England and other countries in Europe.[23]

The leaders and members of the department pursued its international obligations with great sincerity. They sent Hunt as a delegate to every World W.C.T.U. convention and appointed her to represent them at a pure food and drug congress in Brussels in 1897. In 1903, at the request of the Emperor of Germany, Theodore Roosevelt appointed Hunt as the official representative of the United States to an educational conference in Berlin where she delivered a series of lectures. Until her death in 1906, she maintained an impressive correspondence with world leaders and worked with them on reforming their educational systems to include scientific temperance instruction. The prestige of these connections increased the effectiveness of department programs in the United States.[24]

Upon her death, the disposition of the department's property triggered a bitter dispute between the N.W.C.T.U. and Hunt's heirs. Both claimed the royalty funds, the scientific library, her home furnishings, and the *School Physiology Journal*, but the heirs retained legal title because the department's holdings were in Hunt's name. An unpleasant dispute between Hunt's successor, Cora Stoddard, and the National W.C.T.U. officials led to a formal split and separate operations. The two organizations did not reconcile until 1918. Without National W.C.T.U. support, the vitality of scientific instruction in the schools gradually declined.[25]

Regardless, over the 35-year period since its beginning, the department achieved its goal of providing scientific instruction to the 22 million children of school age in the United States. The crusaders secured national legislation and laws in every state and territory requiring the instruction of health and the dangers of substance abuse. They designed courses of study that were widely adopted for all grades and helped to prepare more than 40 textbooks. They conducted ongoing research on the subject, collected medical and other scientific literature from all nations, and classified the material in a large library, that was in constant use by students, authors, and lecturers. They had prepared and distributed well over six million pages of educational literature to the general public, provided instruction and guidance for teachers, and introduced the subject in many European and Asian countries.[26]

The Department of Narcotics

The Department of Narcotics focused more attention on pure food, drink, and drugs during the reorganization period. Faced with the prospect of either extinction or relating the activities of the department more closely to temperance, its leaders began to accelerate their support for food, drink, and drug regulation. Eliza B. Ingalls, the superintendent of the department, explained, "for several years the women have been educating themselves in regard to opium; they have given more thought to the tobacco question, perhaps because it is the most commonly used of all narcotics; but," she said, "now we have taken up the fight against opium in its many forms; also cocaine, ether, hashish, and chloroform." This interest followed the release of the 1890 census report that indicated large increases, over the previous decade, in the importation of opium, Indian hemp, and other habit-forming drugs. The report also revealed concern over a sharp rise in the use of headache powders that were readily available in small packets for as little as five cents.[27]

Ingalls prepared a twelve-phase program for each union, five sections of which pertained to narcotic drugs. Her agenda included encouraging ministers to preach against opium, petitioning state legislatures for better laws to regulate the sale of opium and kindred drugs, and arranging for at least one address on narcotics at every annual W.C.T.U. meeting. Lecturers were asked to condemn the use of narcotics when they spoke on the "broad question of intemperance, to warn persons against using chewing gum, soothing syrups, headache powders, and cigarettes" — all of which reportedly contained opium — and to assist "slaves" to these drugs.[28]

Probably, the practice of adding opium to tobacco products and chewing gum was not as common as W.C.T.U. women were led to believe, but the *Union Signal* published evidence of opium in cigarettes often enough to activate mothers who suspected their children might be smoking. Ingalls reported that the "agitation" had caused some tobacco companies to discontinue adulterating tobacco with opium and some other dangerous drugs.[29]

Cocaine abuse triggered particular alarm among department members. Ingalls reported that cocaine imports had doubled between 1899 and 1904. Alkaloids prepared from the little one- to three-inch leaves of *Erythoxylon coca* and other species of *Erythoxylon* shrubs, which had inhibited the hunger and enhanced the endurance of Andean highlanders for centuries, were being marketed aggressively by German industrialists in alarming quantities to bring euphoria, increased energy, and often agony and death to people in the United States. Cocaine sniffing was becoming stylish among young adults as a "pleasure" drug. It was prescribed extensively by physicians, used in self-medication, advertised as a cure for opium addiction and was a secret ingredient in general tonics and proprietaries. The U. S. Hay Fever Association endorsed it as a decongestant. Sears, Roebuck sold an energizing cocaine wine. Cocaine-containing sodas, mostly in the form of cola drinks, were becoming increasingly popular.[30]

The cocaine-abuse problem was thought to be particularly critical among black populations in the South. Southern shippers had introduced cocaine to stevedores in Southern seaports to increase their endurance and to insure their loyalty to the company. By 1900 cocaine abuse had spread to the general population. Reportedly, some saloons in black neighborhoods had gone out of business because so many of their patrons turned to cocaine. Other saloons exploited the demand by offering the drug for sale on their premises.[31]

Rumors and overblown accounts of cocaine-related violence sounded an alarm for concerned women. By the turn of the century, many pure food, drink, and drug recruits became convinced that the cocaine user was not a normal individual, but a "dangerous and debased" person, obsessed with securing the drug — a paranoid who suffered delusions of persecution, carried knives and firearms, and robbed, raped, and murdered.[32]

Druggists were particularly suspect of dealing cocaine. The Kansas City attorney warned, "There are a whole lot of druggists in this city who are selling cocaine to young boys and making criminals of them." Cocaine was readily available to juveniles in powder form at the drug store as inexpensive as five cents for a small packet.[33]

Ingalls advised members not to center all of their attention on the "vile tobacco habit." It was the duty of W.C.T.U. women to warn people against using any drug containing chloral, opium, and especially cocaine. Ingalls considered cocaine "a most destructive and deadly drug" that outstripped opium, whiskey, or tobacco in its "damaging effects upon the human system."[34]

The Department of Medical Temperance

In 1895, yet another group of W.C.T.U. women joined the crusade. The Department of Medical Temperance gained popularity quickly and by 1903 became the leading W.C.T.U. agency in the fight for pure food, drink, and drugs.

Originally, the Department of Medical Temperance had initiated its national campaign in 1884. Fashioned after a like department in New York State, the National Department of Medical Temperance had concentrated its efforts on persuading physicians to sign a pledge not to use alcohol in their practices. From its beginning, the department had encountered opposition from W.C.T.U. members and physicians alike. Medical use of alcohol was an established practice which few felt justified in abandoning. The majority of W.C.T.U. members considered the idea a fanatic measure, and physicians ridiculed its advocates.[35]

After a few years, the N.W.C.T.U. dropped the department, but the New York State Union retained its program, changing the plan of work to focus on the prescribing and use of all types of narcotics, dangerous drugs, and proprietary medications, and to verifying its claims. Under the leadership of Martha Meir Allen, the department began to amass a large library of research material, confirming the fears that temperance people were among those who consumed vast quantities of alcohol and narcotics in patent medicines, sometimes unknowingly. In an attitude of inquiry and cooperation, rather than censure, women found physicians more willing to talk to them and to supply them with information.[36]

Both the women and physicians knew by the taste and smell that some of the proprietaries contained alcohol, but they did not know how much. The presence of narcotics was difficult to detect. To determine the alcohol content, Martha Allen took suspect samples of widely used proprietary remedies to the Massachusetts State Board of Health for assay. The chemists determined that the preparations contained from five to forty percent alcohol. Allen presented a brief summary of the results at the 1887 N.W.C.T.U. convention, held in Buffalo, New York. The next year the New York *Christian Advocate* published her report and the W.C.T.U. produced a pamphlet entitled "The Danger and Harmfulness of Patent Medicines." These marked the first times the percentages of alcohol in proprietary medications had been printed for the public.[37]

With a broader emphasis, greater credibility, and less abrasive approach, the department achieved considerable popularity in New York State. Most of the unions were able to support departments of non-alcoholic medicine, a number of women physicians joined the ranks, and Martha Allen began to persuade the Massachusetts Medical Association to denounce alcohol, narcotics, and proprietaries as hazardous and useless medications.[38]

Adequate documentation for its claims, and the new popularity of the New York department under its revised plan, convinced the national union that its program might be useful. In 1895 the N.W.C.T.U reinstated the department under the name of the Department of Non-Alcoholic Medicine with Martha Meir Allen at its head. In 1905 they changed the name to the Department of Medical Temperance.[39]

The expanded national program revolved around investigational, organizational, educational, and legislative objectives. The program targeted eight specific areas to alert the public to the latest objections against the use of alcoholic beverages for medical purposes, to show the dangers

of self-medication, and to determine the exact content of the most popular proprietary medicines. Further, the aim of the program was to expose
dangerous "patent medicines" and "liquid foods," to eliminate fraudulent
medical advertising, and to convince physicians that medical authorities
on the leading edge of the profession had discontinued prescribing alcohol and proprietaries. Finally, the program sought to introduce the same
medical literature to nurses and to seek their cooperation in educating the
public against self-prescription, to work for legislation to correct the "evils"
of whiskey drugstores, "quack doctors," and "patent medicines," and to
collect and publish the opinions of physicians who did not use alcohol in
their practices.[40]

This time the program assumed campaign proportions in a short time.
The national department sent 25,000 leaflets to acquaint local and state
unions with its objectives, teachings, and plan of action. After study and
discussion, state and local workers from Maine to California, began organizing to implement Allen's program. In two years, the plan was operative in forty-three state unions.[41]

Allen reported the greatest advances among both the membership and
medical profession in New Hampshire and New York where this department had been operating independently for a number of years. The New
Hampshire superintendent wrote that non-alcoholic medicine was "growing in favor" in local unions and many new members were specializing in
pure food, drink, and drug activism. In New York, physicians and nurses
at the Women's Hospital and at Bellevue were concluding that alcoholic
medications delayed recovery, the Red Cross Hospital was strictly non-
alcoholic, and two medical colleges, the Woman's College of New York
City, under the direction of Dean Phebe J. Wait, M. D., and Syracuse Medical College, under Dean Didama, added classes in non-alcoholic medicine.[42]

Pure food, drink, and drug lectures by department heads, state and
county presidents, physicians, and others, became popular in many areas.
The subject was the theme of discussion in innumerable parlor meetings,
mothers' meetings, and county conventions. Allen attributed the new
enthusiasm to the "fact that this department puts effective weapons into
the hands of workers wherewith they may successfully fight against alcohol and narcotics in medical practice."[43]

The American Medical Temperance Association, whose annual meetings were held in conjunction with A.M.A. conventions, was their ally.
These physicians created an invaluable link between W.C.T.U. crusaders

and the medical profession. Allen held them up as authorities and quoted them frequently in the department propaganda.[44]

In the five years following its reinstatement, the department reported appreciable headway. Between October 1899 and January 1900, approximately 400 pure food, drink, and drugs articles appeared in various medical journals. Allen considered this as an "encouraging sign of the great change of sentiment" in the "leading edge" of the medical profession. She found that cooperation usually replaced opposition when workers contacted physicians. Repeatedly physicians asserted that they would eliminate habit-forming drugs and proprietaries from their practices if their patients, or their associates, agreed.[45]

The department generated an impressive amount of pure food, drink, and drug literature. In 1898 alone it published and circulated leaflets entitled "Safe Remedies," "Railroad Emergency," "An Appeal to Physicians, "A Non-Alcoholic Study," "Doctors and Alcohol," and an updated version of "The Danger and Harmfulness of Patent Medicines."[46]

The "Patent Medicines" leaflet involved Allen in legal difficulties. Dr. Ray Vaughn Pierce brought suit against Allen for listing his favorite prescription among remedies that secretly included alcohol and opium in their formulas, when in actuality the Pierce preparation contained neither. Unknown to Allen, the firm had deleted alcohol and opium from its formula since the last assay. Pierce dropped the suit when the department issued a new edition of the leaflet that omitted reference to all preparations, except those examined by a new assay, and Allen advised those who quoted the leaflet to cite the Massachusetts Board of Health as their source.[47]

In 1900, Martha Allen published *Alcohol a Dangerous and Unnecessary Medicine*, a handbook in which she devoted several chapters to the dangers of drugging and proprietary medicines drawn from the department's research. This was the first published book that provided evidence against fraudulent patent medicine testimonials. Later she published two more leaflets entitled "A Study of Patent Medicines," and "Percentages of Alcohol in Proprietary Medicines, Liquid Foods and Malt Extracts." In January 1903, the Massachusetts Board of Health examined additional medications for the percentages of alcohol. The N.W.C.T.U. published the first report on their findings, with analyses of many of the liquid proprietary foods advertised for people in poor health in Allen's latest edition of the "Patent Medicines" leaflet. Allen's publications furthered the momentum of the crusade by providing information that communities needed to chart plans of action, mark the pitfalls, and suggest guidelines.[48]

Distributing books and pamphlets, and personal contact were still the best ways to reach the general public. The majority of newspapers and magazines refused to print W.C.T.U. articles. The *Christian Advocate* was one of the few national papers to publish articles that attacked patent medicines. The *Epworth Herald* accepted a manuscript in 1900, but did not print it. The *Ladies' Home Journal*, which started its own campaign against proprietary medications in 1904, rejected a W.C.T.U. manuscript submitted in 1899. Frequently W.C.T.U. members produced copy for women's pages, and occasionally newspapers printed their articles, but, as a general rule, W.C.T.U. members encountered difficulty in persuading newspapers and magazines to print items that attacked their advertisers. Occasionally, with some justification, editors criticized the quality and the bias of W.C.T.U. material.[49]

To overcome this disadvantage, in 1901 the national department initiated contests for the best original manuscripts of between 800 and 1,400 words that illustrated the dangers of substance abuse. The contests drew thousands of new participants into the active production of pure food, drink, and drug propaganda, involving newswomen and persons with writing skills in producing a better quality of pure food, drink, and drug literature. The judges expected writers to expound on the dangers of both physician-prescribing and home-medicating with dangerous drugs. Cash prizes of ten to twelve dollars were awarded for the best state report; best short story; best poem; best humorous article, suitable for recitation, showing the "evils and absurdities of the use of patent medicines" containing alcohol, opium or cocaine, or other addictive ingredients; and best oration revealing the evils of the medical use of alcohol, including alcoholic patent medicines, or fraudulent medicines.[50]

The Department of Legislation

Reorganization of the Department of Legislation intensified the W.C.T.U. drive for pure food, drink, and drug regulation. Judith Ellen Foster, the original superintendent and long-time friend of Frances Willard, with a group of fellow dissenters, left the W.C.T.U. in opposition to Willard's endorsement of third-party politics to form a break-off organization entitled The Non-Partisan W.C.T.U. Foster was active in Republican politics and went on to became president of the National Association of Republican Woman's Clubs, in which capacity she led a wide spectrum of reforms.[51]

In 1895, the N.W.C.T.U. elected Margaret Dye Ellis, of Newark, New Jersey, as the new superintendent of the Legislation department. The arrival of Ellis to serve as a W.C.T.U. watchdog in Washington, D.C., advanced the pure food, drink, and drug cause considerably. In a short time, Ellis became a proficient N.W.C.T.U. lobbyist. Mrs. Clinton Smith, president of the D.C. Union, described her as "the bright, particular star" in the "firmament" of W.C.T.U. "influence-makers" in the nation's capital. Well-placed through her personal connections to social reformers and evangelical activists, and through her husband's influence as a senator, Ellis soon learned how to take advantage of their influence to gain access to government officials in executive and legislative circles, developed political tactics, and claimed the right to speak for the women of the world.[52]

Her presence in Washington strengthened the credentials of the W.C.T.U. and widened its network of influence. During the winter of 1898-1899, Ellis crowded her months with the work before Congress — interviewing dignitaries, arranging and presenting petitions, lecturing, apprising the W.C.T.U. departments of the most opportune times to contact their representatives, and contributing occasional articles and a regular column for the *Union Signal*. She worked to influence the Republican political elite at the highest levels, more than once contacting Theodore Roosevelt personally.[53]

In spite of the intense pace of Ellis' political involvement, her affiliation with the W.C.T.U. moderated her influence. Temperance heightened her motivation, but the W.C.T.U. focus on prohibition carried the burden of special-interest-group representation. In addition, as the wife of United States Senator J. H. Ellis, she was careful to promote her own causes with discretion. Much of the time she worked behind the scenes, and often through politicians and other reform lobbyists, such as H. W. Blair from Vermont, Wilbur F. Crafts of the International Reform Bureau, and John G. Woolley of Chicago, who served on her advisory committee along with Lillian Stevens and Mrs. N. White-Kenny of Astoria, Oregon.[54]

The Department of Purity in Literature and Art

Early in the twentieth century, women in the Department of Purity in Literature and Art entered the fight to ban fraudulent proprietary advertising on billboards, barns, pictures, displays, and in newspapers and magazines. This department added a sensational new dimension to the crusade, by classifying proprietary advertising with pornography (for which, at the time, the language and illustrations of many of the ads obviously qualified). Its appeal flamed the outrage of a great many women against proprietary advertising, but, so late in the crusade, most pure food, drink, and drug enthusiasts were occupied in other departments. These crusaders supported the Department of Purity in Literature and Art's anti-ad campaign, but were too busy implementing existing programs to enroll in the department.[55]

Conclusion

For all of their activism, what did the W.C.T.U. pure food, drink, and drug crusaders accomplish? Despite continual criticism they accomplished a great deal. More than in any other organization, the legions of pure food, drink, and drug reformers operating within the W.C.T.U. departments were able to mobilize a vast force of public concern. Through their organization, they were able to reach great numbers of people quickly in remote as well as metropolitan areas, reflect consumer interests accurately, and attack the problem with courage, intensity, and determination. They facilitated cooperation and communication between localities and groups. They did not allow politicians to intimidate them, they were willing to bridge social barriers that had separated them in the past, and they did not hold back from trying to reach their objectives through every method they thought might be effective, including the use of public schools, churches, and political action.

On the negative side of the ledger, although affiliating with the W.C.T.U. provided an effective medium through which pure food, drink, and drug forces were able to conduct their crusade, membership in the W.C.T.U., to a certain extent, circumscribed their freedom of action and limited their ability to push the crusade to its ultimate goal of insuring safe food, drink, and drugs for the American public. Their religious temperance approach provided the impetus necessary to initiate, nurture, and propel the crusade. Adjusting their focus directly toward purely temperance issues changed the public image of W.C.T.U. workers "from the best, most respected, most forward-looking women in town to narrow-minded, anti-libertarians riding a hobby horse."[56]

At the same time it is important to note that the organization's retrenchment was not as "immediate, abrupt, and dramatic," nor as complete after Willard's death as some of her biographers have depicted. It came gradually from the top down, rather than from the bottom up. Many members had joined and were joining the W.C.T.U. for the specific purpose of promoting the varying and diverse aspects of food, drink, and drug reform. Two hundred fifty thousand women did not instantly change their view. The natural tendency was for them to broaden rather than to restrict their activities. Mass support on local and state levels insured continuity of their programs and fostered the rise of strong department leaders who were sensitive to the concerns of the membership in general.[57]

It is also important to realize that the influence of the W.C.T.U. pure food, drink, and drug crusaders extended far beyond the official membership. This influence is evident in unexpected ways that typically have been ignored by historians because W.C.T.U. activities have not been included in a context of specific reforms, other than in regard to feminism and prohibition. They were able to extend their influence into a wide variety of women's organizations and women's clubs. Bureaucrats, legislators, journalists, educators, and medical providers were influenced by, and took advantage of, the public opinion the W.C.T.U. crusaders organized, but they seldom were willing to admit it.

Regardless of the advantages of W.C.T.U. affiliation, the stigma attached to prohibition by many people sometimes ate away at the effects W.C.T.U. women were able to exert in their communities and on local politicians. The link to prohibition alienated some voters and limited the number of women who were willing to work in the W.C.T.U. departments for pure food, drink, and drugs. Historians were not exempt from this attitude. The connection to prohibition and the fact that the W.C.T.U. crusaders were women without the power of the franchise, coupled with the preoccupation of historians with the deeds of great men, help to explain why they received so little credit.

After 1905, partly because of their temperance affiliation, the W.C.T.U. departments lost the leadership of the crusade to the General Federation of Women's Clubs, the National Consumers' League, and ultimately to federal bureaucracies. Regardless, to paraphrase Frances Willard, a large army of women became "attempered" to altruism, inured to "contradiction," and found that they could be useful in "coming invisibly" active in protecting their homes and communities.[58]

The Woman's Christian Temperance Union did not ever abandon the battle against drug abuse. They provided active support for drug regulation for the Pure Food, Drink, and Drug Act of 1906 and for strengthening all federal and state legislation. With the repeal of prohibition, scientific temperance instruction was discontinued in the public schools, but W.C.T.U. members still continued to generate and distribute anti–drug-abuse literature from their headquarters in Evanston, Illinois, and to encourage young people and adults to avoid drug abuse.[59]

6

The General
Federation of Women's
Clubs Crusaders

"Our Goddess, Literature, never comes empty-handed."[1]

The General Federation of Women's Clubs was another national organization through which pure food, drink, and drug crusaders were
able to promote their cause. Like W.C.T.U. women, pure food, drink, and
drug advocates in the Federation marshaled recruits, politicized their cause,
moved from study to activism, and utilized a combination of educational
and political tactics to secure federal regulation. Women in each organization participated in pure food, drink, and drug activism to protect the
American home. Rather than competing for membership or posturing for
dominance, each organization cooperated with and complimented the
other in achieving their common goal.

The differences in pure food, drink, and drug activities between the
two organizations were not always well defined. In general, federated
women concentrated more on adulterated food than on drugs. W.C.T.U.
women focused more on dangerous drugs. Federation women were motivated more by altruism and service. W.C.T.U. women related their concern more toward temperance and religion. Although many individual
crusaders held membership in both organizations, the Federation attracted
those who were not primarily interested in supporting the prohibition
movement and included groups of non–Christian members, as well as
Christian women. Without the stigma many politicians and journalists
placed on temperance activities, federated club women were able to work

more closely with other pure food and drug forces, to establish greater credibility and to receive more recognition for their efforts.

Its founders formed the Federation in 1890 to organize women's clubs nationwide. They envisioned the Federation as a coordinating agency for the cultural, intellectual, and philanthropic interests of individual clubs, and also as a national body of social workers to promote the general welfare by assisting the poor, fighting famine and disease, raising the educational and cultural level, and working for reform. Member organizations could not require partisan political tests for their own membership, must not be secret societies, and must uphold state and national laws.[2]

As discussed earlier, a considerable number of clubs were already involved with pure food, drink, and drug reform on local and state levels. Women in the large department clubs, like the Chicago Women's Club with a membership of over 700, and the Denver Women's Department Club, maintained large committees to fight for pure food, drink, and drugs in their respective cities. Women who had formed health improvement associations and civic clubs for the specific purpose of local regulation were operating actively. Members of the myriad of smaller local clubs had moved beyond their self-improvement programs to address public health needs. Women in these organizations were anxious to expand their pure food, drink, and drug campaigns into a nationwide crusade.[3]

The Federation brought these forces together and, after an organizational and educational "seed time," focused their pure food, drink, and drug activities on securing federal legislation. As Jane Croly observed, the national organization became a "radiation" center for the "diffusion of that which was brought into it."[4]

The Federation created a climate favorable to advancing the crusade. It fostered perceptive writing, speaking, and debating skills to improve societal conditions. It also encouraged open membership; inclusion of all members in club activities; innovation and diversity in thought, but unity in action. Finally, it promoted the development of a cognizant philosophy; and sharpening business methods, executive leadership, and management. All of these policies furthered pure food, drink, and drug activism.

Karen Blair is among the historians who has shown that many women's clubs, federated or unfederated, organized at first for the purpose of self-improvement through the study of literature, history, or art, but soon diversified their objectives into social reforms. Blair found that the Federation expedited this transition. She wrote, "the General Federation diverted clubs from their cultural programs, accelerating the drive toward Municipal Housekeeping which had already begun." Federation leaders emphasized the need for committees to correct problems in the community. As Ohio clubwoman Louise B. Ernst stated, "our Goddess Literature never comes empty-handed." For her the ultimate "mission" of literature was to inspire altruist endeavor. Like many other clubwomen, she found club life "indigent if reserved for self alone."[5]

The Federation encouraged clubs to welcome every woman who wished to join. Many of the early clubs had limited their members to a specific number and had screened enrollment. With some it was a matter of maintaining exclusiveness, in others accommodation was the problem. Sarah Platt Decker, a club leader of Denver, illustrated the absurdity of exclusion by relating an account of her visit to one "wealthy and handsome" clubhouse in which the floor of the meeting room was highly polished and finished with an inlaid border. The president of the club told her that there were 200 members and sometimes as many more on the waiting list. Some of those waiting to join had died before a vacancy opened. When Decker asked why the membership remained restricted, she was told that only 200 chairs could fit inside the inlaid border and setting chairs on the inlay might detract from the decorative effect of the hall. To Decker, this statement suggested that the club considered elegant surroundings more important than the contributions of potential members. Such a concept opposed the spirit of club life. She believed that the ideal club should welcome all women in the community, accommodate them with adequate facilities, and, if suitable, divide the work into departments to meet the interests of all of the members.[6]

Decker reflected the opinion of most Federation leaders in saying that "no spirit of intolerance should be allowed." When considering prospective members, it was "imperative that clubs should ignore social distinctions." All women were "entitled to club courtesies, whether ever before introduced in a social way." The desire to serve should be the criteria that determined club membership, and "the underlying principle of high moral character, without artificial distinction, ... should be the base of beneficial club association." Members should extend sisterhood to any woman regardless of attributes, origin, or station in life.[7]

The obvious advantage of open membership increased the potential of the crusade by bringing greater numbers and a wider heterogeneity of women into the club movement. By 1900 Federation membership rose to more than 150,000 women, organized into 595 clubs and 30 state federations. By 1905 the numbers more than doubled. In Illinois, alone, 242 federated clubs represented 24,000 women. Nonfederated clubs and state federations that did not affiliate with the national Federation totaled an estimated two times that number.[8]

Open membership also served to bridge the religious, sectional, ethnic, and social barriers which had prevented women from uniting in the past. It was an essential key to directing the club movement toward reform activism.

Federation promoted a climate of democracy, cooperation, and community within the clubs by encouraging all members to participate. Repeatedly, the Federation leaders stressed the importance of every member's contribution. One of the most important functions of clubs was to develop language skills and logic through discussion of any subject in a liberal, courteous manner, regardless of how widely opinions differed. Louisa Poppenheim noted, "The club was an instrument in their [women's] hands for giving mental training and moral discipline, as well as social intercourse." She said that club participation lifted women "from their narrow sensitiveness and self-consciousness and taught them practical, candid lessons of everyday life. It was always used as a means to an end."[9]

The Federation officials encouraged clubs to increase the opportunities for members to sharpen their intellectual dexterity through group and individual study; to develop communication skills in debates and public speaking, in writing papers and articles, and in fashioning petitions and legislation. Club activities provided educational and intellectual stimulus impossible for mature women to acquire in any other way. Through a few years of concentrated club study and research, "pursuant to well-digested schemes and carefully prepared programs," they were able to receive the equivalent of postgraduate courses in the best colleges and universities in the world.

The Federation encouraged unity of action along with innovation and diversity in thought. As Mrs. C. J. McClung of Knoxville, Tennessee, wrote, "Harmony of thought" was not possible, "nor desirable even in the best governed club, but harmony of action" was "imperative to the well-being of all organizations, for in unity alone" lay the power to effect societal improvement. "Unity in Diversity" became the Federation slogan and an essential component of every activity. Like those who preceded and succeeded her, General Federation President Rebecca Lowe emphasized the necessity of cooperative effort in her 1900 New Year's message, "Let our dream of the new century be a time when all women of all classes, in all nations, shall stand close together, pushing forward, shoulder to shoulder, for the achievement of all good things in the world where they, the mothers of the race, are ever playing the largest stakes."[10]

A broad body of interrelated club attitudes and beliefs contributed to the pure food, drink, and drug crusade. Through an informal, ongoing process of blending attitudes, which they developed within the crusade itself, with views of their day and ideas from the past, they were able to generate a viable credo for their activism. St. Louis clubwoman Eva Perry Moore, later to become president of the General Federation, was one of many women who observed the growth of thought and purpose that propelled reform. She wrote that by superimposing attitudes cultivated through their own experiences upon popular ideas of the time and "beliefs centuries old," club women were able to develop a congruous, constructive philosophy, "literary, educational, civic, and altruistic — with no line of demarcation, rather each working into and bringing out the most ideal and practical features of the other." This philosophy included a belief that it was the duty of governments, local, state, and national, to protect the general public against the avarice of special interests, that altruism should supersede competition, and that democracy should govern social and political institutions.[11]

Their concept of the role of the national government was vital to the crusade. They believed that insuring purity of food, drink, and drugs was a proper function of the federal government under the Constitution. This function fell within the federal responsibility for promoting the general welfare and regulating commerce. They viewed the role of government as simple and clear cut. It should be more responsive to the needs of the populace than to the pressures of "special interests." This concept seemed elementary and fundamental to democracy's principles. Peoples' rights should take precedence over property rights. If people were more important than property, it made perfect sense to protect people against poison and fraud. In this context, their position became a radical deviation from the established stance of American law that most often protected free trade and business rights above human rights. Politicians, particularly those of the Old Guard and from the South, argued that food and drug regulation, however popular, would set a dangerous precedent of violating the Constitution and threatening free trade. Women argued that reforms, such as food and drug regulation, did not violate either the spirit or the letter of the Constitution, and trade should not be free to prey upon the consumer. If government did not protect the people, then it was useless.[12]

They argued that the real spirit and intent of the Constitution, which guaranteed protection to life, liberty, and property, justified the control of food, drink, and drugs in the public interest. When the secret nature of proprietaries prevented the consumer from determining the ingredients, it was logical to delegate this function to a special agency that had chemical laboratories to check the contents, and because all potential consumers required the same information about the contents of a package, people had the right to expect the government to provide this service.[13]

Altruism and democracy were closely related. Clubwoman Mrs. D. H. Kornhouser wrote that the club concept of democracy included not only a "scheme of government," but a plan of education, a theory of economics, and a "sublime faith in the possibilities of man, a sublime faith in the power that fellowship and brotherhood has to develop individual character." Unless controlled, the commercial spirit of the age threatened to create "a triple aristocracy of birth, wealth, and intellect that counterbalanced character and public service." Abolition of caste and class, the giving of equal opportunity, and the mingling of diverse cultures were the keystones of American democracy. To retain the "true spirit of democracy, women must organize for service and realize that the goal of democracy was to create an environment in which people regarded the welfare of others with the same concern as their own."[14]

In the same vein, Mrs. E. E. Trayer wrote that the elimination of the "privileged class" was paramount to maintaining American democracy. America was built on the concept that "no class of persons" had the right "to do any conceivable thing from which others were barred. The distinctive quality of American society was the equality of rights." Business trusts, private schools, and lack of worker independence violated this right. She believed that the sense of duty, the power of discerning, and doing right broke down barriers between segments and "annihilated all class distinctions."[15]

Finally, the Federation promoted the executive leadership, business methods, and management necessary for an effective national campaign. Its organization was particularly efficient, suggesting directives to each unit on how to organize and focus their activities on the goals they hoped to achieve. In addition they suggested methods by which units could cooperate with other departments, to develop strong leadership skills among the general membership, and to persist in their objectives. Thus, the central committees served as clearinghouses for ideas, developed suggested courses of study, and correlated club activities.

The federated women who were interested in promoting pure food, drink, and drugs concentrated their efforts within the Standing Committees of Domestic Science and of Civic Improvement. These two committees provided pure food, drink, and drug enthusiasts with a nationwide structure for study, the production and dissemination of propaganda, and, eventually, of writing and securing legislation.

Initially, the Committee of Domestic Science (later changed to Household Economics Committee) approached pure food, drink, and drugs from an educational stance and became involved in activism as an application of its studies. The Committee of Civic Improvement was directly associated with political activities and securing legislation from the beginning.

The crusade for pure food, drink, and drugs was always a popular part of the Federation's Domestic Science agenda. Every homemaker had a vested interest in the quality of the food she prepared for her family. Nothing concerned the women of the country more than the purity of food and no question was of greater importance to the home than to stop the traffic in adulterated foods and drinks. As Isabell Churchill, clubwoman of Denver, Colorado, explained, "the quality of food stuff should be a question of paramount interest to every Housewife. It therefore behooves" club women "to thoroughly awake to the need ... for pure food legislation."[16]

Most clubwomen expressed outrage over the magnitude of food adulteration. Commenting on the extant conditions, the editor of *Club Woman* wrote, "As a mere drop of poison will pollute a whole quart of milk, so will one dishonest merchant or manufacturer corrupt" the entire industry." She charged that "the avenues of trade" were poisoned by every merchant who sold "renovated butter to an innocent and unsuspecting customer for prime 'creamery made,' or gluten molasses for that of the sugar cane." She found fraud extensive among food processors, who had "vehemently denied" any incidence of adulteration only a few years previously, and later were arrogant enough to defend and justify their practice by arguing that their adulteration was either "harmless or just as good as the genuine commodity." For her, justifying the use of salicylic acid as a preservative provided a typical illustration of the reckless nature of their claims. Despite scientific evidence indicating that salicylic acid was "deleterious to the human system," its use in food products had become so accepted that manufacturers, "easily to be found," were "brazen enough to declare" its use was harmless. She argued, although, "every intelligent person" knew that salicylic acid arrested digestion, food processors claimed that it's use was "justified by the interests of trade" and opposed efforts to "discourage its employment in food products."[17]

Ella Hoes Neville, chairman of the Household Economics Committee of the General Federation, denounced the adulteration of food as "an enemy which attacks the home whose approach is so insidious that one unprepared is not aware of the presence until death or impaired health is the result." To her, food adulteration was "sinful dealing worse than short weight or dishonest fabric." She wrote, "Give us short measure and we only lose; give us adulterated food and we die." To combat the "great money interests at stake," she called for "the immediate, combined action of every Federation member" in writing or telegraphing the senators and congressmen from her state.[18]

Marian A. McBride, of the N.W.C.T.U. Department of Health, served concurrently as an official of the Federation's Household Economics Committee. She wrote articles for Federation journals, as well as for the *Union Signal*. In her Federation capacity, she led a coalition of pure food, drink, and drug advocates that promoted home economics studies and pure food, drink, and drug regulation. Their activities included encouraging clubs to organize consumer groups and to work for a federal pure food, drink, and drug law. She considered consumer activism an essential ingredient to securing legislation. As she pointed out, chemists, such as A. C. True, of the United States Department of Agriculture, and Harvey W. Wiley, of the Bureau of Chemistry, could set the standards; Senators Brosius, of Pennsylvania, and McCumber, of North Dakota, could defend bills in Congress; but only "diligent effort by the women of the country could organize adequate demand to pass a pure food, drink, and drug law that would insure high standards for their food supply."[19]

At the same time, she considered the United States government their most powerful assistant. In December 1902 when the House of Representatives passed a pure food bill, McBride wrote, "This bill, presented by Mr. Hepburn of Iowa, is a measure of great importance to every housekeeper, because it places the guardianship of the nation's food supply in the hands of national officers. Every woman will feel the benefit of this bill." She was too optimistic. The bill did not pass the Senate.[20]

Like McBride, many Household Economics Committee members supported federal regulation and worked in state and local groups to enforce state food laws, but they did not succeed in initiating a Federation drive for a national food, drink, and drug law separate from other domestic science issues until after the turn of the twentieth century. Part of the reason was that Federation officers believed in organizing activities under large general committees where they clumped the issue of pure food, drink, and drugs together with the study of nutrition, food preparation, and various aspects of good health. With this arrangement, pure food, drink, and drug activism competed with attempts to introduce home economic classes into the schools, along with home decoration, sewing, school sanitation, physical education, and the drive to simplify women's clothing styles to allow greater freedom of motion. In addition, as was the case among some W.C.T.U. members, the cause was burdened by extending the period of study beyond its usefulness, and by opinions that promoted adulterated products and the education of children and adults as adequate measures.

Conversely, the Federation Committee of Civic Improvement worked directly for national regulation from the beginning. Its objectives, as stated by Clara P. Bourland of Peoria, Illinois, was to gather into one body, "for mutual support and combined action, all the forces for good, public and private, existing or at work" in a particular locality. The civics committee fostered the formation of women's organizations, suggested effective methods, united a wide variety of local and state reform agencies, and correlated activities designed to improve local and national situations and environments.[21]

Their work fell under three general classifications: first, training women for activism; second, promoting effective legislation of a "lasting nature" and opposing "mere temporizing expedients"; third, securing public health, civic, and moral reform without regard for "business interests or the parties in power." Here again pure food, drink, and drugs competed with other issues such as electing reform government officials, the disbursement of city funds, civil service, settlement houses, school improvement, clean streets, village beautification, conservation, and pure air.[22]

One of the goals of the General Federation Committee of Civic Improvement was to introduce satellite civic committees into every state federation. In this they were largely successful. By 1904, fourteen state federations reported that standing civic reform committees were functioning and other state federations had given civic work to related committees. Among these, six state federations had delegated civic reform to educational committees: Arkansas, Wyoming, Colorado, and Pennsylvania gave the responsibility to their legislative committees or subcommittees; Georgia entrusted reform to its Social Service Committee; Ohio added it to its conference committee; and in several states it was considered by entire clubs or committees that operated independently of the national Federation. In certain places and at certain times, some local civic reform committees worked exclusively for pure food, drink, and drugs, but not as a general rule.[23]

Working specifically for pure food, drink, and drug regulation was more a function of state civics committees, operating together with the national organization. The national and state committee members worked specifically for pure food, drink, and drugs by advising and coordinating groups that were agitating for state laws and assisting in their enforcement. As a primary line of work in 1901, under the auspices of the Federation civics committee, the Nebraska federation began cooperating with the Nebraska Pure Food Commission in enforcing and extending the provisions of the state's pure food law. The Connecticut federation formed a civic committee that generated interest in enforcing pure food, drink, and drug statutes, and in recommending specific ordinances to reinforce the existing laws. Using recommended Federation tactics and propaganda, Idaho clubwomen introduced and pushed a pure food law through their state legislature, and formed committees to monitor retail and wholesale outlets. Other states carried out similar Federation programs.[24]

The federated Committee of Civic Improvement also launched national campaigns to eradicate "disagreeable and objectionable" medical advertising. With very limited success, they targeted newspaper ads, particularly fraudulent proprietary ads that illustrated news columns with sketches of "a forlorn procession of heart-achy, back-achy, every-kind-achy feminine wrecks" that could be cured with specific remedies. With equal lack of success, they tried to restrict the "big bill posting trust" that extended "from ocean to ocean along the nation's roadways advertising all sorts of exotic cure-alls, and attempted to stem the proliferation of ads on America's "great red barns" for Carter's Little Liver Pills and Dr. Pierce's Favorite Prescription. They tried to remove posters that "desecrated the face of nature by placarding its beauties with proclamations setting forth the merits of hair tonics, face powders, and panaceas for all of the ills that flesh is heir to."[25]

Between 1902 and 1904 the Federation reports indicated considerable nationally supported pure food, drink, and drug activism in a majority of the clubs. A great many literary and other groups were setting aside a portion of their meeting to discussing the problem and a number were adopting various programs to deal with these concerns.[26]

By 1904, the General Federation crusaders were ready to open a vigorous campaign for federal food, drink, and drug regulation. They initiated their drive and marshaled their forces at the seventh biennial federation convention held May 17 through 25, 1904, in St. Louis to coincide with the opening of the Louisiana Purchase Exposition. Planning their agenda around fair activities, the Household Economics Committee and Civic Improvement Committees decided not to prepare a pure food, drink, and drug demonstration that would duplicate a Department of Agriculture exhibit at the fair. Instead, they assisted agricultural chemists in preparing focal points that were designed to appeal to women and directed their delegates to the agriculture display. Mrs. Arthur Courtenay Neville of the Household Economics Committee explained that "an exhibit illustrating every facet of the subject would require the expenditure of unnecessary time and money," and was not advisable, considering "the vast number" of related exhibits at the Exposition in which clubwomen were interested. The planning, labor, and money already expended in the preparation of previously scheduled fair exhibits would "lose value" unless the members of the Federation were free to examine them and gleaned "such lessons as each can make of practical use."[27]

As Neville predicted, the combination of the agricultural exhibit at the fair and an emphasis on pure food, drink, and drugs at the biennial impressed the clubwomen. It reinforced the course of action to which they were already committed. Before they arrived, the delegates were primed to direct every conceivable Federation effort toward securing national and state legislation to eliminate the fraudulent manufacture and advertising of dangerous food and drug products, to authorize the formation of an autonomous pure food subcommittee to expedite the work, and to elect a number of staunch pacesetters to lead the national food, drink, and drug battle.[28]

The president of the Federation, Sarah Sophia Chase Harris Platt Decker of Denver, Colorado, was foremost among these new leaders. Often cited as the most outstanding woman of the early century, Decker represented the most advanced thought and advocated the leading reforms of her time. She was among those who felt that club study should be directed to practical use. Her work served as a model for what millions of American women hoped to achieve. She was a seasoned reformer, experienced in working with men such as Judge Benjamin B. Lindsey for juvenile courts in Denver, and serving as president of the Denver Women's Department Club, where politicians, reformers, and businessmen waited in line for interviews to solicit club support for their causes.[29]

Colorado was one of the four states, along with Wyoming, Idaho, and Utah, where women held full franchise rights. Decker represented the largest block of voters in her state. She knew how to push reform measures through the state legislature and had established powerful personal connections. She had worked alongside her husband, Colonel James H. Platt, a prominent business tycoon, city developer, and behind-the-scenes politician. After he died she married his friend and associate, Judge W. S. Decker, in 1899. When the judge became ill, she managed many of his private, public, and political functions.[30]

She came to the attention of the General Federation of Women's Clubs officers in 1896 when she served on the national nominating committee. She gained the universal admiration of thousands of clubwomen when the Colorado Federation hosted the national convention in Denver in 1898. The nominating committee approached her to fill presidential vacancies on three occasions, but each time she declined because she was too busy managing her husband's business and political affairs. After he died, she accepted the nomination.[31]

General Federation historian Mildred Wells described Decker as a woman of large proportions — physically large, "large-brained, large-hearted," and large-visioned. Rising above the "frills and crimps of fashion" to exemplify the "true woman" of the twentieth century, she had earned a reputation for being a person of uncommonly sound judgment, with an ability to choose effective leaders, to delegate authority, to allow those chosen to carry out duties, and to inspire innovation. Mary I. Wood, who worked closely with her and knew her well, recalled, "Perhaps the greatest gift which the new President possessed was the power, so rare in great minds, of recognizing and calling out the best in others." In Decker's presence, each woman in the Federation, "whether from a small rural club in a hillside town of New England, whose vision was bounded by the limits of the home farm, or from the great departmental club of the largest town," experienced "a surge of self confidence," assuring her that she was a vital part of a great work, prompting her to ignore feelings of timidity or inadequacy, and lending "her best effort to perfect the whole."[32]

Among a wide variety of other reforms, Decker had supported the fight for state pure food, drink, and drug legislation in Colorado. When she became president of the G.F.W.C., she threw the strength of the entire organization behind federal regulation.[33]

The delegates elected Eva Perry Moore of Saint Louis, Missouri, as the first vice-president. Wood declared that Decker and Moore were a perfect combination. Moore complemented Decker's attributes. Wood stated, "it is impossible to consider the success of Mrs. Decker's administration without taking into account ... the need of the times and the admirable assistance rendered by her First Vice-President."[34] Moore was born at Rockford, Illinois, in 1852. After her graduation from Vassar she traveled and studied in Europe. She married, had children, and was a leader in reform activities and in educational, musical, and philanthropic work. She served as a trustee at Vassar, a member and president of the Association of Collegiate Alumnae, and a juror on the Superior Jury at the Louisiana Purchase Exposition.[35]

Moore brought an expansive federation experience to the office of First Vice-President. She had participated in every phase of club life from committee member, to State Federation President, General Federation Secretary, and General Federation Treasurer. She had served as chairman of many committees, including Foreign Correspondence, and as president of the Missouri Federation. She had a remarkable understanding of parliamentary procedure, presided with dignity and poise, and was a master of detail.[36]

Her views of the role of government and the control of big business represented the sentiments of the vast populist membership of the Federation in the Midwest. She believed that government should be the means to promote the welfare of the general public above that of the special interests, that majority should decide how they would be governed, and that participation of the people was an inherent part of the democratic process.

During her fights for food, drink, and drug control in Missouri, she had encountered the political power of the meat packing, liquor, and proprietary drug interests in St. Louis and Chicago, and was familiar with how to deal with their tactics. Regarding the pure food, drink, and drug crusade, she stated, "For our own homes we have insisted upon food pure and clean; we have gone directly to the markets and to the laws of the land, for regulations which will assist the homekeepers in conserving the health of the household."[37]

One of Decker's first acts as President of the G.F.W.C. was to appoint an autonomous Pure Food Subcommittee (commonly called the Pure Food Committee), under the Standing Committee of Domestic Science, with Helen R. Guthrie McNab Miller, of Columbia, Missouri, as chairman; and Elizabeth Foster of Boston, Massachusetts, Mrs. James D. Whitmore of Denver, Colorado; and Alice Lakey of Cranford, New Jersey, as assistants. These appointments brought together a combination of personalities designed to appeal to a wide spectrum of supporters and to promote intensive activism.[38]

Helen Miller was an energetic clubwoman, a pure food, drink, and drug enthusiast, and a home economist at the Agricultural College in Columbia, Missouri. She was born near Zanesville, Ohio, studied at

Stanford and the University of California–Berkeley, the University of Nevada, and abroad. Her husband was a staff member of the Pathological Department of the University of Missouri.

One clubwoman described Miller as a tall, stately, impressive woman and an accomplished speaker with a carefully modulated voice. She had a pleasant personality, an air of self-assurance, and worked comfortably with government bureaucrats and legislators. Her work in Missouri with Frank Waters and other officials for pure food, pure water, and pure milk had given her a vast experience with public service. She understood the advantages and disadvantages of food, drink and drug regulation, realized the realities of the kind of bill women could expect to pass Congress, and was familiar with the ramifications of various federal bills that had been introduced. Miller and her associates developed a viable plan of action and implemented it within less than one year.[39]

The General Federation recruited Elizabeth Foster from the Massachusetts Federation where she served as chairperson of the Pure Food Committee. She was a seasoned consumer advocate and represented a large Federation constituency that had been active in securing and enforcing pure food throughout the New England states. No detail of food adulteration escaped her notice. No collective effort to protect the consumer was too great for her to tackle. No individual effort was too small for her to ignore.[40]

She was able to reduce the complexities of legalese, which floated through pure food circles, to terms with which every consumer could identify. "Pure food," she defined as any "wholesome article of food or drink" that was "sold and consumed under its proper name." Adulteration was the addition of foreign matter. The threat of adulteration fell into three categories, all of which "peculiarly benefited the producer to the consumer's detriment." First, the addition of harmless matter was a "menace to the pocket" that the manufacturer used to accrue profit. Representing cottonseed and corn oil as "pure olive oil" created no danger to the health, but was a blatant example of consumer fraud. Second, adding coloring agents, such as aniline dyes to make the product more appealing and toxic preservatives to retard deterioration, brought high business returns, but endangered the health and life of the consumer. Third, diminishing the food value of natural foods through dilution, or processing to lower the cost to the producer, but not to the consumer, deprived infants and invalids of essential nutrition and swindled the public.[41]

Foster warned consumers that the considerable time and effort spent in passing and enforcing state pure food laws was undermined by the absence of federal regulation. Without federal control of food, drink, and drugs in interstate commerce, state regulations were not adequate to stem the growth of food adulteration.[42]

With the aid of her associates, Foster used every means at her disposal to secure a federal food, drink, and drug law. As a National Federation official, she played a major role in organizing its campaign, outlining plans of action, writing articles, lecturing, and distributing pure food, drink, and drug propaganda.

In her own state Foster led concerted local and regional efforts in her capacities as the State Federation Pure Food Chairman, Second Vice-President of the Women's Auxiliary of the Massachusetts Civil Reform Association, and a board member of the Massachusetts Consumers' League. She secured the endorsement of federal legislation from various other organizations, such as the Women's Educational and Industrial Union of Boston, the Boston Chamber of Commerce, and the Boston medical society, all of whom sent petitions to their U. S. senators and representatives.[43]

On a personal level she had enlisted the support of individual physicians in the cause and solicited the aid of friends and relatives. She persuaded her brother, Dr. Burnside Foster of St. Paul, Minnesota, to recruit the support of the medical associations and journals in his state, but her uncle, a certain Judge Baldwin of New Haven, who she described as having considerable political influence in Connecticut, was more difficult to convince. In desperation, she requested Harvey Wiley to send him a copy of the bill and any other literature "fit for missionary work and converting a constitutional opponent of federal interference."[44]

Mrs. James D. Whitmore was chairman of the Colorado State Federation Legislative Committee and an experienced lobbyist in the state legislature. In each of these capacities, she had initiated and promoted campaigns for pure, drink, and drug regulation in her state. From 1902, she had served as a member of the G.F.W.C. Household Economics Committee, where she took an active part in organizing clubs to work for local and federal food, drink, and drug legislation.

Along with Miller, Whitmore advocated firm, but fair food regulation. In a Pure Food Committee report read to the General Federation Council, Whitmore noted that local and state laws to protect the consumer against food that was adulterated, stale, or spoiled were inadequate and poorly enforced. She urged local clubs to escalate community action towards creating a substantial infrastructure for enforcement of local and federal laws once they were passed. With the future in mind, she advised clubwomen to proceed in a reasonable and equitable manner. In general, when women's clubs were attempting to improve conditions in markets and provision stores, the report recommended using methods to influence just public opinion, rather than a "hasty resort to legal enactment and penalties." Clubwomen should avoid "sudden action" that interfered with business and unduly punished the dealers who were willing to improve when their attention was called to unsatisfactory conditions, and leave legal action to health officials. Instead, Whitmore suggested publishing white lists that advised women in their communities of what and where to buy, encouraging women to patronize only those dealers who were willing to maintain reasonable standards of purity and cleanliness, and devising methods of praising or censoring the individual dealer.[45]

Whitmore did not have time to follow up on her ideas for the national crusade. She served on the Federation Pure Food Committee for only a short time before she was elected president of the Colorado State Federation of Women's Clubs. Among other duties, she continued to support food and drug regulation in a more limited capacity, but Sarah Platt Decker assumed her responsibilities for the campaign in the western states.[46]

Alice Lakey, clubwoman and pure food enthusiast of Cranford, New Jersey, was by far the most outspoken and decisive member of the Federation pure, food, drink, and drug leaders. Because of her rise to prominence in the crusade, we know more about her contributions than those of some of the other leaders. She was born October 14, 1857, in Shanesville, Ohio, to Charles and Ruth (Jacques) Lakey. Her father was a Methodist preacher in Ohio, an insurance broker in Chicago, and an insurance journal publisher in Cranford, New Jersey. Her mother died when Alice was six years of age. Alice attended public schools in Chicago until she was 14, after which she received instruction from a tutor. She studied voice in Paris, London, and Florence and performed on the concert stage in London and Sydenham, England. When her concert career proved too demanding for her health, she returned home, where she taught voice for a few years before she moved with her parents to Cranford, New Jersey.[47]

Frustrated by trying to find clean, unadulterated food for her ailing father and herself, she joined the domestic science unit of the local Village Improvement Association and soon became the president. In 1903 she wrote Federal Secretary of Agriculture James Wilson to request pure food, drink, and drug literature, and suggestions for a qualified lecturer to speak at one of the club meetings. Wilson recommended, among others, Harvey Washington Wiley, head of the U. S. Bureau of Chemistry.

Correspondence and a brief acquaintance between the two marked the beginning of a useful collaboration. Wiley supplied clubwomen with information and Lakey rallied support for pure food, drink, and drug regulation.[48]

In 1904, under Lakey's leadership, the Cranford Association and the New Jersey Federation of Women's Clubs petitioned members of Congress to enact the pure food bill. The same year she drafted a resolution and circulated petitions in favor of a pure food bill at the biennial meeting of the General Federation at St. Louis, which contributed to formation of the Pure Food Subcommittee.[49]

Her unflagging energy in working for pure food, drink, and drugs brought her to the forefront of the crusade. The contacts she fostered were influential in bringing the Federation into direct collaboration with state and federal officials, and her work in New York led to recruiting the National Consumers' League to the cause.

Following their appointments, the committee members set programs into action that involved every federated women's club in the United States. They divided their work into geographic territories, with Alice Lakey and Elizabeth Foster leading the crusade in the East, Helen Miller in the Midwest, and Sarah Platt Decker in the West and South, each adapting the program to the needs and possibilities of her section of the country. State and local organizations arranged for lectures, exhibits, newspaper articles, propaganda distribution, and delegations to commit their national and state legislators to vote for food, drink, and drug regulation. Clubwomen in Missouri, Arkansas, and Colorado brought bills, modeled after the pure food, drink and drug bills pending in Congress before their legislatures.[50]

The committee members traveled, lectured, and activated clubwomen to work for pure food, drink, and drugs, regardless of the orientation of their study and reform programs. In the East, Alice Lakey and Elizabeth Foster were popular speakers. Helen Miller worked with extension stations in the Midwest. Sarah Platt Decker secured the support of women in the West without difficulty and toured the South to draw women into the pure food, drink, and drug crusade.

Women in various national organizations that affiliated with the G.F.W.C. also contributed to the pure food, drink, and drug crusade. The National Congress of Mothers' Clubs, the National Council of Jewish Women, and the Women's Educational and Industrial Union were notable among these.

The National Congress of Mothers' Clubs lent strong support to both G.F.W.C. and W.C.T.U. pure food, drink, and drug campaigns. Its members were concerned with all aspects of homemaking, child health and development, and children's education. The quality of food and medication they gave their children was of utmost importance to them. Often they assisted public health officials, took part in food fairs, and agitated for food and drug regulation. Many state and local Mothers' Clubs joined state and national federations of women's clubs and were active pure food, drink, and drug advocates. Mothers' clubs also functioned in temperance unions, particularly before 1890, and assisted in projects involving the well-being of children, such as introducing and monitoring scientific instruction in schools.[51]

The Montgomery, Alabama, Mother's Circle was one of the earliest proponents of pure food and drug legislation in the South. Organizing on March 10, 1900, under the name of Montgomery Mothers' Union (later changed to Circle) for the purpose of training for motherhood and solving problems of mothers, the Mothers' Circle joined the National Congress of Mothers' Clubs in February 1901 and affiliated with the Alabama State Federation of Women's Clubs in April of the same year. The Circle established a household economics committee shortly after it organized and in April 1902, this committee divided into two subcommittees, one to investigate food values and another to promote pure food regulation. To kick off her organization's crusade in 1902, Mrs. Moritz of the Domestic Science committee presented an extensive and detailed paper on the "Chemistry of Foods." In 1904 she reported that through her correspondence with a Mr. A. A. Wiley in reference to the "Pure Food" bill, that he had promised to push the bill through the Alabama legislature. From 1903 through 1906 the Circle's minute books frequently refer to attempts to influence state pure food and drug legislation. Following animated discussion in the February 1, 1906, meeting, the members petitioned national legislators for federal regulation.[52]

Pure food, drink, and drug advocates were also active in the National Council of Jewish Women. Chapters of this organization in New York, Massachusetts, Ohio, and other states affiliated with the G.F.W.C. and adopted the Federation lines of reform in which they were interested. Members of the New York Council participated in various public health projects and were among the most active pure food, drink, and drug crusaders. On Saturday, December 3, 1905, they held a mass meeting in Mendelssohn Hall in support of pure food regulation. Sadie American, the president of the Council, introduced and endorsed the recommendations of each of the speakers. Among the speakers, a *New York Times* reporter recognized a number of pure food and drug authorities of "national note," including Senator Weldon B. Heyburn, Senator Porter J. McCumber, Harvey W. Wiley, and a bevy of state food commissioners. Under the headline, PURE FOOD ADVOCATES LEAVE LITTLE TO EAT, the newspaper reported, "Every article of food, except eggs, was denounced by the various speakers as being injurious to the human system." Nathan Strauss, a New York City philanthropist and dairy commissioner, denounced raw milk as a leading killer of children. During his service of the past 14 years he had prosecuted an unbelievable number of dairies for filthy milk handling, condemned thousands of gallons of milk for unacceptable levels of bacterial content, and ordered the slaughter of hundreds of diseased cattle.[53]

Senator McCumber, who was co-sponsoring a pure food, drink, and drug law in Congress, told the audience that three million dollars worth of "spurious, misbranded foods" were consumed in the United States each year, enough, in his estimation, to pay off the national debt "three times over." He claimed that the "pure article in the market" was the exception, rather than the rule. Of the items examined by the food commission in his home state of North Dakota that year, not one can of potted chicken and turkey contained the "slightest particle of chicken or turkey." Each pound of meat contained between 40 and 48 grains of boric acid. All chocolates and cocoa contained 10 to 90 percent foreign matter. All canned goods were either adulterated or colored with "poisonous dyes." With food and drug adulteration so extensive, he alleged that only federal regulation could control the problem.[54]

Senator Heyburn recommended a nationwide boycott to supplement federal legislation. He pointed out that if everyone interested in pure food, drink, and drugs refused to deal with "the vendors of deleterious" products, the women could put the "purveyors of fraud" out of business.[55]

Harvey W. Wiley claimed that 20 kinds of supposedly "imported wine" came from the same cask of domestic manufacture. Pure imported olive oil was nothing more than American-processed cottonseed oil. Of 373 samples of phenacetin purchased in New York drug stores, 315 were found to be adulterated. People who used proprietary medications actually drank near-whiskey "worth about 10 cents a gallon," which they purchased "at one dollar a pint." He invited all those present to join the "crusade for honesty."[56]

Federation women considered the meeting a huge success. The number of women who joined the crusade as a direct result of the mass meeting was estimated to be considerable. Pure food advocates reported a notable rise in support of pure food, drink, and drug measures in New York City. As a direct result of increased demand, the city aldermen increased funds for milk inspection, tuberculosis control, and related programs, and authorized erecting additional milk depots at various sites in city parks, where mothers could obtain certified milk at little or no cost for needy infants and children.[57]

Another large associate of the General Federation, the Women's Educational and Industrial Union of Boston, founded in 1877, was a vigorous advocate of pure food, drink, and drugs. Although it comprised elements of both, the Industrial Union was more of an exchange than a club. It provided social, educational, and self-improvement support for its members, but directed its primary activities toward qualifying women for self-support. The Union offered training classes, job counseling sessions, an employment bureau, and salesrooms to market home-manufactured goods for women who did not qualify for work outside the home. Its services were available particularly for women, but also to men, and to residents of New England towns outside Boston. Thousands of persons passed through its three public buildings daily. Any woman could join. In addition to serving as a center for mutual benefit, the Union provided opportunities to donate services, financial aid for specific projects, or such small contributions as magazines and entertainment tickets for the unemployed. It became involved in the pure food crusade to insure the quality of food it served to its patrons. It maintained lunch and tea rooms that fed from 900 to 1,000 persons daily and provided employment for 52 persons — 7 cooks, 6 assistants, 12 servers and kitchen maids, 23 waitresses, and 3 cashiers. In 1903, out of concern for the dangers of contaminated and adulterated food, the Union hired an inspector to monitor its almost 150 food consignors, and many of its contributors joined the crusade to make sure the food it purchased met "clean and healthy" standards.[58]

Between 1893 and 1905 consumer crusaders who affiliated with the General Federation of Women's Clubs laid a solid foundation for their national pure food, drink, and drug campaign. They began by introducing the study of food into the Federation agenda, then reached out to other groups, discussing the problem and cooperating in more formal coalitions to secure pure food, drink, and drug regulation.

Most components of their federation experience strengthened the fight for pure food, drink, and drugs. The study phase led women to realize that their inalienable right of the pursuit of happiness could be realized through an "orderly mind", an "enlightened spirit," and community concern. The study of literature, art, music, history, and social problems gave women the chance to exchange thought and discuss issues of mutual interest. Their study of art, for example, was not a study of things. It was the study of "religions, of history, of science, of climatic effects, of customs, of nations, of men — their heart emotions, their life struggles, their defeats, their successes." These studies provided the educational and intellectual stimulus that was impossible for them to receive in any other way, and gave them the opportunity to develop the skills and confidence to cultivate leadership qualities and to acquire the organizational abilities essential for united action.[59]

The social aspect of federated life allowed women to break down the traditional barriers between groups and enabled them to make new friendships and form useful alliances. It emphasized the value of diversity, aroused a new sense of the worth of every individual, and awakened the spirit of cooperation among women. Alice S. Harris of Ohio noted that the Federation gave women the opportunity to know and appreciate women from diverse backgrounds, to form new and true friendships with companions of "real worth," and to exchange thoughts for their "mutual benefit and delight." For Harris, gaining "high and noble" acquaintances was no "fleeting experience" for she realized that to "awake in them and to arouse" in herself "a new sense of worth" was one of the "great goods of life."[60]

The reform aspect, which the federation accelerated, extended the value of club experience into improving the community, the state, and the nation. As R. J. DeVore, clubwoman from Cincinnati declared, "The educated mind, the brilliant brain, the skilled hand, the swift feet unused for others are the mill-stone of offence hanged to every club woman's neck who fails to see her duty to her neighbor and the community in which she lives."[61]

The G.F.W.C. encouraged clubs to become involved in solving the pure food, drink, and drug problem; to apply the skills, talents, and unity they had developed through study programs toward protecting their families and communities against commercial adulteration and fraudulent advertising. As clubs began to implement the Federation's educational and legislative programs, their involvement had a ripple effect, contributing to the growth of other groups around the country. The General Federation was an effective force in molding mass public opinion into a viable secular mechanism for pure food, drink, and drug activism.

7

The National Consumers'
League Crusaders

The National Consumers' League formalized the emerging coalition of major national forces that were working for pure food, drink, and drugs. By bringing women's clubs, temperance unions, religious organizations, state and federal chemists, public health workers, medical professionals, journalists, and representatives from every state in the union into a single entity, the National Consumers' League consolidated pure food, drink, and drug activities, and created a united consumer front for federal regulation, state statutes, local ordinances, and enforcement at each level of government.

The pure food, drink, and drug advocates introduced their program into the National Consumers' League in 1904. Before then, the League's programs were connected only peripherally with the crusade and concerned primarily with labor conditions under which clothing was manufactured and sold. The League's founders, Florence Kelley, Maud Nathan, John Brooks, Nathan Strauss, and others had organized in 1899 to unite consumers for the purpose of protecting women and children in the garment trades against industrial exploitation. They expanded their program to include pure food, drink, and drugs after they were well established and state consumer leagues joined the crusade.[1]

Because it was able to draw from a wide cross section of consumer advocates, was blatantly activist, and its membership was open to both women and men, many of the pure food, drink, and drug crusaders felt that the National Consumers' League came close to providing the ideal medium for advancing their cause. From the beginning, its organizers had recognized the need to recruit members from religious organizations, labor unions, and both women and men into its ranks. Kelley wrote that seeking support "from as many sources as possible" was "always desirable." By definition a consumers' league was not a "movement of the few." Limited organizations, "however intelligent, conscientious, influential, and wealthy" the members, could not hope to influence shopping behaviors.[2]

Bringing a variety of religious organizations into its ranks was one of its major achievements. By soothing the breach between women's organizations and the religious community, the League was able to relieve both the resentment of women against ministers who, as a rule, had not been particularly helpful in progressive reforms and to bring in new support for the crusaders. In the spring and summer of 1902, Kelley and the other League officers enlisted Protestant congregations — such as the Unitarian Church in Grand Haven, Michigan; the First Methodist Church in Los Angeles, California; the First Unitarian Church in Oakland, California; and the Fourth Presbyterian Church in Chicago. In May they recruited a large group of Jewish organizations in the West to augment the ranks of the Jewish League membership in Chicago and New York City. During the same year, the Catholic Women's League of Chicago, the Catholic Benevolent Society of Pennsylvania, and Bishop Canavan of Philadelphia enrolled in the National Consumers' League, and Cardinal Gibbons of Baltimore became one of the vice-presidents of the Maryland League.[3]

The close association of the League with trade unions was another feature in its favor. League women encouraged working women to organize, took part in their assemblies, and instilled consumer league circles within trade alliances. Concurrently, they tried to establish working relationships with people who employed women. Often they were able to mediate strikes and establish amicable associations between labor and management. These activities were particularly effective in preventing hostilities from erupting in small, local organizations. In one instance, the League persuaded housewives in Oshkosh, Wisconsin, to organize domestic help into a women's union to insure job security and improve the quality of work.[4]

League members infiltrated farmers' institutes and granges, made a systematic effort to enroll farm women in the League, and organized branches in high schools, trade schools, and colleges, such as the Girls' Classical School in Indianapolis, the Casa di Rosas School for Girls in Los Angeles, Miss Spence's School for Girls and the Young Men's Guild in New York City, the normal schools at Los Angeles, and Pomona College at Claremont, California, the University of Chicago, and Johns Hopkins Training School for Nurses.[5]

Perhaps the League's greatest asset was that membership was open to men as well as women. Neither the W.C.T.U. nor the G.F.W.C admitted men. Occasionally the W.C.T.U. granted honorary membership to supportive men, such as Dr. J. H. Kellogg of Battle Creek, Michigan, and Judge W. H. Goodale of Louisiana. Clubwomen accorded partial club privileges, but not full membership, to Judge Ben Lindsey of Denver, novelist Henry James, poet John Greenleaf Whittier, several Unitarian ministers, women's rights advocate Thomas Wentworth Higginson, and a few other supporters. Women's organizations feared that men in their ranks would try to assume leadership roles, dictate policies, and limit activities. Excluding men allowed women to express themselves with greater freedom and to act independent of male dominance. When the organizing federation set its policy, the first president, Charlotte Emerson Brown, noted, "women should work by themselves apart from men. If inexperienced beginners, they have less embarrassment, a greater feeling of responsibility, and are less likely to be thrown into the shade and do more and better work."[6]

New England clubwoman, Caroline Severance, explained:

> We admit our husbands, sons and friends, as associate members, to our literary gatherings and our recreations. We welcome their counsel and sympathy and receive most valuable and generous help from them. But since women pre-eminently need the benefits of such an organization and of practice in directing it, we wish them to be free in debate and in executive detail from the constraining presence of their more experienced brothers.[7]

Organized women did not rule out the possibility of including men in the future after women had "shaped and polished their "armour." Most leaders looked forward to the time when "civilization had advanced" to the point where women and men could work together for reform as equals, as Frances Willard said, "in the natural order of things." Repeatedly, Sarah Platt Decker stressed the importance of "good women and good men" working "side by side" for social reform. In an address at Chautauqua, New York, she told the story of a woman at the St. Louis Exposition who bent down to tie her shoelace, and, not able to see her shoe, found when she stood up that she had tied it to the shoe of a man who stood next to her in the crowd. "I wish we could tie all the men to us with tight shoe laces," Decker explained, "so that we might step bravely out together, side by side, hand in hand. We need the help of the men." Many women, including Sarah B. Visanska, a prominent suffragist and clubwoman, felt that the ideal club of the future would be composed of both sexes. Nevertheless, neither of these organizations were structured to accommodate male members, let alone appeal to men. Most men saw women's organizations as opportunities for women to socialize, or as harmless outlets for female energy. Husbands who took their wives' work seriously often approved of their activities and donated funds to their reforms, but they did not become part of their organizations.[8]

The same was not true of the National Consumer's League. The largest numbers of League members were women. Most of its founders were women. The corresponding secretary, Florence Kelley, led and directed its operations. At the same time, men were encouraged to join and made to feel comfortable working with the women. John Graham Brooks was president and other men made significant contributions to the League's achievements.

By the time the League incorporated the pure food, drink, and drug crusade into its program, a number of state consumers' leagues had joined state federations and the G.F.W.C. A few had added food reform to their agendas. The Massachusetts League, with a membership of over 1000, joined the Massachusetts Federation in 1903. Each organization considered the merger of "great value" in extending its potential for reform. The League's drive to improve the conditions under which products were manufactured and distributed appealed to federated women. Many of them admired its activist orientation and welcomed the opportunity to participate in organizing boycotts and strikes against offending practices. In turn, the support of every club in Massachusetts more than tripled the reform influence of the Massachusetts League.[9]

The National Consumers' League joined the pure food, drink, and drug crusade, at least partly, to accomplish the same goals as the Massachusetts League. In May 1903, the National League had brought the problem of child labor before the Biennial of the G.F.W.C. that was meeting at the Great Synagogue in Los Angeles. At this time Florence Kelley had been functioning as chairman of the Federation Committee on Industrial Problems for three years. She joined Maud Nathan in presenting the work of the National League to the delegates, and Jane Addams in persuading the Federation to confront "the social waste of child labor" by discouraging its members from purchasing non-union merchandise. In this meeting the League enlisted a great number of clubwomen.[10]

As a result, the General Federation adopted the problem of child labor as a primary line of work for the next two years. They organized an industrial committee composed mostly of National Consumers' League members (with Maud Nathan as chairman) and requested that club officers lay the matter before local clubs, organize committees to study child labor conditions in their areas, and work for government regulation and enforcement of child labor laws where they existed.[11]

With Federation support for its programs, members of the National Consumers' League were in a favorable mood to reciprocate when the Federation solicited their assistance in the pure food, drink, and drug crusade, but their response was more than a courtesy between women's organizations, or a bid to increase their membership and power. Improving the conditions under which food was handled and processed expanded their base of operation and was a logical companion cause to their work in the garment industries.

The Federation pure food, drink, and drug advocates approached the League early in 1905 through an open letter from Alice Lakey, followed by her plea for help at the League's biennial convention in March. The League responded to Lakey's summary of the dangers threatening consumers, the extent of fraud in the food, drink, and drug industries, the difficulty of enforcing state and local statutes, and the need for League support of the pure food, drink, and drug bill pending in Congress. The League agreed to conduct an investigation of conditions under which food products were prepared and the working conditions of the employees who prepare them, to disseminate official information relating to the adulteration of foods, and appointed Alice Lakey to head a large Food Investigation Committee (later known as the Pure Food Committee).[12]

The formation of this committee was the key to securing federal regulation. In effect, it created an activist network of the nation's leading pure food, drink, and drug advocates that defined consumer objectives more clearly and spoke with more authority for American consumers than either the N.W.C.T.U. or the G.F.W.C.

Lakey had been trying to organize a pure food, drink, and drug league for over two years. She considered the activities of clubwomen and temperance women commendable, but she felt that an organization that did not have its interest diverted by other issues would be more effective. She had consulted with food officials Ernst Lederle, Harvey Wiley, Willard Bigelow, Robert Allen, and many others concerning the details of its organization and had secured a slate of officers and advisors. In the spring of 1905 at a council meeting in Atlantic City, she submitted a proposal for the General Federation to sponsor such a league, but her suggestion was not "received with enthusiasm." The delegates thought a pure food league would draw members and attention away from the domestic science programs, entail too much "machinery," and accrue too great an expense. After she became chairman of the Consumers' League Pure Food Committee, Lakey became so busy that she felt she could not direct another organization. Instead she decided to incorporate the independent league into the Consumers' League Pure Food Committee. As an established organization with a history of widespread inclusion, the Consumers' League seemed to offer the most attractive alternative at the time. Lakey wrote Wiley, "I have been given carte blanche to do as I like with the Food Com. of the National Consumers' League"; therefore it seemed to her that by combining the proposed league with the Consumers' League Pure Food Committee, she could accomplish the same purpose without expending additional time and money.[13]

The committee included an impressive array of clubwomen, temperance workers, chemists, public health officials, physicians and journalists, each of whom were leaders in the pure food, drink, and drug field. The committee reorganized at times and added new members as needed.[14]

The formation of this committee consolidated a loose networking process that had been surfacing between women's groups and male reformers. Networking among women's organizations had emerged in an informal manner. As individuals began to affiliate with several related reform organizations simultaneously, they developed a system of interlocking chairmanships, then coalitions of men and women.

Affiliating with several women's organizations was not unusual. The crusaders found natural logic in working for a common cause on various different fronts. Sarah Platt Decker, president of the G.F.W.C., was a member of the Denver W.C.T.U. and the National Consumer's League. Florence Kelley and Maud Nathan, officials of the National Consumers' League, were also members of the G.F.W.C. Marian McBride served as an officer in both the N.W.C.T.U. Department of Health and Heredity and the G.F.W.C. Household Economics Committee. Jewish and Catholic women's leagues, and women's business and professional organizations held membership in most state federations of women's clubs. Black women's organizations held membership in a sizable number of state federations and the N.W.C.T.U.[15]

Members in each of these major women's organizations supported and complemented, rather than competed with, members in the others. Frances Willard helped organize the General Federation of Women's Clubs. The Federation supported the programs of the National Consumers'

League. The N.W.C.T.U. and the G.F.W.C. always sent greetings and delegates to the other's conventions, as well as to the conventions of a variety of national women's organizations. The National Congress of Mother's Clubs, which affiliated with the G.F.W.C., included among its members Lillian M. N. Stevens, national president of the W.C.T.U., Anna Gordon, Vicepresident of the W.C.T.U., Mrs. J. W. Porter, superintendent of the Mother's Department of the Texas W.C.T.U., Elizabeth Boynton Harbert of the Illinois W.C.T.U., and Mrs. Lawson and Mrs. Hills of the District of Columbia Colored Union.[16]

Officials of each of these organizations came together at the conventions of the National Council of Women, the largest national woman's suffrage organization. In February of 1899, Lillian Stevens and Anna Shaw spoke at the their annual convention. Rebecca Chambers, president of the Pennsylvania W.C.T.U., served on the resolutions committee. Sadie American, from Chicago, president of the National Council of Jewish Women, made a presentation to Susan B. Anthony. Hannah G. Solomon, an influential member of the same organization, was elected treasurer. Emmeline B. Wells, Salt Lake City, of the Relief Society, was chosen as the recording secretary. Participating in chautauquas and world's fairs also brought women from various organizations together in working relationships.[17]

When she sent Alice Lakey to recruit the National Consumers' League into the pure food, drink, and drug crusade, Sarah Platt Decker deliberately directed this general networking process toward the specific reform of pure food, drink, and drugs. Merger of reform agencies had always been one of Decker's goals. Mergers were the method by which businesses consolidated their influence, and Decker considered mergers the way for women to accomplish their goals. In her 1904 inauguration address, she extolled the virtues of merging reform activities and called attention to the power that mergers had provided business concerns.[18]

The N.W.C.T.U. advocated networking in much the same way. In 1899 the editor of the *Union Signal* suggested that reform agencies would do well to draw a page from the notebook of the capitalists. Interestingly enough, she thought social reformers could counteract the oppression of trusts by using the same methods to control corporations that industrialists used to take advantage of the public. She wrote, "In their present stage and under present conditions trusts are an oppression," but the "trust idea" itself provided the "way of escape from the bondage" into which it had drawn them. Concentration, federation, combination — the financial trends of the age — held the key to the solution of social problems. The concentration of consumer power could form a still bigger trust. Such concentrated power would prove an irresistible combination that eventually attracted industries and producers, not into a society where every person shared equally in the profits of the industrial system, but in a benign cooperative state in which industries harmonized their interests with consumer welfare. This, of course, was a utopian vision, and its advocates did not indicate how far they were prepared to carry this "social evolution," or how it would come about. They did emphasize that it did not involve creating a socialist state.[19]

Uniting food commissioners, representatives from the American Medical Association, and journalists with crusaders from the leading women's organizations brought obvious and immediate advantages. The first of these was greater harmony, fellowship, and unity among pure food, drink, and drug advocates.

Usually, the relationship between women crusaders and food commissioners had been congenial. On state and local levels, women's organizations worked incessantly for adequate food and drug laws, took an active part in their enforcement, and, in many cases, used their influence to secure appointments of food commissioners and chemists to state agencies. As early as 1900, women in Missouri petitioned the General Assembly for a state chemist to identify food adulterations, to work for adequate sanitation measures in food processing, and to protect consumers. Women from Massachusetts to Oregon demanded similar protection. Incorporating food commissioners and chemists into the League committee brought them into a closer alliance with the women so that both could focus more intensely on regulation. It brought official consumer backing to the commissioners and, in turn, established the League as a pure food, drink, and drug authority that government officials and legislators respected and took seriously.[20]

Representatives from the medical community elevated the League's scientific credibility. Lakey and her associates chose prominent physicians who contributed prestige to the committee and were influential in their professions. Equally significant to the crusade, the League had a uniting influence on the A.M.A. When physicians realized the vast consumer support for pure food, drink, and drug regulation, many of the adversaries in the medical profession withdrew their opposition.[21]

Establishing an inroad to the press represented another major accomplishment. With few exceptions, newspapers and magazines had not been receptive to pure food, drink, and drug propaganda. Many publishers and editors deliberately excluded or lampooned anything related to the crusade. Others avoided what they called "women's issues" as insignificant. Lakey considered recruiting Samuel Hopkins Adams into the League as a significant step toward establishing friendly relations with the media.[22]

Apart from the dimensions of solidarity and influence, the pure food, drink, and drug coalition presented the crusade with ready access to the latest research in medicine, to the latest developments in government, and, in some degree, to the press. Lakey selected specific physicians, not only for their influence, but because she considered her choices to be on the leading edge of their profession. Physicians generated literature, helped with reports, and corrected errors and outdated material. Most of the state food commissioners she chose served on federal committees that determined policies and advised legislators. Women no longer had to wheedle information from the Department of Agriculture, or wonder what was happening behind the scenes in Congress and government bureaucracies. The journalists provided the League with an insight into media trends and the best ways to appeal to the public.[23]

Once organized, the League's Pure Food Committee went to work immediately. Before the end of summer 1905, the committee had defined its objectives and completed its investigation into the lack of efficacy of state legislation. The committee determined that an omnibus federal law was essential to protect the health of the nation, and accordingly directed its energies toward political action.[24]

More clearly and completely than any of the other national organizations, the committee set forth the essential goals of the pure food, drink, and drug crusade and divided them from other reform issues. It delineated the fundamental rights of consumers as (1) the right to safety, (2) the right to be informed truthfully, (3) the right to choose, (4) the right to be heard, and (5) the right to be protected by government agencies. Each of these rights had been violated by industrial competition. Each of these rights were basic to consumer protection.[25]

The right to safety presupposed that products offered for sale must not harm consumers or their families. Each year, thousands of people were injured by adulterated food, addictive or dangerous drugs, and unsafe medical devices and practices. Consumers had the right to demand that the products they bought were safe to use.[26]

The right to be informed honestly precluded false or misleading advertising and withholding information. Firms that marketed their product to the public had no right to deceive the public, or to gag the communications media by threatening reprisal if newspapers and magazines investigated and published incidents of fraud, harm, and death caused by dangerous products. Consumers were entitled to more information than sellers were willing to disclose.[27]

Competition in the marketplace had denied consumers the right to choose. Pricing a product at the competitive level had made the use of adulterants so universal that consumers could not depend on brand names to provide quality merchandise. In too many cases, adulterated products were the only products for sale.[28]

Consumers demanded the right to be heard. A consumer had a right to seek recourse in the courts if the product the consumer purchased harmed the consumer or a member of the consumer's family. The judicial system should not favor the producer above the consumer. In the same vein, consumers should be consulted when executive and legislative agencies considered decisions that affected the public.[29]

Consumers had a right to demand that federal and state governments protect their interests. Government agencies of the people had the responsibility to protect the public from unreasonable risk or injury caused by products marketed to the consumer, to assist consumers in comparing the safety and value of various items, to develop safety standards, and to promote research concerning product-related deaths, illness, and injuries. Agencies should ensure that processed foods, drugs, medical devices, and cosmetics were safe and properly labeled; that foods were clean, wholesome, and nutritious; that unsafe products were removed from the market; and that firms that violated safety laws and standards were criminally prosecuted.[30]

Securing the Heyburn federal pure food, drink, and drug law was the top priority on the committees' agenda. Although the proposed legislation applied only to interstate commerce, consumer advocates felt that securing the law would set a precedence for government regulation that would eventually achieve their goal of protecting the health of the nation.[31]

Despite Wiley's initial reservations regarding the pure food, drink, and drug coalition, the League and the U. S. Bureau of Chemistry worked closely together. Members of the League maintained correspondence with Wiley, solicited his advice, acknowledged his expertise in the field, and supported him in Congressional hearings. They recognized the Bureau of Chemistry as the proper government agency to enforce the law, and conceded to Wiley the position of figurehead, and later as the leader, of the drive for pure food, drink, and drug legislation and enforcement. Wiley supplied the League with government bulletins, research, results, and suggestions. He wrote Lakey that the roster of the Leagues' board was a "very strong one." With the possible exception of the representative from the manufacturer's association, he considered the choices "heartily in favor of pure food legislation."[32]

Wiley's assistant, Willard D. Bigelow, was an enthusiastic booster of the pure food and drug coalition. In Wiley's absence he wrote to Lakey on August 18, 1905, "It seems to me that your idea of organizing a Pure Food League is an excellent one." He advised her to select a governing board with considerable care to protect the association from exploitation by commercial or other interests, and offered to prepare a compact collection of samples for use with her lectures. On August 29, he assured her that he would be "very glad" to assist her "in any way" and suggested approaching Elton Fulmer of Pullman, Washington; H. V. Tarter of Portland, Oregon; and Dr. Richard Fischer of Madison, Wisconsin, as committee members to represent the chemists from the West.[33]

The committee members were anxious to have Theodore Roosevelt endorse the bill. His reputation for reform convinced them that the president shared their concern for the dangers of food, drink, and drug adulteration. In New York City, he had worked for health reform while a member of the Sanitary Aid Society of the Tenth Ward and had served as port commissioner with the Health Department. However as president of the United States, he had withheld his support for sweeping legislation.

An unidentified writer for the *Woman's Home Companion*, who claimed to be intimately acquainted and in close touch with the president, assured women that Roosevelt supported the pure food, drink, and drug cause, but that he preferred to allow executive agencies a chance to control the problem through existing statutes before "confessing himself powerless in the face of admitted evils" by "throwing himself on the mercy of Congress" for additional legislation.

Already the federal Department of Agriculture meat inspectors were in place to enforce sanitation in slaughterhouses. The postal system was trying to bar proprietary concerns from sending blatantly fraudulent nostrums through the mail. The commissioner of internal revenue had ruled that various compounds sold as bitters, tonics, cordials, and similar preparations, which were composed chiefly of distilled spirits, without effectual medical ingredients, were subject to the federal distillers and rectifiers tax.[34]

The National Consumers' League coalition considered these measures piecemeal and ineffective. The existing laws addressed only a small segment of offending items and accomplished little. League investigators, such as Harriet Van der Vaart, found federal meat inspectors ignoring filthy and dangerous conditions in the slaughterhouses. Investigations revealed that postal officials were only catching a small percent of fraudulent drugs in the mail, and the tax upon alcoholic medications, although troublesome to manufacturers, was doing nothing to curtail their sales.

In February 1905, before it was organized completely, the Pure Food Committee assembled a delegation of six, consisting of Alice Lakey; Robert M. Allen, secretary of the National Association of State Dairy and Food Commissioners; Horace Ankeney, Pure Food Commissioner of Ohio; J. B. Nobel, Food Commissioner of Connecticut; A. B. Fallinger of the National Association of Retail Grocers; and Sebastian Mueller, of the H. J. Heinz Company of Pittsburgh, to call upon the president. Roosevelt expressed sympathy for their cause, promised to study the need for additional legislation, and asked the delegation to return in the fall.

During the summer, William Frear, another food commissioner who was affiliated with the National Consumers' League Pure Food Committee, wrote to remind the president to include a statement in his annual message that would emphasize the need for federal food, drink, and drug regulation. Secretary of Agriculture James Wilson endorsed this request in a letter written for him by Wiley. Roosevelt consulted with Wiley, with Ira Remsen of Johns Hopkins Hospital, and with his personal physician, Dr. Samuel W. Lambert, who Roosevelt described as an "exceptionally wise man."[35]

With Charles A. L. Reed, M.D., chairman of the Legislation Council and former president of the A.M.A; Mrs. F. V. Covill, of the Twentieth Century Club, representing the G.F.W.C.; and several food commissioners added to its ranks, the League delegation met at a conference in Washington on November 14, 1905. After discussion, they drafted a memorial, which requested that Roosevelt recommend legislation to ban all poisons from food, and to require listing all harmless adulterants on the label. To accompany the memorial, they prepared an exhibit that demonstrated strong public demand for such legislation. On November 15, during an advisory interview, they gave James Wilson the memorial and exhibit to present to the president at the next cabinet meeting.[36]

The following day, November 16, Senator Porter J. McCumber, cosponsor of the pure food, drink, and drug bill in the Senate, presented the delegates at the White House, where they received a cordial welcome. Roosevelt assured them that his message to Congress contained the long-looked-for recommendations, but asked that they let him announce his support. He told them, "I, of course, want to be the first to make my message to Congress public, but I am going to trust you and tell you that it will contain a recommendation for a law to stop interstate traffic in adulterated foods and drugs. But it will take more than my recommendation to get the law passed, for I understand that there is some very stubborn opposition."[37]

In his annual State of the Union message on December 6, 1905, Roosevelt fulfilled his promise in three brief sentences, meant to placate the consumers and not to alarm the opposition unduly. "I recommend," he said, "that a law be enacted to regulate interstate commerce in misbranded and adulterated foods, drinks, and drugs. Such law would protect legitimate manufacture and commerce, and would tend to secure the health and welfare of the consuming public. Traffic in foodstuffs which have been debased or adulterated so as to injure health or to deceive purchasers should be forbidden."[38]

Following their trip to Washington, the committee's agenda escalated. During the rest of the year, Alice Lakey sent out over 500 personal letters and cards requesting greater effort from reform groups, officials, and individuals. She wrote a number of articles for the press, and spoke before many women's clubs and other groups. Early in 1906, she stormed through New Jersey, organizing pure food, drink, and drug support, giving major addresses in Elizabeth, Newport, Jersey City, Metuchen, and Winchester. She illustrated her talks with samples of adulterants and adulterated foods sent from the Kentucky and Connecticut experiment stations, along with a collection of artificial wines, and an assortment of pie and cake fillers seized by Philadelphia food inspectors. Her display included chemical preservatives and spice fillers, adulterated coffee, cocoa, spaghetti, catsup, flour, and fake olive oil. The New York press reported that when she spoke in the Manhattan theater in New York City, Lakey came equipped with a "series of bottles and dyed flannels" containing aniline dyes extracted from various kinds of foods and confections. A piece of brightly colored pink flannel attached to a small box of coconut strawberries, sold to children for one cent, showed the amount of aniline dye in one piece of the candy. A larger swatch of flannel illustrated the amount of coal-tar dye in a bottle of strawberry soda. Another display contrasted the contents of an old-fashioned coffee pot, that made pure coffee like "mother used to make," with coffee containing "an incredible variety of adulterants, including the sweepings from bakeshops." Beside this was an analysis of a "leading substitute" for coffee, "intended to help break the coffee habit," which revealed that the substitute contained more caffeine than the coffee.

Other members of the committee met similar agendas. State chairmen, such as Mrs. Frederick Nation and the Reverend Caroline Bartlett Crane, followed strenuous lecture agendas. As a result, letters and petitions poured into the offices of senators and representatives in Washington, and many states elected candidates who were sympathetic to the pure food, drink, and drug bill.[39]

As another part of its pure food, drink, and drug campaign, the National Consumers' League food committee appointed Mary Sherman to lead investigations into the conditions under which food was manufactured and milk was processed. Beginning in New York City, Sherman and her associates found the Board of Health and the State Department of Labor inspectors bogged down with violations of sanitary standards and handicapped by lack of authority to close offending businesses. The worst violations were among basement businesses in New York City where families lived on the premises, and among unlicensed enterprises hidden among the tenements of Manhattan.[40]

Conditions were particularly unsanitary in home bakeries that often used adulterated ingredients and where persons with communicable diseases assisted in the manufacture and packaging. Children handled the products, and flies swarmed over the merchandise. City food inspectors attempted to supervise the licensed bakeries, but had no access to home industries.[41]

Lack of sanitation in the home manufacture of macaroni products created equal concern. Macaroni was made in every block where Italian immigrants had settled. In many streets, several small shops on each block of apartment houses dried macaroni in doorways and windows. The product was sold from the front room that often served as living quarters for extended families and lodgers. In one shop the League investigators discovered a child ill with diphtheria lying in a dirty back room adjoining the area where the father manufactured and sold macaroni. The father went directly from holding the child in his arms to the macaroni machine, pulling macaroni with unwashed hands and hanging it over racks to dry. In another instance, a child with scarlet fever handled macaroni that was drying in the yard and the windows of her home.[42]

The investigators found conditions in nut factories completely unsatisfactory, and the situation was made more unsanitary because the acid content of the nuts produced suppurating ulcers on the hands of the sorters and shellers. In one of the city's largest nut factories, that specialized in health food products, they found girls with dirty hands and running sores sorting and packing nuts. Some of the workers took piecework home. The investigators were able to accompany a mother and daughter to their residence. They lived in four rooms with a married sister, her husband, one boy of thirteen and three small children. The apartment house, "indescribably filthy and crowded," had several citations pending against it by the city tenement house department, but had not been closed. The family picked the nuts and dried them on a table. Back at the factory, the nuts were not cleaned, but packed into jars and sold to the investigators. This factory advertised the purity and cleanliness of its goods and marketed them to health food fans in the most prestigious retail stores and confectioneries in the city.[43]

Sanitary conditions in candy factories were described as deplorable. On the lower west side, League investigators discovered a thriving candy business housed in two rooms at the top of a dirty tenement house, whose owners had not complied with orders issued against it. A family of mother, father, and two children lived in the same area where they mixed molasses and cooked the candy. The investigators described the family and rooms as "extremely dirty" and "totally unfit" for manufacturing food. In addition, candy factories sent work home with their employees during the rush seasons and in every case the conditions in these homes were substandard. Many of these employees lived in crowded and dirty tenement houses. At one candy factory, the manager refused to admit the investigators, frankly admitting that he was not "at all proud of it" and that it would compare very unfavorably with other factories. Considering the conditions they had already encountered, the investigators had difficulty imagining how this factory might be worse.[44]

The league investigators discovered some of the most dangerous health situations among ice cream manufacturers. Ice cream makers operated throughout the tenement districts and distributed their wares in push carts. Like the nut and candy factories, they were not supervised or restricted by law. With few exceptions, the manufacturing premises were undesirable and the workers equally careless. In most cases, they made their product from uninspected milk. Their product spread tuberculosis and a variety of other dangerous diseases.[45]

Armed with the evidence that home industries spread disease, not only among people in the tenement districts, but to anyone buying food at the most expensive stores, the League began an intensive campaign to secure laws and agencies capable of enforcing the regulations. As a direct result of the League's reports and demands, the New York legislature passed laws to prohibit the manufacture, preparation, or packing of macaroni, spaghetti, ice cream, ices, candy, confections, nuts, or preserves in unclean and unlicensed tenements, and authorized the Labor Commission inspector to close bakeries that they found unclean or unsanitary until they complied with the law. Such efforts, unfortunately, were only partly effective. Although the state legislation empowered inspectors to control the food industries, they touched only the surface of the problem. The investigators found universal non-compliance with the laws and the inspectors unable to cope with increasing caseloads.[46]

The National Consumers' League Pure Food Committee extended its investigations from New York City to locations throughout the country, where League women uncovered similar conditions and tried to correct them with local statutes and inadequate law enforcement. Although the pure food, drink, and drug bill before the national Congress did not apply to home and local manufacture, the committee hoped that securing a federal law would strengthen local regulation and enforcement.

As its third area of pure food, drink, and drug activism, the National Consumers' League initiated a drive to improve the quality of the nation's milk supply. Despite provisions for dairy inspection in most states, consumer investigations found that infant mortality, caused largely by contaminated milk, continued to account for about 35 percent of the total deaths. Health Officer George W. Goler of Rochester, New York, asserted that diseased cows and unsanitary handling were the main causes for the high incidence of infant deaths in his city. One of the chief sources of Rochester's milk supply came from a dairy outside the city limits. Goler complained that the barn was poorly drained and cobwebs "festooned" the walls and sides of the milking shed. According to Goler, the farmer, who cared for the cattle, milked them, and distributed the dairy products, was ignorant of "even the first principles of cleanliness." His clothing and hands were dirty, and he was careless in preventing contamination of the milk with barnyard refuse. Lack of adequate water precluded cleaning his milk buckets and cans. Insufficient amounts and poor quality of cattle feed lessened the nutritive value of the milk. A large percentage of the cattle were in poor health and a number were infected with tuberculosis. The bacterial content was far above the acceptable count of 100,000 bacteria per cubic centimeter. Because the dairy was outside his jurisdiction, however, Goler could do little except attempt to intercept, test, and condemn each batch of milk as it came into town. Because of inadequate personnel, he could prevent only a small percentage of contaminated milk from being sold in the city.[47]

Consumer investigations revealed that such conditions in dairies throughout the country were more the norm than the exception. In large cities, grocery milk averaged from 50 to 100 million bacteria per cubic centimeter, the nutritive value of the milk fell below standard, and milk inspectors often accepted bribes to ignore unacceptable practices.[48]

As an option to fresh milk, the League considered recommending, but then rejected, the idea of using condensed milk. Processing lowered the bacterial content to an acceptable level, though the other contaminants remained. The same objection applied to sterilization and pasteurization. If milk was dirty, no process of sterilizing or pasteurizing removed dirt, manure, or urine from the product. In addition, heating the milk made the curd tougher and more difficult for small children and the elderly to digest.

In New York City, consumers had been concerned with their milk supply throughout the nineteenth century. During the 1850s and 1860s, the public had become aroused over the production and sale of so-called swill milk, produced by cows fed on the by-products of whiskey distillation. Under duress, the Board of Health drove these dairies out of business, but a problem with milk dilution persisted as the profits from adding large quantities of water and preservatives to milk far outweighed the penalties. At the same time, the role of contaminated milk in spreading disease became clear. Concerned public opinion forced enactment of various state laws to protect consumers. After the passage of each law, state agencies declared that they had the milk problem under control.[49]

Bacteriological and chemical tests indicated exactly the opposite. As late as 1902, the report of the city health department indicated that state dairy laws fell short of protecting the public in every respect. The state laboratory reported a consistently high bacteria count in New York's milk supply and found some form of adulteration in over 50 percent of the samples tested.[50]

Within the city, the state authorities were singularly ineffective in enforcing the laws. The health and dairy departments were chronically understaffed and too many of the inspectors accepted bribes. A department chemist indicated that "all was not well" in the city. He pointed out that although the department had authority over the five percent of milk produced locally, it had no control over the 95 percent produced outside of the city, or its handling in transit. Milk producers invented endless ways to evade the law. As one example, a law banned the sale of milk from tubercular cows and required that all cows having the disease be destroyed. The only way the Board of Health could track down diseased dairy herds was by inspecting cows sold to the slaughterhouses. To avoid the danger of having the city health department condemn their milk, farmers who knew their herd was infected had only to avoid sending diseased cows to New York City for slaughter.[51]

For these reasons, the Consumers' League demanded more careful and systematic regulation of all milk sold to condensed milk factories, as well as for the fresh milk supply. They were searching for permanent solutions, instead of the usual palliative and sporadic responses to consumer demands.

How could this be accomplished? The Consumer's League submitted a long list of suggestions. In the smaller cities and towns, citizen's groups could insist that inspectors be chosen by merit examinations, rather than by political appointment. To lessen bribery, inspectors from two agencies should be required to work in pairs. Rigid standards of cleanliness could be established. Offending dairies could be closed. Milk that did not meet the minimum standards must be discarded. Women's organizations could secure the right to monitor inspectors, dairies, and laboratories to enforce compliance. Permits could be required for retail outlets and vendors. Dealers found guilty of selling adulterated milk would automatically lose their permits. Consumers could urge ethical milk dealers to form a milk association to help raise standards in the industry by expelling any member convicted of selling adulterated milk. State supervision was necessary to control dairies outside the jurisdiction of cities and towns, to supply technical services that the towns could not afford, to provide legal advice, and to train new inspectors.[52]

Federal intervention was a prerequisite to controlling interstate commerce in milk as in other foods. Federal laws would strengthen the authority of local inspectors and help to insure the stability of local laws. Federal agencies were more able to maintain large laboratories and employ competent personnel. Milk should be mentioned specifically in the federal pure food bill. Harvey Wiley and other federal officials assured women's organizations that the bill before Congress covered milk as well as other foods. The Consumers' League was not as confident however, and made plans to introduce supplementary legislation as soon as the federal food, drink, and drug bill passed.[53]

The Pure Food Committee formed a loose alliance with the People's Lobby, a national political action organization of men reformers that was supported by private subscription funds. As their title indicates, the People's Lobby influenced legislation in the interests of the American public. Many of the Lobby's members were also members of, or were closely associated with, the National Consumers' League. Mark Sullivan was the president of the organization and James B. Reynolds was the chairman of the executive committee. The board of governors numbered among its members such influential reformers as Robert M. Allen, Louis D. Brandeis, Samuel L. Clemens, Benjamin B. Lindsey, Lincoln Steffens, and William Allen White. Heavily represented by men who had the "ear of the President," had an inside line to the power of the press, and, because of their prominence, were able to contact legislators without undue difficulty, the People's Lobby was often able to detect trouble before it became serious. Their lobbyists, together with W.C.T.U. lobbyists, often contacted Alice Lakey in time for consumers' advocates to organize their forces against opposition.[54]

Taken together, the League's drive for passage of the federal food, drink, and drug bill, its attempts to clean up the conditions under which food was manufactured, and its drive for safe and unadulterated milk represented a more comprehensive program than the crusaders had conducted before. More closely focused activism, wider participation, greater centralization, and networking allowed them to pursue more of their goals, but convinced them, more than ever, that federal regulation was necessary.

Their campaign was both imaginative and realistic — imaginative in the variety of methods they used and the goals they hoped to achieve — practical in the sense that they knew that national legislation was reached partly by numbers, partly by focusing on specific goals, and partly by compromise. They backed a bill that they knew was incomplete and imperfect with faith that it would be a precursor to stronger and more inclusive legislation.[55]

8

The Southern Crusaders

"We trusted our Southern Gentlemen."[1]

The participation of women in the pure food, drink, and drugs crusade was not limited to Northern and Western women. Despite stereotypes that characterized the South as indifferent to progressive reform, considerable evidence indicates that Southern women were equally concerned with pure food, drink, and drugs as their Northern counterparts. The differences in sectional activism were more in demeanor than in substance.

In most respects, the patterns of pure food, drink, and drug activism arose and advanced in the South in much the same way as they did in the North, with the exceptions that the Southern crusade lagged a few years behind the Northern crusade. Southern temperance workers approached the problem in a more populist mode; clubwomen were not so open in their demands, and many of the Southern reformers felt that they encountered greater difficulties. These differences stemmed from a combination of realities and proprieties in the South that, at first, required crusaders to maintain a lower profile, but did not deter their participation in food, drink, and drugs reform. The methods they devised to overcome seemingly insurmountable opposition are a tribute to their ingenuity, determination, and altruistic aspirations.

Southern Clubwomen

Louisa B. Poppenheim, editor of *Keystone* and secretary of the General Federation of Women's Clubs, supported the point of view that social conditions in the South required women to utilize a more subdued approach. She refuted the claims of critics who alleged that Progressive reform had not "taken a strong hold on the Southern mind," and described the position of Southern clubwomen as more circumspect, but equally as strong as that of women in the North. According to Poppenheim, Southern women encountered similar problems, but faced greater obstacles in trying to overcome them. Deeper isolation in the South kept women out of the limelight. Preoccupation with supporting themselves occupied more of their time. A universal desire to support the economy of the New South, distaste for Northern regulation, and a belief that the South could take care of its own problems tempered their activities. The desire of a defeated people to project a positive image of Southern unity, virtue, and progress kept them from airing any defects in their society. The dependence of Southern women's publications on the advertising of proprietary medicine companies and food manufacturers precluded media attacks upon their main means of support. The faith Southern women placed in their legislators, before their "Southern gentlemen" betrayed their trust, delayed open activism.[2]

According to Poppenheim, sectional advantages made up for many of the obstacles. Southern clubwomen learned how to circumvent some of the obstructions they encountered and devised means to turn them to their advantage.[3]

Most clubwomen agreed that the cult of true womanhood was entrenched more deeply in the South than in any other section of the country, creating a stronger barrier against public reform activism by women, but strengthening their personal influence. Convention and good taste demanded delicacy in trying to influence political issues. Poppenheim wrote, "in legislative matters Southern club women are not openly as active as other club women. They are, however, in close touch with their legislators, and often through private talks and personal influence important questions are carried through" with no "visible effort from the club women themselves."[4]

Mrs. A. E. Smith concurred:

> Public sentiment discourages the American woman from seeking actual service in political affairs. It is not her privilege to cast a vote for reform, but she can restrain the demoralizing tendencies at the polls by proxy, and in all the relations of life she can, by precept and example, give precedence to those qualities of mind and heart which shall make every American citizen

a champion of good government, from the home circle to the President's cabinet....

Woman's influence over fathers, brothers, husbands, and sons must put forth its most gracious and indomitable power to make men see the better standard and use their best efforts to place the public interests in the keeping of true statesmen, whose private lives entitle them to the confidence of the people — men of patience, courage, dignity and personal integrity, who mourn the lack of noble principle in high places of our nation, and are willing by conscientious and self-sacrificing labor, to serve their country from honorable motives, and not for the love of fame or monetary aggrandizement."[5]

The South was predominately agricultural, "dotted over with small towns" and isolated plantations. Greater distances kept women farther apart and made organizing more difficult. On the other hand, greater distances made club participation all the more important to Southern women. The club relieved women's isolation and gave them opportunities for cooperative effort. Southern women appreciated the social opportunities that the club provided.

According to Poppenheim, women's clubs were a leveling influence in the South. Although some women of high social position were leaders, she found most women's clubs to be democratic. This characteristic made the movement valuable in the South. Federations strengthened the sympathy between the country woman and the city woman, and women's clubs were a boon to newcomers in old established communities where the social lines were sharply defined. Rural clubs were as active as urban clubs in pure food, drink, and drugs work.[6]

Depressed economic conditions following the Civil War demanded the entire attention of a majority of Southern women "in looking after the stern necessities" of sustaining life and in restoring their institutions, leaving little time for other activities. At the same time, the necessity to contribute to the support of their families brought women into direct contact with food contamination in the slaughterhouses and factories, and with the increasing incidence of substance abuse in response to defeat and despair following the war.[7]

A desire to protect the Southern economy was another factor affecting open support of pure food and drug legislation by women's clubs. The New South was still recovering from the devastation of the Civil War. Landmark legislation, such as the pure food and drug bill, might establish a precedence for regulating businesses and stifle gains in the Southern economy. Despite the social problems they brought with them, cotton mills and new industries in the South seemed to be a blessing. They created employment for those who, otherwise, would be idle and poor, and promised a new era of prosperity. Lucy Bramlett Patterson wrote, "We pride ourselves, and justly so, upon our great cotton factories, and look upon their promoters as public benefactors."[8]

The farmers who produced corn, wheat, and hops for distilleries and breweries and those who sold their produce to cottonseed oil companies might be adversely affected by regulation. Packinghouses would have to submit to closer inspection. The cottonseed oil firms, which misrepresented and added preservatives to their product, and the self-designated "importers" who added flavoring and marketed cottonseed oil as "pure imported olive oil" would lose by the labeling provisions of the law. The sections of the bill that pertained to regulating alcoholic beverages and preparations would cut into the profits of Southern distilleries and breweries that contributed to the economy.[9]

If passed, the bill threatened to jeopardize the thriving proprietary medicine industry that opened up in the South after the Civil War. Before the war only a few patent medicines, such as Black-Draught and Wine of Cardui, were produced locally, and even those old standbys were not marketed aggressively. A sudden spurt of medicine-making to replace Northern products began shortly after the end of the war. The new Southern medicine manufacturers made their products available in every village and crossroads in the South by placing them on the shelves of the numerous country stores that sprang up during Reconstruction. They advertised extensively, linking their product with sectional loyalty and printing false testimonials from Robert E. Lee, Jefferson Davis, and other Confederate leaders. Southern women approved of Southern medicines supplanting the Northern drug trade, but they knew that adulterated and dangerous products threatened their homes and families. Rebuilding their society depended upon the health and well-being of themselves and their children.[10]

Another argument for not supporting the bill was a distaste for Northern regulation. Reconstruction was still a vivid memory in the South. Southerners felt that they should and could deal with their own problems. They wanted to reaffirm their ability to attend to their own business and legal matters without interference from the federal government, "with all the attending evils of spies and informers and pestiferous agents running around meddling with the business of the people." Sally F. Chapin, an avid crusader, asserted, "the right of the State to regulate its own internal affairs without let or hindrance from the general government is one of the cardinal doctrines in the Federal constitution." [11]

Ida Marshall Lining expressed the same opinion:

> To keep in the van of progress in either matters financial, educational or philanthropic, the South must work out her own salvation. Common sense should teach us that an alien element cannot have at heart the best interests of a community. Interest to be real must be born within us and love of home must be there to give the right stimulus to patriotic effort....
>
> Let the South alone ... and she will take charge of her own affairs ... there is no need ... to look abroad for a "Moses" to lead her out of the wilderness....
>
> Year by year the wealth of the South increases; year by year we are becoming more independent.... Only the Southerners can know the situation ...
>
> Let us study more seriously to meet these new conditions. Let us not become mendicants, but keep ourselves what we always have been, self-respecting Southerners. Let us ... move slowly and all will be well with us when the South "is let alone" and we manage our own affairs. [12]

In general, Southern women felt that the general assemblies of the South were capable of enacting statutes as the need arose.

The counteracting tendency was a desire to heal the wounds they had suffered, to become less provincial and to gain back some of the national influence they enjoyed before the war. Louisa Poppenheim noted, "since before the Revolution, generations of Southern people had given their best thought to the careful study of forms of government and to the management of affairs, the men in United States politics, the women on plantations, caring for a dependent race." An intense sense of civic responsibility and the development of management abilities "formed the foundation of the ideal club woman," and made the woman's club movement an effective force in the South. [13]

Southern clubwomen felt a need to preserve their image of Southern unity. After the divisive forces of the Civil War and Reconstruction, they did not want to appear to be at odds with their politicians. Many influential Southern politicians objected to federal regulation of food, drink, and drugs on constitutional grounds. Some of the most convincing arguments opposing the bill in Congress came from Southern legislators who claimed that such a law violated states' rights and individual responsibility. [14]

Congressman William E. Adamson from Georgia and Congressman Henry from Texas felt that regulating industries was outside the scope of the constitutional federal domain. Candler from Mississippi opposed standard fixing as a dangerous precedent, and Pagett from Tennessee tried to protect the liquor and proprietary industries by working to limit the provisions of the act. Senator Hernando DeSoto Money of Mississippi led a Southern bloc that deplored the bill as encroaching on police powers of the state and depending on rules that could be defined and applied by bureaucratic officials with discretionary and arbitrary powers.[15]

Many Southern women agreed with their politicians either out of their own states' rights convictions, or out of a concern that an open stance against declared political policies by Southern women would not only shatter the image of a united South, but would jeopardize their chances of influencing legislation.

On the other hand, not all Southern congressmen were against pure food and drug legislation. William Richardson of Alabama, for one, was a devoted advocate of food and drug legislation. As a member of the House Committee on Interstate and Foreign Commerce, he was able to keep some of the proposed amendments from weakening the bill. He represented the views of women reformers in his district and they supported his efforts.[16]

Projecting the image of a solid, moral, progressive South was important to Southern women. Pointing to the prevalence of drug addiction among Southern women created a poor impression of their character. In an earlier chapter it was shown that a striking aspect of nineteenth-century drug habituation was that the rate of substance abuse was higher among Southern white women than any other group. This disproportionate rate of addiction persisted in the South well into the twentieth century. In 1912 women comprised 68.2 percent of Jacksonville, Florida's opium and morphine addicts. Tennessee reported that 66.9 percent of its morphine users, 75.0 percent of laudanum users, and 66.7 percent of gum opium users were female, and Memphis, Tennessee, indicated that 57.0 percent of its morphine addicts were women. Exposing Southern weakness projected a negative idea of Southern morality.[17]

Still, Southern women wanted to correct the problems threatening their society. Exposing adulteration and fraud was one step toward controlling the difficulties they faced.

Dependence on proprietary medicine advertising was a disagreeable consideration for Southern women's journals and magazines. Poppenheim claimed that most women's publications in the South operated on even smaller margins than those in the North and depended more heavily upon proprietary medicine advertisements to remain financially solvent.

The *Southern Woman's Magazine* of Atlanta, Georgia, was the official organ of the Georgia Federation of Women's Clubs. Dispersed among the short stories, poetry, fashion, domestic topics, recipes, society sketches, book reviews, and needle work, the *Southern Woman* published articles about current concerns, such as food and drug adulteration, and at the same time, carried occasional proprietary medicine advertisements. In the May 1904 issue, Mrs. Mary A. Mason, a health and beauty columnist, began a series of articles advising women against the use of health-destroying practices. The first article summed up the onset of health problems of women in the South as she saw them, "At birth begins an insurrection against the laws of nature. Babyhood is a record of over-dressing, over-feeding, paregoric, and soothing syrups, and the transition from childhood to womanhood" was marked by substance abuse and other health-eroding practices. When the magazine retained the services of a certain G. P. Talbott to alleviate its financial difficulties, Mason dropped the series abruptly and Talbott inaugurated a vigorous campaign to increase circulation and advertising. Despite an editor's statement that the magazine did not "care for and would not accept any advertising of a questionable character," Talbott openly courted proprietary medicine and miracle cure ads, assuring prospective clients that "the South offers today a better field for profitable returns to reputable advertisers than any other section of the country." By May the advertising pages bulged with new advertisements for patent remedies such as Asteco, a surprising new cure for asthma in America, and for alcoholic beverages, such as Steinerbrau beer. In June, the editor wrote an explanation describing the fiscal realities of publishing a woman's magazine in the South.[18]

The Keystone, of Charleston, South Carolina, encountered similar financial stress. This popular woman's club journal began publishing in June 1899 under the direction of Ida Marshall Lining, and the Poppenheim sisters — Mary, Louisa, and Christie — all prominent clubwomen of Charleston. The avowed purpose of the journal was to unite Southern women and to provide a literary vehicle for "advanced thinkers among women." Southern women had the reputation for being the most conservative element of society, and Charleston the most conservative city of the most conservative state in the Union. A Charleston woman's club publication that encouraged women's activities outside the home took the

South by surprise. The first issue carried reviews of the activities of the Colonial Dames, the Daughters of the American Revolution, the United Daughters of the Confederacy, King's Daughters, and the South Carolina Federation of Women's Clubs. Women's organizations recognized the potential of *The Keystone* at once. It soon became the official organ of various groups in the Carolinas, Virginia, Florida, and Mississippi. In its first year it expanded from 12 to 20 pages and doubled its circulation.

Despite its popularity, circulation alone could not support the paper. *The Keystone* carried regular ads for proprietary medications until the editors discontinued the practice in hopes that the magazine would be accepted as the official organ for the G.F.W.C. After the Federation selected *The Federation Magazine* of Massachusetts, *The Keystone* returned to running a few selected proprietary ads with an editorial explanation that the publication would accept advertisements from reputable clients only.[19]

Finally, a large majority of Southern women did not want to interfere in politics. They thought it unwomanly and unnecessary. Southern politicians had assured women that they did not need to agitate for legislation because the votes of Southern men represented women. Politicians promised that they would grant whatever reforms women desired if apprised of their wishes privately and quietly. Southern women trusted the promises of their legislators. Mrs. Abby Crawford Milton, a clubwoman from Tennessee remembered, "We yielded to the men. We had confidence in our Southern gentlemen." The net effect was to delay public activism and temper open demands.[20]

Notwithstanding, state federations and local clubs promoted pure food, drink, and drugs in a quiet and determined manner. As in the North, Southern clubwomen incorporated its principles in domestic science departments, discussed the problem in their meetings, and circulated and distributed pure food and drink literature. A number of civic and village improvement societies worked for local pure food statutes. Visiting nurses, trained and employed by benevolent associations, cautioned their patients against dangerous drugs and adulterated food. Some of the 200 civic leagues in Texas adopted the line of work. Maryland and other states organized consumers' leagues to deal with the problem.[21]

At the 1905 convention of the South Carolina Federation of Women's Clubs, the president, Mrs. W. K. Sligh, appointed a committee of three "to take charge" of pure food legislation and recommended that the clubwomen of her state use their influence among the representatives in Congress on behalf of the pure food bill. Mrs. Robert Zahner of Atlanta noted that the Atlanta Women's Club had organized a pure food subcommittee to correlate its activities with the G.F.W.C. In Florida and Louisiana various women's groups, who felt the effects of dangerous medications and adulterated food "close at hand" among relatives, neighbors, and friends, worked for federal regulation.[22]

After the failure of effective pure food, drink, and drug legislation in a number of the Southern states and opposition to federal regulation by Southern legislators in Washington convinced them that they had misplaced their trust in Southern politicians, Southern clubwomen became more vocal in their demands. The number of articles promoting pure food, drink, and drug laws in the society pages of newspapers and in magazines increased. Monthly *Keystone* articles, written by Sarah Platt Decker, encouraged clubwomen to organize every possible means to support federal regulation, and state federations to strengthen food committees.[23]

Rhetoric in the women's section of the *Mobile Daily Register* was among the most colorful and incriminating of any in the nation. The editor, Mrs. J. Sydney Robbins, a member of the Alabama Federation of Women's Clubs which, at that time, was not affiliated with the G.F.W.C., repeatedly expressed support for federal regulation. She considered the problem of dangerous drugs in proprietary medications of vital concern to the entire American public for, as she stated, "at one time or another there is scarcely one of us who has not been deluded into drenching our long-suffering stomachs with some of the quack cures, whose fearless advertisements run riot all over our library tables."[24]

She wrote with the same directness concerning the need to address the problem of adulterated food:

> No subject should engage the closer attention of women, nor enlist their more united strenuous efforts for reform than the conditions now surrounding our food supply. It is a matter which strikes directly home and an appalling state of affairs is menacing our dearest interests...;

and became more indignant when she described the condition of the nation's meat supply:

> From the height of our lofty civilization, we shudder at the sight of the savage Igorettes feasting upon their dogs, when in truth, the dogs they ate would turn in disgust from much of the food now being used by the American nation could they behold it in its pristine repulsiveness before it has been "skillfully prepared"

for the consumers. The well-authenticated charges brought
against the meat kings of the West, notably of Chicago, are well
nigh incredible, so abandoned is the state of morals shown and
so infamous are the impositions now being practiced upon innocent people. The most nameless abominations of foul and
tainted meats, laden with germs of cancer and tuberculosis, are
disinfected and "embalmed" with dangerous chemicals, adorned
with a showy label of some great trust or multi-millionaire and
bearing a fraudulent government stamp, are sent forth into the
market as fit food for the people. Few are the homes where some
of the products of these concerns do not appear.

She advocated immediate and drastic action:

Now, are we women so helpless in this matter that we should
sit supine. Who purchases the bulk of food supplies of the country? The housewives. How can the women of the country best
be aroused to the enormity of the evil in question? "In unity is
strength." ... women of this country deserve to know the source
and the extent of the contamination. They should demand of
Congress a searching investigation of the methods of every great
food concern in this country. Let them demand that fullest publicity be given the results of these investigations. Women should
convince their husbands, sons, and brothers that the problem
of pure food is a "vital question, affecting their daily bread," they
should boycott the offending industries, and pledge their legislators to vote for regulation.

No offending trust nor combinations of trusts could possi-
bly stand up under the storm of universal indignation and boycott that would ensue. It would become a great political issue
and men's careers in public would depend upon their pledge to
protect the lives of their people from the iniquitous frauds now
being perpetrated upon them.

To Mrs. Robbins the danger went beyond damage to health and fraud.
Adulterated food threatened the fiber of American morality:

Who knows how much of the moral decadence so distressingly
evident and apparently on the increase is being brought about
by the insidious evil effects of the poisons and powerful drugs
being daily introduced into men's systems through the medium
of adulterated and doctored foods.

Subtle and intimate are the relations between mind and body,
and the healthy body that the healthy mind demands can never
be built up from debased and degraded sustenance.[25]

The Robbins articles articulated the opinion of Southern clubwomen everywhere. Along with other state federations, the Alabama Federation of Women's Clubs commended President Theodore Roosevelt for supporting the legislation. Individually and collectively, they bombarded congressmen with letters and petitions requesting passage of the bill and confronted their representatives personally.[26]

The Temperance Crusaders

As it had in the North, the Woman's Christian Temperance Union in the South provided an effective medium for mobilizing pure food, drink, and drug forces at the grassroots level. The Southern pure food, drink, and drug crusade took root with the introduction of the W.C.T.U. into the South and grew rapidly following Frances Willard's three Southern tours in the winters of 1881, 1882, and 1883. Its growth was part of, and contributed to, the rise of the W.C.T.U. as a major source of Southern social reform. Within the W.C.T.U., Southern crusaders were able to organize without intruding gender roles or attracting undue opposition. After the Civil War, food adulteration and sanitation became a serious problem, and the rise of drug habituation created considerable concern. Few Southerners doubted the need for promoting nutritious food and combating substance abuse. The W.C.T.U. presented an acceptable format for attacking the problem.

As in the North, pure food, drink, and drug activism was an integral part of W.C.T.U. activities. All aspects of the W.C.T.U. appealed to Southern women, but, more in the South than in the North, W.C.T.U. adherents tended to pursue the entire aggregate of temperance issues together. This tendency was particularly evident in local and smaller unions where the membership did not warrant dividing the unit into departments. How much emphasis they gave pure food, drink, and drugs in proportion to prohibition and other reform issues is difficult to assess. W.C.T.U. reports from the South entangle pure food, drink, and drug efforts with the other temperance activities. As in the North, the members believed that each problem fed upon the other. They equated proprietary medicine companies with liquor interests and felt that adulterated food was a main cause of substance abuse. On the whole, with the exceptions of Maryland, Texas, and Arkansas, the State Departments of Narcotics and of Health did not appear to be as highly organized and activist as some of those in the North, and the State Departments of Medical Temperance did not have a chance to gain a foothold before about 1903. From Georgia in 1886, Dr. S. M. Hicks, the State Department of Health Superintendent, reported that she pursued the work under difficulties, but had held one institute and secured one session of the monthly meeting of the local union for the presentation of health topics. In 1898 Selena S. Butler noted that the unions of her race were "too poor to buy literature" for circulation.[27]

The pure food, drink, and drug advocates seemed to concentrate most of their efforts in the Departments of Scientific Instruction. Vast numbers of W.C.T.U. women brought scientific instruction bills before Southern legislatures, and pushed for pure food and drug education and regulation, often with more optimism than they held for prohibition legislation.[28]

Historian Anne Firor Scott characterized the W.C.T.U. as "one of the most significant social forces in the South," and Frances Willard as "one of the most magnetic personalities of the nineteenth century." Southern crusaders observed that Frances Willard came to the Southern states "like a meteor" and left "sparks" behind which "kindled into a flame" that "illuminated" the South.[29]

Perhaps their observations were a bit overstated. Historians who have considered the activities of the W.C.T.U. in the South differ in their opinion of Willard's influence. Ruth Bordin agreed with Scott. Bordin pictured Willard's Southern travels as "triumphant journeys" that enhanced her self image and introduced the W.C.T.U. programs to an enthusiastic populace. Richard W. Leeman was more conservative in his estimation. He stated that Willard's visits only helped to organize the W.C.T.U. in the South. Most likely the actuality lies between the two positions. Probably, Southern women would have joined the W.C.T.U. without Willard's presence. Temperance forces were gathering strength already and Southern women were launching pure food, drink, and drug campaigns when she arrived. But, certainly, Willard made a significant impact on the activities of large numbers of Southern women.[30]

Anna Gordon, her secretary and confidante, accompanied Willard on her first tour. When Gordon became ill and returned home to recover, Georgia Hulse McLeod, a cultured Southern lady of Baltimore, took her place as Willard's companion. In Charleston, South Carolina, they added Sallie F. Chapin to their entourage.[31]

McLeod and Chapin were women of wide influence in religious, social, and political circles. McLeod's husband was a well-respected judge and active in behind-the-scenes politics. Chapin was a prominent

Charleston publisher, philanthropist, and socialite. They tutored Willard in Southern mores, introduced her to ministers and reform leaders, provided for her travel expenses, made arrangements for her to be a guest in private residences, publicized her cause, and scheduled her to address large audiences in Maryland, Virginia, North and South Carolina, Georgia, Florida, Alabama, Mississippi, Tennessee, and Kentucky. On Willard's subsequent tours, in the winters of 1882 and 1883, they included small towns, as well as the major cities, in Arkansas, Texas, Louisiana, and other Southern states.[32]

Willard found the Southern field "ready to harvest." She attracted large sympathetic audiences and strengthened the convictions of thousands of women that the sphere of the mother included improving the community. At first, some came to hear her partly from curiosity, partly because her cause was seen as worthy and respectable, and partly because she was sponsored by churchmen and judges; but, once assembled, her audiences listened with respect. They saw her as a "womanly woman" who was "simply yet tastefully dressed." Noting that she spoke in "soft, sweet tones," that she wore a conservative black suit and bonnet, that she did not posture or gesture, and her arguments were convincingly logical, the South Carolina *Baptist Courier* described her speech to an audience of 500 in Charleston as a "literary gem."[33]

The enthusiastic response to her person and to her message exceeded her fondest expectations. Willard felt that the experience "reconstructed" her. Of one tour, she wrote in her autobiography, "That trip was the most unique of all my history." Not only was she well-received and had arrived in time to witness Gulf State legislatures vote funds for Negro education, but she was encouraged and helped by Southern whites to address black audiences.[34]

Willard arrived in the Southern states at an opportune time. Southern women were anxious to provide adequate education for their children. At the end of reconstruction, prominent white Southerners had regained control of the political process. The fear of Populist militancy had not yet led to disbanding public assemblies. Willard moved easily between white and black audiences. She spoke on the campuses of white and black schools and in black churches. She avoided suggestions of integration in favor of assisting blacks to form separate W.C.T.U. unions and Southern whites to aid them.[35]

Her companions, McLeod and Chapin, proved to be women of exceptional insight and ability. They were utterly fearless, and frank in addressing large audiences and presenting the many-faceted W.C.T.U. programs as the answer to the South's post-war social problems.

In the summer of 1881, Chapin traveled to New England to study the entire range of W.C.T.U. programs and methods in action, and to evaluate each to determine how it might be implemented in the South. The popularity and potential of the Departments of Hygiene and of Scientific Instruction excited Chapin most. The Department of Franchise activities impressed her least.[36]

From October 26 through 29, 1881, she led a delegation of Southern women at the national convention of the W.C.T.U. in Washington, D.C., where she asked for a "place" for Southern women in the National Union, a chance to heal their differences, and for unity between Northern and Southern women. In poetry, she proposed they build a platform of reform to draw them together to replace the platforms of political parties that had led to the Civil War and had separated them:

> Then let us build what men in vain
> Have sought to rear these hundred years,
> And failed in throes of heart and brain,
> And torture deep and blood and tears;
> A platform broad as all the land,
> Where North and South and East and West
> In grand and high accord may stand,
> Arm linked with arm and breast with breast,
> Where Maine may bring her plank of pine
> To mortise with palmetto beam,
> …No North, no south, no alien name,
> Firm in one cause we stand,
> Hearts melted in the sacred flame
> For God and native land.[37]

The convention accepted the overtures of the Southern delegation and their platform with enthusiasm, created a Department of Southern Work with Sally Chapin as superintendent, Georgia H. McLeod as secretary, and charged them and their "coadjutors" to appoint lecturers in the Southern states.[38]

Before the winter of 1882 set in, the officials of the newly formed Department of Southern Work influenced Mrs. J. C. Johnson of Tennessee, Caroline E. Merrick of New Orleans, Mrs. W. C. Sibley of

Augusta, Georgia, Belle Kearney, and Rebecca Latimer Felton, along with scores of other women, to put aside their reluctance to appear in public and become aggressive organizers. Their goal was to form unions in every village, town, and city in the South. This preliminary work of organizing W.C.T.U. unions was prerequisite to their pure food, drink, and drug activism.[39]

The lecturers swept through the South, pulling independent local temperance groups, which had sprung up spontaneously, into the N.W.C.T.U. and organizing unions where none existed. They found little difficulty forming unions among whites and blacks throughout urban and rural areas, becoming role models of selfless service. Thousands of Southerners of all descriptions flocked to churches and schools to hear them, and came away members of the W.C.T.U. Between 1882 and 1885, there was a union of some kind enjoying considerable outside support from church and temperance men in almost every town they visited. The unions were often small, usually from 10 to 50 women, and the activities varied according to the needs of their communities. Individual experiences of these lecturers illustrates the popularity of their cause and indicates how they mobilized pure food, drink, and drug activism in the South under the W.C.T.U. banner.

Eden C. Bryce, superintendent of the Alabama Department of Scientific Instruction, reported that Southern women came to Chapin as "tides to the moon," and that she "carried everything before her like a whirlwind." In 1885 she spoke 40 times in Alabama, addressing large audiences throughout the state. At Evergreen she spoke to great audiences of both white and black people. At Greensboro sixty-five students and the entire faculty of Southern University signed petitions. She spoke to the children and teachers of public schools in Birmingham and other places, establishing unions and Bands of Hope wherever she went. Black people flocked to hear her and formed large unions. More than 2,000 people joined the W.C.T.U. in Alabama in that year, and uncounted others subscribed to their cause. Articles written by staff editors and reporters in two Atlanta papers, the *The Atlanta Constitution* and the *Sunny South*, devoted considerable space to W.C.T.U. proposals.[40]

Like many women in small Southern communities, the women of Gadsden, Alabama, knew nothing of the existence of the W.C.T.U. when they organized. They were typical of many groups that sprang up spontaneously in the South. After reading about the W.C.T.U. in a newspaper, the president, Marietta Sibert, named her baby boy Willard and contacted the National Union, which sent Sally Chapin to affiliate the group with the N.W.C.T.U.[41]

In Louisiana, Sally Chapin spoke 14 times in one week. In churches, in halls, in universities, and among white and black people, she secured thousands of pledges, not only to uphold personal abstinence standards, but to vote for prohibition and scientific instruction. At Monroe, where she arrived on April 26, she formed a very large union among influential white adults, a Band of Hope for the children, and addressed a mass-meeting of black people. As was her custom when so many attended, she pledged the entire audience by a rising vote and registered individuals after the meeting.

She described the courtesy of black congregations at Monroe in sending a handsome carriage and an entourage of black ministers and influential white citizens to take her to the church. The building was packed to its utmost capacity. Those who could not get standing room climbed the outside walls to watch through the windows. In the best tradition of Southern Baptist preaching, she told them now that God had given them their freedom, they had no masters to blame their sins on. They had gone over in a body to Satan, and she had come down to call a halt, and they would be sent into a bondage far more terrible than they had known before, if they did not repent and serve the Lord. In the best tradition of Baptist congregations, they loved her message. Women joined W.C.T.U. ranks and men promised to vote for temperance issues. The audience was so effusive in their praise that the minister whisked her out the back door to prevent her hands from being shaken off. To Chapin this one meeting was worth all the hard stage-riding of her entire trip, and even reconciled her to the chill and fever she had contracted "in this malarial country."[42]

In Georgia, Sally Chapin visited six key locations in the state, speaking 15 times. At Covington, the Methodist minister, with only a few hours' notice of her arrival, arranged for a lecture at his church. The Baptist and Presbyterian ministers, with their congregations, attended, and the mayor introduced Chapin. At Oxford, the university staff, students, and union members greeted her with a large reception. At Rome, not only the temperance people, but groups of citizens generally, "vied with each other in their attentions to Chapin." All denominations united in the public exercises at her lectures. Audiences were large and enthusiastic. Chapin spoke to a large white audience at the Gainesville Baptist Church, and black congregations responded with fervor to her address to that meeting.[43]

Her home state of South Carolina responded with equal enthusiasm. In Laurens, two temperance groups invited her to affiliate them with the state W.C.T.U. Ministers of all denominations endorsed the work and assisted with the organization of several large unions among white and black congregations. In one Laurens location, the principal of the high school marched in with his students. Each one signed the pledge and pinned on the white ribbon. A colt and a baby were named Sally in her honor. In Newberry, the mayor and town council sat on the platform in body and 500 people signed the W.C.T.U. polyglot pledge. At Edgefield, a town considered to be an anti-temperance stronghold, a congressman took up their cause and black men pledged to "Stand up for God at the polls." When the rector and the bishop of the Episcopal church sponsored W.C.T.U. meetings, the "whiskey men" vandalized the seminary and broke into the school. The principal found her Bible in the creek, and her supplies scattered, but used the incident to prove that the liquor interests were conducting a war against women and children. In Lexington, Greenwood, and Hodges, Chapin added 1,180 members to the W.C.T.U. roll in ten days.[44]

Born and reared among black people, she claimed to love them and understand their needs, enjoying the same popularity among black audiences everywhere she went. One minister said that Chapin was raised in black laps, one of them — "an angel from Heaven," sent to help them in their hour of need.[45]

Consistently, she demonstrated her concern for the black people and recognized the necessity of their participation to social reform. In one attempt, she petitioned the federal government to appropriate money to the W.C.T.U. to use among blacks because private funds had dried up. The people most able and willing to donate to the cause were those who staked their all in the war, and lost. She claimed that with $1,000 dollars the W.C.T.U. could do more to help the blacks than one million dollars in the hands of politicians. Above all, she wanted to help Southern blacks. She could not bear to see substance abuse "sweeping" them by thousands down "the moral scale." Like most Southern women, once she had attributed the use of narcotics among both blacks and whites to personal weakness. After working more closely with persons from all backgrounds, she and they began to realize that the reason many people used dangerous substances was because of the disorganization of the South. They were destitute and could see no hope for improvement. It was the socioeconomic conditions that were at fault, not the individual.[46]

Chapin's attitude toward universal participation explains much of the acceptance of W.C.T.U. programs in the South. In two Florida cities where she formed unions, the ministers whispered to her that she must be careful. The W.C.T.U. officers had all been elected from the aristocracy. Chapin ignored their warning. Because she did not either nominate or elect, she left matters as they stood. Above all, she declared, the idea of the W.C.T.U. was for everyone to merge their individuality for the general good. Class was not relevant.[47]

Lesser-known W.C.T.U. organizers experienced situations similar to those that Chapin encountered. They found some women eager to implement W.C.T.U. programs and some who needed convincing. Mrs. Walter Gwynn discovered a group of women reformers in Tampa, Florida, who affiliated with the W.C.T.U. as soon as she told them about it.[48]

Women in Selma, Alabama, were not so sure that they wanted to affiliate with the W.C.T.U. Helen H. Rothrock told what happened when the first W.C.T.U. organizer came to Selma. People there were wary of women lecturers. Rothrock did not know how it came about, whether a certain Miss H. G. Moore invited herself or someone invited her, but the newspapers announced that Moore would speak at Gilman's Hall on the following Sunday. Because no one had offered their home to "so controversial a figure," Moore stayed at a boardinghouse. Rothrock and several of her friends were appointed to accompany her to the hall. Rothrock described following Moore onto the platform embarrassed "to occupy so prominent a position" beside a woman speaker. After Moore spoke for about a half an hour, Rothrock's discomfort turned to mortification that she had not offered the lecturer the hospitality of her home. Moore soon convinced the audience that the W.C.T.U. was a worthy reform society and that a woman could speak in public "without seeming to be out of her sphere."

When they dined together the following day, Rothrock asked Moore if she thought that they could organize a union in Selma.

Moore answered, "Certainly, haven't you?"

"No indeed," Rothrock replied.

A meeting at the First Presbyterian Church vindicated Moore's optimism. After Moore's address, the women in the audience organized a union on their own with Mrs. Brooks, the wife of a local judge, as president and Helen Rothrock as corresponding secretary.[49]

In similar situations, a Miss I. C. DeVelling addressed as many as five congregations in 36 hours in Arkansas. In several localities no one had ever heard a woman speak in a public place before, but they came to hear her out of curiosity. After they heard her message, a considerable number, both men and women, who had disapproved of women speaking publicly, changed their minds and accorded her a "kind and respectful" reception. After receiving advance notice of her message and speaking ability, a group of men and women at Magnolia met her at the depot with a brass band with which they escorted her through the streets to an informal reception at the local hotel. Such experiences were typical of the reception of W.C.T.U. organizers throughout the South between 1883 and 1885.[50]

Southern audiences accorded the same courtesies to lecturers from the North. Reportedly, Lucia Kimball, of Chicago, Illinois, was one of the first Northern women to speak in any of the churches in Rome, Georgia. She was greeted with cordiality and respect. In Atlanta she gave 12 addresses and reluctantly declined a number of others, because she had previous engagements elsewhere. *The Atlanta Constitution*, the largest paper in the city, along with other newspapers donated unsolicited notices of the meetings and Kimball attracted "earnest" audiences from "all classes" of the people to whom she introduced various lines of W.C.T.U. reform. The Fulton County Sunday School Association lauded her as "a lady whose goodness of heart was only equaled by the eloquence of her tongue," and newspapers reported that she "made a signal impression for the honor and good of the cause." At Oxford, Kimball received invitations to meet with the State Sunday School Convention, the State Teachers' Association, and a member of the legislature, who offered to secure a hearing for her before the General Assembly. Like Chapin she found the black people particularly interested, appreciative, and eager to be included in the W.C.T.U. activities.[51]

With this tide of momentum, Southern women were able to marshal considerable support for departments of health and compulsory scientific instruction. To suggest ways and procedures, Virginia crusaders invited Mary Hunt to visit their second annual convention held at the Lutheran church of Staunton on September 16 and 17, 1884. A Department of Scientific Instruction, with a Mrs. Payne of Charlottesville as superintendent, and a State Department of Hygiene and Heredity were organized and activated.[52]

Mary Hunt and others reported the experiences of scientific instruction crusaders in Louisiana and North Carolina. These accounts are particularly helpful in providing a step-by-step profile of the processes through which Southern women were able to translate their concern for pure food, drink, and drugs into regulation.[53]

At its March 1884 convention, the Louisiana W.C.T.U. adopted a resolution to introduce physiology and hygiene into the Louisiana schools as its first plan of work. Caroline E. Merrick, the president, addressed a large audience assembled at the St. Charles Avenue church. She was the first woman to speak there. The audience listened with undivided attention as she assured the delegates that the sphere of their duty was limited only by the sphere of their capacity, and that they were taking the time away from their home duties for the sake of their children. She did not boast that any "bonfires were lighted in their honor," or "knights in glittering armor were ready to march out to the sound of trumpets to do battle in their cause," but they were "surrounded by staunch and true friends — men wise and strong," ready "to become a good and reliable committee of responsibility," who would guarantee that no harm came to them.[54]

The first item of business was to find a superintendent of scientific instruction, who was capable of directing the work for the state through the local unions. Her duties included securing a hearing before all teachers in institutes and conventions. In order to act judiciously, she must be familiar with the school laws of the state. She should endeavor to secure the "sympathy and co-operation of all moral and religious assemblies, presenting this phase of temperance effort before church conferences, synods, and associations as the opportunity presented itself." Mary Reade Goodale of Baton Rouge fit their qualifications.[55]

Their aim was to secure legislation to place the study of physiology, along with other required studies, under state control. Because they knew that they could not expect legislators to pass laws that public sentiment did not sustain, their first effort was to attract public support.[56]

Not more than one-fifth of the people of the state lived in cities. Widespread support required contacting people in rural areas and small towns. To accomplish this, they established a tight-knit department of scientific instruction in every parish to visit the outlying areas, to introduce the subject to school boards, and to influence law-makers to vote for scientific instruction legislation. In cities such as New Orleans, where larger concentrations of voters lived, the department assigned all W.C.T.U. members to give scientific instruction top priority. With the help of the entire state W.C.T.U., the department conducted a vigorous campaign, distributing propaganda, giving lectures, and making personal contacts. One-by-one the state medical societies, the New Orleans Sanitary Association, the press societies, education associations, and church conferences recommended passing the law.[57]

Judge W. H. Goodale, Mary Goodale's husband, and president of Louisiana State University, stated that petitions "by the thousand were circulated in all parts of the State, and came back to the legislature of 1886 black with the names of the best citizens of Louisiana." The W.C.T.U. was able to marshal considerable support, but the bill was tabled, "snowed under completely beneath the white flakes of less important measures," and had to wait for two more years before it could be reintroduced. In the interim, the W.C.T.U. continued to gather advocates. Judge Goodale reported that "public sentiment" sufficient to "insure success" grew as silently "as the daisies on the hillsides."[58]

When the bill came before the legislature a second time, the Louisiana W.C.T.U. crusaders invited Mary H. Hunt, the national superintendent of Scientific Instruction, to travel from Washington, D.C., where she had been working for a law to introduce the subject into the territories and other federal jurisdictions. Day after day "for a solid month," Hunt, Goodale, and other members of the department attended sessions of the legislature, following every step of the passage of the bill through the committee, House, Senate, back to the House, through the "dangerous vortex" of the negotiating committee, to the signature of the speaker, president, and Governor Nicholls, who gave Hunt the pen with which he signed the bill.[59]

The North Carolina W.C.T.U. waited until the state and local unions were well organized and functioning before campaigning for a scientific education law. Miss Aston, the state superintendent of Scientific Instruction, and other members of the department consulted with Mary Hunt at the Interstate Summer School at Asheville, North Carolina, in August 1891, concerning the possibility of securing a strong scientific education law for their state, and subsequently designed their plans accordingly. Members went "up and down" gathering signatures for petitions. They committed the candidates running for the next legislature and, as soon as each was elected, the white-ribbon women of his locality reminded him of his promise to support the law. Apparently they encountered little difficulty. Aston reported that the candidates were mostly "Farmers' Alliance men accustomed to straightforward ways of doing things." As such, they saw "the wisdom and reasonableness of this request from the motherhood of the State." When the legislature convened, the state crusaders sent telegrams requesting Hunt to go to Raleigh to present the scientific instruction bill to the legislature, and to explain the reasons for its various specifications. Hunt remembered that she left the "snow-clad north" and found herself on February 15, 1892, in the "balmy air of North Carolina, surrounded by scenes and atmosphere of opening spring, that typified the warm greetings of waiting friends."[60]

Her first appearance was a hearing before a joint session of the House and Senate committees on education. With the aid of a large map showing the states with scientific instruction laws in white and those without in black, she explained the characteristics of effective laws, why such features were necessary, and how easily the law was evaded if any part of the program was eliminated. Professors from the state college system and the State Superintendent of Public Instruction reinforced her plea.[61]

In retrospect, Hunt recalled, "It was a tender and solemn hour and as we plead for the education of the children of that State ... the assurance fell upon us all, that it would not be in vain." They were not surprised when a representative from Raleigh moved for the proposition, it was unanimously carried. The committee requested the chairman to confer with Hunt regarding the details, and instructed him to prepare the bill for immediate report.[62]

The next day Hunt addressed a joint session of the House and Senate, after which she replied in committee to certain questions regarding the practical working aspects of the bill. Toward evening, Hunt began to "scent the old battle cries" she had heard so many times in previous campaigns from opposition against the clause that allocated one-fourth of time allotted to scientific instruction to temperance matter, and from the "special interests" who were accusing the W.C.T.U. of trying to raise funds by selling textbooks.

Hunt explained that she was not "a third party prohibitionist who had come down there to destroy their party organizations," that she was not a book agent, and that what was in the texts made "no financial difference to her or the Woman's Christian Temperance Union." The children of North Carolina were the ones that would suffer if the temperance issues were eliminated. The committee dropped the matter and told her, "That is enough; we are not accustomed down here to doubt the word of a lady."

At eight o'clock on Monday evening, the W.C.T.U. committee and friends of the measure filled the galleries of the House in Raleigh. Hunt wrote, "the members were all in their seats and an expectant air was hanging over everybody." A copy of the bill, with a miniature of the scientific instruction map and a plea from the North Carolina W.C.T.U. for his vote was on every member's desk. The Honorable D. D. Gilmore came to the front and moved to pass the bill in a "logical and earnest" speech in which he referred to passage of the national law and urged North Carolina "to come into line" with the other states by requiring this education for her children. Four other legislators endorsed the bill. It passed by a unanimous standing vote and went to the Senate. On Thursday morning, Hunt, Aston, and several Department of Scientific Instruction members went to the Senate gallery to witness the final proceedings. As in the House, the measure passed without dissenting votes. North Carolina became the first state to pass the law by unanimous consent.[63]

Throughout the South, W.C.T.U. women repeated variations of this activity pattern. Between 1885 and 1888, women in most Southern states organized departments of scientific instruction, introduced bills into their legislatures, and solicited the support of lawmakers, although many found that making their wishes known to politicians did not produce results. Their first attempts succeeded in only a few states. Passing legislation required intense activism and widespread support.

At the Virginia legislative session of 1887-1888, when W.C.T.U. women asked for scientific instruction law, the legislators did not take the bill seriously. The *Richmond Times* reported that their failure was "an eye-opening experience." The indignant women walked out of the congressional halls and began a vigorous public campaign. A few years later, when they came back to Richmond with a stronger law and more support, they succeeded.[64]

In Florida and Mississippi, the measure was not reported out of congressional committee. Crusaders in Georgia and Texas were not able to secure laws until after 1890. In these and some other states they enjoyed greater success on a local level. School boards often introduced the subject into their schools, and individually, teachers taught physiology and hygiene lessons from one to three times a week. Often parents were too poor to afford books. Much of the instruction was oral. In general, teachers were enthusiastic and the subject was a favorite among students.[65]

In the spring of 1885 the Alabama legislature passed a law that required teaching the effects of harmful substances in all public schools and stipulated that teachers pass an examination in hygiene and physiology with special reference to the effects of stimulants and narcotics upon the human system.[66]

The Maryland Union hoped to secure a law to educate their children in the same way, but preferred to strengthen their power base to be sure that they were able to introduce the type of scientific instruction they felt would be effective. Part of their campaign was to gain the backing of influential legislators, another part was to solicit popularity for their cause. They broadened their base by involving satellite organizations, such as the Woodbridge Young Woman's Temperance Union, male temperance organizations, religious groups, and the N.W.C.T.U. Their determination was rewarded in 1886 when the Baltimore Yearly Meeting of Friends, with other advocates of the bill, united behind them in petitioning the legislature for the enactment of a law that required teaching the nature and effects of stimulants and narcotics upon the human system in the public schools. Mary Hunt, accompanied by officers of the Maryland Union, held two meetings at the state house at Annapolis, in which she presented the merits of the bill "to attentive and appreciative hearers ... in an eloquent and impressive manner." The scientific instruction bill, as written by W.C.T.U., and a "stringent and comprehensive" act to outlaw the nonmedical use of opium, passed by large majorities.[67]

In Georgia they encountered severe opposition. They presented a petition to the legislature for temperance instruction in Georgia schools in 1885, drew up an exemplary bill, fashioned after the Pennsylvania law, and eight of their most influential members appeared in person before the Joint Committee on Education, where they received a respectful hearing. The Georgia Teachers' Association, the Grand Lodge of Georgia, and all temperance organizations in the state had endorsed the bill and the Georgia Joint Committee on Education recommended its passage. Mrs. J. C. Keyes and Mrs. J. Norcross left the papers and petitions in the hands of the educational committee chairman with every expectation that the bill would pass. On the Senate floor, several legislators spoke in favor of the bill. When the bill reached its third reading, the W.C.T.U. delegates detected subtle hostility among the Senate leadership. The most devastating opposition emerged from persons determined to undermine any change in the public school system, backed by the liquor and proprietary medicine industries. One observer stated that scientific instruction "furnished matter for much disgusting amusement among the senators." One of the senators, who she characterized as a "liquor champion," ridiculed the textbooks, particularly the *Health Primer*, and the illustrations accompanying them. Others attacked the W.C.T.U. for introducing an expensive and "unconstitutional measure," objected to teaching physiology to children, and declared that Southern teachers were not prepared to teach the subject. In the tide of ridicule, support of the bill collapsed and its friends in the Senate spirited the women away from the taunts of the opposition.[68]

The conduct of the Senate aroused cries of "foul" from the press. In a Cartersville *Courant* article entitled "The Reason Why," the editor accused senators of being puppets of the liquor industry:

> The liquor party would not have the truth taught to the children, and their obedient servants in the Senate of Georgia dare not disobey their mandates. The good people of the state desire the plain, unvarnished, truth of science taught to the children: but the red-nosed bacchanals of the state need but raise a warning finger and the average senator falls into line with an alacrity that would be amusing if it were not disgusting and humiliating. The truth can not be taught in any institution under state control, provided it may militate against the interests of the dram-seller. Was ever the slavery of a great state more abject?"[69]

In a letter to the *Wesleyan Christian Advocate*, Walter B. Hill, a reporter of Macon, wrote:

> Great things have been done in Georgia, but let us not forget that in this year of grace a Senator could be elected in this state which denied the prayers of the Christian women of the land who asked that the chemistry of intoxicants should be taught to the children in the public schools.[70]

In the face of such a humiliating defeat, the Georgia W.C.T.U. crusaders did not give up. Gradually, through the influence of the mothers on school boards, county school commissioners, and teachers, they introduced physiological temperance textbooks into public and private schools in the absence of a state law.[71]

Without doubt, the obstacles that Southern women faced muted and delayed their pure food, drink, and drug activities, but the crusaders were nevertheless able to achieve many of their goals. Their experience exploded the myth that Southern gentlemen entered politics to protect women and children, and that women were the silent constituency of every man. Political opposition to state laws that promoted pure food, drink, and drugs sorely strained the sacred trust that women placed in their Southern gentlemen and convinced them that indirect representation did not represent.

As a result, Southern women became much more closely united, vocal, and militant in their demands. By the time the federal pure food, drink, and drug law passed in 1906, they were organized and ready to conduct open campaigns to enforce it in the South and to build on its provisions.

9

Profiles of Pure Food, Drink, and Drug Protagonists

"The most diverse elements ... work harmoniously together because they have a common impulse, and a common pleasure in the result."[1]

O ne notable characteristic of the crusade was the extent to which women in diverse occupations became involved in pure food, drink, and drug activism. Because adulterated food and dangerous drugs was a consumer issue that threatened every person in the country, women who engaged in a wide variety of pursuits were interested in rectifying the situation. This aspect of the crusade challenges the idea, proposed by Paul Starr, and shared by other historians, that pure food, drink, and drug activism was limited to a narrow clique of professionals to gain control over the market for their services as well as the various organizational hierarchies that governed their profession's practice, financing, and policy.[2]

The vast majority of pure food, drink, and drug activists were homemakers who found crusading for pure food, drink, and drugs a necessity to protect their families and neighbors from the dangers of adulterated food and dangerous drugs. They learned to practice the arts of politics and administration through club, union, and league activities, and they devoted endless hours and energy without expectation of recognition or compensation. They received none. Only a few of their names were recorded and little is known of their individual contributions. Mary Hunt called them the "great army of battalions in every State and territory, regiments and companies in all counties, with pickets at every outpost."[3]

This army of invisible women elected the most innovative and able women that they could find to lead and to represent them. The leaders emerged from their ranks. One clubwoman observed that organization brought forth hidden capacities "from their concealment," and leaders arose with "the blessed variety of human endowments," to address the endless "variety of human needs." Rather than attempting to impose middle-class value systems upon reluctant members, the leaders reflected the values of their constituents. Frances Willard reminded delegates to a W.C.T.U. convention as early as 1883, "you who are gathered from every quarter of this vast republic, are not self-constituted, but elected delegates with a great constituency behind you, and chosen leaders," for reform.[4]

True, the leaders recruited members, but not from among the apathetic throng. The hundreds of thousands of women who joined the crusade were receptive to its message and eager to unite with others who were attempting to do something about a danger that threatened themselves and their society. A few of the leaders, such as Sarah Platt Decker, Alice Lakey, and Mary Hunt, rose briefly to national prominence among women, but they were soon forgotten and, for the most part, the few remains of the records they generated lie dormant in local archives and special collections of university libraries.

The leaders of the pure food, drink, and drug crusade did not achieve the kind of status that traditionally attracts historians. The significance of the crusade leaders lay in their typicality, rather than in their singularity. Primarily the crusade gained ground because it organized public opinion, not because any particular leader attained prominence or distinction. It was the rank and file who educated the children, who formed the vanguard to the movement, who organized grassroots outrage, who brought the interested forces together, and who persisted in the fight. Not only did the leaders carry out the wishes of their constituents, they absorbed, reflected, and synthesized the thought of those they represented with startling fidelity. They were links that connected the chains of progressivism, not an engine that drug the chain along.

The extent to which housewives united with women who worked outside the home was particularly beneficial to the pure food, drink, and drug cause. Often professional women provided a pool of public experience upon which organized women drew ideas and propaganda. Within clubs, unions, and leagues, they often served on committees, exposing the homemaker to the facts and problems of the working world of which she had little personal knowledge. More than their male counterparts, women professionals fused improvement of the community with their work. They promoted pure food, drink, and drug principles in the associations to which they belonged, in the institutions in which they served, in their practices among their clients, and among their social contacts.

The records that have been preserved suggest that next to housewives, elementary school teachers comprised the second largest group of pure food, drink, and drug crusaders. Educating and nurturing the young created a bond of interest between mothers and teachers. The desire to protect children against dangerous food and drugs brought them together, and working in a common cause created strong associations. As we have shown previously, teachers were often partners with housewives in distributing propaganda and influencing school boards to adopt physiology classes.

The response of educators in Santa Barbara, California, to include scientific instruction in their classes was typical of teachers in other states. Within the city limits, local W.C.T.U. representatives contacted over seventy teachers in two days to sign petitions for a state law. Of the teachers visited, only one refused to sign because he said that he "would not insult the teachers of California" by implying that they did not already teach physiology and hygiene. Sixty-four of those who signed were public school teachers, five were from the University of Southern California (Methodist), and one from St. Vincent's College (Catholic).[5]

Articles in women's journals and other accounts frequently mention the contributions of teachers, but few are identified by name. Of course, Mary Hunt and Frances Willard were notable exceptions. They led and designed programs, but it was the large corps of local elementary school teachers that carried out the programs and taught children pure food, drink, and drug principles.[6]

Narcissa Edith White was one of these teachers. A native of Pennsylvania, she entered Edinboro State Normal School near Erie while in her early teens. She began teaching elementary students at age 15. Later she accepted a position on the teaching staff of her alma mater, became superintendent of the Edinboro Union School, and county institute instructor. In 1880 she acquired an interest in scientific instruction and, according to Frances Willard, taught the subject with "the divine fire of enthusiasm" to her students. Subsequently, she served as president of the local W.C.T.U. and superintendent of the New York State W.C.T.U. Department of Scientific Instruction. She lectured, wrote, taught at teachers' institutes, and pledged legislators to vote for state scientific education laws in her state.

In 1886 she graduated from medical school in Baltimore and became a strong pure food, drink, and drug advocate.[7]

Clara Cleghorn Hoffman, from Kansas City, Missouri, was another teacher who worked for pure food, drink, and drugs. She came from a northern New York farm family of thirteen children, and as a child, learned the value of hard work and strong convictions. At age 16 she entered a high school at Springfield, Massachusetts. After graduating, she went to Keokuk, Iowa, then to southern Illinois to teach in elementary schools. In Illinois she married Dr. G. Hoffman and had two sons. She moved to Kansas City where she found employment as first assistant and then principal of the Lathrop School. She joined the local W.C.T.U. and became president of the Kansas City Union. In 1882 she was appointed president of the Missouri Woman's Christian Temperance Union, and in 1884, after her sons were grown, gave up her home and her position at the school to serve full time as a W.C.T.U. organizer and lecturer. She took an active interest in all of the W.C.T.U. programs. Her primary interest was educational work among the youth. In Missouri, she worked tirelessly for a scientific instruction law that applied to every level of education and worked equally as intensely for pure food, drink, and drug legislation. Clara Hoffman continued to write and plan for the Missouri W.C.T.U. through seven years of poor health before her death on February 13, 1908.[8]

Like homemakers and educators, other professional women viewed the solution to adulterated food and dangerous drugs in the broad context of solving social ills. They attacked a wide range of these problems by participating in many projects. Rachel Yarros, M.D., a Chicago physician and director of the Chicago Lying-In Hospital, reflected such an attitude. She wrote, "the physician is also a citizen [and] should not be ignorant of economics, of political science, of history, of philosophical ethics, of literature" and should "sympathize with labor, with victims of exploitation and industrial autocracy, with the juvenile, and adult delinquents — products of the slums."[9]

The career of Martha Hughes Cannon illustrates the same phenomenon. She was born in Llandudno, Wales, on July 1, 1857, and, as an infant, was brought to America by her parents. Her father died in 1861, a few days after settling in Utah. At 14 years of age, she became an elementary school teacher. The following year she apprenticed as a typesetter to the *Deseret News* and the *Woman's Exponent*. In 1878 she graduated from the University of Deseret and, on her twenty-third birthday in 1880, from medical school at the University of Michigan. After continuing her education with bachelor's degrees in pharmacy from the University of Pennsylvania, and in oration from the National School of Elocution and Oratory, she established a successful medical practice, founded the first nurses' training school in Utah, and became the second resident physician at Deseret Hospital in Salt Lake City. She married Angus Munn Cannon in 1894, had three children, and earned a reputation for being an exemplary wife and mother.[10]

Martha Cannon was a human rights activist and suffragist. She maintained active memberships in the Relief Society and the General Federation of Women's Clubs, for which she served as a pure food, drink, and drug lecturer and authority on narcotic addiction. She was also a member of the National Medical Association, the Psychological Section of the Medics Society of New York, and the National Genealogical Society. She campaigned in the West with William Jennings Bryan, frequently speaking "in the interests of free silver."

Running on the Democratic ticket in 1886, she won election as a state senator over her Republican husband and four other candidates. As a senator she worked for pure food, drink, and drugs; sanitation; disease control; and fair labor practices. She sponsored laws that prohibited the sale of adulterated vinegar, created a seven-member board of health, improved working conditions for women salesclerks, established schools for deaf and blind children, and provided for teaching the dangers of alcohol and narcotic abuse in the public schools. In her later years, she worked in the Orthopedic Department of the Graves Clinic at the University of California in Los Angeles, where she died at 75 years of age on July 10, 1932.[11]

The urgent need for physicians in Utah inspired Martha and Ellis Shipp to study medicine at the Women's Medical College in Philadelphia. Ellis supported Martha and cared for her children while Martha attended medical school. After she graduated, Martha reciprocated. Both practiced medicine in Salt Lake City and established nursing schools where they emphasized the importance of pure food, drink, and drugs. Martha published a periodical, the *Salt Lake Sanitarian*, which warned against contaminated food, milk, and meat, the habitual use of drugs, and fraud. Ellis taught medical courses, sponsored by the Relief Society, to women who could not afford to attend medical schools in the East and issued certificates that entitled the graduates to practice medicine in their communities.[12]

Part of the duties of the Relief Society doctors entailed teaching the dangers of adulterated food and dangerous drugs. They adopted selfless service as part of their creed. Phoebe Campbell, one of the Relief Society physicians, made home visits to the ill and delivered babies whenever she was called. In lieu of cash, she accepted chickens, suckling pigs, produce, or family gratitude when that was the best the family could afford.[13]

Physicians were the most visible professional women who worked as consumer advocates for pure food, drink, and drugs. Often they were active in a wide variety of community affairs. Their opinions carried sway. Their position attracted greater audiences at lectures. They generated an immense amount of health literature, and newspapers tended to accept their articles as more authoritative than those submitted by homemakers.

Cordelia A. Green, a physician practicing in Castile, New York, wrote that during a "constant and laborious practice of nearly a half century" she avoided using any type of medication containing addictive drugs. She warned women that those who depended on patent and proprietary medicines — headache powders, tablets and tonics — were "running a foolish and dangerous risk" of becoming subject to "the power of narcotics."[14]

Dora Green Wilson, a Kansas City physician, became the Missouri State W.C.T.U. superintendent of Narcotics from 1904 to 1906, for the express purpose of activating the women of Missouri on behalf of the federal pure food, drink, and drug law. She wrote and circulated pamphlets, which detailed the necessity for federal regulation from a medical viewpoint, and sent them to every teacher in Missouri, however remote the school, to distribute to their communities. She helped secure the endorsement of Governor Joseph W. Folk, lobbied representatives and senators from Missouri, and marshaled medical providers behind the bill.[15]

Sarah Hackett Stevenson, M.D., attained prominence as a leader in the Illinois and National W.C.T.U. Departments of Health and Heredity, and was an active clubwoman. She was the first woman delegate to attend a convention of the American Medical Association. When the State Medical Association appointed her to represent Illinois at the A.M.A. meeting in Philadelphia in 1876, the secretary submitted only her initials with her last name. The arrival of the only woman at the convention was a surprise to the other delegates. Regardless, when a motion to refer names of women delegates to the Judicial Council was tabled, Stevenson became the first woman accepted by the A.M.A. She served as the first woman on the staff of Cook County Hospital and the first woman to serve on the Illinois State Board of Health.[16]

Elizabeth Wiley Corbett, M.D., Harvey Wiley's sister, was also a pure food, drink, and drug advocate. She often referred to herself as the originator of the Pure Food Act because at the age of 11 she brought up her brother on pure milk when their mother became seriously ill after his birth. She was born in 1833 in Ohio, and educated at home and at the Eleutherian Institute, an interracial, coeducational school in Lancaster.[17]

Elizabeth Wiley studied for a term under Horace Mann at Antioch College in Ohio, then entered the Hygeo-Therapeutic College in New York. Her degree from this college was not accredited in most of the eastern states, but California had no bars to prevent her from practicing. In 1859 she set sail for San Francisco where she established a practice and married another physician, Samuel J. Corbett, M.D.[18]

In 1879 she traveled to Vienna for a year's study. On the way home, with letters of recommendation, she enrolled at the University of Michigan, earning a degree in medicine from that institution. Back in California, she became an active pure food, drink, and drug advocate in several women's organizations. She died on June 4, 1914.[19]

Temperance unions and women's clubs actively recruited women physicians into their ranks. Louise C. Purington, M.D., encouraged local unions to elect as many practicing physicians as possible to serve as W.C.T.U. Department of Health superintendents. She felt that physicians contributed greater authenticity, vitality, and innovation to the crusade. In addition to practicing their professions, Dr. Ellen A. Wallace and Dr. Elizabeth Hofma wrote and directed distribution of numerous pamphlets and articles and directed active campaigns. Dr. Annette Shaw of Wisconsin wrote a regular health and home column for local papers. Dr. Shaw also served, along with Mary Allen Wood and Sarah Hackett Stevenson, both administrators and physicians at the National Temperance Hospital in Chicago, as a lecturer for the W.C.T.U. Department of Health.[20]

Temperance unions and women's clubs provided medical scholarships and other financial support to promising women students. One of the recipients, a Miss Epsie Patterson, was the first graduate among the beneficiaries of the Mississippi Federation of Women's Clubs Scholarship fund. She was teaching 20 students at a little country summer school when she "received the good news" that she had been awarded the scholarship. She wrote, "You cannot know how much that message meant to me — a girl working for means to return to school…. I hope to make a physician of myself, for I'm sure that in that way I can be a true helper to mankind." After Patterson graduated she "passed on a part" of what she had received by helping to educate her two sisters and younger brother.[21]

Temperance unions established similar scholarships. Kate Bushnell, and other pure food, drink, and drug advocates, were among the physicians educated through W.C.T.U. funding. Such graduates established their own practices, or found employment at the National Temperance Hospital in Chicago, at other women's hospitals and clinics, and in health departments, where they practiced pure food, drink, and drug ideals and promoted them among their patients.

Although not as much in limelight, nurses were among the most valuable crusaders. Often they attended schools and found work in facilities that supported food, drink, and drug regulation. They came from diverse backgrounds, worked with all levels of American society, and encountered numerous health problems among their patients that related to adulterated food and dangerous drugs. Women's organizations realized the potential of nurses to promote pure food, drink, and drugs early in the crusade. Women had become involved in nursing on a large scale during the Civil War through their efforts to relieve the conditions of servicemen in disorderly and unhygienic military hospitals. After the war, nursing became closely associated with social reform as various groups of women established training schools to supply the growing need for nurses in hospitals, clinics, dispensaries, schools, infant welfare stations, and visiting nurses.[22]

In 1880, under the leadership of Sarah Stevenson, Lucy Flower, and Sarah Peck Wright, a group of reform-minded women opened the Illinois Training School to provide nurses first for the Cook County hospital and later for Presbyterian Hospital in Chicago. The need for pure food and the dangers of proprietary medications were part of the curriculum that Sarah Stevenson and other pure food, drink, and drug advocates taught.[23]

The National Temperance Hospital in Chicago, established by N.W.C.T.U. superintendent of Health and Heredity, Dr. Mary Weeks Burnett, also began a nurses training program soon after its opening in 1886. This was a model hospital designed to demonstrate that pure food and good nursing care were more effective in the practice of medicine than the use of alcoholic preparations and potent drugs.[24]

The Philadelphia School for Nurses, a branch of the Supply and Medical Dispensary was another such center. Finding many young women in the city's churches who expressed a desire to help the "sick poor," the administrators offered a free practical nurse program to all of those willing to donate their services to relieve suffering. More than one hundred young women volunteered and were trained by graduate nurses.[25]

Settlement houses, such as the Henry Street Settlement in New York City, under the direction of Lillian D. Wald, became centers for visiting nurse training and deployment. Two of the settlement house nurses, Lina

L. Rogers and her assistant, specialized in the treatment of minor disorders among school children, visited the homes of the children with more serious illnesses, and advised their mothers in treatment and care. The free treatment of colds, sore eyes, skin disorders, and other maladies was most valuable to the mothers. The improved physical condition of the children convinced the New York City Board of Health to engage 10 more trained nurses at $75 a month to look after more than 40 schools in the poor sections of the city.[26]

As historian Susan Armeny has pointed out, Wald, and nurses like Annie Goodrich, who worked at the Henry Street Settlement, came from wealthy families. Often they entered nursing out of a sense of altruism and a desire to accomplish something purposeful in their lives. Other settlement nurses, like Martha Kulberg and Caroline Gull, chose nursing as a career to support themselves and their families. Most of the nurses came from cities and towns, but a few, like Jean Edmonds and Ida Hadden came from farm families.[27]

Nurses managed milk stations that supplied infants of poor families with certified milk. In the summer of 1897, Annie E. Kennedy, a graduate of City Hospital in Rochester, New York, was appointed to the first milk station in Rochester. At that time the city did not have its own milk farm, but dispensed the milk furnished from a herd of cows that was under the supervision of the health department. The milk was brought to the station and either sterilized or pasteurized on the premises.[28]

In addition to the preparation of milk, Kennedy gave advice to mothers about the medical care of their children. At the close of one season, because the advice she gave was not always followed and she had serious misgivings concerning her effectiveness, she considered changing her employment. However, she decided to stay on when she found out that the mothers had taken a deeper interest in the benefits of the station than she had realized. The mothers organized and as a result of their activism, the health department established three substations, and by 1902 increased the number to five.[29]

In 1903 the Health Department of Rochester assumed control of the milk farm, located about three miles out of the city, where 15 cows were kept. Kennedy's duties were extended to include superintending the cleanliness of the stables, cows, and men during the milking process. This required her to rise at four o'clock every morning, rain or shine. The strainers and all utensils used in the substations had to be sterilized and ready for use as soon as needed. About one hundred quarts of milk were sent out daily from this farm, in four, five, seven, and eight ounce bottles. Washing and sterilizing bottles became a daily ritual at these stations.[30]

Visiting nurses were among the most notable pure food, drink, and drug crusaders. The visiting nurse program grew out of the compassion of religious groups and women's organizations for the poor. Individual congregations collected donations to hire suitable women in need of employment to visit and care for the poor in the patient's home. Often, women's clubs and temperance unions adopted similar programs. The King's Daughters, a philanthropic, nondenominational religious organization, trained and employed a large number of poor women as visiting nurses, as did Associated Charities and the Ladies' Benevolent Societies. In 1903 the Ladies' Benevolent Society of Charleston, South Carolina, reported assisting 132 sick persons, of which 10 were chronic cases, one 99 years old. In 1906 they assisted 1,983 persons. During the same year, one of their visiting nurses, Anna D. Banks, with the help of a part-time assistant, visited 168 persons, under the direction of 30 physicians.[31]

Throughout the South, similar opportunities opened for needy women. Women's clubs and temperance unions contributed sizable grants. Many young women without funds to educate themselves applied for these stipends. Such training schools for black women were scattered in various communities throughout a number of states. Women's organizations established schools in the mountains of North Carolina and Tennessee where poor girls learned the basics of an elementary education. Here, they also came into contact with more affluent ways of living than they had experienced in the past, acquired the skills of nursing, and found employment in sanitariums for nervous and tubercular patients.[32]

Nurses trained in such schools were taught to direct patients away from proprietary medications and to encourage their families to provide them with unadulterated and nutritious food. Associated with or influenced by women's clubs and temperance unions, visiting nurses often joined the pure food, drink, and drug organizations, left pure food and drug literature in the patients' homes, and recruited poor women to the cause.[33]

As illustrated by the careers of Helen Miller and Marian McBride, working for pure food, drink, and drugs was a part of the professional activities of home economists. They included the study of how to avoid adulterated foods and dangerous drugs in the courses of land-grant colleges and high schools where many of them taught.

Ellen Richards, probably the most prominent home economist of the time, served on the faculty of the Massachusetts Institute of Technology and took the opportunity to further the pure food, drink, and drug cause on many fronts. She edited *Home Sanitarian* a manual for housekeepers that, among other subjects, apprised homemakers of products that contained adulterants. She took part in fairs and exhibitions that encouraged manufacturers to improve the quality of their products. She supported health boards and assisted women's clubs and temperance unions that worked toward regulation. She wrote many articles on the subject, such as the one published by *Science* magazine that advocated legislation against food adulteration.[34]

Marion Talbot worked on the staff of the *Home Sanitarian* before she went to the University of Chicago in 1892 as dean of women and assistant professor of sanitary science. By 1895 she was a professor in the new Department of Household Administration and was working with the pure food and drug forces in Chicago Women's Club.[35]

Political activism often required the services of attorneys. Judith Ellen Foster, Iowa attorney and suffragist, advised the W.C.T.U. in legal and legislative matters until she broke with Frances Willard. Attorney Sophia Breckenridge was a member of the University of Chicago Department of Household Administration, where she taught home economics with an emphasis on family legal problems. She became dean of the Chicago School of Civics and Philanthropy, later annexed into the University of Chicago. She resided part time at Hull House where she studied and conducted research.

Breckenridge became one of the foremost social reformers of Chicago. At the instigation of the Illinois Consumers' League, Breckenridge and Harriet Van der Vaart, secretary of the Illinois League and member of the National Consumers' League Food Investigation Committee, were appointed special, impartial state agents to investigate food conditions in Illinois. Their appointment covered all food trades, including canneries and stockyards. They had access to the stockyards — to all of their buildings, to the payroll and employee records, to the holding, slaughtering, and processing areas, and to all of the industries in the complexes. Working in the yards and canneries for more than one year, these agents prepared data for a report to the legislature and consumers. The results of their investigation were published in the annual report of the Illinois State Bureau of Labor Statistics and their recommendations became the basis for regulative legislation.[36]

Attorney and Populist lecturer Mary Elizabeth Lease, "the Red Dragon of Kansas," famous for her admonition to farmers to "raise less corn and more hell," was a prohibitionist and the organizing president of the Hypatia Club in Wichita, which worked for pure food, drink, and drugs in Kansas.[37]

Social workers furthered the crusade with remarkable fidelity. Social workers continually ran into problems related to adulterated food, drinks, and dangerous drugs. The Henry Street facility in New York City was not the only settlement house that worked to improve the quality of foods and drugs. Mary E. McDowell, who worked for scientific instruction in schools, encountered various problems related to drug abuse, and fought against meat contamination in the Chicago stockyards. The editor of the *Federation Bulletin* wrote that McDowell had "done a noble service for the women of her day." She cited one of McDowell's most notable contributions as the "whole incident of her work in Chicago," which illustrated "what can be done by consummate greed on one hand, as it works with a will which seems absolutely irresistible," and, on the other hand, what could be accomplished "to set at defiance even such unimagined powers of greed and selfishness as ran the Chicago stock yard and packing interests."[38]

A number of women and men interns worked with them. Upton Sinclair resided near Hull House while researching material for *The Jungle*. Various settlement houses in the South engaged in similar activities. Jane Addams urged women everywhere to participate in pure food, drink, and drug activism. She warned women that they could not expect protective regulation until legislators understood the determination of American women to protect their families against adulterated food and dangerous drugs.[39]

Women writers and journalists became caught up in the crusade. Jane Croly, who formed the Sorosis Club when she was excluded from a press conference because she was a women, expressed considerable interest and gave support to the women who attacked the slaughterhouses in New York City. Louisa and Mary Poppenheim, and Ida Lining, publishers and editors of *The Keystone*, became the Southern links with the Pure Food Committee of the G.F.W.C. Women journalists for newspapers in Atlanta and Montgomery devoted columns to pure food, drink, and drugs.[40]

Mary A. Livermore, journalist, suffragist, editor of *Women's Journal*, a major organ of the women's movement, and W.C.T.U. organizer, supported pure food, drink, and drug measures. Mary Alden Ward and Helen A. Winslow, editors for the *Federation Bulletin*, wrote and published pure food, drink, and drug articles that rivaled the tirades of the muckrakers; writers for the *Union Signal*, *Club Woman*, together with women's journals and magazines throughout the country, advocated forcing manufactures and processors to be more careful and honest in producing and advertising their products.[41]

Sarah A. Evans, literary editor of the Portland *Evening Journal*, was chairman of the Press Committee of the G.F.W.C. At the same time, she served as president of the Oregon Federation. Her reputation as a model homemaker and an avid promoter of the state pure food bill, led to a position as food inspector for the city of Portland.[42]

Women in various other professions also participated in the crusade. Pharmacists, such as Ida Roby of Chicago, joined several departments of narcotics and advised patients to avoid addictive medications. Chemists, like Mary E. Pennington of Philadelphia, conducted research on food and provided assays of proprietary medications and foods to women's clubs. Factory and food inspectors enforced state and local legislation. Pastors, such as the Reverend Anna Shaw and Antoinette Blackwell, Methodist preacher Jenny F. Willing of Chicago, and the Reverend Caroline Bartlett Crane of Kalamazoo, Michigan, preached the gospel of pure food, drink, and drugs. Legislators, like Colorado's Martha Conine, introduced regulatory bills into state legislatures.[43]

Librarians made significant contributions to the cause. One universal method of reaching the public was to place pure food, drink, and drug literature in libraries, to hold meetings in libraries, and to enlist librarians in the crusade.

The activities of these women illustrate the diversity of reformers, but only a small sample of those who participated in the crusade. Because they were addressing a consumer issue that affected every person in the country, women from a wide variety of social, occupational, ethnic, and religious backgrounds were able to cooperate across the barriers in their society that industrialization had intensified. The unity they displayed was one of the remarkable features of the pure food, drink, and drug crusade.

PART III:
SECURING THE ACT

From about 1902, until federal food, drink, and drug legislation was passed by the United States Congress in 1906, the crusaders faced an additional challenge. They had organized as consumers. They had formed alliances with public health officials and bureaucrats. They had committed enough legislators to vote for a federal law. Their remaining hurdle was to bring consideration of effective legislation onto the floors of the Senate and the House.

They encountered seemingly insurmountable opposition. In the White House, Theodore Roosevelt sympathized with their cause in principle, but he considered pure food, drink, and drug regulation one of the "unrealizable ideals" of "radical" reformers. In the Senate, the Republican political leadership — Henry Cabot Lodge, from Massachusetts, Nelson W. Aldrich and Thomas C. Platt from New York, Orville H. Platt, from Connecticut, and Hernando DeSoto Money, from Mississippi — prevented consideration of any effective pure food, drink, and drug bills. These senators were the center of a political machine that was elected by state caucus to defend the business interests of their respective states. Members of the House of Representatives, elected by popular vote, were more responsive to the pulse of the people, but the congressmen were subject to the iron rule of Speaker Joseph G. (Uncle Joe) Cannon from Illinois, who, like the senate leadership, opposed all legislation intended to control manufacturing and marketing. Bills came to a vote in Congress only through the auspices of those congressional leaders. Parliamentary procedure dictated that bills be considered in order. In each session the congressional leaders made sure that food, drink, and drug legislation fell far enough down the list to prevent its coming to the floor. Consideration of any bill ahead of calendar order required unanimous consent.

Overcoming this obstacle entailed securing legislators dynamic enough to advance strong bills and powerful enough to protect those bills against weakening amendments. In addition, it required conducting an intense publicity campaign to place irresistible pressure on the Republican leadership. The ability of organized women to establish a working relationship with the press, the members of Congress, and the federal bureaucracy was crucial to accomplishing their goal. Partly by chance, but mostly by design, the women crusaders were able to muster the resources necessary to secure the legislation.

10

Breakthrough: Partners in the Pure Food, Drink, and Drug Crusade

"In this crusade for the family we begin to find a glorious company: 'ministers of grace' not only, but legislators, magazine writers and observant people of all classes."[1]

An examination of the contributions of other participants in the crusade, from the women's point of view, reveals that the battle for pure food, drink, and drugs was more of a team effort than has been depicted in other accounts. Working alone, no single person, group, or association was strong enough to secure regulatory legislation. Women's organizations did not have adequate political power, and other groups did not have the organization and public support. Reaching their common objective required the collaboration of a number of forces, many of which emerged in response to the activism of associated women.

By 1903 the women crusaders had organized enough public demand for national regulation to attract a combination of forces that helped to bring an effective bill before the United States Congress. A few influential journalists, bureaucrats, politicians, and businessmen began to promote the pure food, drink, and drug cause to further their ambitions and interests. Each group functioned independently at first, but eventually joined forces with the coalition of crusaders within women's organizations who were accelerating their push for federal pure food, drink, and drug legislation. In response, the opposing interests gathered for an all-out battle. Drug companies, brewers, distillers, meat packers, and food manufacturers pressured congressional leaders to protect their interests and retained million-dollar-a-year attorneys to argue their cases before congressional committees.

The Muckrakers

Beginning in 1903, investigative journalism became an influential factor in securing federal regulation. Previously, magazines, such as *Popular Science Monthly, Outlook, Christian Advocate*, and a few trade journals, had carried occasional articles condemning food adulteration and dangerous drugs, but it was not until editor Edward William Bok began his tirade against proprietary medications in the *Ladies' Home Journal* that the exposé reached muckraking proportions. In 1870, at age seven, Bok had immigrated with his family to the United States from Holland. Settling in Brooklyn, New York, Bok's father found work as a translator for the Western Union Telegraph Company, then owned by Jay Gould. Bok's mother took in boarders, while Bok and his older brother helped with household chores and hustled for any odd jobs they could find.[2]

Although Bok did not admit that Gould influenced his passion for financial success, Gould took an interest in Bok's business career. According to his autobiography, *The Americanization of Edward Bok*, Bok drew his entrepreneurial inspirations from accounts of poor boys who became industrial giants through hard work, thrift, and innovation. At age 13 he left school to become an office boy at Western Union for $6.25 a week. To save bus fare, he walked five miles to work and went without lunch to buy books. He established contact with prominent people by writing to request autographs and advice. Emerson was one of his heroes. Against the wishes of his mother, who wanted him to become a preacher, and following the advice of Gould, he decided to become a journalist. He learned the trade working as a stenographer with the Henry Holt publishing house, then, at age 18, set up his own business. The Bok Syndicate Press achieved instant success by circulating "Bab's Babble," a woman's gossip column in the *New York Star*. With a syndicate of 90 newspapers, Bok engaged a popular novelist, Ella Wheeler Wilcox, to write the column under her own name, and solicited enough contributions from leading women writers to fill an entire page of women's topics.[3]

Bok's woman's page led to a position with Scribner's and, eventually, to an offer to become the editor of *Ladies' Home Journal*, a magazine founded by the wife of the publishing mogul, Cyrus Curtis, and holding over 400,000 subscriptions in 1890. Bok hired an "expert in every line of feminine endeavor" to enrich the articles with answers to letters that were sent to them for advice. These experts included qualified doctors and nurses who wrote medical information for regular departments of the magazine. For problems too delicate to print, he engaged Mrs. Lyman Abbott, wife of the famous preacher, to advise women through personal correspondence. He reserved the front page for his own editorial domain. In addition, he was the first editor to devote large sums of money to advertising upcoming feature articles. Such innovations added a million readers to the magazine's adherents and propelled the *Journal* to a position as one of the leading women's magazines of the time.[4]

By today's standards, it is difficult to understand the magazine's popularity. Its columns were excessively instructive and paternalistic. Bok wrote down to women. He disapproved of woman suffrage because he felt that American women were not ready to exercise the privilege intelligently. He attacked women's organizations and stereotyped women as ignorant, prudish, and in need of guidance. In his autobiography, Bok admitted that although he did not dislike women, neither did he like them. They had never interested him. He knew little of their likes and needs, and he had no desire, even as the editor of the *Journal*, to know them better, or to seek to understand them. What he did understand was that his success hinged on addressing personal issues that confronted women in their daily lives. He hired women to accomplish that goal by employing them to write columns that interested women. Perhaps his attitude toward women explains the way in which he approached the pure food, drink, and drug crusade.[5]

In November 1902, the editor of *American Medicine* had commented upon a paper about patent medicine that was presented to the Colorado Medical Society. The editor wondered why the W.C.T.U. did not oppose the alcohol in patent medicines. Spending so much energy in opposing beer, while paying no attention to proprietary medications which contained a higher alcohol content, seemed absurd to her. Martha Allen, of the N.W.C.T.U. Department of Medical Temperance, answered the criticism in a letter that outlined the over-twenty-year W.C.T.U. crusade against dangerous drugs and enclosed a copy of her book and a number of pamphlets. *American Medicine* published her letter, praised the W.C.T.U. for its pure food, drink, and drug work, and said that the leaflet "Patent Medicines" should be read by "every citizen of the United States, especially every legislator."[6]

The matter did not drop there. The question of why the W.C.T.U. did not fight the patent medicine "enemy" appeared in a number of medical journals and periodicals. Allen wrote a reply to each and sent copies of the "Patent Medicines" leaflet to every medical publication in the country, after which a number of comments favorable to the W.C.T.U. crusade appeared in print.[7]

Maud Banfield, one of the nurses who wrote a health column for the *Ladies' Home Journal* was among those who had picked up on the articles in *American Medicine*, repeating the question, "Why does not the W.C.T.U. oppose alcoholic patent medicines?" She neglected to mention Mrs. Allen's letter to the editor of *American Medicine*. Allen wrote the *Journal*, asking for a correction, but the letter was not answered, nor was a retraction printed. Instead, Edward Bok wrote a letter to W.C.T.U. headquarters in Evanston, Illinois, asking for everything the W.C.T.U. had published on the subject. Martha Allen sent him copies of her book and the pamphlets written by herself and others concerning the subject, accompanied by a letter explaining the W.C.T.U. crusade against proprietaries. Always quick to grasp opportunity, Bok recognized the potential of the W.C.T.U. research in launching himself into the center of the exposé in competition with his main rival, Sam McClure, and his staff of investigative reporters — Ida Tarbell, Lincoln Steffens, Ray Stannard Baker, and others. Bok borrowed generously from the W.C.T.U. publications, but neither he, nor any of his journalists gave the W.C.T.U. credit. Quite the opposite. Although he knew he was attacking the W.C.T.U. without justification, he repaid Allen's generosity with another blast at the W.C.T.U. for not directing its efforts toward proprietary medicine.[8]

In his disclosure of the ingredients of Dr. Pierce's Favorite Prescription, Bok tripped and fell into the same trap that caught Martha Allen several years previously. As Bok described the incident, he "slipped a cog in his machinery." Among other material supplied by Allen, he published the 1886 Massachusetts State Board of Health analysis of 27 medicines by name and revealed their ingredients. Dr. Pierce's Favorite Prescription, he claimed, contained digitalis, opium, and 17 percent alcohol. Most of the alcohol had been eliminated from the Pierce formula after the Massachusetts assay. Pierce sued the Curtis Publishing Company for libel, recovered $16,000 in damages, and forced Bok to run a retraction.[9]

This misadventure did not stop Bok. He hired a young attorney, Mark Sullivan, as an investigative reporter to research the marketing practices of proprietary medication companies, and continued his exposés in a series of articles running from September 1904 to January 1905. Bok avoided naming Dr. Pierce's remedy again, but referred frequently to "favorite patent medicines," contending that proprietary medications fell into two classes, "absolutely worthless," and "absolutely dangerous."[10]

Following one of Allen's suggestions, and with the investigating skills of Sullivan, Bok exposed Lydia Pinkham as a fraud. Beside a reproduction of a recent advertisement which indicated that Miss Pinkham would answer personally all letters for private advice, the *Journal* printed a clear photograph of Lydia Pinkham's gravestone in Pine Grove Cemetery near Lynn, Massachusetts, which revealed that she had died 23 years earlier on May 17, 1883. Bok's article included an assay of the alcohol content of the Pinkham preparations. It also contained interviews with several male employees who admitted that they had read with "profane amusement" the "most intimate details of women's lives" in the confidential correspondence, and had sent back stock answers as their advice.

In an article entitled, "Why 'Patent Medicines' are Dangerous," Bok accused any physician who marketed proprietaries of violating "the highest medical ethics" and "sacrificing his moral right to practice as a physician for mere self-gain as a trader." In "A Diabolical 'Patent Medicine' Story," he illustrated how fraudulent advertising convinced people that they were suffering from diseases they did not have. Again borrowing from Allen's material, the February 1906 issue printed a sample pure food and drug bill for women to send to their state legislators. In other articles, he castigated women for using home medication, becoming addicted to dangerous drugs, and poisoning their families with proprietaries.[11]

Following Bok's instructions, Sullivan wrote to Martha Allen for more assistance and used her information to launch a fresh series of articles against patent medicines under his own byline. One article exposed a number of widely advertised testimonials for patent medicines from senators and congressmen as the scheme of a group of Washington journalists who obtained testimonials by trickery, fraud, and misrepresentation. The article disclosed that the testimonial mill charged $75 for a senator's endorsement, $40 for that of a congressman, and accepted no contract for less than $5,000. Succeeding articles revealed how letter brokers bought and sold requests for medical advice to provide proprietary firms with susceptible victims.[12]

With Martha Allen's help, Sullivan managed to secure a copy of the minutes of a Proprietary Medicine Manufacturing and Dealers Association meeting in which the president, Frank J. Cheney, described how he incorporated a clause in his contracts with magazines and newspapers which canceled their advertising agreement if their state or the federal government passed any law adverse to the proprietary interests. Sullivan included this "red clause" in an article that condemned the power of proprietaries over the news media. After Bok rejected the article, *Collier's Weekly* published it without byline under the title of "The Patent Medicine Conspiracy Against Freedom of the Press."[13]

Sullivan's revelation was not new to *Collier's*. In a previous issue, a *Collier's* article had echoed Bok's criticism of the W.C.T.U. for not exposing the alcohol content of proprietaries. When Martha Allen advised the editor, Norman Hapgood, of the error, he retracted the statement and apologized. One of Allen's comments in her correspondence with Hapgood became the basis for a series of articles in *Collier's*, later republished as a book, entitled *The Great American Fraud*, by Samuel Hopkins Adams. Allen had informed Hapgood that the reason the public did not know more of the W.C.T.U. crusade for pure food and drugs was that the press refused to print anything against the patent medicine trade because of the "red clause."[14]

Adams has been labeled the consummate muckraker. Before he wrote the *American Fraud* series that brought *Collier's* and himself to the forefront of reform, Adams wrote for the *Sun* of New York City and *McClure's Magazine*. His language was far more aggressive and intemperate than any W.C.T.U. member or clubwoman cared to employ.

Adams exposed the names and addresses of no less than 19 nostrum manufacturers, which he categorized as "Brothers in Villainy," and attacked their marketing strategies. "At the very bottom of the noisome pit," he wrote in one article, "crawl the drug habit specialists — scavengers delving amid the carrion of the fraudulent nostrum business. The human wrecks made by the opium and cocaine habits come to them for cure, and are wrung dry of the last drop of blood."[15]

Collier's defended and, in fact, amplified Adams' position. When under attack from the proprietaries, the editor summarized his series, claiming that, although Adams had written bluntly, he had been careful and fair. He had called some of the proprietary medicine dealers "murderers because they were taking their profits at the cost of human lives." Others he designated "merely as thieves" because "no other term described them." Only two suits for libel against the magazine materialized. One was dropped before it came to trial. The makers of Pink Pills for Pale People litigated the other after 1907.[16]

After achieving national attention for his series in *Collier's*, Adams continued to write articles about the subject and promote the cause. As a member of the National Consumers' League Pure Food Committee, he lectured frequently and worked constantly to pave the way for Alice Lakey and other members of the committee to gain access to the press and receive favorable mention in news coverage.[17]

In a less sensational mode, *Woman's Home Companion* writers joined the ranks of journalists that attacked proprietaries. Margaret E. Sangster advised women that the temptation to "spur lagging energy or drive away an attack of nerves by taking a pill or powder" inevitably led to "the last state ... worse than the first." Home economist, Mary Taylor-Ross, offered alternatives to the use of proprietaries. In cooperation with Dr. W. D. Bigelow, chief of the Division of Foods, Bureau of Chemistry, and in typical muckraking tradition, Henry Irving Dodge wrote a series of three articles intended to "strike a blow at the very heart" of the national food adulteration "crime," delineating "How the Baby Pays the Tax" for contaminated milk and baby foods, how the Bureau of Chemistry microscopes uncovered graft, and the "poison squad" exposed the dangers of preservatives, and how "tricksters" doctored alcoholic beverages.[18]

A number of other popular magazines printed drug exposés. Articles dealing with drug abuse and the facts about nostrums appeared in *Popular Science Monthly*. *Nation* carried a report of the crusade against proprietary medications. *Outlook* published an article that showed how false advertising attracted customers for dangerous drugs.[19]

A few large newspapers started to address the problem. Louise Purington reported that the crusaders were "steadily moving toward better things." She felt fortunate that at least some of the "leading dailies" were "keeping pace" with boards of health, public health associations, social science and household economic clubs, and civic clubs, and the Woman's Christian Temperance Union.[20]

New York Times reporters began following the fight for federal food, drink, and drug regulation about 1903. Consistently sympathetic toward public health issues, the *Times* became one of the leading newspapers in the country to support the crusaders. Between February 1903 and December 1904, the paper ran numerous articles exposing addiction, the dangers of using proprietary medications, and medical fraud. They covered congressional and Senate hearings, Harvey Wiley's food experiments, the International Food Congress in St. Louis, and meat investigations. They accused physicians and fakirs of collusion in bilking their patients. They charged the Proprietary Association of forming a trust-like organization to perpetuate fraud, and food processors of poisoning the public. In 1905 and 1906 they reported the progress of food, drink, and drug legislation in Congress, criticized opponents of the bill, and applauded when the bill passed.[21]

In the June 8, 1905, issue, a *Times* editor asked, "What is the matter with this Republican House of Representatives? Do they on the whole believe it to be good party policy to leave the cheats and swindlers, the poisoners and the adulterators unmolested?" He placed the blame for lack of progress in pure food and drug legislation on a combination of giving in to the pressure of a powerful lobby and to half hearted support. He accused William P. Hepburn, sponsor of the bill, of offering only "lamb-like resistance" to opposition and Speaker Joseph Cannon of "in no wise" using his influence to protect "his countrymen against swindling and adulteration." According to the editor, pressure from "Packingtown ... reduced this powerful officer of the House [Cannon] to a condition of infantile nervelessness in respect to the Pure Food bill."[22]

The Federal Bureau of Chemistry

In 1903 Harvey Washington Wiley, chief of the Bureau of Chemistry in the U. S. Department of Agriculture, began to attract widespread public attention. As his biographer, Oscar Anderson, has shown, throughout his career Wiley had been interested in food properties and standards. As chief chemist of the Bureau, he supervised investigations of foods and their adulterants. Legislators consulted him and food congresses retained him as an expert witness, but the press of other considerations in his profession and his concept of professional proprieties limited his participation in the pure food and drug crusade until about 1902.[23]

Typical of most historians, Robert Crunden depicts Wiley in much the same light as Anderson viewed him — as the chief exponent of the pure food, drink, and drug bill. Crunden's analysis is correct in noting that Wiley was the intermediary between congressmen and the industrial interests and in depicting Wiley as a chemical fundamentalist, primarily interested in the ethics of pure food. Crunden errs, however, in giving the impression that Wiley aroused indifferent public opinion. The evidence previously presented here indicates that the public was already demanding congressional action before Wiley entered the public arena.[24]

About 1902, the growing public outcry for food and drug regulation prompted Wiley to focus his attention on a national campaign for pure food as his lasting contribution to society. During a summer trip to Europe in 1902, he conceived the idea of starting his attack with an eye-catching investigation of the effects of preservatives on human digestion and health, and in November he began to implement his plan. The experiments involved setting up a kitchen and dining room in the basement of the chemistry building of the Department of Agriculture, recruiting 12 healthy young male employees to undergo a series of tests, and undertaking extensive laboratory measurements. Members of Wiley's test group pledged to take no food except from the "hygienic table." After a "fore period" of determining the quantity of food necessary to maintain body weight at a constant level, the volunteers were fed foods preserved with boric acid, their body excretions were weighed and analyzed, and they were given frequent physical examinations to determine the effects. An "after period" restored their health to normal levels. The results confirmed Wiley's hypothesis that "both boric acid and borax, when continuously administered in small doses for a long period, or when given in large quantities for a short period, created disturbances of appetite, of digestion, and of health." In 1903 and again in 1904 Wiley repeated the experiment with other preservatives — salicylic, sulphurous, and benzoic acid; formaldehyde; and alum.[25]

Critics challenged both Wiley's methods and his interpretations of the data, but Wiley achieved the public attention he desired. From the first newspaper announcements that Wiley had recruited volunteers to receive free board for doing nothing but eating food that, at times, would contain commonly used preservatives, the newspapers followed his progress in a humorous vein. George Rothwell Brown of the *Washington Post* was his main publicist.

To begin with, the press accounts were reasonably accurate and based on interviews with the Bureau's chemists, but when the reports became so rash that they threatened to undermine the Bureau's reputation in the scientific community, Secretary of Agriculture James Wilson forbade Wiley further contact with newspapermen. Without sources, Brown invented humorous accounts that were repeated in scattered newspapers across the country.[26]

Regardless of Wiley's professed humiliation when he read about preservatives as "poisons" and his volunteers as the "poison squad," his public discomfort did not interfere with his private pleasure in his new popularity. Reportedly, women wrote for information when they read that volunteers developed a beautiful pink and white complexion from taking borax. Minstrels composed ditties about the poison squad. Speaking and writing articles on adulterated food and testifying as an expert at congressional hearings became major responsibilities of his position. The moniker "old Borax," which senators coined for him, was less to his liking. For better or for worse, the experiments launched his reputation as a leading pure food expert.[27]

Despite Wiley's flamboyant bid for recognition, most women crusaders welcomed the pure food and drug publicity, but many held reservations about his emphasis. Relying on results of his limited investigations, Wiley concluded that the issue was not so much that adulteration injured the health of the consumer, but that it constituted widespread fraud. For him, the problem was mainly ethical. As he reiterated on several occasions, "I am not one of the people who think there is a very great increase in the attendance at the graveyard due to the practice of food adulteration. In other words, the injury to public health, in my opinion, is the least important question in the subject of food adulteration, and it is one which should be considered last of all. The real evil of food adulteration is deception of the consumer." Women crusaders believed the opposite. They contended that adulterated food was a definite threat to the nation's health and that adulterated drink and drugs were a major part of the problem.[28]

The W.C.T.U. and clubwomen were concerned about Wiley's neglect of drug adulteration and proprietary medicine abuses. As a physician, Wiley opposed both, but, because he felt adulterated food affected more people, he considered the question of food fraud more important. It was not until March 1903 that the Bureau of Chemistry equipped a drug laboratory and delegated its research to Lyman F. Kebler, M.D., a Philadelphia chemist from the pharmaceutical firm of Smith, Kline, and French. Retained at first to study the properties of chemicals and crude medicinal plants, Kebler became involved in analyzing nostrums and cooperating in the fight against drug abuse. Wiley left the entire direction of the drug laboratory to Kebler and did not keep abreast of developments. When he accepted an invitation to speak on drug adulteration at the Society of Medical Jurisprudence in New York, he wrote to Kebler to ask for printed matter and suggestions. He found it necessary to consult with Kebler when he spoke on the same subject on other occasions.[29]

Wiley's regard for certain business interests disturbed the women crusaders. They found Wiley too willing to compromise principle for exigency. They were not always sure of where he stood. At one moment he claimed to represent consumer interests, and at the next he seemed to support "practically the whole of every trade concerned." As his biographer observed, Wiley represented "a heterogeneous army bound together in a curious amalgam of self-interest and principle." He served as "a coordinator who sought by compromise and concession to keep his strange alliance intact." On one side, the leaders of reform expected him to support effective legislation; on the other, industry found him receptive to amendments that weakened food and drug legislation. On most occasions he maintained a moderate approach, refusing to become an alarmist. He preferred a law that fell short of consumer ideals to no law at all.[30]

His deal with the National Association of Retail Grocers was one case in point. State laws had interfered with what grocers could sell and held them libel for adulterated and dangerous goods. Grocers feared that federal legislation would create an additional hardship for them. Wiley traded a promise that he would use his influence to introduce federal regulation that applied only to manufacturers in exchange for their support. Women felt that retailers should bear at least some of the responsibility for what they sold.[31]

His efforts to calm opposition from proprietary medicine and whiskey rectifiers provide other examples. To avoid jeopardizing the bill, he counseled Heyburn to eliminate clauses that applied to proprietary remedies. To appease the rectifiers, he recommended allowing certain adulterations in whiskey and deleting the provisions that required ingredients, processes, and storage details to be listed on the label, as long as the blends were distinguished from straight whiskey. The consumer advocates felt that Wiley had sold out to the proprietary medicine and whiskey interests.[32]

Another problem associated with trying to work with Wiley was that he tried to channel the activities of women's organizations into a mode he visualized for them. He resented the "new ideas, rhetoric, directions, combinations, and configurations" constantly erupting out of the "unconfined" enthusiasm and energy of the women's crusade. Wiley envisioned using women's organizations to disseminate his propaganda, to lobby U.S. congressmen, and to strengthen the Bureau. Women expected a cooperative alliance in which all of the forces for pure food, drink, and drugs drew upon each other's resources and strengthened the cause — the kind of alliance that Silena M. Heiman, president of the Tennessee W.C.T.U. described as "the variety that can heartily and actively cause organizations to work with each other toward a common end without either suffering from absorption."[33]

Wiley found Lakey and her associates inexhaustibly innovative, repeatedly proposing new ideas, pestering the Bureau for information, and going out on their own without consulting him. Lakey offended Wiley in 1904 by publishing and distributing an excerpt from one of his letters, commending clubwomen for their pure food activities and encouraging them to expand their efforts for regulation, at the Louisiana Purchase Exposition without his permission.

Actually, Lakey did not view his communications to her as private, but addressed to her as the representative of the Cranford Women's Club. Although she could not see anything wrong with publishing the letter and could not understand why it should subject Wiley to criticism, she apologized profusely; but Wiley, however, was suspicious of her from then on. She persisted in her requests for information, advice, and to have him speak at various women's meetings, often with limited results. When he procrastinated sending government information, Lakey obtained the information from his associate, Dr. Willard D. Bigelow.

On one occasion, when Wiley declined an invitation to speak at the Cranford Women's Club, she invited Dr. Ernst J. Lederle from New York. Yet, throughout the drive for food and drug regulation, they maintained a lively, if sometimes constrained correspondence, in which she asked Wiley's advice and sometimes he gave it. She conditioned herself to ignore his rebuffs. Eventually, he came to recognize the value of her contributions.[34]

One of Wiley's greatest personal weaknesses was his insistence on preserving credit for himself. This led him to disregard the contributions of other crusaders. It hampered the progress of food and drug legislation by antagonizing state chemists and health officials, and frustrated women whose efforts began earlier, and were more comprehensive, more contiguous, and more energetic than his own. He enjoyed the reputation of being the "father" of pure food and drugs, took delight in claiming that consumers were indifferent to food adulteration before he aroused public opinion, avoided any suggestion that he had espoused a "women's issue," and chose not to share credit for the initiation and growth of the crusade with "organized motherhood" or women's clubs. Years later, he wrote in his autobiography that "there seemed to be a distressing apathy in the public mind relative to these glaring evils. It took many years of education on the part of my bureau before ... public opinion swung in behind the passage and enforcement of a general food and drugs law." Mary Hinman Abell, a home economist, who wrote a food column for the *Delineator*, thought that Wiley was exploiting the pure food, drink, and drug issue "to build himself a department" and that women's organizations were wrong in contributing to his efforts.[35]

Many women did not appreciate his wit, particularly when it lampooned women. He was fond of composing satirical verse, often at the expense of the feelings of others. One example, which women who were trying to establish dignity in their professions and working for pure food, drinks, and drugs found more offensive than clever, appeared in the Boston *Herald* about October 19, 1906, and, in Wiley's words, referred to "ladies in drug stores":

Feminine Pharmacy
There in the corner pharmacy,
This lithesome lady lingers,
And patent pills and philters true
Are fashioned by her fingers.

Her phiz behind the soda font
Is often seen in summer
How sweetly foams the soda fiz
When you receive it from her.

When mixing belladonna drops
With tincture of lobelia,
And putting up prescriptions
She's fairer than Ophelia.

Each poison in its proper place,
Each potion is her chalice,
Her daedel fingers are so deft
They call her digitalis.[36]

The Politicians

In 1903, the crusaders for pure food, drink, and drugs derived an unexpected boost from the appointment of Weldon Brinton Heyburn, freshman senator from Idaho, to replace Porter J. McCumber, as chairman of the Committee on Manufactures. At first, the pure food, drink, and drug advocates were dismayed. They had every reason to believe that

Heyburn would block any pure food, drink, and drug legislation referred to his committee. Heyburn had a reputation for being a straight-line Republican and an ally of the "Old Guard" that opposed progressive reform in Congress. Their fears were unfounded. As it turned out, Heyburn was a conspicuous, articulate, and capable pure food, drink, and drug advocate whose dedication and determination proved essential to bringing the bill to a Senate vote in 1906.[37]

Heyburn was born in Delaware County, Pennsylvania, on May 23, 1852, to parents of English Quaker descent. After attending public schools, he studied law, civil and mining engineering, metallurgy, and geology at the University of Pennsylvania. In 1876 he was admitted to the bar and began his law practice in Media, Pennsylvania. His interest in mining led him to Leadville, Colorado, then to Wallace, Idaho, where he practiced law, became a judge, invested in mining and lumber ventures, and became active in politics. In 1903 he was elected to the United States Senate and married Gheretien Yeatman of Chester County, Pennsylvania.[38]

An attorney for the timber and banking conglomerates headed by David Eccles in his state, the new senator from Idaho was well-placed in the Committee on Manufactures to keep regulatory legislation from reaching the Senate floor. Considering his opposition to other Progressive issues; from conservation, the direct election of senators, the initiative, referendum, and recall, to the child labor law, and woman suffrage; and his close ties to the Old Guard, the Senate leadership had no more reason than the women to suspect that Heyburn would lead the fight for a pure food, drink, and drug law.[39]

Heyburn's biographer was at a loss to explain his fervor for pure food, drink, and drug regulation. In the absence of other evidence, the biographer felt that despite his loyalty to business interests, in his heart, Heyburn was resolved to do what was right.[40] There is some credence to support such an opinion. Congressman Bartholdt from Missouri called Heyburn a "standpatter" when "asked to go wrong" and "a progressive when progress was in the right direction." In Bartholdt's judgment, Heyburn believed the "high mission of his party to be an instrument for sane progress and reform."[41]

Heyburn gave one explanation for the quirk in his political philosophy in a congressional address. He declared that he had always been "aggressively against proprietary advertisement." To illustrate one of the reasons for his concern, he related an experience:

Some time ago a friend of mine, a very old fellow, had reached the age and condition of dependency. I succeeded in getting him a comfortable pension that would pay his bills for household provisions. Once, when I found he was very poor, I said to his wife, "What are you doing with your pension?" She said, "Don't you know, Mr. Heyburn that it takes at least one-half of that pension for patent medicine?" Then she enumerated the proprietary medications they were taking. Fraudulent newspaper advertisements convinced them that they were the victims of ills that they were not troubled with, and that they could find relief through these different medicines. I am in favor of stopping the advertisements of these nostrums in every paper in the country.[42]

Undoubtedly Heyburn's sympathy for consumers was strengthened by a commitment to the women of Idaho, who enjoyed and exercised full franchise rights. Before the 1902 election, Idaho clubwomen had advised every candidate running for office in their state that women would vote as a block against anyone who did not support pure food and drug legislation. Once committed, Heyburn carried through.[43]

Unlike Wiley, Heyburn approached pure food and drugs from the consumer standpoint; his tactics were rarely conciliatory, and he directed his remarks directly to the heart of the matter. Consistently he described the pure food and drug bill as "a measure to protect the health of the consumer, not to conserve the comfort of the producer." When food retailers stressed the need for amendments to protect business, Heyburn reminded them,

...I should like to call your attention to the fact that all of the discussions we have had before us have been from the standpoint that it is the dealer who is to be protected. I would suggest that the object of this bill is not to protect the dealer. It is to protect the persons who consume the articles. It is against the dealer that we are seeking to protect the purchaser, the consumer.[44]

He reiterated his position to the drug interests:

I would suggest that all of the considerations in respect to the ... bills before us have been presented by the dealers. Now, it is proper that they should be heard and heard fully, and we have been only anxious that they should present every possible phase of this question, but ... I should like very much to hear from those who you represent dealers, the other side of the

> question — the effect that these medicines have upon the users
> of them. They do not affect the man who wraps them, sells
> them, taps the till, and makes the change. They are not delete-
> rious to his health, no matter what they contain. It is the per-
> son who consumes them who is to be protected by this bill. We
> are not trying to protect the jobber against the wholesaler, or
> the retailer against the jobber, or the wholesaler against the
> manufacturer, except as it may be incidentally.[45]

His hard-line approach led the press and his contemporaries to depict Heyburn as egotistical, opinionated, pompous, abrasive, temperamental, "utterly without a sense of humor," unyielding, and unable to take criticism. In turn, Heyburn characterized Senate reporters as "joke sifters" who, "as guests of the State, had no right to make disparaging remarks about senators." At the same time, Heyburn played to the press in his speeches, and reporters applauded his courage, patience, and tenacity in resisting the pressure tactics of opponents of pure food, drink, and drug regulation and in creating opportunities to bring the bill before the Senate.[46]

James R. Mann, congressman from Illinois and member of the Committee on Interstate and Foreign Commerce, became a convincing spokesman for the pure food, drink, and drug bill in the House. Unlike Heyburn, he supported the views of a large constituency of Midwestern Progressives. He advocated protecting the farmer against discriminatory hikes in railroad rates, regulating mergers, social reforms, and later, in 1910, sponsored the Mann Act, that prohibited transporting women across state lines for the purpose of prostitution. He was a strong advocate for food, drink, and drug regulation, but, at the same time, he had to consider the political clout of the Chicago jobbers, manufacturers, and meatpackers. From 1900 to 1904, he proposed placing enforcement in the hands of a food commission appointed by the president. Under Mann's plan, the commissioner would have absolute authority to determine what was harmful and what was not. If the commissioner rejected the product, his decision was not subject to review from any other agency. When he approved a product, it was safe under federal and state law. After Mann's proposal failed, he turned to the Bureau of Chemistry as the next best regulatory agency.[47]

Neither William P. Hepburn of Iowa, chairman of the Committee on Interstate and Foreign Commerce in the House, nor Porter J. McCumber of North Dakota, cosponsor of the bill in the Senate, were as dynamic as

Mann and Heyburn, but their experience with trying to pass pure food, drink, and drug legislation proved invaluable.

Hepburn represented strong agricultural and consumer support in the Midwest for pure food, drink, and drugs, but he was not forceful enough to push the bill to completion. Eager to secure a pure food, drink, and drug law and in an effort to be fair to all parties concerned, he had allowed "special interests" to weaken each of the bills, often losing support from proponents and gaining a reputation for being an easy mark for the opposition.

McCumber represented constituents that demanded federal regulation to protect the strong pure food, drink, and drug statutes that had been written into their constitution when North Dakota became a state. As chairman of the Committee on Manufactures from January 1902 until Heyburn replaced him in 1904, McCumber had introduced a series of bills into the Senate, but powerful opposition kept them from floor consideration. By 1904, both Hepburn and McCumber were wise to the tactics of the opposition, but still wavered in the kind of bill they expected Congress to pass.

The Louisiana Purchase Exposition

The Louisiana Purchase Exposition that opened in St. Louis in May 1904 gave a tremendous boost to the prospects of the pure food, drink, and drug bills. Devised by a congressional decree to celebrate the one hundredth anniversary of the purchase of the Louisiana Territory by holding an exhibition of arts, industries, manufacturers, and the "products of the soil, mine, forest and sea," this gigantic world's fair occupied most of the area now known as Forest Park.

The fair commission invited large organizations to hold conventions and to build exhibits at the fair. Many declined to meet at the Exposition, reasoning that the attractions might pull members away from their meetings and deflect attention away from the issues they wished to address. Among those organizations involved in pure food, drink, and drug reform who accepted the invitation were the General Federation of Women's Clubs, the National Congress of Mothers' Clubs, the International Council of Jewish Women, the Daughters of the American Revolution, the National Society of the Colonial Dames of America, the Woman's Christian Temperance Union, and the National Association of State Dairy and

Food Commissioners. The conventions of each of these organizations were well attended. The leaders expedited business and social affairs in order to allow members time to view the exhibits, to attend the fair events in which they were interested, to interact with the public, to distribute propaganda, and to establish contacts with members of the other organizations.[48]

At their convention, the Dairy and Food Commissioners voted to give official support to the pure food, drink, and drug bill pending in the Senate. Although individual state commissioners — Robert M. Allen of Kentucky, William Frear of Pennsylvania, and Edwin Fremont Ladd of North Dakota, among others — championed strong national legislation, the National Association, as a whole, feared that federal legislation would interfere with state regulations. Moreover, those who were pioneers in the enforcement of state food laws felt that a national food commissioner, chosen from their own ranks and answerable only to the president, would execute the law with greater dispatch, more efficiency, and less interference than the Bureau of Chemistry. By the time they attended the convention at the fair, the reluctant state officials were ready to admit that they could not control the problem without federal assistance and that their concept of a food czar was unpopular. They decided to support the Senate bill as the best method of reaching their public health goals. Uniting the commissioners behind the Senate bill strengthened the crusaders' chain of proficiency and their case for regulation.[49]

In connection with their meeting, Robert M. Allen, secretary of the National Association, with the aid of other state chemists, designed a huge international pure food congress to which they invited scientists, public health officials, manufacturers, distributors, and other interested parties, including Alice Lakey to represent consumers. Their intent was to exhibit safe methods of preservation, discuss practical problems in distribution, expose fraudulent and unfair business practices, illustrate methods of detecting adulteration, and determine the most effective means of regulation.[50]

Marian McBride and other pure food, drink, and drug advocates were dubious of the outcome. The 1898 and 1900 food congresses had provided manufacturers an opportunity to emasculate food and drug bills, stimulated bitter debates, pitted manufacturers against their rivals, and sharpened opposition to regulation.

The 1904 pure food and drug congress proved to be no exception. Adopting firm positions in favor of regulating preservatives and whiskey solidified hostilities. Suggesting that processors show the need for preservatives and list the amount of each preservative used on the label validated the fears of food firms. Setting standards of quality for alcoholic beverages and requiring labeling to apprise the consumer of age, place, and method of manufacture heightened the antagonism of the whiskey rectifiers. Questioning the safety of baking powders triggered heated exchanges between the alum and the cream-of-tartar baking powder companies. The result was that the associations representing these interests withdrew what little support they had given the bill in the past.[51]

The National Association of State Dairy and Food Commissioners' exhibit was a main attraction at the fair. The commissioners grouped their pure food, drink, and drug displays together in a two-acre area in the center of the agricultural section. Ella Hoes (Mrs. Arthur Courtenay) Neville stated that no exhibit at the fair was of more interest to women. Food value charts, analyses, and examples of preservation techniques, coloring matter, and fictitious labeling warned women about the nature of the food they fed their families. Chemists demonstrated household tests to enable housewives to determine the presence of harmful substances. Charts illustrated what protection women could expect from the various state agencies against the "insidious attack" of adulterated food and drugs. Various manufacturers displayed their products, but not under trade labels, to illustrate how food could be processed under sanitary conditions and without harmful preservatives. Despite the size of the distilling industry, whiskey exhibits were banned from the fair. R. M. Allen wrote that the B. I. B. [bottled in bond] people accused him of being unfair because he would not permit their "fat men, owl signs, and trade literature to be exhibited," nor their trade representatives to display their wares.[52]

Paul Pierce, superintendent of the food exhibits and editor of the Chicago magazine *What to Eat*, stated that the plan and scope of the "unequaled and matchless agricultural" exhibits made him feel "like throwing his hat in the air and shouting." Mark Sullivan observed visitors by the thousands filing by the food manufacturers displays, then pausing at the pure food booths to study a number of the same cans and bottles displayed with a placard naming the dangerous substances used in their coloring and preservation. Silk and woolen swatches that had been colored with aniline dyes extracted from artificially colored food attracted intense scrutiny. Americans who had studied the colors of healthy and diseased human tissue in scientific instruction classes experienced acute distress when they visualized what effect the dyes might have on their internal organs. According to Sullivan, the average visitor to the fair "examined the display with intentness and minuteness, and passed on with a readiness to listen favorably to any agitator" who advocated government regulation.[53]

Robert Allen wrote, "State legislatures, delegations from women's clubs, newspaper and magazine writers and editors flocked to the exhibit. Some of the food manufacturers considered getting injunctions against us and against the management of the fair, but decided this would only increase public interest."[54]

The exhibit made a significant contribution to the pure food and drug cause. Several firms agreed to discontinue the use of colors and false labels after their products appeared on the display of adulterated goods. Requests from every section of the country for reports, information concerning the adulteration of foods, and model state food regulation laws indicated a widespread public interest. As a result of the exhibit, the City of St. Louis added a food inspection section to their health department and employed the chemist in charge of the exhibit to head the city's enforcement agencies.[55]

The Opposition

Transcripts of the 1904 House and Senate committee hearings on pure food, drink, and drug legislation clarify the positions of the opposition. Far from supporting the legislation as a means of controlling competition, as various historians have suggested, the involved business interests initially opposed the law, then tried to offset its provisions when they realized that the public demanded protective legislation. Wiley observed that the legislation had a "peculiar history. The agitation ... was started at first solely by the consuming interest." The first bills were "promoted by the Grange and by the consumers and by the people at large." Gradually, as manufacturers became aware that federal intervention was imminent, the opposition intensified and became more subtle.[56]

By the time the Senate Committee on Manufactures convened its hearings on January 6, 1904, consumer agitation and public opinion had convinced the affected businesses that a pure food law was inevitable. They retained attorneys to defend their interests and appointed agents to propose amendments that would exempt them from rigorous regulation.

Opposition to the bill fell into three categories — opposition to the principle of federal regulation, opposition to some of its provisions, and opposition to the methods of enforcement and selection of enforcement officials.

Opposition to the principle of federal regulation was based upon broad constitutional issues of the role of government, the rights of states, and free trade. Opponents argued that the bill was unconstitutional, that it would create a precedence for transferring the power of states to the federal government, and that it would restrict industrial development.

Opposition to specific provisions of the bill came mostly from industries that stood to be regulated if the bill became law. Few of those who testified at the hearing were willing to admit that they objected to eliminating harmful ingredients, but they argued that certain provisions were unfair to their specific industry.

Concern for methods of enforcing the bill centered around how the evidence for prosecution would be collected, how the standards for adulteration should be set, and how to define potential court decisions. Many industrialists and professionals considered the Department of Agriculture to be the wrong agency to set standards and feared that the proposed legislation did not protect them against unfair charges and indiscriminate prosecution. They felt that committees from their own ranks were more capable of deciding who should be regulated, what offenses should be covered, and how violations should be controlled.

Alexander J. Wedderburn, still secretary of the National Pure Food and Drug Congress, notified the concerned interests of the hearings and sent them copies of the bill that they had approved for presentation to Congress during their pure food, drink, and drug convention in 1898 to compare with the new bill that was introduced into the 1903 United States Congress by Hepburn in the House and Heyburn in the Senate. Wedderburn advised them to state their objections to the changes in writing, or to attend the hearings in person. All of the parties replied, except the National Association of Retail Grocers, which could not decide on the position it wished to pursue.[57]

In light of the recent publicity, none of the opponents felt comfortable in admitting outright that they opposed the bill, but each objected to specific provisions. Wedderburn supported a pure food, drink, and drug law, but objected to vesting standard-setting and enforcement in the Bureau of Chemistry under the direction of Harvey Wiley. He considered that too much power to give any one organization or any one man. He preferred the earlier compromise bill that provided an appointed referee board consisting of five medical experts — one from the Army, one from the Navy, one from the Marine-Hospital Service, and two from the public at large — and five commercial experts with whom the Secretary of Agriculture was compelled to consult before taking any action. Wedderburn felt that commercial interests had a right to participate in setting standards that effected them and to decide which violations to prosecute.[58]

Wedderburn's second objection pertained to assigning the responsibility for selling adulterated or mislabeled products. He did not think that the proposed legislation provided adequate protection for retailers. Under the proposed legislation, he felt that retailers were subject to rulings by the Department of Agriculture that might find them culpable of dealing in defective merchandise, when the manufacturer was at fault.[59]

The Association of Manufacturers and Distributors of Food Products in the United States decided that their best course of action was to approve the bill, "absolutely," then to work with the Bureau of Chemistry and courts to hold enforcement to a modest level.

The National Food Manufacturers Association — formed by some 50 dissenting manufacturers of food, glucose, and preservatives mainly based in New York, Chicago, and St. Louis, "but extending from the cod fisheries of Massachusetts to the canning factories of California" — opposed the bill as written. The members of this association included manufacturers who feared restrictions in the production of adulterated foods or provisions requiring them to label and market their product honestly. Among these were firms who used $500 worth of saccharine as a substitute for $10,000 worth of sugar to sweeten their products, those who used coal-dyes to enhance the color, formaldehyde to deodorize stale eggs, and alum in pickles to keep their product crisp.[60]

Their attorney, Thomas E. Lannen, stated that their object was "to secure a proper national food law" that would "protect the people of the United States against fraudulent, unwholesome, and adulterated food; and at the same time recognize and conserve the legitimate constitutional rights of the food manufacturers of the United States." Their petition stated, "Pure food and pure drugs are vital to the public health. No honest man can oppose legislation designed to secure that end in any captious spirit," and "Pure food and pure drugs are so highly essential in every view that argument in their favor is needless," but the power conferred under the pending bills was too vast. Lannen contended that it was open to abuse "through malice, mistake, lack of information, misinformation, scientific belief creating unjust prejudice." The property rights and reputation earned through "years of honorable dealing" might be destroyed by adverse publicity or at the "caprice of unfair authority."[61]

As an alternative, Lannen proposed a substitute bill to protect manufacturing interests. Its provisions permitted the use of the most commonly used preservatives if they did not exceed liberal minimums, limited the definition of drugs to those covered by the *United States Pharmacopoeia* and the *National Formulary*, provided for action against unwholesome or injurious substances if they were added intentionally or occurred naturally, and assigned enforcement to the Department of Commerce and Labor.[62]

Food, drink, and drug advocates rejected his proposal out of hand because it did not restrict proprietaries in any respect, nor food adulterations to any degree. Moreover, it gave whiskey concerns free rein and placed enforcement in the hands of the businesses which were to be regulated. Lakey thought that its intent was to defeat all food, drink, and drug legislation. The committee did not give Lannen's proposal serious attention, but the issue appeared again when Senator Hernando DeSoto Money from Mississippi introduced it into the Senate during the Fifty-ninth Session of Congress in 1906.[63]

Warwick Massey Hough, a St. Louis attorney, represented the National Association of Wholesalers and Distillers, an organization of all of the leading liquor interests. Hough claimed that the firms which he represented were "heartily" in favor of pure food, drink, and drugs in principle, but claimed that fixing standards and requiring contents to be listed on the label discriminated against whiskey blenders and placed unnecessary burdens on the industry. He asserted that setting standards was unnecessary because the reputable distillers he represented complied voluntarily with the *U. S. Pharmacopoeia* standards of quality of alcohol sold for compounding medications. Exposing the "character and constituents" of their products would embarrass the trade and destroy the business of selling spirits to blenders. Blenders did not want their competitors to know how they mixed, in what proportion they mixed, or what kinds of "spirits" they used. Fusel oil, tannic acid, saccharine, and caramel were natural products of storing whiskey in charred barrels and improved the flavor of the product. If these ingredients were listed on the label, consumers would not buy their product.[64]

Outside committee hearings, the Wholesalers and Distillers' communications to its members indicated that its alleged support for pure food, drink, and drugs was far from sincere. On October 25, 1904, they sent out a circular warning that "inimical state and national legislation threatening the trade, together with constant annoyances from other quarters" required organized opposition to the bill. They expected that the "hostile measures" which they had prevented from passing Congress at the previous session would be introduced again. In part, the circular read, "We must continue our active opposition, and we need your support. *Don't hold back.* Your adhesion *means more power to us and added protection to you.*"[65]

In December they sent out another circular assuring their members that the organization was working to protect their interests. They wrote, "Congress is now in session. Conditions require us to be watchful of trade interests, and our best efforts are being exerted in your behalf." They claimed that their association had "accomplished a great deal for the entire trade" by preventing "passage of the Hepburn-Doliver-Prohibition Bill, aimed at National Prohibition, and the McCumber substitute for the Hepburn Pure Food Bill, containing certain provisions discriminating against whiskey."[66]

Like the whiskey interests, the drug industry — manufacturers, wholesale distributors, and druggists — separately and in concert, expressed support for consumer food, drink, and drug protection, but they opposed the bill as a "great and radical departure" from the measures they had approved in the 1900 National Pure Food and Drug Congress. Previous bills had limited government jurisdiction to drugs that were recognized by the *United States Pharmacopoeia* as safe and effective for both internal and external use. The Heyburn-McCumber bill expanded the definition of drugs to cover any substance intended for the cure, mitigation or prevention of disease, thereby including the "tens of thousands" of other preparations, mainly proprietary medications, not listed in the *Pharmacopoeia*. Their attorneys — Joseph W. Errant of Chicago and J. C. Gallagher of Jersey City representing the National Association of Retail Druggists, George L. Douglas of Chicago representing the National Proprietary Medicine Association, Frank C. Henry of the American Pharmaceutical Association, Mahlon N. Kline of Philadelphia, representing the National Wholesale Druggists' Association, and John F. Queeny, president of the Monsanto Chemical Works, representing his company and the Meyers Brothers Drug Company of St. Louis — felt the Senate bill applied to too many products to be manageable. Further, they believed the bill invested too much authority in the Bureau of Chemistry, and would "disturb the peace of mind and the business practices" of retail druggists who were ethical professionals "above reproach for their honesty, integrity, and fair-mindedness." They were patient, skillful men who held the "issues of life and death" in their hands, "faithful purveyors of medicinal agents" who provided the "universal application of the great discoveries of modern science in medicine and surgery" to the American public, and who were capable of judging the merits of their merchandise without outside interference. They suggested that the consumer advocates "had worked themselves up into such a state of mind that they believed" the public was in danger, when little or no danger existed. In addition, much of what the bill hoped to regulate came within the scope of family medicine for which the government could never hope to succeed in fixing standards. Such stringency would do no good and would jeopardize passing any kind of pure food, drink, and drug legislation by unnecessarily unleashing a flood of opposition, not only from the pharmaceutical interests, but from political statesmen who resisted introducing new fields of lawmaking power to the federal government.[67]

Pure food, drink, and drug advocates were quick to note that the "faithful purveyors" whom pharmaceutical attorneys hoped to protect included businessmen Frank J. Cheney, president of the Proprietary Medicine Association, who manufactured Hall's Catarrh Cure, introduced the "red clause' to gag the press, and thought it "silly" to require him to label his products; James Cook Ayer, M.D., of Lowell, Massachusetts, who marketed a line of cures for pulmonary ills, ague, falling hair, and tired blood; and the incredible Drs. Pierce — the father, Ray Vaughn Pierce, and the son, Valentine Mott Pierce — who plastered advertisements of their medical discoveries on barn roofs and billboards across the country.[68]

The Drs. Pierce exemplified the kind of proprietary manufacturers the crusaders hoped to regulate. A graduate from the Eclectic Medical College of Cincinnati in 1862, Ray Vaughn Pierce practiced medicine in Titusville, Pennsylvania, for four years, then moved in 1868 to Buffalo, New York, where he set up a small laboratory and began to compound proprietary medications. Following the philosophy of the college from which he graduated, he avoided the use of powerful mineral remedies and leaned toward "botanicals," or "herbals," derived from plants. His first proprietary was an emmenagogue, designed to "combat the many ills that women suffer with" because of "prolonged existence of invalids to exposure, lack of care" during childhood and puberty, "too much brain work, and too little exercise out-of-doors." He called his preparation "Dr. Pierce's Favorite Prescription." Then he concentrated on formulating an all-purpose tonic to cause a "favorable change in the disordered functions of the body." Reportedly, Dr. Pierce's Golden Medical Discovery, as he named his tonic, was a mixture of cinchona (quinine), colombo, guaiacum, licorice (mostly for flavoring), opium (narcotic), podophyllin (laxative), and alcohol. It was a compound meant to "tone, sustain, and regulate the body functions ... while increasing the discharge of noxious elements accumulated in the system." Pierce claimed that it stimulated "the liver to secrete," changed "the sallow complexion," and transformed "the listless invalid into a vigorous and healthy being." He advertised in newspapers, presenting testimonials of persons claiming to be cured by his preparations and inviting sick persons to "consult with Dr. Pierce by letter *free*."[69]

By 1875, he had expanded his laboratory and found time to finish an enormous 1,008 page manual of health and medicine, *The People's Common Sense Medical Advisor in Plain English; or, Medicine Simplified*, profusely illustrated with several hundred pictures in black and white and four full-page plates. During the next thirty years, the *Advisor* underwent 66 editions and Pierce sold or distributed over 2,140,000 copies. About this time he began painting the barns of rural America with advertisements of his Favorite Prescription and his Golden Medical Discovery.[70]

Henry W. Hill's *History of Buffalo* lists Pierce as one of the most prominent citizens of that city. He built the imposing Pierce's Palace Hotel, facing Buffalo's Prospect Park, where he entertained such prominent personalities as President U. S. Grant, President James A. Garfield, and Senator Roscoe Conkling. He served as a state senator in 1877 and as a U.S. Representative in the Forty-sixth Congress. In 1891, he achieved his lifelong ambition by founding the elegant Invalid's Hotel and Surgical Institute, equipped with the latest scientific apparatuses and a large dispensary of botanical drugs. The Institute was staffed by eminent specialists, including his son Dr. Valentine Mott Pierce, A.B., Harvard, 1888, and M.D., University of Buffalo, 1891.[71]

Valentine Mott Pierce operated the Invalid's Hotel and Surgical Institute from his father's death in 1914 until it closed in 1941. He was an adroit businessman and a community leader. He was president of the World's Dispensary Medical Association, member of both the Erie County and New York State Medical Societies, and president of the National Proprietary Medicine Association in 1900 and again in 1923. He opposed government drug regulation in any form. Samuel Hopkins Adams rated Valentine Mott Pierce as the most aggressive member of the Proprietary Medicine Association in its war against state and federal laws to restrict patent-medicine advertising and labeling.[72]

Convinced that such powerful opposition might jeopardize the entire bill, Senator McCumber and Wiley leaned toward granting some concessions. True to his reputation, Weldon Heyburn "stood pat." The committee recommended the bill to the Senate floor with the expanded drug definition that included nostrums.[73]

The pure food, drink, and drug hearings of the House Committee on Interstate and Foreign Commerce proceeded in much the same manner as they had in the Senate, with the majority defending the consumer interests and a minority preoccupied with the problems such a law might cause industry. In the committee recommendation to pass the law, the majority reported that there should be "no question as to the power of Congress to enact such legislation." The Constitution vested the national government with the right to regulate commerce between the states. Furthermore, precedence for the right to exercise police power far enough to prevent frauds and injuries through interstate commerce had been set in the interstate commerce railroad law.[74] Representing the minority, Congressmen W. E. Adamson and John B. Corliss disagreed. Adamson objected to imposing "burdensome, annoying, and expensive" subjects of legislation and litigation on the federal government. He saw no reason why the state courts could not handle the punishment of "common cheats" and "swindlers" more "certainly and effectively" than federal agencies.[75]

Corliss claimed to approve of legislation to insure pure food for the consumer, but considered the bill an attempt to embarrass honest manufacturers and dealers. He felt that the bill would create "confusion" in the states. Because it authorized federal agents to set standards and fix label requirements at will, the rules would be subject to change as one authority succeeded another, and such changes would cause "no end of confusion and embarrassment to trade."[76]

In spite of the fact that the most effective journalists, bureaucrats, and politicians entered the fight for pure food, drink, and drugs late, and at least partly for selfish reasons, they paved a path along which women crusaders advanced regulation, although their assistance did not always accomplish what the women wanted. The new recruits brought a baggage train of modifications with them and attracted opposition that the crusade would have been better without, but most women found cooperating with them more beneficial than harmful.

Marian McBride advised W.C.T.U. women to support Harvey Wiley and requested that they write to their representatives in Washington, D.C., "urging co-operation and active endeavor" that the bill might become law.[77]

Dr. Louise C. Purington wrote,

> This department [the National W.C.T.U. Department of Health and Heredity] is fortunate that the leading dailies publish matter for study and thought, keeping pace with Boards

of Health, Public Health Associations, Social Science and Household Economic clubs.

We are steadily moving toward better things. The liquor interests and commercial greed may again defeat the Pure Food Bill in our National Congress at Washington ..., but what of it! Defeat may help show up the business in its true light. A great educational campaign is in progress. The Pure Food committee of the National Federated Women's clubs, joined with us in the battle against poisonous food; especially against false labels which give little conception of the real nature of goods, packages, cans and even barrels, brought into our homes.... A little more or less adulteration of liquor does not so much matter — it is poison anyway — but when it comes to the home supply and the daily rations? Also the supply for invalids and children, it is another matter.[78]

11
Io Triomphe!

"A Great Victory for the American Home."[1]

The women crusaders followed the course of pure food, drink, and drug legislation through the convoluted avenues of congressional maneuvering with intense interest. Between 1889 and 1902, over twenty food and drug bills were introduced in the Senate and twenty-five in the House. One or two passed in one of the chambers, but failed in the other. Usually, organized women did not play a prominent role in trying to secure their enactment. They found these earlier proposals too piecemeal and discriminatory to protect the general public. Instead, they held out for legislation designed to ban traffic in all harmful substances, including drinks and drugs, as well as food, and to require those that were not injurious to be sold for what they were. They insisted that honest businessmen, farmers, professionals, and politicians should not fear regulation and those living off the misery of the public should be punished.[2]

Before the early 1900s, efforts to secure the kind of general pure food, drink, and drug law that organized women advocated were mostly frustrated. Consistently, in one house or the other, regulatory legislation failed to emerge from committee. In 1886 the House Judiciary Committee ruled that two such bills did not fall within the constitutional authority of Congress to regulate commerce. In 1888, meat inspection and general pure food bills died in Senate and House committees. In 1890 and again in 1900 Algernon S. Paddock, senator from Nebraska, introduced a comprehensive bill that organized women felt they could support. It passed the Senate in March 9, 1892, but the producers of cottonseed oil and food processors kept it from being considered in the House. On December 18, 1897, Senator Marriott Brosius, from Pennsylvania, proposed a similar bill that received some support in the House, but was not considered in the

Senate. The version Brosius reintroduced in 1898, 1899, and 1900 was cut so drastically to accommodate retailers, manufacturers, and food officials that it lost the support of the women.[3]

Eventually, in 1903, encouraged by the public demand for a law to protect the consumer, McCumber in the Senate, and Hepburn in the House introduced bills which women crusaders decided to approve. Because they had committed a large majority of legislators to support their cause, the women felt that these bills would pass if brought to a vote. Again, the bill passed in the House, but, true to form, languished in Senate committee.[4]

On March 5, 1904, Weldon B. Heyburn reported a substitute bill that appealed to the women crusaders. It included proprietary medications and required manufacturers to label alcoholic beverages as blends, compounds, combinations, or imitations, to indicate their character and ingredients.

Although a majority of legislators in the nation's capital considered the pure food bill the most important measure before Congress, they realized that it had no chance of passing until after the fall elections. Both political parties relied on contributions from the interests that opposed the bill. James R. Mann lamented, "While there ought to be no politics in a bill of this character, still it is perfectly plain that if a law like this goes into effect and is enforced just before a Presidential election, so as to interfere with commercial business, it will have a very deleterious effect on the party in power [Republican party]."[5]

In December, after repeated failures to advance his bill for consideration on the Senate floor, Heyburn called up the Hepburn Pure Food Bill, H.R. 6295, which had been referred from the House to the Senate, as an alternative. His move came too late. Opponents quibbled over minor points and sentence structure, until Heyburn decided to delay further debate of the bill until the following year.[6]

As early as January 1905, the press was predicting that the law would not pass the Senate. On the editorial page of the New York *Evening Journal*, William Randolph Hearst called it the kind of law that could not be passed. He wrote:

> There is a bill in the Senate of the United States called the Pure Food bill. Its purpose is to prevent food adulteration, the swindling and poisoning of the public. Nobody in the Senate says a word against this bill, nobody dares go on record, of course, in behalf of adulteration.

YET IT IS CERTAIN THAT THE BILL WILL NOT BE PASSED....
The explanation is that Congress must not interfere with BUSI-
NESS.
    Very respectable business men are making their fortunes by
the manufacture of shoddy, by adulterations of every kind.[7]

In the spring and summer sessions of 1905, despite frequent attempts
to bring the bill to a vote, Heyburn and McCumber had no success. As
Hearst had predicted, the Senate leadership shoved the bill aside for other
legislation.

The failure of the 1905 bill disheartened pure food, drink, and drug
crusaders. They asked each other what more they could have done. They
had committed enough legislators to pass the bill, presidential elections
no longer stood in their way, public opinion was aroused, and scientific
evidence supported their stand.[8]

Helen Miller wrote to Wiley, "What Now? Does this mean the defeat
of the Pure Food Bill or shall we keep on with our petitions and letters? If
this Bill is lost ... the united women of these United States might well stop
all other work until such a law is passed." Hoping that intense activism
directly following the bill's demise might influence future legislation, she
asked all state federations and clubwomen to send protests to the senators
of each state, to the sponsors, and to as many newspapers as possible.[9]

Federation and W.C.T.U. crusaders spent the rest of the year promoting pure food, drink, and drugs by lectures, demonstrations, contacting legislators, circulating more recent propaganda, and correlating their
efforts. Members of the Pure Food Committee prepared a "white list" of
canned goods, which they found to be pure and honestly labeled, and circulated a bulletin showing the extent of adulteration and describing simple tests for housewives to check the integrity of the food they purchased.
For the Federation lectures, the National Association of State Dairy and
Food Commissioners provided a new travel exhibit of adulterated food
with an explanatory leaflet more graphic than the one in St. Louis at the
Louisiana Purchase Exposition display.[10]

During the summer Heyburn and McCumber wrote a new bill, which
they introduced on December 6, 1905, and reported from committee on
December 14, 1905. To appease legislators who felt that the bill was unfair
to retailers, they inserted the word "knowingly" in respect to dealer violations, but strengthened the law by prescribing heavier penalties for
infractions of the law, which, for the first time, held corporate officers

responsible for violations, and involved the Secretaries of Treasury, Agriculture, and Commerce in enforcement. Crusaders feared that including the old bugaboo word "knowingly" weakened the bill, but felt that the defect was offset by provisions for prosecuting corporation officials.[11]

Early in 1906 the bill bogged down. Heyburn suffered an attack of appendicitis. In his absence from the Senate, Hepburn was unable to overcome the opposition. On January tenth and eighteenth, the Senate brought up the bill, but dropped the matter without discussion.[12]

Suddenly during the second week in February, in an unexpected reversal of his position, Nelson Aldrich sent word to Heyburn that he would no longer block a Senate debate. Albert J. Beveridge, senator from Indiana, recalled that Aldrich yielded to pressure from his colleagues to allow consideration of the bill. According to Beveridge, "The Senate was in a jam and public feeling had become intense. Aldrich came to me one afternoon and said: 'Tell Heyburn if he asks consideration for the Pure Food bill there will be no objection.'" At the time, Beveridge thought the request an obvious maneuver to save something else Aldrich considered more important, or perhaps that the Republican leadership planned to kill the pure food bill later in the House. Regardless, he conveyed the message to Heyburn that if he presented the pure food bill instantly the Old Guard would not resist. Heyburn thought the message was "some kind of a joke" and said that he was tired of "being made a fool of by asking useless consideration for which he had asked so many times before." Beveridge insisted. About mid-afternoon a reluctant Heyburn rose to ask that the bill be considered. True to Aldrich's promise, the Senate scheduled the bill as the next item of business.[13]

As its advocates expected, opposition to the bill was loud and strong. Aldrich spoke against the measure. This was unusual. He rarely made speeches. Aldrich was not a persuasive speaker. His expertise lay in parliamentary procedure and political maneuvering. Breaking his precedence attracted attention.[14]

Like Aldrich, most of the opposing senators prefaced their remarks by admitting that public opinion demanded some kind of legislation, but the Heyburn bill was unconstitutional and unfair. Hernando DeSoto Money from Mississippi noted the "general demand everywhere for some reform" in the manufacture and preparation of food, drinks, and drugs. A "great many frauds" were practiced which enriched "very hastily" the guilty parties, but robbed "the people of health and strength." He assumed that "there was not a Senator" present who did not "sincerely desire that there should a pure-food bill of some sort." His problem with the Hey-burn bill was that it would paralyze trade and infringe upon the jurisdiction of the states. Money proposed that the Heyburn bill be replaced by the National Association of Manufacturers bill that had been rejected by the 1904 Senate committee hearings.[15]

McCumber countered that the sole motive of the Association of Manufacturers was to kill pure food legislation. Money's substitute would be "just as successful in stopping it [adulteration] as a sieve would be in stopping the flow of water." The intent of Money's proposal was to "curtail the power of the officers of the States to protect a State against the influx of ... spurious articles" by stifling federal intervention.[16]

John C. Spooner, from Wisconsin, was among the most outspoken opponents. He tried to obstruct the bill through every available means and criticized most of its provisions. Heyburn countered by pointing out that although Spooner had said a great deal about the shortcomings of the measure, he had produced no amendments to correct them. Spooner's reply that he had not suggested alternatives because he had not read the bill defused the force of his arguments. James A. Hemenway, of Indiana, introduced an amendment that the Proprietary Medicine Association had prepared to weaken labeling requirements for drugs. Jacob Galliger from New Hampshire accused the sponsors of the legislation of trying to ruin the patent medicine business. Jacob B. Foraker, of Ohio, supported by Henry Cabot Lodge, of Massachusetts, and Boies Penrose, of Pennsylvania, attempted to amend the section on liquor to relieve manufacturers of blended and rectified whiskey from identifying their products. Such arguments carried little weight with senators who had already decided to vote for the bill as written. In each case, the amendments were decisively defeated.[17]

Wiley always maintained that many of the opponents were sincere in their desire to protect the Constitution. Women were not so sure. They were quick to note a correlation between what certain senators claimed was best for the country and the needs of the "special interests" among their constituents. Aldrich was a wholesale grocer and an officer in the grocer's organization. Lodge received much of his support from the liquor interests and the codfish industry, which packed and shipped hake throughout the country as codfish and used dangerous preservatives to keep them from spoiling. Senators Hale and Frye from Maine represented the packers of "fancy French sardines, caught in quantity off the coast" of their state. Jacob B. Foraker came from Cincinnati, a headquarters of the rectifiers.

Penrose relied upon rectifiers to support his campaign. James A. Hemenway of Indiana spoke for the makers of patent medicines. Hernando DeSoto Money of Mississippi represented the food and packing industries.[18]

The official endorsement of the American Medical Association for the Heyburn bill at its annual convention in January after years of reservations and disagreements in its ranks was not a decisive factor in securing the bill. But it served, however, to counteract allegations that physicians, as a group, objected to drug regulation, and it helped to offset the opposition from the pharmaceutical interests. The senators were impressed by the enthusiasm of 2,000 physicians requesting passage of the bill, but most of the lawmakers had decided to vote for the bill already. At ten minutes to six on February 21, 1906, the bill passed in the Senate. Sixty-three senators — including Lodge, Money, Foraker, Hemenway, and Penrose answered "yea." Aldrich and 21 others abstained; four — Bacon, Bailey, Foster, and Tillman — all Southern Democrats who objected to the centralization of power in the Department of Agriculture — cast negative votes.[19]

The Federation and Consumers' League crusaders were ecstatic. Alice Lakey wrote that the time and energy she had devoted to "spreading the Gospel of Pure Food" had been more than rewarded and that it was only a matter of course before the bill passed the House. Helen Miller wrote Wiley that "of course it [the bill] will pass the house without delay," but that in the interim the Federation would continue their crusade.[20]

The pure food, drink, and drug advocates encountered stronger opposition in the House than they expected. Twice in the past, the House had passed pure food laws, only to have them tabled in the Senate. Now, finally, after the Senate acted, the House delayed.

The success of the Senate bill had brought the full pressure of the opposing forces to soften the bill's provisions. Liquor interests, food processors, and the drug industry were heavily represented in the House. Prominent scientists and businessmen confirmed their objections, and even former Senator William E. Mason, who had introduced pure food legislation in 1900, defended their position. Under intense pressure, Mann and other committee members wrote a revised draft and reported it as a substitute for the Senate bill. The bill was scheduled for April 10, at which time it was delayed by debate on an appropriation bill. On May 17, Hepburn moved to take up the pure food, drink, and drug bill, but the House ruled in favor of a naturalization measure.

As the House prepared to complete its year's work without signs of considering the bill, the pure food and drug advocates became alarmed.

Upon hearing disquieting rumors that the lobbyists for the opposing interests were packing their bags and leaving town, they dispatched a journalist to investigate. He reported back that the Republican leaders had decided
to leave the bill in committee because they expected extensive and controversial debate from representatives defending the business interests.
Lakey had not heard from Heyburn, and Wiley was depressed. On May
15, Lakey wrote to Bigelow, "the failure of the Bill to pass is very hard to
hear after all of us have worked so hard. We must however prepare for a
fight next season." She wrote Wiley a few days later, "I think we shall have
to enlist in another campaign next season for the Pure Food Bill, evidently
the preservative people have stopped its passage this session."[21]

The crusaders decided to unleash a series of eleventh-hour efforts.
This final push tipped the balance in favor of the bill.

St. Paul Minnesota. May 30 through June 8, 1906. The first volley
of telegrams to Congress came from delegates to the eighth biennial
convention of the General Federation of Women's Clubs convened at the
spacious armory in St. Paul, Minnesota. The drill room, which had been
converted into a "scene of beauty" and utility for the occasion by a professional decorator, was filled beyond its 6,000 seating capacity. People
were standing at the back, and hundreds were turned away. On the
immense stage, Sarah Platt Decker sat in the presidential chair, flanked
by Eva Moore, the Federation officers, committee heads, numerous
guests of honor, and dignitaries from various states, London, Oxford,
Cambridge, Düsseldorf, Paris, and Rome. The governor of Minnesota,
the mayor of St. Paul, the president of the Commercial Club, state and
local Federation officials, and clergymen were there to welcome the delegates to the city. Business meetings were scheduled for mornings, conferences in the afternoons, and general assemblies and receptions in the
evening.[22]

As the first order of business, Helen McNab Miller, chairman of the
Pure Food Committee, rose to request that each delegation send telegrams
to its representatives in the House, its senators, the sponsors of the pure
food, drink, and drug bill, Speaker Cannon, and the president of the
United States urging immediate passage of the pure food bills pending in
the House and advise the members of their clubs to do the same. She read
a summary of the deplorable state of food, drinks, and drugs across the
nation while committee members distributed a complete statement of the
condition of pure food legislation in the various states. The response
was astounding. Members of the House of Representatives reported

receiving floods of telegrams. Most of the congressmen confirmed their support.[23]

In their departmental meetings, both the Civic Improvement and the Pure Food Committees elaborated upon the necessity for federal food, drink, and drug legislation. In the civics session, St. Paul Health Commissioner Dr. Justus Ohage emphasized the need for regulation in large cities and small towns. In the Pure Food Committee meeting, where attendance was so large that the session was transferred from its scheduled room to the Central Presbyterian Church, Helen Miller reported "splendid interest everywhere." In 25 states clubwomen had worked for pure food and planned to include it in their next year's agenda. The delegates were disappointed when Senator Heyburn and Congressman H. C. Adams from Wisconsin (who had been scheduled to speak about the legal aspects of food and drug regulation and the difficulties of passing federal food, drink, and drug legislation) sent word that they were unable leave their congressional duties because of a meat scandal breaking in Washington. The Reverend Caroline Bartlett Crane discussed meat inspection problems and South Dakota Food Commissioner James H. Shepard enumerated dangers from adulterations that were hidden from consumers: dangers from goods spoiled in the package, lead poisoning from improperly prepared cans, and foods treated with antiseptics and chemical preservatives. The delegates were especially attracted by his display of cotton and wool swatches colored with dyes from common food products, one of which was a nine-inch square of cloth, colored a bright red with the dye that he had personally extracted from eight ounces of red candy.[24]

The pure food, drink, and drug exhibit at the Old State House captivated people from the entire area and excited journalists. Lakey and her staff had worked on it for months and advertised it in the local papers. To draw immediate attention, they had filled the old flag stand and plastered the walls of the capitol with immense posters printed in large black type proclaiming the principal dangers of the most common adulterations. Rows of glass cases, identified as the "Adulterators' Publicity Gallery," displayed hundreds of cans, together with boxes of spices, syrups, baking powders, and other foodstuffs in their original package form "just as they were sold in the retail stores," each attached to its official chemical analysis that revealed its contaminants. An entire department which flaunted the advertising frauds and dangers of the "patent-medicine evil," reinforced all that had been disclosed in the recent rash of magazine exposés. Of all the displays, the St. Paul *Pioneer* found the "tubercular beef" display the most impressive and important, particularly "in keeping" with the meat scandals that were breaking in Washington. One reporter described it "horrible enough to make one forego forever the uncertainties of meat-eating." In cooperation with the Minnesota State Live Stock Board, the committee had arranged this segment of the exhibit to illustrate that inspection of carcasses, as well as beef "on the hoof," was essential to consumer safety. At that time, federal inspectors examined only the live cattle brought to the stockyards for signs of disease. The beef display showed examples of meat on its way to markets, from animals that appeared to be free from disease when they were alive, but when slaughtered showed discernible tubercular ulcers.[25]

The editor of the St. Paul *Dispatch* was similarly awakened. Discovering that the Federation was a "commanding influence in progressive reform," he marveled, "The Federation has done and is doing things." Through mobilization, they added a "decided power" to public opinion, demanding that the men, who retained "the honor of legislating for women," must protect women's interests.[26]

New York City. May 28, 1906. The *New York Times* launched an attack against Speaker Joseph Cannon for blocking the pure food, drink, and drug bills against the wishes of a majority of representatives in his own party. According to the *Times'* Washington correspondent, no Speaker in history had misused his power in such a "despotic" manner.

One week later, on June fourth, the *Times* reported that Republican legislators feared that Cannon's stand would throw the fall election to the Democrats. The reelection of representatives who had been sent to Washington to pass progressive legislation depended on passing the bills that the Speaker, in "defiance of the House and his party," picked out "for slaughter." Congressmen pleaded with the Speaker to no avail, telling him that they were "doomed to defeat" unless the bill passed. When they returned home that summer, they would be at a loss to explain to their constituents that they had been unable to do anything about the food, drink, and drug problems. By ignoring their requests, the Speaker jeopardized retaining the Republican majority.[27]

In the June fifth edition, the *Times* printed a statement from the Speaker's office claiming that Cannon was "really in favor of the bill, though perhaps not without amendments," but was "unable to get it through because the House of Representatives would not let him." On June eighth the editorial page of the *Times* questioned Cannon's statement. If Cannon was in favor of the bill, it asked, why did both the "very attentive observers of the proceedings upon the floor" and the "gentlemen of the press" receive the opposite impression? Why did the pure food bill make no progress? Why did the Speaker push it aside in favor of less vital legislation every time it came to the floor? Why was Hepburn so intimidated that he did not take advantage of opportunities to bring the bill to consideration when they arose? The editor's answers indicated that the influence of the Speaker was "in no wise exerted for the protection of his countrymen against swindling and adulteration," and that he was the pawn of the powerful industrial interests that opposed food, drink, and drugs regulation.[28]

Washington, D.C. June 4, 1906. Under duress from pure food, drink, and drug advocates and Republican legislators, Theodore Roosevelt released the Neill-Reynolds Meat Inspection Report to the Senate. The report touched off a meat scandal of unprecedented proportions.

In February, Doubleday, Page and Company had released Upton Sinclair's *The Jungle,* an inflammatory fictional account that exposed deplorable working and unsanitary conditions in Chicago meatpacking plants. Sinclair had researched the book under the auspices of the Socialist weekly *An Appeal to Reason* while he was living in an apartment in the stockyard district of Chicago and taking his meals at Hull House. There he consulted with settlement-house workers, physicians, and attorneys who were familiar with stockyard conditions. Sinclair observed the packinghouse employees at work and talked with them and their families at night to make his account as "authoritative as if it were a statistical compilation." Within weeks the book became a best-seller by sensationalizing conditions in the packinghouses. Sinclair wrote the novel as a propaganda tool to induce workers to became Socialists, but was disappointed in its impact. He complained, "I failed in my purpose. I wished to frighten the country by a picture of what its industrial masters were doing to their victims." He had become a "celebrity, not because the public cared about the workers, but because people objected to eating tubercular beef."[29]

At first, Theodore Roosevelt had dismissed the book as muckraking propaganda, but, because it accused federal meat inspectors of accepting bribes, he instructed Secretary of Agriculture James Wilson to investigate. The president directed his energies to the Railroad Rate Bill and executive affairs — until Doubleday sent him proofs of three follow-up articles that they intended to run in the May issue of the *World's Work.* The articles, which were based on an independent investigation conducted by the publishing company before it accepted Sinclair's book, amplified Sinclair's findings. Sensing criticism with the additional publicity, Roosevelt summoned Mary McDowell, whom he considered an expert witness, to Washington to determine how much of *The Jungle* was based on actual conditions in the stockyards. McDowell told the president that Sinclair had exaggerated a few minor aspects, but, in essence, his account was accurate. At her suggestion, Roosevelt appointed Charles P. Neill, the U.S. Commissioner of Labor, and James Bronson Reynolds, a New York reformer and settlement-house manager, to inspect the Chicago stockyards and submit an impartial report.[30]

When the preliminary Neill-Reynolds Report revealed that conditions were worse than Sinclair depicted, Roosevelt asked Senator Albert J. Beveridge to introduce an amendment to the agricultural appropriation bill that provided for postmortem examinations, inspection of all meat products, dates of inspection on the labels, sanitation control, and exclusion of harmful chemicals and preservatives. The amendment further required packers to pay costs. At first, Roosevelt decided to suppress the results of the Neill-Reynolds Report, but finally released it to Congress and the press when legislators representing the packing industry threatened to amend the bill by eliminating the dating clause, requiring a court order to condemn carcasses, and reverting costs to the government.[31]

On June 5, 1906, the *New York Times*, the *Mobile Daily Register*, and other newspapers printed the first part of the text that Roosevelt sent to Congress, including his introductory message in which he characterized the conditions in Chicago as "revolting." The report indicated the "urgent need of immediate action" to provide for "a drastic and thoroogoing [sic]" federal inspection of all stockyards, packinghouses, and their products. It described meat handling as indescribably filthy. Scraps of offal, entrails, and decayed meats adhered to unwashed wooden tables, tubs, and conveyers. Water mixed with blood and entrails dripped from the ceilings. Unventilated privies were located in corners of the workrooms. The facilities provided no water for cleaning. Workers cleaned carcasses with dirty aprons and wiped their hands on their pant legs. The investigators observed:

> ... meat shoveled from filthy wooden floors, piled on tables ..., and pushed from room to room in rotten box carts, in all of which processes it was in the way of gathering dirt, splinters, floor filth, and the expectoration of tuberculous and other diseased workers.[32]

When the investigators called attention to the situation, the floor superintendents replied that sterilization during the canning process removed
any danger from its use.[33]

The investigators determined that such assurances were not "wholly
true." Much of this meat was prepared for hamburger or "sent out as
sausages that were prepared to be eaten without being cooked." Some of
the meat scraps were "dry, leathery and unfit to be eaten; and in the heap
were found pieces of pig skin and even bits of rope strands and other rubbish." Neill and Reynolds did not see dead rats shoveled into the carts, as
Sinclair described, but the presence of rat poison scattered near the walls
of the cutting rooms convinced them that Sinclair's account was plausible.[34]

The report left little to the imagination of the consumers, except the
identity of the packinghouses. Inadvertently the packers themselves supplied that missing detail when they signed a letter to Congress denying all
of the charges leveled against them, and which the *Times* and other newspapers were more than happy to publish. Now consumer advocates could
cite irrefutable evidence that eight leading packing companies in Chicago—
Armour and Company, Swift and Company, Nelson Morris and Company,
G. H. Hammond Company, Omaha Packing Company, Anglo-American
Provision Company, Libby, McNeil and Libby, and Schwarzschild, Suls-
berger and Company — all processed and marketed contaminated meat.[35]

The editor of the *Times* denounced the packinghouses for filth and
impudence —filth in food handling and processing, impudence in denying "in sweeping terms the filthy and polluting condition of their buildings, of their special rooms, of their modes of handling meat, and the
unspeakable foulness of the persons and habits of their employees." To
him, their denial of guilt, despite the overwhelming evidence to the contrary, indicated that they showed little concern for the health and lives of
consumers. Rather than deny the charges, the packers would have been
"better advised" to confess their guilt, clean up their operations by replacing their "disgusting structures" with sanitary facilities, train their employees in clean processing methods, and gradually try to overcome "the awful
repugnance to buying their products."[36]

Meat outlets felt immediate effects. Trade in lard, sausage, and canned
goods came almost to a standstill. Hundreds of consumers who usually
bought steaks and chops contented themselves with fresh fruits and veg-
etables. Restaurants reported a vast decline in business. The governor of
Illinois and the mayor of Chicago initiated separate investigations, and
inspectors received notice that they would be monitored. [37]

The Illinois state inspectors, one of which was Mary McDowell, reported frenzied activity in packingtown. In every department of the stockyards they found gangs of carpenters, plumbers, and cleaners removing every vestige of the conditions condemned in the Neill-Reynolds Report. Within days, the city investigators noticed a "50 percent" improvement. Armour and Company installed tiled washing facilities, lavatories, separate rest rooms, and lunchrooms on every floor. Swift and Nelson Morris ordered new fixtures to replace wooden tables and receptacles. Throughout the country, other packing companies assessed their facilities, and state food commissioners ordered inspectors to increase their vigilance.[38]

Boston, Massachusetts. June 1906. Calling attention to the "revolting methods" used in the selection and preparation of meat and "the impurities" in food products, nostrums, and other remedies for the sick, the A.M.A. convention in Boston sent a petition to the House urging passage of the pure food and drug bill during the coming week. Charles Reed, secretary of the A.M.A. and member of the National Consumers' League Pure Food Committee explained:

> No legislator can explain his opposition to the measure on any theory consistent with either intelligence or honesty. This fact becomes all the more important, all the more significant, when the character of the opposition is taken into account, — an opposition which, with exception, is made up of people interested in manufacturing and selling rotten and poisonous foods and liquors with which to make the well sick and adulterated medicines with which to make the sick sicker. These people, the very vultures of society, possessed of enormous sums of ill-gotten money, are organized into a powerful lobby, which falters at no scheme of corruption.
>
> Their boast, unblushing made under the roof of the Capitol in Washington, is that they represent over a hundred millions of capital, and that the pure food and drug bill shall simply not pass. Yet it is simply a safeguard such as the government of every other civilized country has provided for the necessary protection of society. There is no doubt but that the people at large demand the reasonable protection to their health and lives.[39]

Washington, D.C. June 19, 1906. The House of Representatives approved the meat inspection amendment. Senate members voiced strong misgivings concerning a concession that reverted the expenses of inspection to the federal government, but voted to approve the appropriation.

Washington, D.C. June 24, 1906. The pure food, drink, and drug bill passed in the House. After congressional approval of the meat inspection amendment, under the barrage of intense publicity and pressure from politicians in both parties, Cannon had not been able to delay debate on the pure food, drink, and drug bill any longer. On June 21, 1906, Representative James R. Mann had arrived at the Capitol building with a truckload of Department of Agriculture and Consumers' League exhibits, which he spread out on tables in front of the Speaker's desk. According to a Washington correspondent for the New York *Times*, the exhibit attracted considerable attention and comment. Attendance was unusually large that day and "hardly a member of the House" failed to examine the exhibits and weigh the samples. They were also joined by a number of senators who came from the other side of the building to view the exhibit.[40]

After his opening statement, during which he kept up a "running fire with interruptions, relating to the need for pure food, drink, and drug legislation, from all over the house," Mann moved to the exhibits, using specific examples to illustrate dangerous and fraudulent marketing practices. He denounced the way in which members of the Proprietary Medicine Association marketed their medications, included intoxicants and poisons without revealing their identity, and falsified provisions of the House bill to deceive the public. He claimed that the Proprietary Medicine Association was powerful because it was the largest advertiser in the country. It was "endeavoring in every way possible" to eliminate labeling the content of "opium, cocaine, acetanilid" or any other poisons on the label. He described how peppercorns were simulated by coloring tapioca with lamp black; how sawdust was marketed for coffee; how imported rotten eggs were used to color oleomargarine; and waved a swatch of brilliant red cloth soaked in the juice of cherries which were bleached with acid and colored with aniline dye. He did not take the time to read, but placed into the record, a long list of dangerous and addictive ingredients in popular proprietary medications and numerous instances in which proprietaries had caused deaths. Apparently, Mann's demonstration was highly entertaining. According to the reporter, several times when Mann seemed ready to conclude his remarks, members of the House cried out, "Go on! Go on!"[41]

Debate began late on June twenty-second with consideration of the amendments. Adamson of Georgia, Henry from Texas, Smith from Maryland, Bartlett from Georgia, and others registered the same objections and proposed the same amendments that the opponents had aired in committee hearings and Senate debates, but the success of the bill was insured from the time Cannon allowed its consideration. The overwhelming majority of representatives had already decided to vote for the law. Richardson of Alabama, Cochran from New York, and Slyden of Texas countered the objections and amendments. With briefs in hand and cases in point, Joseph T. Robinson from Arkansas defended the bill in every legal and ethical particular. He conceded that in some instances, private enterprises might suffer from the enactment of the law, "but an enterprise that thrives by fraud, and poisons while it pretends to feed, does not deserve to prosper and can not demand the aid of government to continue its existence." Congressman Goulden contended that the "character of the evil and the suggested remedy" was so "plain and simple" that the opposition could be "concentrated" easily and "analyzed" for what it was worth. He found that it consisted exclusively of interests that had "fattened for years upon fraudulent goods imposed upon a patient people," of interests which had "grown so large and powerful" that they resented interference "as meddling with sacred property rights" and felt "the superstructure" which they had "erected upon the gullibility of the people" was "sacred by reason of its existence."[42]

Henry M. Goldfogle from New York suggested, "Let us in the interest of the public health, in the interest of honest dealing, in the interest of life itself" end "the frauds practiced on an unsuspecting public ... to preserve the life of our fellow-countrymen." Noting that the packinghouse scandals and the proof of "putting on the market" unwholesome and adulterated food and drink had weakened the confidence of the public and "shocked" Congress, Goldfogle advocated passing the bill to restore public confidence and to tell "the fraud and the evil doer that the day of money getting at the expense of life and health of the consumer is at an end."[43]

Speaker Cannon submitted the question to a vote. The bill passed 241 to 17, with 9 answering "present" and 112 abstaining. As in the Senate, those who voted in the negative were Democrats who claimed to oppose the law on the grounds that it violated states' rights. They included, John Sharp Williams, the minority leader; Adamson and Bartlett of Georgia; Hill, Humphreys and Candler of Mississippi; Burleson, Gillespie, Henry, Moore, Russell, Sheppard, and Smith from Texas; Aiken of South Carolina; Garrett of Tennessee; Lelther of Massachusetts; and Sherley of Kentucky.[44]

Washington, D.C. June 30, 1906. After the Senate and House reconciled their bills in conference committee, the House adopted the conference report and returned it to the Senate where it passed without difficulty.

On June 30, Theodore Roosevelt signed the pure food, drink, and drugs bill into law.[45]

In some respects the federal pure food, drink, and drugs law emerged from the controversy better than its advocates anticipated. It prohibited interstate and foreign commerce in any adulterated or misbranded food, drink, or drug. The manufacturer could not misrepresent the ingredients of his product. The label could not indicate the presence of ingredients that the preparation did not contain, or claim the absence of ingredients if they were present, and it must list the content and amount of specified dangerous drugs — alcohol, opium and its alkaloids, chloral hydrate, acetanilid, and several others. Inspectors could seize suspect products, send them to the Bureau of Chemistry for analysis, and refer violators to the proper district attorney for prosecution in local courts. The law specified fines, imprisonment, or both, but the dealer was protected from prosecution if he produced a guaranty from the manufacturer or wholesaler that its product did not violate the law.

At the same time, the law addressed only part of the problem. It did not protect consumers against products which were marketed in the same state as their manufacture. Congress made no provisions for its funding or determination of its standards. Uniform regulations for prosecutions were to be formulated by a cumbersome board under the direction of the Secretaries of Agriculture, Treasury, and Commerce and Labor. The law required blended whiskey to be identified, but did not require dangerous substances to be listed on the label. It did not restrict the sale of addictive or dangerous drugs, and it did not address issues of sanitation in dairies, bakeries, and food handling.

Regardless of the law's limitations, some newspapers and politicians proclaimed that the law was the most important piece of legislation ever passed by Congress. The New York *Times* announced that the law would stop trade in adulterated or misbranded articles. Senator William E. Borah of Idaho called it a "monumental piece of work ... of incalculable benefit to the country and a widespreading blessing to mankind."[46]

Roosevelt was happy to take the credit. Later he said, "This was one of the great achievements of the Progressive Era." During the Bull Moose Campaign in 1912 he claimed, "The Pure Food and Drug bill became a law purely because of the active stand I took in trying to get it through Congress." Wiley and its other supporters, he declared, had "wholly failed to get even the smallest support for it ... partly because some of them, although honest men, were so fantastically impractical that they played right into the hands of their foes."[47]

The newspapers acclaimed Wiley as the father of the pure food, drink, and drug law, an honor he did nothing to discourage. They pictured him as initiating the law, educating public opinion to the need for legislation, recruiting women's organizations to support regulation, and pushing the law through a reluctant Congress.

Weldon Heyburn received his share of accolades. His longtime political opponent, Borah of Idaho, observed that Heyburn's name would be "most conspicuously associated" with the pure food law for his "tireless effort and determination" in whipping a "great principle into a practicable, workable measure" and accomplishing what no other senator had been able to do. Senator Jones of Washington stated that Heyburn's persistent energy and comprehensive mind gave the American people the first law "to guarantee that sooner or later every person in the United States" would be "completely protected against adulterated food and drugs." Wiley suggested that the state of Idaho erect a monument to Heyburn for one of the greatest fights ever made in the United States Senate.[48]

Organized women knew better than to claim exclusive credit for the law. They realized that driving the bill through Congress had required close cooperation among a number of forces in long, intense campaigns. Harvey Wiley, a corps of agricultural chemists, and state food and health officials had provided the bureaucratic support and the scientific expertise. Weldon Heyburn and Porter J. McCumber in the Senate and James R. Mann and William P. Hepburn in the House, with the support of other Federal legislators, sponsored and propelled the bill through Congress. Theodore Roosevelt backed the bill at the last minute. The A.M.A. jumped in to confirm that the bill was necessary to effective medical practice. Journalists sensationalized the problem. A few business interests lent enough sporadic support to indicate that at least some of them might welcome qualified legislation. Some of the groups contributed more than others and each had its diversions. Passage of the pure food, drink, and drugs law was a product of the interaction between women's organizations and all of these other forces.

Women-consumers were aware that their confederations had mobilized the great body of public indignation that secured the law.

Throughout the country, women crusaders expressed gratification in their achievement. From Washington, Margaret Dye Ellis, of the National W.C.T.U. Department of Legislation, wrote, "passage of the Pure Food Bill is a great triumph for the home. The patent medicine interests are completely routed," despite the "desperate efforts of a powerful lobby in their behalf." Both Ellis and her readers were painfully aware that neither the proprietary medication dealers nor food adulterators were "completely routed," but they were convinced that the heyday of food and medical fraud was over. From that time on they knew that food and drug industries could never reach the heights of freewheeling market practices they had sustained in the past. For the first time, manufacturers had to deal with a new control over their desire for profit and self-interest.[49]

At the annual convention of the N.W.C.T.U. Lillian Stevens applauded passage of the Pure Food, Drink, and Drug Act as a product of women's endeavors. She asserted:

> We have reason to be glad that the public demand for national legislation bearing upon the character of foods sold in markets has secured the passage of the pure food bill ... since the developments of the last year the people have been and are fully aroused to the importance of having adequate national legislation, and they welcome the new Congressional law which certainly is needed to check fraudulent and unwholesome practices.... Since everybody has to eat, the question of pure foods is one of vital interest and importance.[50]

From Massachusetts, Elizabeth Foster, reported that a general consensus of public opinion attributed the Pure Food Act primarily to the "persistent and intelligent" efforts of women's organizations. Even their critics conceded that Massachusetts women had "done their part" in organizing enthusiastic effort and attributed the success of the bill to like efforts throughout the country.[51]

From Missouri, Dr. Dora Green Wilson reflected the gratification of W.C.T.U. workers in every state when she reported that women, aroused by "the enormity of the crime of adulterated food and drugs," had refused "to be put off any longer," and brought "such pressure to bear" that the Pure Food Act of 1906 passed after years of "ceaseless effort." She lauded the law as "a wedge for the entrance of amendments" that would "surely follow."[52]

Speaking of the participation of federated clubs in pure food, drink, and drugs activism, Annie Laws, newly elected president of the Ohio Federation, stated that the General Federation's greatest advance was not merely in its healthy growth in members, but "in the place it had taken among the helpful forces of modern civilization." She noted that its success with the Pure Food, Drink, and Drug Act had brought pleas from "all sorts" of national associations for Federation support of their causes and that "the general public recognized it a force to be reckoned with." She quoted an outside observer of the 1906 General Federation convention at St. Paul, who, after seeing the replies that came from Washington in answer to the flood of telegrams delegates sent their senators, said "the legislators of the country are keeping tabs on the club women and are awakening up to the fact that they would rather have this force for them than against them." Laws left no doubt of her confidence in the effect of G.F.W.C. support:

> The strength which this organization was able to wield was shown in the struggle that preceded the final passage of the Pure Food bill after a warfare of seventeen years. Members of Congress assert openly and warmly that it was the interest shown by the club women of the country that brought victory to the friends of that measure.[53]

Mrs. J. Sydney Robbins, editor of the Alabama Federation of Women's Clubs page in the *Mobile Daily Register*, writing of the campaign against tainted meat, stated that clubwomen wielded a power that "wrong-doing, graft and impure politics" could "well dread." Florence Kelley, executive secretary of the National Consumers' League, referred to the "successful effort of the food Committee" of the League "to promote enactment of the Federal pure food bill" and to block an amendment "designed to cripple" the law. Anna Kelton Wiley, Washington, D.C., clubwoman, later assessed the Federation's efforts as a great battle for "the lasting good of the Nation," and the law as "a real prop on which to build the health of the people." In her estimation, the law made food the "staff of life," instead of a "means to enrich the pockets of unscrupulous manufacturers."[54]

A few women expressed disappointment at the law's shortcomings. Although Martha Allen felt that the law hurt the drug traffic seriously, it was only a "small restriction" on the sale of nostrums. The public needed more protection. Only later she conceded that the law opened the way for an era of W.C.T.U. victories.[55]

In July 1906, the *Union Signal* expressed the official opinion of its sponsoring organization by referring to the new law as a major victory for the American home. The *Federation Bulletin* asserted that passage of the bill was a reason for great rejoicing and announced that once the bill became effective, American women would assume new duties of enforcement and of bringing state laws up to the standards of the federal law to protect consumers from dangers that threatened them from within the borders of their own states. *Consumers' Reports* hailed the law as a successful finish to a prolonged struggle in which women's clubs and consumers' leagues had participated, and outlined ways that the National Consumers' League intended to build on their victory. The editor of *Club Notes* left no doubt that she considered the law a consumer victory. She pointed out that the pure food law was "no idle whim and no momentary spasm of discontent or disgust," but a "well-matured purpose" of consumer refusal to submit to "pecuniary losses and physical danger" from food, drinks, and drugs that were "notoriously not what they seemed." She felt the law would put restrictions on the business of anyone attempting "to defy or evade the law at the expense of the consumer."[56]

Bureaucrats and legislators finally gave credit to organized women for mobilizing consumers in the pure food and drug cause. Their praise was direct and straightforward, more than a gracious expression of good will. Harvey Wiley wrote Alice Lakey that the law was "certainly a great victory ... grand, encouraging and far beyond our most sanguine expectations." He called it "a victory of the women of this country, whose influence was felt as irresistible." Wiley's letter to Helen Miller expressed much the same sentiment. He wrote that clubwomen's work for pure food legislation in both the states and the U.S. Congress had been "wonderfully effective," and added that their pure food and drug crusade had convinced him that women's clubs could accomplish "great work" in whatever they undertook "towards the betterment of the conditions of society." He expressed awe at their accomplishment: "There is something wonderful in the power which organized effort can develop, and the women of this country through organized effort" could "secure any good thing" they demanded. Later, referring to the advocates of pure food, drink, and drugs legislation, he wrote, "Perhaps the greatest and most forceful were the Federated Women's Clubs of America and the Consumers' League. They took up the program with enthusiasm and great vigor." He named Helen McNab Miller and Alice Lakey as outstanding leaders of the crusade. In a 1911 address he said that the women's federated clubs passed the pure food law after a 25 year fight to preserve the health of the public against fraud and misrepresentation:

> I have seen during that fight representatives so beset by lobby-
> ists arguing for and against the bill that the poor fellow did not

know which way to turn. Then along came the women who had been the first of the public to wake up to the impurities being sold in the market for food, and all they had to do was to whisper to the representative and he voted as they said. Then he did not care what the lobbyist wanted. The women made him feel what was right and just. The passage of the bill was due the women's federated clubs of the country. Trust them to put over the goal line every time. The enactment has proven the finest example of political education I have ever seen.[57]

Robert M. Allen, who had worked more closely with Lakey and Miller, gave them greater credit. He wrote, "I speak knowingly when I say that the interest and support which the women have given the Bill have been one of the strongest, if not the strongest, influences in accomplishing last Wednesday's big victory."[58]

Letters from the two U.S. senators who sponsored the legislation were as open and warm in their praise. Senator Porter J. McCumber wrote that Federation women must be gratified with the results of their efforts and thanked them for their "great assistance."[59]

Weldon B. Heyburn had written Alice Lakey that she and her associates in the National Consumers' League and the General Federation of Women's Clubs had "assisted materially" in representing public sentiment when the bill was being considered by the Senate in 1905 and requested they "spare no effort" until the bill passed the House. After the law passed he sent an evaluation of their work:

> I think I very inadequately expressed my appreciation of the value of the co-operation and assistance given by the women of the country in enactment of this legislation, through their creation of sentiment local to every community, culminating in the final opinion by Congress. I certainly have no objections to making it known to the women of this country that their co-operation in the passage of this measure is appreciated, and in my judgement the conservative and practical co-operation of the women of the country would materially aid the law makers in every department of local, state, and national government in enacting legislation.[60]

Among journalists, the influence of women in securing the Pure Food Act became a subject of considerable interest, occasional amusement, and some alarm. An editorial in the New York City *Sun* stated that the club women of the country were the main force behind the pure food and drug bill. An article in the *National Civic Federation Review* attributed the final success of the pure food and drug bill to the "vigorous and immediate action" of women telegraphing their lawmakers from the 1906 Federation convention. The editor of *Good Housekeeping* wrote that the "lion's share" of credit for the national pure food law was due to American women and that their activities heralded the beginning of vast improvement in the quality of American goods and in moral advancement. He anticipated that "the new ideals and broader concepts of civic duty, social relations and personal responsibility, which now animate our people, especially American women" would make "American products the standard of excellence at home and abroad." The American character was a model for all that was "best in humanity, in the family, in industry, and in government."[61]

An article in the January 1907 issue of *Good Housekeeping* announced that the women had captured Congress. The author, L. D. Gibbs, credited women with organizing interest all over the country in pure foods and "free alcohol" legislation, claiming that women had been the prime movers in passage of the pure food and drug law. He observed that even though the "granges" represented by the Department of Agriculture apparently took great interest in the matter, the majority of petitions were signed by women. Members of Congress from every state and district had received a flood of communications from women's organizations and many groups had written repeatedly.[62]

Gibbs said that legislators were taken by surprise. Those who had "only dim recollections of Frances Willard's and Susan Anthony's crusades, came up with a jolt" when confronted with the immense volume of personal communications from women in their own districts. Gibbs quoted one representative as exclaiming, as he clutched his bundle of daily mail, "Heavens! The women are after us now in dead earnest; the Lord only knows where we'll fetch up."[63]

Gibbs reported that the bulk and continuity of the pure food, drink, and drug mail was the talk of everyone employed in the capital. Petitions were "displacing the weather as a subject of conversation at the boarding house and on street cars, in the corridors, committee rooms, and on the floors of the Senate and House of Representatives, congressmen discussed the subject with more than passing interest." Newspaper correspondents in the capital city "took it up," and before anyone realized it, women had mobilized "that indefinite but forceful commodity known as public sentiment."[64]

Gibbs' claims might have appeared extravagant if Wiley had not described the same phenomenon. Of the excitement in Washington, Wiley said that the "force of the movement" had gone beyond "all restraining influences" and that opposition from "the vested interests" had lost its potency in the furor. Like Gibbs, he described people discussing the matter in the streets and in their clubs.[65]

Gibbs found the activities of women's groups "premeditated, organized and timed to exploit the most advantageous position." He explained how the G.F.W.C. worked through its state branches, which, in turn, inspired the separate clubs. Civic clubs, health improvement leagues, the "numerous sections of the Council of Jewish Women," the W.C.T.U., "the Free Art League, humane societies, and the Patrons of Husbandry" all "united in pouring a flood of communications upon congress." He marveled that "the ebb and flow of the volume" was timed to discussion in committee rooms and on the floors of the Senate and House, and that their timing indicated the petitioners were "on the watch." Gibbs observed that the interest extended throughout the country and "thousands of women who had never done such a thing before" were following the news from Washington.[66]

In a less favorable tone, a Washington, D.C., paper quoted another unnamed senator as warning that the federal government was "fast becoming a government of the women, for the women's views, and by the women's clubs." The senator complained that "men do the voting and elect candidates to positions, while the women assume the duty of telling us afterward what they want us to do." He said, "The women's clubs, federated, amalgamated, consolidated, nationalized, organized, with general committees and boards of consulting agencies and investigating branches" were more active in shaping public policies than any other agency in the nation, and added that anyone who declared women unfit for a part in government because they were not qualified by training, interest, and study was "taking long chances of being discredited." He warned:

> ... if the women of the country should suddenly decide that they wanted the tariff revised, or a rate bill passed, or the coal mines nationalized, we should have before the men would wake up to know what had happened.... petitions from the women's clubs would do the work.... And they have never been known to quit.[67]

Conclusion

Basically, the force of consumer demand was responsible for passing the meat inspection and the pure food, drink, and drug laws in June 1906.

As Hunt, Allen, and Willard had predicted, Congress enacted regulatory legislation when public agitation became loud and strong enough that it could not be ignored. Women's organizations proved to be surprisingly effective in advancing the issues and in keeping a constant pressure on legislators. Their stress on consumer danger struck home with a force that the exposure of fraud alone could not inspire. More than any other factor, their campaigns against slaughterhouse filth, addiction, and the harm and deaths related to proprietary medications explain the drive for federal regulation.

Despite Harvey W. Wiley's expertise and prominence, he limited his influence by placing his primary emphasis upon food fraud at the expense of adequate attention to consumer health protection and diverted attention away from consumer objectives by becoming involved in relatively insignificant and controversial issues. The newspapers which addressed the problem, muckraking articles in periodicals, and Upton Sinclair, all of whom sensationalized an issue already entrenched in public concern, livened interest in pure food, drink, and drug regulation, but they did not create or organize that interest. *Outlook* evaluated the meat-inspection scandal as a "draft" that blew "the smoldering fire into flame." Carl Alsberg, Harvey Wiley's successor, stated, "The enactment of the Federal Food and Drugs Act was the crystallization of a sentiment developed during a period of approximately twenty years, during which time the question was actively agitated." Mark Sullivan said "much more than the effects of *The Jungle* entered into the storm that rose throughout the country." Sinclair's novel "struck such a chord" because it "confirmed and publicized what people already knew or suspected" about commercialized food and drugs. *The Jungle* was "merely the final, spectacular, fictionalized climax" to the "long agitation" by "patient investigators"— women's organizations, food chemists, journalists, and other reformers and altruists."[68]

Presidential support fortified the consumer's position. Without Roosevelt's help, the pure food, drink, and drug bill might have been delayed longer, but the president was not an enthusiastic advocate of prosecuting offenders. Roosevelt was a skilled politician who took advantage of his opportunity to win public approval by supporting pure food, drink, and drug legislation at the last minute, and once it passed he preferred mediation to regulation.

Neither were commercial and manufacturing interests responsible for passing the law. Initially and fundamentally, in most cases, they opposed federal regulation. They used every means at their disposal to keep pure food, drink, and drug bills from congressional consideration, proposed emasculating amendments, and evaded the law once it passed. Whatever support they expressed came as an attempt to mollify public opinion, or as a ploy for trade advantage. When specific provisions favored a particular group, that group supported the bill; when regulatory stipulations controlled its activities, it fought against them. A few sectors of the business community supported the bill consistently, but most withdrew their support when an effective bill became imminent. The majority of business interests became resigned to federal regulation, but few were willing to accept the trade restrictions that applied to their industry.

The support from professionalizing physicians came too late to be decisive. Individual physicians, particularly women, lent significant support to the crusade, but, until the final few months, the A.M.A. was too divided on the issue to take a definitive stand.

In the final analysis, it was organized women that initiated the crusade, defined its objectives, took the lead, nourished the issue through discouraging times, and endured in their commitment. Protecting the physical and moral health of their families and communities was their primary concern, and pure food, drink, and drugs was vital to achieving their ultimate goal of building a better society. Women crusaders were willing to cross lines to accept help from all quarters that offered it in good faith. They were the ones who forged the connecting link between consumer, professional, and legislative forces, and were able to consolidate support for general, nondiscriminatory legislation.

12

"The Augean Stables
Are Still Unclean"[1]

What happened after the federal pure food, drink, and drug bill passed is one of the most intriguing aspects of the crusade. An extraordinary explosion of activism accompanied attempts to implement the law. Throughout the country, consumers began to demand adequate appropriations, standards to establish culpability, uniform state laws, measures to abate communicable diseases, and laws to restrict the sale of dangerous and addictive drugs. Citizens formed committees to aid government officials in enforcing the laws, restrain drug advertising, encourage consumers to read labels, and boycott products that violated the law. The increased activity brought favorable results. The quality of the food, drink, and drug supply improved as firms began to comply with consumer demand. At the same time, endless obstacles plagued the consumers. To recoup their loses and to obstruct enforcement officers, the opposing forces became more sophisticated in their marketing techniques and rallied their forces more effectively. Eventually, a gradual decline in activism followed the initial burst of enthusiasm, but this did not occur until after food, drink, and drug standards were better established, the Federal Trade Commission was empowered to prosecute adulteration and mislabeling, and the Harrison Narcotic Act was passed to limit access to addictive drugs.[2]

Increased Activity

The fresh eruption of consumer activity was not unplanned. While Congress was still considering the bill, the Pure Food Committee of the National Consumers' League had designed and distributed plans for a comprehensive program to redress the shortcomings of the law and to insure

266

its enforcement. They completed arrangements to publish regular bulletins designed to alert consumers to new adulterations and to prepare a traveling pure food exhibit that would be available upon request to unions, clubs, and consumers' leagues.[3]

Pending passage of the bill, and Lakey's signal, women's organizations in every state and section of the country stood poised to insure enforcement, to consolidate their gains, to build on the law's provisions, and to enlist new recruits. At Wiley's request, Lakey held back. In July 1906, Wiley had asked Florence Kelley to be patient, saying the best thing women could do was to keep quiet until he requested their help. By late summer 1906, their patience was exhausted. Lakey informed Wiley that the women were anxious to resume the crusade, and the Consumers' League activated its plan. As Louise Purington announced, it was time to turn back to the states to work "for enforcement of laws regulating interstate commerce, state laws, laboratories of hygiene and milk inspection, improved sanitary conditions in factories, markets and stores, clean food, clean surroundings, clean handling."[4] Lakey's signal unleashed an explosion of activity. Providing adequate appropriations for the Bureau of Chemistry was of immediate concern. Congress had allocated funds to administer the meat inspection amendment, but not adequate provisions for pure food, drink, and drug enforcement. Without resources to augment its staff, the Bureau could not begin to cope with its vastly expanded case load. The *New York World* reported apathy in the Congress:

> Although Congress has been in session seven weeks, nothing has been done toward making provision for the enforcement of the Federal pure food laws. The appropriation needed to set in motion the wheels of the Agricultural Department, which is charged with the administration of the regulation, is not forthcoming.
>
> As a consequence, Dr. Wilie [sic], the department official in Washington, who is immediately in charge of the administration of the new law, is powerless to employ inspectors or bring prosecutions.[5]

Lack of funds and inertia left the Department of Agriculture woefully unprepared. No standards had been set, no inspectors had been appointed, and the Bureau of Chemistry had not been expanded. An inadequate staff floundered under the deluge of specific inquiries, requests for advice, invitations to lecture, and squabbles over what constituted adulteration. Wiley delayed funding further by alienating the president and the Secretary of

Agriculture over relatively minor and controversial issues, such as the use of borax as a preservative.[6]

From the outset, the Pure Food, Drink, and Drug Act floundered for lack of direction. Setting standards was essential, yet the standards board, led by the Secretaries of Treasury, Agriculture, and Commerce and Labor, moved too slowly and was too divided in opinions to stem the momentum of the opposing forces. The Bureau of Chemistry was beset by intense opposition from the preservation and whiskey interests. The Consumers' League thought that inflexibility, indecision, and lethargy of the standards board encouraged evasion of the law.[7]

In contrast, consumers' leagues, women's clubs, unions, and civic organizations in every corner of the country were beehives of activity, defending the Pure Food, Drink, and Drug Act against encroachments, trying to expand its provisions, researching, writing, assembling workers, coordinating efforts, agitating for better laws and better enforcement, and continuing to update consumers to new developments. Louise Purington reported that Alice Lakey was "much in the field," lecturing on the objectives of the Pure Food Act, what it had accomplished, what realms of activity it had opened up, how consumers could help food commissioners, and what consumers could do for safe milk. In addition to addressing temperance unions, women's clubs, and consumers' leagues, she spoke at national and international food fairs, teachers' conferences, and various kinds of conventions and assemblies. At the same time, she worked with the New York City Board of Education, conducted research, wrote articles and pamphlets, organized workers, and prepared editorial material for *Outlook* and other magazines and newspapers.[8]

Lakey was engaged in trying to amend the Frelinghuysen Bill in New Jersey. Fashioned after the federal bill, this state bill made no provision for meat inspection, milk standards, or protection against the use of harmful preservatives. It was of the greatest importance to Lakey that the law of her home state serve as a model to protect the consumers by addressing these shortcomings of the federal law. Lakey and her associates encountered intense resistance from meatpackers, druggists, dairymen, and canners. Through the activism of Lakey and the New Jersey Consumers' League, women's clubs, and temperance unions, Senator Frelinghuysen recommended the desired changes himself, the amended food bill became law, and Frelinghuysen became an enthusiastic supporter of the Consumers' League.[9]

Improving the quality of milk was a top priority on Lakey's agenda. In New York and New Jersey she accompanied health officials in their inspection rounds of dairies and slaughterhouses. With two exceptions, they found the dairies in "a filthy condition" and cows showing symptoms of tuberculosis. Eventually the worn out and diseased cows from the approximately 10,000 dairies in New Jersey ended up in slaughterhouses. Lakey and her associates observed slaughterhouses in New Jersey still operating in much the same way as the Beekman Hill women had found conditions in New York City 29 years earlier. The cattle were kept tied up in low, dark, dirty sheds and fed on garbage from New York hotels. The garbage was cooked in great vats and the smell of rancid grease added "horror to the scene." In New York State, conditions were similar.[10]

Consumers' reports of analogous conditions in every state led to activism for a standard slaughterhouse inspection bill. Developed by James B. Reynolds and Dr. John Huber of the Leagues' Pure Food Committee, this bill proposed supplementing federal inspections by passing more exacting state laws, better screening of inspectors, and restricting the number of local slaughterhouses to one in each county where the state health agencies could maintain detailed antemortem and postmortem inspections with minimal expense. The plan was implemented in Indiana, Michigan, Pennsylvania, and other states with favorable results.[11]

In groups and as individuals, consumers throughout the country inspected places where food was manufactured, processed, and sold. Wisconsin women reported filthy slaughterhouses to the State Board of Health. After inspecting grocery stores, vendors' markets, fruit stands, and push carts, New York City women secured the cooperation of the New York City Retail Grocers' Union to promote better sanitation, and reported scores of violations to the board of health. In response to Kansas State Food Inspector Fricke's appeal, the clubwomen of that state aided enforcement by acting as official volunteer inspectors. In Wheeling, West Virginia; Tacoma and Seattle, Washington; Portland, Oregon; and other cities; clubwomen secured the appointment of professional food inspectors from their own ranks. Chicago women's clubs initiated personal inspections and prepared a report on dairy products during the National Dairy Show. After inspecting bakeries, fruit stands, meat markets, and dairies, Louisiana women demanded that fruit stands and open markets be screened.[12]

The Grand Forks, North Dakota, Pure Food Committee of the North Dakota Civic League, in consultation with Edwin Fremont Ladd, the State Pure Food Commissioner, inaugurated a program to use what they termed "just and reasonable" means to deal with food inspection that safeguarded the interests of both merchants and consumers. Under the leadership of

Dr. May Sanders, the committee initiated a general educational campaign and sent copies of the state pure food and drugs act, with a personal letter outlining the provisions of the law and requesting cooperation in its enforcement, to each of the 128 food stores in the city. The women gave the merchants 10 days "to clean house" and prepare for state inspection. After 10 days, Mrs. R. A. Sprague, a league representative, accompanied by the state inspector, rated each business on a score card. The results convinced her that the only way to insure the quality of the city's food supply was to conduct sanitary inspections at frequent intervals. After considerable agitation from the Civic League, the city appointed Mrs. Sprague as the city inspector.[13]

Unions, clubs, and consumers' leagues continued to alert the public to dangers. In an effort to help women from diverse ethnic groups protect their families' health, the New York City and New Jersey Consumers' Leagues translated pure food, drink, and drug pamphlets into Italian and Yiddish for women's club departments of domestic science to distribute among immigrant populations. Food commissioners in Pennsylvania and Wisconsin reprinted the leaflets in their regular publications. Women's groups sponsored classes on pure food at settlement houses, and nurses at milk stations and food distribution centers taught its principles to those who came into their facilities.[14]

Consumer agitation became particularly intense, expanding the law to aid in abating communicable diseases, beginning with tuberculosis, but also including scarlet fever, diphtheria, pneumonia, and other life-threatening infections. This involved an ambitious program of demanding sanitation at all levels of food processing and handling, from the manufacturer to the kitchen. It meant state and local regulation, not only of slaughterhouses, but of all types of food, drink, and drug processors and dealers, such as bakeries, food markets, drug stores, restaurants, and saloons. It meant banning public expectoration, improving light and ventilation in work places and schools, giving tuberculin tests, replacing water buckets and dippers with public drinking fountains, and controlling insects. Most important, it meant securing a safe milk supply by rigid regulation of dairies and milk handlers — keeping dairies clean and sanitary, cooling milk, inspecting cattle for disease, barring additives, and preventing persons who were ill from handling milk and milk products.[15]

The Pure Food Committee of the General Federation made pure milk the primary subject of its activities in 1907. Women considered this phase of pure food activity paramount to the health of the nation. Helen

McNab Miller reported an infant mortality rate in cities where vital statistics were kept to be in excess of 20 percent in the first year of life and 40 percent among those who were fed on ordinary dealer's milk. Lack of sanitation and the use of preservatives were responsible.[16]

The committee recommended that every club in the federation appoint a milk investigating committee to prosecute through existing government agencies when possible, to investigate conditions in the absence of local health officials, to solicit expert assistance, and to take the matter before the "court of enlightened public opinion."[17]

The majority of the states needed additional legislation to meet the women's standards. In her home state of Missouri, Helen Miller appeared before the General Assembly at Jefferson City to introduce a state law for more effective milk regulations. Eva Moore, who accompanied her, reported that Miller's confidence and statistics convinced the legislators. In the District of Columbia, an Association for the Prevention of Tuberculosis lobbied Congress to enact a law requiring the pasteurization, under official supervision, of all milk and cream sold in the District. In Massachusetts, the Consumers' League, in conjunction with the State Board of Health, conducted a vigorous campaign for clean milk, which included distributing circulars and enacting statutes in cities and towns.[18]

In other aspects of their crusade for pure food, drink, and drugs, groups of women developed publicity campaigns to encourage consumers to scrutinize labels. Making adulteration illegal tended to give people the mistaken impression that any food or drug the government allowed to be sold was safe and clean. In an effort to correct this misconception, the crusaders organized into committees to make sure that consumers were aware of ruses to circumvent the law, to report violations, and to publish white lists of products and businesses that had complied.[19]

Unions, women's clubs, and consumers' leagues conducted extensive campaigns against soft drinks, particularly the colas and soda fountain mixtures, which contained cocaine, caffeine, and other habituating drugs. Bills regulating or forbidding the sale of such drinks were introduced into the legislatures of several Southern states. None became law, but the agitation for laws in the South, where colas were particularly popular, and every state in the union made the public aware of the ingredients that soft drinks might contain.[20]

The fight for pure drugs expanded into a campaign against quackery in all forms. Once content to protect consumers against secret ingredients, the crusaders came to believe that the danger could not be addressed effectively without confining the sale of dangerous drugs to the prescription of a qualified physician.[21]

The Bureau of Chemistry frequently lagged behind. When the National Consumers' League requested that the Bureau of Chemistry investigate the common practice of misbranding condensed milk, Wiley informed Alice Lakey that his department was not organized to take up the matter, that her letter would be filed with others of a "kindred nature" which had been received, and that the matter would receive attention when the inspection forces were in order. When Lakey requested a decision on the question of preservatives, Wiley replied that the whole question of preservatives and dyes was awaiting the decision of the Secretary of Agriculture. Personally, Wiley was strongly against the use of preservatives, but thought one or two violations should be allowed for a short time to give manufacturers a chance to change their methods of manufacture. When Lakey asked for help in preparing an exhibit on adulterated milk, the chief of the dairy division of the federal agricultural department, wrote that he could give her no assistance. When she solicited opinions regarding the bleaching of flour and the use of sulphur compounds in dried fruits and syrup, Wiley was unable to give a satisfactory reply pending investigations.[22]

Improved Conditions

Despite the difficulties of the Bureau of Chemistry, the renewed activism among organized women brought a number of favorable results. The women's coalition and the People's Lobby defeated several attempts to weaken the law. Consumers began to read labels and boycott fraudulent products. The federal government improved its meat inspection policies and its inspectors, and special investigative committees reported considerable voluntary improvement in the packinghouses. State chemists noted a marked voluntary reduction in the narcotic and alcohol contents of proprietary medications, especially among those marketed in interstate commerce. To avoid prosecution, many of the drug firms modified their labels, formulas, and occasionally the claims of curative properties of their products.[23]

Each of the national, state, and local units of the W.C.T.U. sent out hundreds of appeals for newspapers to discontinue advertising secret proprietary medications. Not many publications dropped the ads, but the women felt they had made some headway. In most cases, they were treated with courtesy and received many encouraging replies. A few papers and magazines dropped the offensive advertising despite a significant loss of revenue. Many publishers expressed sympathy with the measure and agreed to consider discontinuing the ads once their contracts with the proprietary medicine companies ran out.[24]

By 1912 Margaret Dye Ellis was able to report that the Department of Agriculture was having better success in enforcing the Pure Food, Drink, and Drug Act. In April, May, and June of 1911, government agents turned over nearly 1,000 cases to the U.S. Attorney General for prosecution. In several instances, the courts assessed the maximum penalty, a $200 fine for the first offense and imposed the first jail sentences under the statute. Inspectors seized and destroyed several hundred consignments of food stuffs that were fraudulently labeled and condemned thousands of food and drug imports that were adulterated or misbranded. Such measures served as a deterrent to manufacturers who were tempted to ignore the law.[25]

In conjunction with women's clubs and temperance unions, the consumers' leagues expended enormous efforts to secure state laws similar to the federal pure food, drink, and drug law. California women secured an effective state pure food, drink, and drug law shortly after passage of the federal law. Martha Conine wrote and introduced such a law into the Colorado legislature, and women throughout the country presented similar laws into their legislatures. With six exceptions — Georgia, Minnesota, Mississippi, Delaware, Arizona, and New Mexico — by 1912, every state in the union had a law conforming to and supplementing the National Pure Food, Drink, and Drug Act. Arizona had a pure food law, but it did not cover medications. Georgia had an exemplary drug law, but its food law did not conform to national standards. Laws against false advertising, aimed especially toward medical advertising, had been passed in Kansas, Louisiana, Michigan, North Carolina, North Dakota, Rhode Island, and South Dakota. Chicago and New York City had similar city ordinances. Some states and a considerable number of cities forbade the distribution of drug samples. All of these measures were, to a considerable extent, the results of the women's crusade for pure food, drink, and drugs. These local, state, and city ordinances were necessary to supplement the federal law.[26]

The federal law had the effect of strengthening state laws and giving confidence to state officials. In a single year, New York State Food Commissioner Darlington reported one million pounds of adulterated food were detected and condemned by his inspectors during one week. In 1908, among other enforcement measures, six carloads of adulterated corn syrup were seized and condemned at Little Rock, Arkansas, and unsanitary slaughterpens were fined out of existence. Numerous reports from other states described dramatic increases in prosecutions for diverse violations of state laws.[27]

The issue was popular enough to prompt medical practitioners, druggists, and educators to embrace pure food, drink, and drug legislation as if it had been their own idea all along. The American Medical Association advised its members to support "publicity and honesty" in all that pertained "to medicines and medical preparations" and to avoid prescribing proprietary preparations. Physicians were developing a keener responsibility regarding habituating substances. The Proprietary Medicine Association instructed its legislative committee to advocate legislation to prevent the use of alcohol in proprietary medicines for internal use "in excess of the amount necessary as a solvent and preservative" and "continue their efforts to control the sale of cocaine and of other narcotics and poisons." The *American Journal of Pharmacy* advised its readers that it was the responsibility of the pharmacist to prevent fraud and quackery by advising their patrons to avoid addictive drugs and to promote pure food, drink, and drugs.[28]

The National Education Association advocated teaching children and parents to avoid the use of alcohol, tobacco, tea, coffee, sodas, and proprietary medications. The teachers agreed to teach anti-drug sentiment, the dangers of self-medication, and work to eliminate proprietary advertising.[29]

Consumer response to the law in the South was particularly spectacular. Long muted beneath the surface, the crusade suddenly erupted into the open in July 1906. The *Mobile Daily Register* blared the headline "Pure Food Bill Passes Congress," with the subheadings, "Food and Drink Will Now Be Pure" and "No More Bogus Drugs."[30]

Once quiet and invisible, Southern women's clubs and unions became public in their demands for clean bakeries, clean water, clean air, and drug regulation. Women wrote articles, demanded legislation, and spoke in public forums to publicize the cause.

Maryland was the first state in the Union to conform its pure food, drink, and drug laws to the federal statutes. Under pressures from women's organizations, the Baltimore Canned Goods Exchange, among other food firms, abandoned the use of coloring matter, improved its canning processes, and guaranteed the quality of its products.[31]

Georgia was among the first states to pass a stringent narcotic act to strengthen the federal law. Asserting that the indiscriminate use and sale of addictive drugs was growing at an alarming pace, the women of Georgia demanded state legislation to regulate drugs and the state pharmaceutical association broke with its national counterpart to endorse the bill. The Georgia act preceded the federal Harrison Narcotic law by seven years and served as a model for the federal legislation.[32]

Across the country women crusaders arranged for the introduction of more effective state pure food, drink, and drug laws. State Senator Martha Conine wrote the Colorado law. Helen Miller introduced the law into the Missouri General Assembly. Clubwomen in New York, Pennsylvania, Louisiana, and almost every state in the union initiated legislation to supplement the federal law. In 1911 the editor of the *Federation Bulletin* wrote:

> The work the women of the country have accomplished for pure food has been really remarkable and it is growing more and more important each day. With their efforts in the National Congress, before the State Legislatures, their expositions of pure foods, their talk and their writing, they will during the next five years wipe out of existence the curse of impure and adulterated foods.[33]

Dr. Carl L. Alsberg, who replaced Wiley as chief of the Bureau of Chemistry, noted considerable overall progress:

> The enforcement of federal and state laws and municipal ordinances has produced a marked improvement in the quality of food and drugs.... Practically all the grosser forms of adulteration which were in evidence at the time of the beginning of food legislation have been eliminated ... or are only occasionally found...[34]

Overcoming Obstacles

Despite improvement, some of the gains were limited. In 1907 Samuel Hopkins Adams wrote Wiley, "I find a general disposition to obey the law in letter, though to evade it as far as possible in spirit." Wiley answered, "Our experience is in accord with yours."[35]

Although Wiley thought the law had "worked a revolution" in labeling, he discouraged strengthening it until it had "passed the ordeal of the courts." He felt the law encouraged a slight rise in voluntary compliance among "honest firms."[36]

Alsberg noted that "newer and more refined forms of adulteration," that were developed "from time to time by unscrupulous manufacturers," required "constant vigilance and development of new methods of analysis to detect the forms" as they emerged. Like the older types of adulteration, Alsberg felt that the newer forms were developed for "the purpose of cheapening the product." Accidental adulteration still concerned him. He found a decided need to prevent contamination from metals during the processes of manufacture and the introduction of pathogens during the handling of food products.[37]

Although much of the advertising for mislabeled liquors disappeared temporarily on the day the Pure Food, Drink, and Drug Act became effective on January 1, 1907, a *New York World* reporter observed displays of the "poisonous stuff" back in the windows of retail outlets three weeks later. Throughout the east, he observed mislabeled products advertised as the "Best French brandy, 75 cents per full quart," and "Finest French claret, 35 cents per full quart." Absence of provisions to prosecute retailers and in-state manufacturers, induced liquor dealers to revert to making imitation goods.[38]

Martha Allen would have liked to report to the pure food, drink, and drug advocates that an unqualified triumph had crowned their efforts. If the federal law had solved their problems, the crusaders could have moved on to other reforms with the confidence that the Bureau of Chemistry could insure the quality of their food and the safety of their medications. Unfortunately the political solution was not that simple. Although numbers of manufacturers complied with the law and made sincere efforts to have their problems clarified, the most blatant offenders before the bill passed continued to make every attempt to evade it after it became law by clogging the bureau with trifles, manufacturing their products as closely as they dared, circumventing the intent of the law, and often ignoring it outright.[39]

The first serious legislative test to the Pure Food, Drink, and Drug Act came in late January 1907, when James A. Tawney, from Minnesota, succeeded in attaching an amendment to the House Agricultural appropriation bill that threatened to render the Pure Food, Drink, and Drug Act ineffective. On the pretext of preventing the national government from diverting funds to state enforcement, Tawney's amendment frustrated Wiley's plan to relieve the shortfall in funds and staff in his department and to promote cooperation with state officials through a reciprocal agreement to share work and facilities. The intent of the amendment was to cripple the pure food, drink, and drug law. The editor of *Club Notes* wrote:

> In the fight over the pure food bill the "special interests" oppos-
> ing the measure did everything to create a feeling of antago-
> nism between State officials and the advocates of a Federal law.
> By this means it was hoped to divide the force of reform and
> bring about a conflict of opinion regarding the issues involved.
> The plot failed. The pure food law has approved unqualified
> approval from State officers. It would now appear that the same
> thing is being attempted in a different way — that is, by practi-
> cally prohibiting all plans for co-operation between the National
> and State authorities.[40]

The Consumers' League, in cooperation with the federated women's
clubs, the N.W.C.T.U., and the People's Lobby (a national organization
supported by popular subscription to protect the public), exposed it as a
liquor-instigated ploy, calculated to impair efficient administration of the
Food and Drugs Act, making execution of the law much more costly and
requiring the creation of another unwieldy national bureau. The Tawney
amendment failed enactment.[41]

This was only the first of numerous attempts to weaken or nullify the
effects of the law. Anna Kelton Wiley remembered that many such measures were made by powerful corporations with "their own interests at
heart." Women everywhere remained on guard against weakening amendments, and alerted members of Congress. As Anna Wiley observed, women
were aware that any amendment that weakened the law made an entering
wedge for some "favored industry" and created a precedence for legislation that would entirely nullify the law.[42]

The persisting problem of adulterated liquors, whiskey, and beer
caused Alice Lakey great concern. Under consumer pressure to determine
what constituted whiskey adulteration, Roosevelt submitted the matter to
Attorney General Charles J. Bonaparte, who ruled that a mixture of two
or more straight whiskeys should be labeled a "blend," straight whiskey
mixed with ethyl alcohol should be marked a "compound," but flavored
and colored neutral spirits must be labeled an "imitation." This ruling
supported the consumer's position, but invoked such a hue and cry from
the whiskey trust that in May 1907 the women crusaders sent letters to Roosevelt urging him to endorse Bonaparte's opinion. Roosevelt signed the
decision. The question of whiskey as whiskey did not concern the Pure
Food Committees. Like Lakey, most of them felt that "every member of
the human race would be better off if its manufacture were stopped" altogether. The problem was that misleading labeling of any kind undermined
the law.[43]

An opinion handed down by Solicitor General Bowers in the opening months of the Taft administration rescinded all of the consumer
gains made by the Bonaparte decision. Consumers sent telegrams to
Taft requesting he revoke the Bowers opinion. The president responded
with an opinion of his own which Lakey termed "the severest blow ever
aimed at the Pure Food Law." In effect, it permitted the mislabeling of
neutral spirits and allowed alcohol that was adulterated with colors,
flavors, and preservatives to be marketed as whiskey, thus overturn-
ing the labeling provisions of the Pure Food, Drink, and Drug Act.
Food commissioner Dr. Harry E. Bernard of Indiana wrote that "if Taft's
decision were seriously considered by the courts," setting standards
would "go by the board and every manufacturer of imitation or adulterated food could put his wares on the market almost without restriction."[44]

In 1909 through 1910, one of the chief efforts of the National Consumers' League's Food Committee was to secure the truthful labeling of
beer. Like the issue of whiskey, the Consumers' League had little interest
in the question of beer as beer. Their interest lay in the principle of enforcing the law. As Alice Lakey said:

> For if the great brewing industry with the enormous financial
> interests back of it can escape the rigid interpretation of the
> pure food law, then the manufacturers of all other articles of
> food, drink and medicine, should also be exempt from the pro-
> visions of the law, or we have class legislation. We, therefore,
> asked the Board of Food and Drug Inspection to pass such reg-
> ulations for the labeling of malt liquors as would be in accord
> with the pure food law. If beer is not made from barley malt
> and hops, the label should tell the truth.[45]

Commissioned by the committee, a Mr. J. R. Mauff, of Chicago, filed a
brief with the Board of Food and Drug Inspection in Washington to com-
pel brewers to comply with the Pure Food, Drink, and Drug Act. At first
there seemed little chance of consideration, but after several months'
activism by leagues, women's clubs, and temperance unions, the Remsen
Referee Board agreed to require truth in labeling for all brewing industries.
Despite Mauff's assertions that the timely action and resolution of organized women did more "to arouse the attention of the authorities in Washington than all the other work put together" for what seemed a hopeless
case and a great deal of favorable publicity, the matter was not settled to

the League's satisfaction. Lakey complained, "The government enacted the law and now piece by piece tears it apart. This committee stands for the principle of truthful labels whether on whiskey, beer, jam, or baking powder." She added, "When we are truly civilized the truth must be told not only on labels but on every placard or poster and by every advertisement."[46]

Perhaps the most questionable action taken by the committee was its unqualified support of Harvey Wiley. From the passage of the law, the Pure Food Committee of the National Consumers' League tied its destiny to the success of the Bureau of Chemistry. In the first respect, Wiley influenced the league to emphasize aspects of the crusade that appealed most to him, to the neglect of aspects with which the public was most concerned. Second, the consumer cause suffered with Wiley's difficulties. When Wiley's affluence began to fade, the Pure Food Committee lost much of its influence.

The Bureau of Chemistry's fight to regulate drugs under the 1906 law was never as vigorous as the fight for pure foods. Part of Wiley's neglect of drugs stemmed from his primary interest in foods, and the belief that his tenuous political position precluded attacking powerful proprietary interests. As a result, he concentrated on the smaller drug manufacturers who were not able to create as many difficulties. He wrote Lakey that he preferred to maintain a low profile in the matter of drugs to avoid too much opposition.[47]

Sometimes reluctantly, the women crusaders followed Wiley's advice. Lakey could see the wisdom of Wiley's decision to delay targeting the powerful drug interests until the Food, Drink, and Drug Act was on firmer ground. Like Wiley, she was more interested in pure food than in pure drugs. She hesitated to jeopardize the pure food cause by a too vigorous campaign for pure drugs. On the other hand, she was under continuous pressure from Louise Purington to do more to promote pure drug activism. In contrast to Lakey's stand, the primary interest of the W.C.T.U. lay in stemming the violations of proprietary medicine, large and small offenders alike.

The failure of the courts to uphold the Bureau of Chemistry's decisions undermined the law. Many of the pure food, drink, and drug advocates had a mistaken notion of the power granted Wiley. Many of his duties had been shifted to a referee board, called the Remsen Referee Board, whose aim was to negotiate solutions with manufacturers and dealers, and to commissions that determined standards. In a letter to Lakey, dated February 8, 1909, Senator Heyburn stated:

> Some people are taking it for granted that the appointment of
> a Bureau of Standards and Commissions of Chemists, etc., is
> authorized by law and that their action is binding in the deter-
> mination of what constitutes a violation of the pure food law.
> Such was not the case. The law as enacted leaves to the courts
> to determine what constitutes a violation. These fancy boards
> have no legal status. The Board of Chemists has none. They
> only constitute evidence of his opinion.[48]

In particular, one court ruling effectively undermined enforcing the
law with one blow. As originally passed, the law stated that any preparation was misbranded if the label carried any statement which was false or
misleading "in any particular." The crusaders and the enforcement officials
assumed that this included claims for curative effect. Most proprietary
companies interpreted the law in the same way and modified their labels
to conform to the law. One manufacturer of a "cancer cure" demurred.
When prosecuted by the federal officials, he contended that the law did
not apply to curative claims. The trial court ruled for the defendant on
the grounds that under the law the Bureau of Chemistry could not prosecute people simply for false therapeutic claims, but had to prove intentional fraud. The Supreme Court upheld this decision.[49]

This overwhelming defeat brought a burst of nationwide protest and
immediate demand for an amendment to redress the weakness in the law
that had allowed legal maneuvering around its intent. However, because
of a compromise with the "patent medicine" interests, the resulting Sherley Amendment of 1912 did not remedy the situation.[50]

After the election of Woodrow Wilson in 1912, the pure food, drink,
and drug crusaders recouped some of the losses that they had accrued during the Taft administration and achieved some of the goals they had been
working toward since the passage of the 1906 law. Foremost among these
achievements were the establishment of the Federal Trade Commission
(1914) to replace Roosevelt's Bureau of Corporations and the passage of
the Harrison Narcotic Act to regulate the sale of addictive drugs.

The Federal Trade Commission was given power to procure data from
corporations and to issue cease and desist orders against certain corporate
abuses, among which were mislabeling and adulteration of products. The
Harrison Narcotic Act restricted the sale of opiates, cocaine, and other
addictive drugs to licensed providers. It also separated the control of narcotics from the general provisions for food and drug regulation by shift-
ing enforcement of narcotic laws from the Department of Agriculture into

the Department of the Treasury. Margaret Dye Ellis explained the law's stipulations for stricter supervision of commerce in narcotic drugs:

> After six years of persistent labor, at home and abroad, the United States is about to be placed in a position where her revenue officials can trace to its source the supply of morphine, cocoa leaves, opium, and cocaine with which victims of the drug habit feed their cravings. The powerful influences which for years have been able to prevent legislation looking to interstate regulation of opium, etc., have given in and agree to submit to strict Federal regulation of the traffic in these drugs and their derivatives. After exacting a few minor alternatives, the National Drug Trades Conference, representing a large number of drug and pharmaceutical associations, has agreed not only not to oppose the movement further, but to support the bill prepared by Representative Harrison of New York, which provides for this strict supervision of all licensed handlers of the drug. The new bill requires the keeping of record of sales or disposition by retailers, wholesalers, of professional men legally entitled to handle drugs, which records must be available to collectors of internal revenue at all times and kept in a form prescribed by the Secretary of the Treasury. One not registered and paying the tax of $25, is liable to a fine of not more than $2,000 or imprisonment for not more than five years or both in the discretion of the court.[51]

Eliza B. Ingalls called 1914, when the Harrison Narcotic Act went into effect, a "red Letter" year for the American home. It was the "most far-reaching law yet enacted to stem the drug evil," a most "fortunate measure to protect people against the drug habit."[52]

Decline in Activism

Beginning about 1912, the crusade lost some of its impetus. Specialization into the various aspects of the pure food, drink, and drug crusade broke up the coalition of national forces and eroded its power base. Mildred Wells, a General Federation of Women's Clubs historian, observed that the diversity of the organization was its greatest weakness, as well as its greatest strength. She wrote that after 1912 the Federation's efforts to meet the needs of its "widely diversified membership, with all-inclusive programs," scattered the energies of its members, and the central committee was unable to maintain universal concentration on its multiple reforms.[53]

Anna Stees Richardson, of the *Woman's Home Companion*, saw a "strange process of disintegration" taking place:

> As happens in every family, every home, many of your younger daughters became restless or ambitious. They wanted to specialize in study and work. Those interested in child study formed mother's clubs, and the real parent-teacher movement was established. Others wanted to specialize in civics, government, and the National League of Woman Voters was organized. More young women were graduated from universities and the American Association of University Women forged to the front. More graduates came from conservatories and the National Federation of Music Clubs set up its machinery.[54]

Noting that all of these groups sprang from the Federation and that the Federation provided their inspiration and example, Richardson lamented that the Federation "paid with its life blood." The influence that once made the Federation a "great woman power in the country," a leader in culture, good works, and "betterment of home and community, dissipated into specialized organizations and its power was taken over by municipal, state, and federal agencies."[55]

The old leadership began to leave the scene. Sarah Platt Decker yielded the presidency of the Federation of Women's Clubs to Eva Moore. Decker became occupied with improving working conditions for women and children, and died in 1912. The Federation Pure Food Committee merged with the Physical Education Committee to form the Health Committee under a new leader. Helen McNab Miller lectured frequently, led a successful fight for pure milk in Missouri, then moved to Kalispell, Montana. Elizabeth Foster returned to Massachusetts to strengthen public health measures in her home state. Louisa and Mary Poppenheim retired from publishing the *Keystone* and traveled extensively in Europe.[56]

Louise Purington retired from the N.W.C.T.U. Department of Health in 1914, after outlining an elaborate plan for continuing its multifaceted programs. Her final words were an impassioned plea for union members to continue their fight for their lives, homes, and their communities; for a moral and physical environment "pure, holy, and undefiled"; for sanitary details, fresh air, sunlight, pure water, cleanliness and purity in their markets, shops, and bakeries; for pure milk, food, and meat; for disease prevention of all kinds; to encourage people to examine labels; and to support food and drug reform. After she left, the department increased its emphasis on prohibition at the expense of pure food, drink, and drugs.[57]

Other W.C.T.U. crusaders joined the trend toward submerging pure food, drink, and drug issues in alcoholic temperance. Frances Willard had died in 1897, followed by Mary Hunt in 1906, before the pure food, drink, and drug law passed. Ella Kellogg turned her attention to the social purity crusade. Martha M. Allen continued to fight for pure drugs until the Harrison Narcotic Act passed in 1914, when she also became more absorbed in securing a prohibition amendment.[58]

Although the National Consumers' League retained its Pure Food Committee, it transferred much of its emphasis to the conditions of workers in the food industries, except for flurries of pure food, drink, and drug activity when these concerns were under attack, and during campaigns to restrict the sale of dangerous drugs to the prescription of a licensed physician. The chemists and food commissioners returned to work in their respective states, or accepted positions with the federal government.[59]

Alice Lakey led the Pure Food Committee of the National Consumers' League until 1912. She helped organize the New Jersey and the New York State Milk Committees, and the National Health Defense League. She was a member of the New York City Board of Health, and maintained a lively lecture circuit for the New York Board of Education, the Woman's Christian Temperance Union, the International Congress of Mothers, and other groups. In 1914, she and other pure food and drug advocates founded the American Pure Food League, and Lakey served as its executive secretary until financial difficulties forced it to suspend its activities. When her father died in 1919, Alice Lakey took his place as manager of *Insurance*, the trade journal he had founded in 1883, but she remained active in the New Jersey and National Federations. She supported the various attempts to strengthen the food, drink, and drug laws, including the movement for a new pure food and drug act in the 1930s. She died in Cranford, New Jersey, from heart failure on June 18, 1935.[60]

Harvey Wiley, never popular with the Republican administration, lost its support. Roosevelt thought Wiley lacked diplomatic discretion and considered Wiley's zeal for banning preservatives the work of an impractical crank with few, if any redeemable traits.[61]

Without unqualified support from the administration, Wiley suffered a long series of reverses, which included a charge that he had mismanaged the food, drink, and drug law. Wiley was exonerated from any wrongdoing, but he felt hog-tied by political necessities. Eventually most of his

duties were shifted to the Remsen Referee Board during the Taft Administration.[62]

Lakey and the National Consumers' League supported Wiley throughout his trials, but often wished he would abandon what they considered
the trivial matters and instead concentrate on amending the Food, Drink,
and Drug Act to include a food standards clause, and on prosecuting issues
that were of great danger to the nation's health. In 1911 when Lakey
informed Wiley of her intention to campaign for the amendment, he
requested that she not take any steps at the present. His position was too
tenuous to risk offending Taft at that moment.[63]

Lakey complied. She thought the loss of Wiley would kill the pure
food law. She barraged Taft and Congress with night letters (telegrams) and
petitions requesting Wiley be retained, and the Secretary of Agriculture
and the Remsen Board dismissed. She persuaded the leaders of consumers'
leagues, temperance unions, women's clubs, and suffrage organizations to
do the same, and arranged for newspaper articles and distribution of thousands of pamphlets endorsing Wiley to the public. The food commissioners tried to warn Lakey that continued support of Wiley was a "weak spot
in the wall" and that working for a proper amendment to the law would be
a better course of action. Much to her detriment, Lakey did not take their
advice. Although Taft retained Wiley as chief of the Bureau of Chemistry,
so much of his power had been given to other agencies that he felt he could
not function effectively. He resigned his post on March 15, 1912.[64]

The women's organizations were devastated. With Wiley's departure,
they lost their contact with the government agency in which they had
placed their future. They had antagonized the officials who remained, and
their cause was seriously crippled. They tried to get Wiley reinstated, but
Wiley made no effort to recover his position. He married Anna Kelton,
who had worked with him for a short time in the Department of Agriculture and who became President of the Consumer's League from 1911
through 1912, had two children, and joined the staff of *Good Housekeeping* where he administrated the seal of approval. Wiley authored eleven
books, wrote numerous newspaper and magazine articles, and supervised
the production of over 60 government pamphlets and 225 scientific papers,
as well as numerous newspaper and magazine articles. He died June 30,
1930, still bitter over what he called the "crime against the pure food law."[65]

Weldon Heyburn's successful fight for the Pure Food, Drink and Drug
Act secured his reputation as gifted orator, aggressive debater, efficient
legislator, and one of the most virile and forceful figures of the Senate. He

fought against joint statehood for Arizona and New Mexico, guided the Philippine tariff laws through committee onto the Senate floor, opposed enactment of the reciprocity treaty with Canada, and supported railroad regulation. He led a joint committee that codified and revised the Criminal Code and the Judiciary Title of the United States. In March 1912, at the close of a speech in the Senate opposing the arbitration treaties with France and England, he collapsed from a stroke and later died on October 17. With Heyburn's death, the pure food, drink, and drug crusaders lost one of their most influential and conscientious supporters.[66]

Once the crusaders lost their primary points of contact with the government bureaucracy and the Congress, their efforts became less effective. Although they noted some progress, the consumers' league felt that the Remsen Referee Board had prevented the law from being as effectively enforced as they had desired, that the chief executives were too sensitive to the complaints from big business, and that the legislature had tossed them a bone without completing their task.

Pure food, drink, and drug activism was further eroded by the suffrage movement. By 1915 the crusaders had diverted much of their energy toward woman suffrage as the last remaining way to protect their families and communities. This attitude was a reversal of the majority position in the past. Woman suffrage had always been a controversial issue, often threatening to split national women's organizations. Francis Willard and Lillian Stevens favored supporting suffrage, but most W.C.T.U. members did not. General Federation presidents, particularly Sarah Platt Decker, were officers in suffrage organizations, but they did not promote suffrage in the Federation. As Eva Moore explained, they felt it was better to keep the support of women who would withdraw if suffrage became an issue. Although they favored woman suffrage, they did not see it as a panacea. A great many women considered the suffrage movement superficial because it left basic social disorders untouched. They believed that a woman's influence in politics was more valuable than the power of the ballot.[67]

The majority of Southern white women opposed woman suffrage because they thought that, if given the vote, most black women would support the Republican Party. When the W.C.T.U. organized on a state level in Virginia in 1883, the state president made her position unmistakable. "We ... have nothing whatever to do with the ballot for woman. My own opinion is that its advocacy in this State could lose us many sympathizers, and seriously imperil our usefulness."[68] Although as late as 1906, the G.F.W.C. refused to become involved in suffrage issues, an equal number of women crusaders, especially in the North and the West, supported woman suffrage as a means to secure societal reform. This trend was evident among the rank and file, as well as among the leaders.[69]

As women engaged in activism for pure food, drink, and drug activism and other public reforms, they began to perceive ways in which their usefulness was limited. In Virginia, the W.C.T.U. president protested that women without the vote were severely handicapped when they tried to influence the General Assembly, and crusaders throughout the country came to the conclusion that persuasion, education, petition, and indirect democracy were too slow, too uncertain, too cumbersome, too time-and-energy consuming, too humiliating, and required too much compromise. Many of them began to feel that if they had been able to vote, the pure food, drink, and drug law would have been more effective. They began to see their votes as a last resort in protecting society against the excesses of industrial greed. Alice Lakey felt that evasions of the law could have been prevented if women had been given the vote before the law passed. She said, "It seems a far cry from the hobbling of women's skirts to the hobbling of the food law, and yet as fashion has the power to do one, so the special interests ... has the power to do the other." Political power gave manufacturers the advantage over unenfranchised women. If women had been able to vote, Lakey felt that they could have forced Congress to pass a more rigid and comprehensive law at the onset and to provide adequate provisions for its enforcement.[70]

Mrs. William M. Ellicott, president of the Arundell, Iowa, women's club, agreed. The women she knew wanted suffrage, not as an "abstract right," but as a tool to further the social reform in which they were engaged. The Reverend Anna Shaw wrote that woman suffrage was not a "question of whether men wish women to have certain privileges or opportunities, or whether all women agree in desiring them, but whether, in performance of the duties women undertake, they need these privileges in order to obtain the best results."[71]

Many women throughout the country felt betrayed by politicians who did not support rigid pure food, drink, and drug enforcement. In a letter to the *New York Times*, Marinda C. Butler Robinson vented her frustration with the Taft administration and indicated that after every other effort had failed, women's vote was the last remaining remedy. She wrote:

> It was due to the women of the country that the Food and
> Drug Act became a law, and it has been a source of unspeak-
> able sorrow to see the systematic betrayal of it during this
> Administration, in spite of the fact that the last biennial of
> the great Federation of Women's Clubs a year ago stands on
> record as invoking the Federal and State authorities to protect
> the health of the American home and Nation from the practices
> of unscrupulous manufacturers.
>
> Mr. Taft has not lifted his finger in response to this appeal
> which represents more than 300,000 American women, and
> largely mothers. We women ask for the only sure weapon which
> can protect our homes and interests — the ballot.[72]

The sacred trust of Southern women for their Southern gentlemen had
been sorely strained when the few votes against the pure food, drink, and
drug bill came from Southern senators and representatives in June of 1906.
Mrs. Robert Zahner, Mrs. O. A. Granger, and other Georgia delegates,
along with hundreds of Georgia clubwomen had sent telegrams to their
congressmen requesting support of the bill. Their lack of success in
influencing the congressmen or any recognition of their telegrams
prompted Zahner to report to the Atlanta Federation:

> Mrs. Granger and I telegraphed to Georgia's four representa-
> tives and two senators this message: "Georgia delegation over
> 50 clubs request support passage of pure food bill." ... Our
> short message could not have been misunderstood by our rep-
> resentatives. Other states had immediate affirmative replies,
> Louisiana receiving the first message, but not a single reply came
> to either Mrs. Granger or myself. I have kept the names of our
> representatives. The bill passed over the opposition of 12 South-
> ern senators. The day was saved, but to no thanks to the regard
> of the Southern gentlemen to the desires of organized women.[73]

This incident was one of a series in which Southern politicians ignored the
wishes of Southern women. Such experiences convinced women in the
South that without the vote they had no real representation in political
affairs and prompted them to work for woman suffrage. As Passie Fenton
Ottley wrote, if the men could not make indirect representation work, "the
women would have to find some other way."[74]

Although the change in attitude over the rest of the country was not
as dramatic as in the South, women throughout the country found their
situation untenable. They were tired of representation that did not

represent. Mrs. Ellicott expressed the growing opinion of a great many women when she stated, "I should like to expose the fallacy that woman can vote through her husband, wheedling him into voting as she desires." Not only had the concept become demeaning to both sexes, but women's influence was often futile. Increasingly women resented expending years of energy toward reforms that politicians could nullify or compromise in a few minutes time. Women discovered that the unrepresented were likely to be given less than they needed by legislators who wished merely to placate them.[75]

As a final factor in the decline of pure food, drink, and drug activism, World War I diverted the energies of organized women into war efforts such as selling war bonds, knitting stockings for soldiers, food conservation, humanitarian efforts, and trying to Americanize immigrants through classes in the English language and American customs. Entrance into World War I made criticism of government unpopular and suggestions that the country could improve sound un–American. After the war suspended the crusade, the pure food, drink, and drug crusaders never regained the vigor and momentum of the preceding decades.

Consumer indignation flared up in occasional responses to specific catastrophes. The Elixir of Sulfanilamide disaster of 1937, in which its solvent, diethylene glycol, caused over 100 deaths, mostly among children, precipitated passage of the Federal Food, Drug, and Cosmetic Act of 1938. The thalidomide tragedy of the 1950s and 1960s, which left children with phocomelia — a condition that prevented the growth of the long bones of the arms and legs — created public demand for tighter drug regulation. The meat scandals in 1967, which exposed contaminated meat — horsemeat and flesh from sick animals in hamburger; eyeballs, lungs, hog blood, and chopped hides in bologna and hot dogs; bone particles, hair, sawdust, and entrails, finely ground and mixed with seasonings and preservatives, and marketed as, "Sausage products with that old world taste," — in Delaware, Nebraska, Colorado, and Oklahoma, triggered a rash of consumer outcries for tighter government regulation. At various times, consumers have decried abuses of the law, but they have never attained the unity of purpose that held them together in the Progressive Era. In large, they have depended on government officials to detect and remedy situations.[76]

Conclusion

"In the sober, somber afterthought of mature deliberation."[1]

The noted historian Edward Hallett Carr has said that modern man is "conscious of history." We "peer eagerly back into the twilight" from which we came hoping that it will "illuminate the obscurity" into which we are going. In turn, our "aspirations and anxieties" about the future "quicken" our "insight into what lies behind. Past, present, and future are linked together in the endless chain of history." Carr's observation applies to the value of examining what the experience of the pure food, drink, and drug crusaders means to us, today.[2]

The experience of the pure food, drink, and drug crusaders contributes a more complete understanding of the past in three related fields of historical study—the history of the Progressive Era, the study of women's issues, and the history of democratic movements. It shows that the extraordinary potential of which every ordinary man and woman is capable can make a difference. With vision and innovation, with struggle and energy, with cooperation and determination, their ideals and hopes shape events, past and present.

Progressivism

A comprehensive view of the crusade for pure food, drink, and drugs — one of the hallmarks of progressivism — suggests that the Progressive Era began earlier, was more pervasive, and ushered in a process of reform more profound and sweeping than is commonly thought.

Confining the Progressive Era to the years between 1900 and 1916 is too short a time period. Organized activism for reform, such as the pure food, drink, and drug crusade, began more than 30 years before the turn of the century, and the accelerating economic, social, technological, and aesthetic trends of the later 1800s continued to spiral into the new century, becoming stronger with time and amplifying the urgency for societal improvement. The beginning of the twentieth century did not mark any sudden breach with the past. The period that has been designated as the Progressive Era was characterized by the continuation, rather than an eruption, of reform activities.

Loss of status does not seem to be a major factor in triggering demand for Progressive reform. Activism for pure food, drink, and drugs extended across lines of class, sex, religion, and ethnic origin that had divided people in the past, and which industrialism had amplified. Of necessity, the crusade was inclusive, rather than elitist. The cooperation of every segment of the American society was needed to improve the quality of food, drink and drugs in the United States.

Perhaps the orientation of historians, more than what actually happened, has been responsible for reducing our understanding of the Progressive Era to an issue of class. Social historians have long recognized the tendency of academicians, among others, to exclude the rank and file of American society and to perpetuate an illusion, if not an arrogance, regarding leadership. People at the time understood this problem. Frederick Law Olmsted (1859) wrote:

> Men of literary taste ... are always apt to overlook the working-classes, and to confine the records they make of their own times, in a great degree to the habits and fortunes of their own associates, and to those of superior rank to themselves.... The dumb masses have often been so lost in this shadow of egotism, that, in later days, it has been impossible to discern the very real influence their character and condition has had on the fate of the nation.[3]

Olmstead's observation reflects an enduring tendency. Traditionally, historians have preferred to concentrate on the rich and famous because writing about the affluent is less difficult, less expensive, safer, and more prestigious. Comparatively, data concerning public figures are more readily available in books and library collections. Writing about the lesser known often involves expensive travel and tedious research in obscure and scattered manuscripts. It requires time, which those who teach for a living find difficult to allocate, and money that is not always available in grants.

In addition, some historians prefer not to risk exploring depths and breadths with which they are not familiar. The politician, businessman, and the celebrity often fit into a thesis, but when one begins to investigate the common person, he cannot know what he will find. Name-dropping is an old and time-honored custom, which if handled subtly still attracts attention. Historians are not immune. If honest with oneself, almost everyone has to admit greater interest, at least initially, to the participation of Mary Elizabeth Lease, Jane Addams, and Charlotte Perkins Gilman, than in more obscure women.

Like the rest of humanity, historians become intoxicated with their own opinions. They become too easily convinced, either by sincere or feigned admiration for something they tossed out as a possibility, that their postulation is gospel. This tendency is encouraged by an academic inclination to admire the novel at the expense of honest evaluation of the evidence.

More extensive research and careful consideration suggests that the essence of progressivism lay in the determination of the people in general to remedy the upheavals of industrialization and at the same time to enjoy the technology, discovery, and ideas of the time. Progressivism embraced all segments of society—recent immigrants, factory workers, slum dwellers, housewives, farmers, teachers, physicians, social workers, journalists, politicians, and socialites. It was truly a mass movement that began in the grassroots of America, took hold in the rural communities, towns, and cities, expanded to the state and national proportions, then moved back to the localities to solve specific issues.

Progressivism was not as loosely connected as has been portrayed. By ignoring women's involvement, historians lost sight of where Progressive reform originated, resided, and grew.

Women's Studies

The heart, mind, and drive of progressivism lay not with emerging professionalism, nor the attempts at business monopoly, but within women's organizations. Organized women were the most active workers for social, political, and economic reforms. Women's innovation introduced them, promoted them, nurtured them through difficult times, propelled them into the political arena, and secured legislation to put them into effect. Women comprised the largest number of participants, supplied the most effective leaders, organized the campaigns, and defined the scope of reform that would protect themselves, their communities, and their society. Historian Anne Firor Scott has gone so far as to state that progressivism could not have emerged without the efforts of organized women.[4]

Organized women redefined the political norm in twentieth-century America. The breakdown of the monopoly in men's influence in politics was a lasting, if only a limited, achievement. Still, we do not understand the process through which this was accomplished. Historian Paula Baker has noted that "there is much more we need to know about the political involvement of women of all classes in the years prior to suffrage." Baker has shown that organized women domesticated American politics. Other historians, including Karen Blair, have explained that women developed the skills, competence, confidence, and value of cooperation that propelled them into political activism through organizing into sisterhoods. The experience of the pure food, drink, and drug crusaders reveals more details of the mechanisms of political and social activism through which women effected reform. These day-to-day reform activities of organized women makes our concept of the past infinitely more comprehensive and more logical. As innumerable historians have observed, the more closely scholars view the stream of events from different viewpoints, the more closely their view of the past approximates what really happened.[5]

Equally important, the crusaders' experience emphasizes service over success — a dimension of Progressive Era feminism that is only beginning to be explored in women's studies. It develops a more comprehensive concept of what feminism means. Equal rights, suffrage, and prohibition were significant aspects, but only part, of the broader issue of protecting the home, family, and community against the dangers that came with industrialism. Albert Einstein, who was a great philosopher and humanitarian in the Progressive Era, as well as an outstanding scientist, observed that mankind places too great an emphasis on success and not enough on service.[6] Altruistic service, spanning all lines of society, has been submerged under the narrower aspects of feminism, yet ultimately selfless service may prove to be the most enduring legacy of the progressive generation. The activities of organized women became more significant, both to themselves and to others, when they began to elevate the need to serve above their desire for personal achievement.

In assessing the accomplishments of progressive reformers, historian Irwin Unger wrote a short commentary which pertains to the experience of the pure food, drink, and drug crusaders. The crux of Unger's message was that progressive reformers did not achieve complete success, even judged by their own terms. Such was the case with pure food, drink, and drug reformers. They did not end all of the dangers inflicted on society by the desire for wealth and power. They did not end all of the anxieties concerning the physical and moral health of the nation. Many of their gains were too easily eroded by the opposition they encountered from many sources. They left problems for later generations to tackle.[7]

In retrospect, it appears that, like other Progressive reformers, the women crusaders should have demanded more from their legislators than they did. Probably, while their causes were popular, they could have secured more comprehensive, well defined, and better-funded laws. They could have insisted upon more clearly delineated stipulations for enforcement, and provisions for new and continuing industrial abuses.

Why did they not demand more? In their cooperation with politicians and bureaucrats, they were persuaded that their cause would be lost by demanding more. They gambled on being able to build upon the provisions of the pure food, drink, and drug law. In many respects the chance paid off well. In others, it did not.

Like many Progressive reformers, they allowed too much influence to fall into the hands of a government bureaucracy that had limited vision and limited mobility. Lakey and some other pure food, drink, and drug advocates relied much too frequently on Wiley's advice, which hung on political exigency and, to a certain extent, depended too heavily on his influence, which was shaky at best.

Clearly, they were taken in by some of the politicians who claimed to be progressives, but were not as much in the forefront of reform as the women crusaders. Many who were more conservative in nature than the women climbed aboard the Progressive bandwagon once it began to roll and abandoned it once it encountered rough terrain.

The inadequacies of their campaign cannot be blamed solely on the progressive women themselves. They were innovators. Their vision was unlimited. Their support was exceptionally wide but sometimes thin in spots. It was in these weak areas that the "special interests" moved in. As Unger has observed, "much progressive legislation proved inadequate, not because of a failure of the progressive vision, but because of insufficient power."[8]

Progressive women found their power limited not only by the power of those who placed economic profits before human welfare and by politicians who were willing to compromise, but also by the prophets of efficiency who tried to rationalize government along business lines and by federal courts not yet accustomed to the idea of an affirmative state — a state strong enough to override entrenched rights if the necessity arose, and which overturned and undermined Progressive regulation on a continuing basis.

Success, like beauty, seems to be in the eye of the beholder. If their gains were weighed against what they failed to accomplish, the balance would be in favor of their achievements. Even if success is measured by lasting results, many of the Progressive reforms, including pure food, drink, and drugs, come up well ahead. Although the limitations of their power placed limitations upon their achievements, the pure food, drink, and drug crusaders and other Progressives left a legacy that has benefited mankind in significant respects. They were the first generation to visualize the extent to which dedicated women could improve the conditions of their society, the first to grapple collectively with the massive social problems that industrialization was placing upon them, and the most determined to reconcile wholesome living with technological advancement.

Participatory Democracy

Perhaps the most important aspect of the experience of the pure food, drink, and drug crusaders was the extent and vigor of their participation. As democracy in America has expressed itself, the activities of Progressive women were exceptional in the importance of the role played by the average person. Mark Sullivan wrote that the average person was not only the "principal spectator" of the Progressive drama, but "largely determined the actions of those who from time to time were upon the stage, regulated the length of their tenure in the spotlight, retired them to the wings, or summoned them back." The whim, applause, disapproval, or indifference of the average person "dictated the entrances and the exits." The average person was "one of the performers — was in fact the principal performer in a more fundamental sense and more continuously than any of the principals; for the drama consisted essentially of the interactions between the vocalization and the audience. In short, the average person was pretty near the whole show."[9]

The crusaders were effective because they could see the broader perspective — able to look beyond the past and the present into the future. They were flexible, ready to deal with change and criticism, and able to cooperate well with their coworkers. They were risk-takers, self-starters, independent problem-solvers, and well-balanced, responsible adults who recognized socioeconomic and political exploitation of the consumer as an evil, and were concerned enough to do something about it. Out of necessity they empowered themselves and practiced a philosophy of leadership that recognized the ability of the people to decide on policies and to elect leaders who reflected their thought, responded to their needs, and depended on the rank and file to carry out their mutual agendas.

The crusaders propagated the idea that the government, as the agent of the people, was responsible for protecting the consumer by offsetting and controlling concentrations of private power — a concept that became increasingly popular as the century advanced. The crusaders' activities aimed at balancing the power between the consumer and big business. They could not have known, and would have been appalled, at how far this concept would take the country, and that toward the end of the century many people would want to retreat from the implications of big government. The problem of wanting regulation and at the same time not wanting government interference in their affairs was not addressed; they could not have anticipated how far government interference in private life would later go.

Their Legacy

As we encounter the perplexities and problems of the twenty-first century, the experience of the pure food, drink, and drug crusaders becomes increasingly significant. A more complete understanding of what worked and what failed in the past provides encouragement to our generation. That is the purpose of history.

It is impossible to escape the modern parallels. Food, drink, and drug problems still plague us, and food, drink, and drug reform is still a living phenomenon. We try to cope with a whole Pandora's box of modern threats to our homes and communities. Our problems seem to multiply. We hear arguments over the legitimacy of drugs, the relevance of regulation, the relationship of drug abuse to violence in our streets and in our homes, and carelessness in the spread of disease. We wonder what to do about growth hormones, insecticides, fraud, false advertising, boodling (bribery), salmonella in our egg and poultry products, and *Escherichia coli* in our hamburger. The cost and caliber of medical care, air and water quality, and the ozone layer are political, economic, and social issues. Sometimes government agencies alleviate our anxieties, more often they do not.

On the face of it, our circumstances may seem more complex than those the crusaders encountered, but there are similarities. How many times are we told that regulation stifles business and costs jobs, that alternative methods of manufacture are too expensive or impractical, that feeding livestock without hormones is not cost effective, and that insects cannot be controlled without toxic chemicals? How often do we hear that consumers are apathetic and need to be educated to their own needs? How frequently do politicians and the media ridicule and malign reformers?

The experience of the pure food, drink, and drug crusaders can serve as a lesson to us. True reform begins at the grassroots and reflects the will of the people. It takes shape through intense cooperative effort and requires patience and determination. As long as the people retain leadership of the cause, the democratic process allows them to utilize political parties and bureaucracies as tools to achieve their goals. When the people allow politicians and bureaucrats to take charge, reform becomes the tool of party politics and industrial greed. Democracy goes down the drain and politicians throw out scraps of reform to appease the "masses." The cause becomes irrelevant to the people and advocates fall away. Pure food, drink, and drug reform was not an isolated case. Partial reform occurred when the Populist cause fused with the Democratic Party, when political forces diluted the goals of the Conservation movement, when various other Progressive Era concerns were incompletely addressed. The same thing still happens today.

Nevertheless, the pure food, drink, and drug crusaders provide inspiration for present-day reformers. Despite a poisoned ideological atmosphere, professional and institutional restraints, and a deep-seated fear of societal censure, the crusaders found the courage to expose and make an attempt to correct the worst of the food, drink, and drug evils of their day. Despite limitations, they broke important ground in proving that food, drink, and drug adulteration was a national issue, that social problems were within the venue of the national government, that commercial interests were not invincible, and that cooperative effort could accomplish the impossible. That is the legacy they left us.

Notes

Introduction

1. The other two listed achievements were beginning the construction of the Panama Canal and the Hepburn Act, which, for the first time, gave a government agency the power to set rates for private business.

2. Peter Temin, *Taking Your Medicine: Drug Regulation in the United States* (Cambridge: Harvard University Press, 1980), 28–29; Paul Starr, *The Social Transformation of American Medicine* (New York: Basic Books, 1982), 131.

3. Robert M. Crunden, *Ministers of Reform: The Progressives' Achievement in American Civilization, 1889–1920* (New York: Basic Books, 1982), 163–99; Arthur and Lila Weinberg, *The Muckrakers* (New York: G.P. Putnam's Sons, 1964), 175–212.

4. Harvey Washington Wiley, *Harvey W. Wiley: An Autobiography* (Indianapolis: Bobbs-Merrill, 1930), *The History of a Crime Against the Food Law: The Amazing Story of the National Food and Drugs Law Intended to Protect the Health of the People Perverted to Protect Adulteration of Foods and Drugs* (Washington, D.C.: Privately published by Harvey W. Wiley, M.D., 1929), 52, and *Foods and Their Adulteration*, 2nd ed. (Philadelphia: P. Blakiston's Son, 1911); James Harvey Young, *The Toadstool Millionaires: A Social History of Patent Medicines in America Before Federal Regulation* (Princeton: Princeton University Press, 1961), 235, 243, and *The Medical Messiahs: A Social History of Health Quackery in Twentieth-Century America* (Princeton: Princeton University Press, 1967), 161.

5. Oscar E. Anderson, Jr., *The Health of a Nation: Harvey W. Wiley and the Fight for Pure Food* (Chicago: University of Chicago Press, 1958), 156–57, 169–70, 179.

6. Richard Hofstadter, *Age of Reform: From Bryan to F.D.R.,* Paperback ed. (New York: Vintage, 1955), 135; George E. Mowry, "The California Progressive and His Rationale: A study in Middle Class Politics," *Mississippi Valley Historical Review* XXXVI (September 1949): 239–50; Samuel P. Hays, *Conservation and the Gospel of Efficiency; The Progressive Conservation Movement, 1890–1920* (Cambridge: Harvard University Press, 1959), 4, 265–66, 271.

7. Robert H. Wiebe, *The Search for Order, 1877–1920* (New York: Hill and Wang, 1967), 112–17, 166, 191.

8. Gabriel Kolko, *The Triumph of Conservatism: A Reinterpretation of American History, 1900–1916* (New York: Macmillan 1963), 285, 305.

9. Mary Ritter Beard, *Woman's Work in Municipalities* (New York: D.

Appleton, 1915); David P. Thelen, *The New Citizenship: Origins of Progressivism in Wisconsin, 1885–1900* (Columbia: University of Missouri Press, 1972), and *Paths of Resistance: Tradition and Dignity in Industrializing Missouri* (New York and Oxford: Oxford University Press, 1986); Karen J. Blair, *The Clubwoman as Feminist: True Womanhood Redefined, 1868–1914* (New York: Holmes and Meier, 1980); Anne Firor Scott, *The Southern Lady: From Pedestal to Politics, 1830–1930* (Chicago: University of Chicago Press, 1970); Paula Baker, "The Domestication of Politics: Women and the American Political Society, 1780–1920," in Linda Gordon, ed., *Women, the State, and Welfare,* (Madison: University of Wisconsin Press, 1990).

    10. Pure Food Act, *United States Statutes at Large,* 34 Stat. 768 (1906).

    11. *Keystone* (Charleston, South Carolina), March 1904, 3, and October 1905, 3.

Chaper 1. The Vanguard

    1. Frances Willard, "Annual Address of Frances E. Willard, President of the National W.C.T.U., at the Tenth Annual Meeting at Detroit, Michigan, October 31–November 4, 1883," *Union Signal,* November 8, 1883, 6.

    2. Jane Cunningham Croly, *The History of the Woman's Club Movement in America* (New York: Henry G. Allen, 1898), 119–22; "Work the Woman's Health Protective League Has Accomplished," *The Club Woman's Weekly* 4, no. 19 (April 18, 1908): 17; John Duffy, *A History of Public Health in New York City, 1866–1966,* Vol. II (New York: Russell Sage Foundation, 1974), 130.

    3. Croly, *History,* 119–21.

    4. Ibid.

    5. Ibid.; Seymour J. Mandelbaum, *Boss Tweed's New York* (New York: J. Wiley, 1965), 111–13; A certain General Alexander Shaler was president of the New York City Board of Health from June 13, 1883, to March 4, 1887. According to one alderman, Shaler was appointed through a package deal in which the mayor's son was made the chief sanitary inspector. Shaler was removed from office after a series of scandals and two indictments for bribery were placed against him. For a detailed account of his tenure, see Duffy, II:76–82.

    6. Stephen Smith, "The History of Public Health, 1871–1921," in Mazyck P. Ravenel, ed., *A Half Century of Public Health* (New York: American Public Health Association, 1921), 7–9, and "New York the Unclean," reprinted from *The City That Was* (New York: Allaben, 1911) in Gert H. Brieger, ed., *Medical America in the Nineteenth Century: Readings from the Literature* (Baltimore: The Johns Hopkins Press, 1972), 263–77; John Duffy, *A History of Public Health in New York City, 1625–1866,* Vol. I (New York: Russell Sage Foundation, 1968) and Duffy, II, present a detailed account of the origins, and activities of the Metropolitan Board of Health.

    7. Croly, *History,* 920–21.

    8. Ibid.

    9. Ibid. The member of the board was not named; Duffy, II: 777–82.

    10. Upton Sinclair, *The Jungle* (New York: Doubleday, Page, 1906); Mark Sullivan, *Our Times: The United States, 1900–1925,* Vol. II, America Finding Herself (New York: Charles Scribner's Sons, 1927), 496; Croly, *History,* 921; Duffy, I: 428.

11. Croly, *History*, 921; Duffy, II: 131–32.

12. Croly, *History*, 921.

13. Ibid; Duffy, II: 2, 130.

14. Croly, *History*, 921.

15. Ibid.; Editorial, "Work the Woman's Health Protective Association Has Accomplished," *Keystone*, October 1905, 3; Wilson served as president of the New York City Board of Health from 1890 to 1897. Despite opposition from the *New York Times* and the New York Academy of Medicine to the appointment of a businessman, rather than a physician, during Wilson's leadership and the goading of The Ladies' Health Protective Association, the Board of Health moved aggressively against slaughterhouses, milk and poultry contamination, contagion, and extensive adulteration and large-scale fraud in proprietary medicine, Duffy, II; 79–239, 638.

16. Duffy, II: 2, 128–30.

17. Sullivan, *Our Times*, II: 492–93.

18. Ibid.

19. Croly, *History*, 75, 922; Mary E. McDowell, "A Quarter of a Century in the Stock Yards District," *Transactions* 27 (1920): 72–83.

20. *Keystone*, March 1904, 11; Croly, *History*, 922; "Women and the Packing House," *Woman's Standard*, Waterloo, Iowa, July 1906, n.p.

21. Frances E. Willard, *Woman and Temperance: or, The Work and Workers of the Woman's Christian Temperance Union*, 3rd ed. (Hartford, Connecticut: Park 1883), 251–54.

22. Ibid., the sketch of Mary Hanchett Hunt opposite p. 142; Ernest Hurst Cherrington, ed., *Standard Encyclopedia of the Alcohol Problem, Vol. III* (Westerville, Ohio: Privately published, 1928), 1268; Mark Edward Lender, *Dictionary of American Temperance Biography from Temperance Reform to Alcohol Research, the 1600s to the 1980s* (Westport, Connecticut: Greenwood, 1984), 248–49; Edward T. James, Janet Wilson James, and Paul S. Boyer, *Notable American Women 1607–1950: A Biographical Dictionary*, 3 vols. (Cambridge: Harvard University Press, 1971) 2: 237.

23. Mary H. Hunt, "The Beginnings of Scientific Temperance," *School Physiology Journal* 15, no. 6 (February 1906): 83; "Mrs. Mary Hunt," *Union Signal*, May 3, 1906, 1.

24. Mary H. Hunt, *An Epoch of the Nineteenth Century* (Boston: PH Foster, printers, 1897), 6–8; Hunt, *A History of the First Decade of the Department of Scientific Temperance Instruction in Schools and Colleges, of the Woman's Christian Temperance Union*, 2nd ed. (Boston: Washington Press, 1891), 3–6.

25. Willard, *Woman and Temperance*, 251–54.

26. Secretary, Batavia, New York, "News from the Field," *Union Signal*, November 1, 1883, 10.

27. Ibid.

28. Ibid.

29. "An Early Reformer," *Union Signal*, February 19, 1885, 2; "She Yet Speaketh," *School Physiology Journal* 15, no. 10 (June 1906): 153.

30. *Union Signal*, March 12, 1882, 2; Mary Tilden M'Call, "An Address to the Semi-annual Convention of the California W.C.T.U. held at San Jose, Feb. 9, 10, 11, 1884," *Union Signal*, April 10, 1884, 8–9.

31. Mary H. Hunt, "Scientific Temperance," *Union Signal*, August 6, 1885, 9.

32. Ibid.

33. "Mrs. Mary Hunt," *Union Signal*, August 5, 1885, 9; Willard, *Women and Temperance*, 251, 254.

34. "The New Departure," *Union Signal*, February 28, 1884, 4.

35. Ibid.

36. Ibid.; At the time of her marriage to Dr. Kellogg, Ella Eaton Kellogg lived in Alfred Center, New York. At the age of 19, she received an A.L. degree at Alfred University, and later an A. M. degree. She married John Harvey Kellogg, M.D., in 1879. They had no children of their own, but reared a number of orphan children in their home. Clara C. Chapin, ed., *Thumb Nail Sketches of White Ribbon Women* (Chicago: Woman's Temperance Publishing Association, 1895), 116. John Harvey Kellogg was born at Tyrone, Michigan, February 26, 1852, attended Michigan State Normal School, University of Michigan, and received an M.D. at Bellevue Hospital Medical College, New York, in 1875. He studied in Europe in 1883, 1889, 1902, 1907, and 1911. He received an LL.D. from Olivet College in Michigan. He established a health sanitarium at Battle Creek in 1875, and was a member of the Michigan State Board of Health in 1878–1890 and 1912–1916, and secretary of the American Medical Temperance Association from 1885–1902. He wrote a number of books, articles, and pamphlets, was editor of several magazines, was a popular lecturer, invented surgical instruments and appliances, developed processes for improving and successfully manufacturing cereal foods, which his brother William Kellogg, the cereal tycoon, marketed. Funk and Wagnalls *New Encyclopedia*, 1985 ed., Vol. 15, 201; Cherrington, III: 1447; see, for example, Frances E. Willard, "The Workshop. No. 1," *Union Signal*, February 21, 1884, 5.

37. "The New Departure," *Union Signal*, February 28, 1884, 4; Bessie Cushman, "Health Talks: The Way We Live Now," *Union Signal*, July 5, 1885, 5.

38. Ibid.

39. Mrs. J. H. Kellogg, "Health Talks," a series of articles in *Union Signal*, January 11, 1883, 5, January 25, 1883, 5, February 1, 5, April 5, 1883, 5, October 4, 1883, 3.

40. "The New Departure," *Union Signal*, February 28, 1884, 4.

41. Ibid.

42. Ibid.

43. Kellogg, "Health Talks" *Union Signal*, November 20, 1884, 3.

44. Mrs. J. H. Kellogg, "Health Talks: Household Hygiene," *Union Signal*, October 4, 1883, 3.

45. "The New Departure," *Union Signal*, February 28, 1884, 4; Mary J. Safford, M.D., "Health Talks: Physiological Effects of Alcoholic Beverages," *Union Signal*, March 8, 1883, 5; Joel Dorman Steele, *Hygienic Physiology* (New York and Chicago: A. S. Barnes, 1884, 171–72; Dr. Lucinda H. Carr, "Health Talks: Health and Heredity," *Union Signal*, April 12, 1883, 5; "Health Talks: Heredity," *Union Signal*, October 11, 1883, 4; Henry M. Hurd, M.D., President of Johns Hopkins Medical School, "The Hereditary Influence of Alcoholic Indulgence Upon the Production of Insanity," *Union Signal*, August 6, 1885, 7; Mrs. T. C. Garner, "Heredity," *Union Signal*, October 11, 1883, 4; "An Averted Evil," *Union Signal*, June 14, 1883, 3.

46. "An Averted Evil," *Union Signal*, June 14, 1883, 3.

47. "The New Departure," *Union Signal*, February 28, 1884, 4.

48. Frances Willard, "Annual Address to the 1883 W.C.T.U. Convention," *Union Signal*, November 8, 1883, 2–6.

49. Ibid.; Willard, "President's Annual Address," *N.W.C.T.U. Minutes,* 1885, 77.

50. For the best account of this incident see Mary E. McDowell, "The Chief Hindrance to Juvenile Work," *Union Signal,* January 6, 1887, 7–8.

51. Ibid.

52. Willard, "Annual Address to the 1883 W.C.T.U. Convention," *Union Signal,* November 8, 1883, 2–6.

53. Ibid.

54. Ibid.

55. Ibid.; Frances E. Willard, "A Plea for Mrs. Leavitt," Official Communications, *Union Signal,* March 12, 1885, 12.

56. Ibid.; "The Opium Trade and Habit," *Union Signal,* August 25, 1887, 8.

57. Louisa B. Poppenheim, "How Shall We Use the Club," *Keystone,* October 1899, 10–11. For a discussion of how women's clubs served as a training ground for activism, see Blair, *Clubwoman as Feminist,* 70–71.

58. Ibid.

59. Mary I. Wood, *The History of the General Federation of Women's Clubs for the First Twenty-two Years of its Organization* (New York: The History Department of the General Federation of Women's Clubs, 1912), 253.

60. Minutes of the Shakespeare Club of Clinton, Missouri, Vols. I, II, and III, December 18, 1901, October 15, 1902, and May 28, 1904, joint collection of University of Missouri, Western Historical Manuscripts Collection, Columbia, and State Historical Society of Missouri Manuscripts, Columbia.

61. Paula Baker, "The Domestication of Politics," 640; Karen Blair, *Clubwoman as Feminist*; Anne Firor Scott, *Making the Invisible Woman Visible* (Urbana and Chicago: University of Illinois Press, 1970), 152.

62. Mildred White Wells, *Unity in Diversity: The History of the General Federation of Women's Clubs* (Washington, D.C.: General Federation of Women's Clubs, 1953), 459.

63. "The Department of Medical Temperance, and Its Part in Patent Medicine Agitation," *Union Signal,* May 31, 1906, 3.

64. Willard, "Annual Address to the 1883 W.C.T.U. Convention," *Union Signal,* 6; For the phrase, "building better than we know," see also Wells, *Unity,* 456.

Chaper 2. The Pure Food, Drink, and Drug Dilemma

1. James, James, and Boyer, *Notable,* 1: 18.

2. Barbara Leslie Epstein, *The Politics of Domesticity: Women, Evangelism, and Temperance in Nineteenth-Century America* (Middletown, Connecticut: Wesleyan University Press, 1981), 90, 101.

3. Ruth Bordin, *Women and Temperance: The Quest for Power and Liberty, 1873–1900* (Philadelphia: Temple University Press, 1981), 29.

4. Dr. Butler, "Help Those Women" *Union Signal,* October 22, 1895, 4–5.

5. Sarah Platt Decker, "Up-to-date Notes," *Keystone,* December 1905, 6; Mary Sherman, "Manufacture of Foods in Tenements," *Consumers' Reports,* 1906, 35; Mrs. F. Merrick, "Home and Church" *Union Signal,* February 19, 1885, 7; Clara Hoffman, "News From the Field: Missouri — President's Annual Address," *Union*

Signal, July 3, 1884, 4; J. Ellen Foster, "Department of Legislation," report of the Corresponding Secretary, *N.W.C.T.U. Minutes,* 1883, 124; "Backward Glances at the National Convention: The View of a Detroit Resident," *Union Signal,* December 10, 1883, 8; Wood, *History,* 4.

6. Ecclesiastes 10:1; Ernst Stieb, *Drug Adulteration: Detection and Control in Nineteenth-Century Britain* (Madison: University of Wisconsin Press, 1966), 4, 5, 19, 215; George M. Beringer, "The Evolution of Nostrum Vending and its Relation to the Practice of Medicine and Pharmacy," *American Journal of Pharmacy,* April 1905, 168–71. Frederick Accum, *A Treatise on Adulteration of Food and Culinary Poisons....* (Philadelphia: Ab'm Small, 1820); George A. Bender, *Great Moments in Pharmacy* (Detroit: Northwood Institute, 1966), 36–38; On the history of proprietary medicines in America before the Civil War, see Young, *Toadstool Millionaires,* 3–89.

7. Jennie Stevens Elder, M.D., "Drug Intemperance," *Union Signal,* August 20, 1885, 4–5.

8. Ibid.

9. David Paulson, "The Wealth of Health," *Union Signal,* May 21, 1903, 4.

10. Ibid.; M. A. L., "The Higher Law of Health," read at a meeting of the Baltimore W.C.T.U., June 9, 1885, *Union Signal,* July 16, 1885, 7.

11. Paulson, *Union Signal,* May 21, 1903, 4.

12. Alsberg, in Ravenel, 213.

13. Ibid.; Ravenel, 76, 211; There are a number of publications that deal with the extent and kinds of food and drink adulteration. For example, see U.S. Department of Agriculture, Division of Chemistry, Bulletins 13 and 25, and Alexander J. Wedderburn, *A Popular Treatise on the Extent and Character of Food Adulteration.* I draw from Wiley, *Foods Adulteration,* and Congress, *Senate Report* [*S. R.*] *516,* Vol. 3, 56th Cong., 1st sess., 1902, 1899-1900; Congress, Senate Hearings, 1904, Hearings before the Committee on Manufactures, *S. R. 1209,* 58–62.

14. Ibid.

15. Ibid.

16. "President's Threat with Meat Report," *New York Times,* June 5, 1906, 1–2.

17. Cited in Sullivan, II: 541.

18. Wiley, *Food Adulteration,* 544, 610; Charles E. North, "Milk and It's Relation to Public Health, in Ravenel, 244–55, 288–89; Wiley to Wilson, October 16, 1907, Harvey W. Wiley Papers, Manuscript Division, Library of Congress; *Union Signal,* June 7, 1883, 1, and July 16, 1885, 8.

19. Jacob Spahn, "Beer — The Fatal Beverage," *Union Signal,* February 28, 1884, 2–3.

20. *Union Signal,* June 4, 1885, 3.

21. "Correspondence: California Wines," *Union Signal,* January 15, 1885, 6.

22. Rev. Wilbur F. Crafts, "What a Century of Temperance Work Has Made Certain in Regard To The Curse and Cure of Intemperance," *Union Signal,* January 15, 1885, 5.

23. Wiley, *Food Adulteration,* 544, 610; Sullivan, *Our Times,* I: 509

24. *Union Signal,* 5 June 1884, 13; "A Disgusted Smoker," Miscellaneous Selections, *Union Signal,* 9 October 1884, 14.

25. U.S. Bureau of the Census, *Thirteenth Census of the United States, Vol. VIII, Manufacturers, 1909: General Report and Analysis* (Washington, D.C.: Government Printing Office, 1913), 40.

26. Temin, *Taking Medicine*, 26; Weinberg, *Muckrakers*, 176; *N.W.C.T.U. Report*, 1905, 108.

27. Champs Andrews, *Union Signal*, May 31, 1906, 1; Martha M. Allen, *Alcohol a Dangerous and Unnecessary Medicine* (Marcellus, New York: Department of Medical Temperance of the National Woman's Christian Temperance Union, 1900), 301.

28. David T. Cartwright, *Dark Paradise* (Cambridge: Harvard University Press, 1982), 38–41, 46.

29. Ibid.

30. Ibid.

31. Ibid.; Claudia Bushman, *"A Good Poor Man's Wife"* (Hanover and London: University of New England, 1981), 152. *St. Louis Mirror*, September 1904.

32. Cartwright, 46.

33. Sullivan, II: 497–98.

34. Alice Lakey, *Federation Bulletin*, November 1906, 87.

35. Alsberg, in Ravenel, 209.

36. Sullivan, *Our Times*, 497, 502, 509.

37. Ibid., 501–10.

38. Ibid., 501–02.

39. Mrs. J. H. Kellogg, "Health Talks," *Union Signal*, June 14, 1883, 5; Anna Kelton Wiley Papers, Manuscript Division, Library of Congress, Box 182.

40. Alsberg, in Ravenel, 209.

41. Wiley, *Food Adulteration*, 251–54; Mrs. J. H. Kellogg, "Health Talks: Good Cooking, No. II, Baking Powders," , *Union Signal*, June 14, 1883, 5.

42. Allen, *Alcohol*, 323, 335–39.

43. Ibid.

44. For one detailed account, see Young, *Toadstool Millionaires*, 93–204.

45. Editorial, *Keystone*, March 1906, 3.

46. *Union Signal*, April 24, 1884, 8, and October 28, 1897, 8; *Keystone*, August 1900, 11, 12;

47. Wilbur Crafts, "The Church and the W.C.T.U.," *Union Signal*, January 26, 1899, 6.

48. Ibid.; from an article in *Unity*, cited in *Keystone*, October 1905, 12; "The View of a Detroit Resident," *Union Signal*, December 20, 1883, and January 26, 1899, 6.

49. Temin, *Taking Medicine*, 29; Starr, *Social Transformation*, 109.

50. *Druggist's Circular* 49 (1905): 30, cited in Young, *Toadstool Millionaires*, 209; Henry P. Hynson, "Ethical Pharmaceutical Practice and Recompense," *American Journal of Pharmacy*, April 1905, 155; William C. Alpers,"Professionalism vs. Commercialism in Pharmacy," *American Journal of Pharmacy*, April 1905, 162.

51. Missouri State Archives, Box 310, 13873–13876.

52. Charles H. La Wall, "The Effects of Publicity on the Standing and Use of Nostrums," *American Journal of Pharmacy*, January 1907, 29–30.

53. *Journal of Proceedings of the Third Annual Convention of the National Association of State Dairy and Food Commissioners*, 1899, 49; "The Adulteration, Misbranding, and Imitation of Foods, etc., in the District of Columbia, etc.," 56th Cong., 1st sess., 1902, *House Report 1426* (hereafter cited as *H. R. 1426*); Congress, House Committee on Interstate and Foreign Commerce, *Hearings ... on the Pure Food Bills*, 56th Cong., 1st sess., (Washington, D.C.: Government Printing Office,

1902), 70–92, 112–13, 117–18; National Association of State Dairy and Food Commissioners, Memorial to the 57th Congress HR; *Journal of Proceedings of the Sixth Annual Convention of the National Association of State Dairy and Food Commissioners,* 1902, 17–23; *Senate Report 1209* (hereafter cited as *S. R. 1209*), 3–33; "Adulteration of Foods, etc.," 58th Cong., 2nd sess., 1905, *S. R. 301*; For a more detailed discussion of the alternating opposition and support of the bill, see Anderson, *Health,* 131–63.

54. *Collier's,* November 4, 1905, 13–16, 25.

55. Young, *Toadstool Millionaires,* 212–13.

56. *Proceedings of the Association of Official Agricultural Chemists, 1885* (Division of Chemistry, Bulletin 7), 25, and *1886* (Bulletin 12), 16; *Report of the Commissioner of Agriculture,* 1885, 11, 109–18.

57. Josiah Strong, "Women and Betterment," *Keystone,* August 1902, 12.

58. *Union Signal,* December 20, 1883, 7, and October 28, 1897, 8.

59. F. L. H. W., "Club Contrasts," *Keystone,* June 1889, 11; Florence Stephenson, "Beware!" *Keystone,* April 1906, 11; E. G. Routzahn, secretary of the Bureau of Civic Corporation, "A Tribute to Women's Clubs, Letter to the Editor," *Unity,* Chicago, April 28, 1905, reprinted in *Keystone,* October 1905, 11.

60. For a discussion of women's historic commitment to the nurturing and protection of life, see Eleanor Lenz and Barbara Meyerhof, *The Feminization of America: How Women's Values Are Changing Our Public and Private Lives* (Los Angeles: Jeremy F. Tarcher, 1985), 179.

61. Starr, *Social Transformation,* 32; Young, *Toadstool Millionaires,* 9.

62. Ibid.

63. Catherine Beecher, "Treatise on Domestic Economy," cited in Mary Ryan, *Empire of the Mother: American Writing about Domesticity, 1830–1860* (New York: Haworth, 1962), 25; Catherine Clinton, *The Plantation Mistress: Woman's World in the Old South* (New York: Pantheon Books, 1982), 143–45; Joseph Kett, *The Formation of the Medical Professions: The Role of Institutions, 1760–1860* (New Haven: Yale University Press, 1968), 14–30.

64. Starr, *Social Transformation,* 32–33.

65. Sophie F. Grubb, "Civics: Have Women an Interest in them?" *Union Signal,* October 7, 1897, 4.

66. Jane Addams, "Why Women Should Vote," *Ladies' Home Journal,* January 1910, 21–22.

67. Anna E. Dickinson, "Shall Women Help?" *Union Signal,* July 31, 1884, 2.

68. Mrs. C. S. Burnett, of Tullahoma, Tennessee, "Women in Politics," *Union Signal,* July 5, 1883, 3.

Chapter 3. The State Crusaders

1. Carl L. Alsberg, "Progress in Federal Food Control," in Ravenel, 214.

2. Louise Purington, "Report of the Department of Health and Heredity," *N.W.C.T.U. Minutes,* 1906, 212–13.

3. Bessie Cushman, "Health," *N.W.C.T.U. Minutes,* 1886, Appendix, xvi; Charles V. Chapin, "History of State and Municipal Control of Disease," in Ravenel, 155.

4. Elizabeth Foster, "Pure Food," Massachusets State Federation, *Federation*

Bulletin, November 1905, 84; Alice Lakey, "Food Laws and Their Enforcement," *Consumers' Reports*, 1906, 59, 69–71.

    5. Ibid.

    6. Ibid.; Charles V. Chapin, "History of State and Municipal Control of Disease," in Ravenel, 155. Charles V. Chapin, M.D, Sc.D., was superintendent of health in Providence, Rhode Island; lecturer, School of Public Health at Harvard and Massachusetts Institute of Technology; and professor of physiology, Brown University.

    7. Lakey, "Food Laws," 69–71; Ravenel, 155.

    8. *N.W.C.T.U. Minutes*, 1883, Appendix, lvii; *N.W.C.T.U. Minutes*, 1885, Appendix, lxxxii.

    9. Allen, *Alcohol*, 310.

    10. Ibid., 312–13.

    11. Ibid.; Martha Allen, "Non-Alcoholic Medicine," *N.W.C.T.U Reports*, 1903, 203.

    12. *N.W.C.T.U. Minutes*, 1882, Appendix, lxxxviii and lxxxix; *W.C.T.U. Minutes*, 1883, Appendix, lxxxi, lxxxii, lxvii.

    13. Lakey, "Food Laws and Their Enforcement," *Consumers' Reports*, 1906, 55, 59.

    14. Croly, *History*, 589; Elizabeth Foster, "Pure Food in the Senate," *Federation Bulletin*, December 1904, 69. Foster, "Pure Food," *Federation Bulletin*, November 1905, 84, 87.

    15. Ibid. *Federation Bulletin*, March 1906, 308.

    16. Ibid.

    17. Laws of Missouri, II General Assembly (G.A.) 1822, 42; VI G.A. 1830-31, 96; VIII G.A. 1834-35, 33; XI G.A. 1840-41, 133; XII G.A. 1842-43, 118; XIV G.A. 1846-47, 186; XXIII G.A. 1865-66, 285–86.

    18. Alsberg, in Ravenel, 212–13.

    19. Ibid., 214.

    20. Ibid., 214; Lakey "Food Laws and Their Enforcement," *Consumers' Reports*, 1906, 54–71.

    21. Lakey, "Food Laws," 55.

    22. Ibid., 60–61; *N.W.C.T.U. Reports*, 1902, 235.

    23. *Consumers' Reports*, 1906, 61–62; *N.W.C.T.U. Reports*, 1902, 235.

    24. *Consumers' Reports*, 1906, 61.

    25. Ibid., 63.

    26. Ibid., 59; *N.W.C.T.U. Minutes*, 1886, lvi; *N.W.C.T.U. Reports*, 1902, 235.

    27. *Consumers' Reports*, 1906, 57.

    28. *Consumers' Reports*, 1905, 62; *N.W.C.T.U. Minutes*, 1886, lv; *N.W.C.T.U. Reports*, 1902, 236.

    29. *N.W.C.T.U. Minutes*, 1886, lv.

    30. *Consumers' Reports*, 1906, 55; 1902 newspaper clippings, Denver, Colorado, Public Library, Manuscript Division; Denver *Business Woman's Magazine* 5, no. 4 (November 1905): 404.

    31. *Consumers' Reports*, 1906, 54–67; 1902 newspaper clippings, reportedly from *The Atlanta Constitution*; Denver *Business Woman's Magazine* 5, no. 4 (November 1905): 404; Congress, House, Joseph C. Richardson of Arkansas speaking for the Pure Food, Drink, and Drug Bill, *Congressional Record* (*Cong. Rec.*), 59th Cong., 1st sess., 1906, 8976–77.

32. Martha Allen, "Medical Temperance," *N.W.C.T.U. Reports*, 1905, 232, and Lillian Stevens, "Address of the President," *N.W.C.T.U. Reports*, 1905, 109.

33. *Union Signal*, April 5, 1883, 5, and September 9, 1885, 9; Petition from the Frankfort Men's Club to the Honorable Members of the House of Representatives, Washington, D.C., Frankfort, Kentucky, April 20 1906, copy in the letters to Elton Fulmer, Washington State Chemist's Records, Washington State Universities, Pullman, Washington.

34. Congress, Senate Hearings, "Adulteration of Foods, etc.," 1904.

35. "Pasadena, California," *Union Signal*, October 23, 1884, 10; Clippings from Georgia Newspapers, 1902, Special Collections, University of Georgia, Athens; *Union Signal*, April 6, 1899, 6, and April 2, 1885, 3.

36. Willard, *Women and Temperance*, 286.

37. Russell Land Carpenter, "Is It Poison? The Band of Hope Lesson," *Union Signal*, September 20, 1886, 7.

38. Allen, *Alcohol*, 345.

39. *Colorado W.C.T.U. Messenger* 10, no. 12 (December 1903): n.p.; Allen, *Alcohol*, 304–09, 314.

40. *Colorado W.C.T.U. Messenger* 8, no. 12 (December 1902): n.p., 10, no. 12 (December 1903): n.p.; Allen, *Alcohol*, 346.

41. Allen, *Alcohol*, 346–54.

42. Ibid.

43. Ibid.

44. Ibid., 338.

45. Canon Farrar, "The Intemperate Language of Temperance Advocates," *Union Signal*, November 20, 1884, 2; H. W. Hardy, "Calling Names," *Union Signal*, August 19, 1886, 5.

46. Ibid.

47. Ibid.

48. *Union Signal*, April 30, 1885, 2, November 15, 1883, 2, November 8, 1883, 11.

49. *Keystone*, October 1899, 8.

50. Professor Phillip Graham Taylor, "Address Before the Buffalo Convention," *Union Signal*, December 9, 1897, 3.

51. *Keystone*, December 1899, 4.

52. *Colorado W.C.T.U. Messenger* 4, no. 3 (February 1898): n.p., and February 1912, 6; *Keystone*, January 1900, 3; Mrs. Esther T. Housh, "All Things Are Yours," *Women at Work*, cited in *Union Signal*, March 20, 1884, 3.

53. Mrs. Ella Dare, "Women's Strength," *Union Signal*, January 10, 1884, 3; "The W.C.T.U. Declaration of Principles: Our Methods," *Union Signal*, May 24, 1906, 9.

54. Editorial, *Keystone*, July 1903, 3; Sarah Hackett Hunt, convention correspondence, *N.W.C.T.U. Minutes*, 1882, Appendix, cxxix.

55. Allen, *Alcohol*, 25–6.

56. See, for one example, Rowena B. Troop, of Mount Pleasant, Iowa, "Two Essential Conditions," *Union Signal*, February 14, 1884, 4; Mrs. Judge Merrick, "Women and Temperance," annual address before the Louisiana W.C.T.U., *Union Signal*, March 27, 1894, 2.

57. Joseph Pulitzer, cited in Morton Mintz and Jerry S. Cohen, *Power, Inc.: Public and Private Rulers and How to Make Them Accountable* (New York and London: Bantam Books, 1977), 62.

58. Merrick, "Women and Temperance," *Union Signal*, March 27, 1884, 2; Elizabeth Foster, "The Pure Food Question," *Federation Bulletin*, April 1905, 224.

59. *Union Signal*, December 20, 1883, 7.

60. Editorial, *Keystone*, July 1899, 3, and August 1899, 3.

61. J. Ellen Foster, "Department of Legislation," *N.W.C.T.U. Minutes*, 1883, 125.

62. Missouri State Board of Agriculture, *32nd Annual Report*, 1900, 30–31; Missouri *Senate Journal*, XLIII General Assembly, 1905, 140, 582; Missouri Federation of Women's Clubs, *Minutes*, 1899–1902, business session of the annual convention held at Joplin, Missouri, 7–9 November 1900, 9:30 session, November 9, 1900, 93, Western Historical Manuscripts, Ellis Library, University of Missouri, Columbia; Missouri Federation of Women's Clubs, *Proceedings of the First Biennial Convention*, May 1905, 51, 53.

63. Wiley's role in the crusade is well-documented in Anderson, *Health*, Young, *Toadstool Millionaires*, and Wiley, *Autobiography* and *Crime*, as well as in a number of other publications.

64. Wiley, *Crime*, 16, 52, 250, 267.

65. House, *Cong. Rec.*, 59th Cong., 1st sess., June 22, 1906, 8976; R. M. Allen to James B. McCreary, 25 March 1904, Bureau of Chemistry letters, National Archives, RG 97; *Consumers' Reports*, 1906.

66. *N.W.C.T.U. Reports*, 1903, 200–04, 243; *N.W.C.T.U. Reports*, 1905, 105, 110.

67. Foster, *Federation Bulletin*, December 1904, 68.

Chapter 4. The N.W.C.T.U. Crusaders, I

1. "The W.C.T.U. Declaration of Principles," *Union Signal*, May 24, 1906, 9.

2. For a discussion of the N.W.C.T.U. transition to politics, see Ruth Bordin, *Frances Willard: A Biography* (Chapel Hill and London: University of North Carolina Press, 1986), 78–79, 106; Frances E. Willard, *Glimpses of Fifty Years: The Autobiography of an American Woman* (Chicago: Woman's Christian Temperance Publishing Association, 1889), 368–69.

3. Contrary to what historians believe, and many have written, it was neither Harvey Washington Wiley, the government chemist, who initiated food and drug reform as Anderson suggests; nor was it muckraker Samuel Hopkins Adams who fired "the opening gun in the first overall campaign against patent medicines" in *Collier's* October 7, 1905 issue, as Stewart Holbrook asserts; nor the A.M.A. spurred on by the "catastrophe" of contaminated diphtheria antitoxin in St. Louis, as Harry F. Dowling contends, who initiated the pure food, drink, or drug crusade. Anderson, *Health*, 1; Stewart H. Holbrook, *The Golden Age of Quackery* (New York: Macmillan, 1959), 14; Henry F. Dowling, *Medicine for Man: The Development, Regulation, and Use of Prescription Drugs* (New York: Alfred A. Knopf, 1970), 188; Mary J. Tucker, "Vermont," *Union Signal*, October 9, 1884, 11.

4. Alice M. Guernsey, "Alcohol A Narcotic — Not a Stimulant," *Union Signal*, December 4, 1884, 3; *Union Signal*, January 6, 1887, 8, and March 24, 1887, 4.

5. "The American Health Propaganda," *Union Signal*, April 6, 1899, 60.

6. Willard, quoted in *Union Signal*, January 9, 1913, 1; "The Twelfth Annual Session of the N. W. C. T. U.," *Union Signal*, November 19, 1885, 4; Willard, *Women*

and Temperance, 42; "The W.C.T.U. Declaration of Principles," *Union Signal*, May 24, 1906, 9.

7. Willard, "Annual Address to the 1883 W.C.T.U. Convention," *Union Signal*, November 8, 1883, 5.

8. Hunt, *Decade*, 7.

9. "Matters to Consider at St. Louis," *Union Signal*, October 9, 1884, 8.

10. Jonathan Zimmerman, "The 'Queen of the Lobby': Mary Hunt, Scientific Temperance, and the Dilemma of Democratic Education in America, 1879–1906," *History of Education Quarterly* 32, no. 1 (Spring 1992): 14, 17.

11. Mrs. J. H. Kellogg, "Suggestions for Work for Local Unions in the Department of Hygiene," *Union Signal*, October 30, 1885, 4–5.

12. Ibid.

13. Ibid.; Willard, "Annual Address, 1884," *Union Signal*, October 30, 1884, 6.

14. *Union Signal*, May 8, 1884, 1; Georgia Hulse McLeod, "Southern Gleanings: Washington, D.C.," *Union Signal*, May 22, 1884, 11.

15. Mary Ellen West, "Illinois' Hygiene and Heredity: State Normal Institute at Lake Bluff," *Union Signal*, August 28, 1884, 12; "Lake Bluff: Where and What Is Lake Bluff?" *Union Signal*, May 17, 1883, 14.

16. M. P. M., "News from the Field: Vermont — County Institute," *Union Signal*, August 21, 1884, 11; Mrs. J. H. Kellogg, "Hygiene," and Mary Weeks Burnett, M.D., "Heredity," *N.W.C.T.U. Minutes*, 1885, Appendix, xlix, l, li, lxxxi–lxxxvi.

17. Mary Whitall Smith, "Correspondence: A Girl's Heredity Institute," *Union Signal*, February 28, 1884, 4; McLeod, "Southern Gleanings: Washington, D.C.," *Union Signal*, May 22, 1884, 11.

18. "Resumé of the Report of the Corresponding Secretary," *Union Signal*, November 26, 1885, 8; *Union Signal*, November 15, 1883, 2.

19. *Union Signal*, November 15, 1883, 2.

20. "Our New Superintendencies," *Union Signal*, November 20, 1884, 9; Bessie V. Cushman, M.D., "Health," *N.W.C.T.U. Minutes*, 1886, lv–lviii.

21. Josephine R. Nichols, "Report of Superintendent, Department of Heredity," *Minutes of the National Woman's Christian Temperance Union, at the Tenth Annual Meeting in Detroit Michigan, October 31st to November 3d, 1883* (Cleveland, Ohio: Home Publishing, 1883), Appendix, xviii– xix; Mary Weeks Burnett, "Report of the National Superintendent of the Department of Heredity," *N.W.C.T.U. Minutes*, 1886 and 1887, clxxxii–clxxxiii and cclii; Willard, *Union Signal*, October 30, 1884, 6; "National W.C.T.U. Convention", *Union Signal*, November 11, 1886, 22.

22. Frank Waldo, "The Scientific Period of the Temperance Movement," *School Physiology Journal* 15: 8 (April 1906): 114; Mary H. Hunt, "The Beginnings of Scientific Temperance," *School Physiology Journal* 15: 6 (February 1906): 81; Willard, *Women and Temperance*, 253; Hunt, *Decade*, 6–7; Hunt, *Epoch*, 6–9.

23. Hunt, "Scientific Temperance," *Union Signal*, August 6, 1885, 9.

24. Hunt, *Epoch*, 6; *Union Signal*, June 7, 1883, 1.

25. Hunt, *Decade*, 9; Waldo, "The Scientific Period of the Temperance Movement," *School Physiology Journal* 15, no. 8 (April 1906): 81.

26. Hunt, *Decade*, 3, and *Epoch*, 6.

27. *Union Signal*, March 15, 1883, 13; Hunt, *Epoch*, 7.

28. Hunt, *Epoch*, 8.

29. Ibid., 9.

30. Ibid.; Hunt, "The Department of Scientific Temperance Instruction," *N.W.C.T.U. Minutes*, 1885, 13; *Union Signal*, November 19, 1885, 25.

31. *Union Signal*, January 18, 1883, 4; Mary J. Tucker, "News from the Field: Vermont," *Union Signal*, October 9, 1884, 11.

32. Julia Lathrop, "News from the Field: Michigan," *Union Signal*, May 3, 1883, 11; C. C. Alford "IO TRIOMPHE!" *Union Signal*, May 3, 1883, 12.

33. *Union Signal*, February 21, 1884, 1; J. S. T., "How to Win a Victory," *Union Signal*, March 27, 1884, 4–5.

34. Ibid.; Elizabeth W. Greenwood, "It Was a Famous Victory," *Union Signal*, March 13, 1884, 4–5.

35. Elizabeth W. Greenwood, "Is the Compulsory Temperance Educational Law in New York State Enforced?" *Union Signal*, January 25, 1885, 5; Mrs. H. A. Perrigo, "Stereoscopic Temperance," *Union Signal*, November 6, 1884, 6.

36. Mrs. Wm. Patten, "News from the Field: Pennsylvania," *Union Signal*, April 19, 1884, 11; "News from the Field: Pennsylvania," *Union Signal*, November 20, 1884, 11; Ellen M. Watson, "News from the Field: Pennsylvania," *Union Signal*, March 19, 1885, 10; Narcissa E. White, "On the Wing," *Union Signal*, February 28, 1884, 5, and "News from the Field: Pennsylvania-educational," *Union Signal* March 12, 1885, 11; Hunt, "Remarks at the 12th Annual Session of the N.W.C.T.U.," *Union Signal*, November 19, 1885, 25; *Union Signal*, June 19, 1884, 11, March 5, 1885, 3, November 20, 1884, 11, March 19, 1885, 10, November 19, 1885, 25, November 19, 1886, 22; Hunt, *Decade*, 14–17.

37. Ibid.

38. Ibid.

39. "Legislative Pleasantry," *Union Signal*, April 16, 1885, 4.

40. "The Legislative Gains of the Season," *Union Signal*, April 16, 1885, 2; Hunt, *Decade*, 14–17.

41. Narcissa E. White, "News from the Field: Pennsylvania-educational," *Union Signal*, March 12, 1885, 11; "The Legislative Gains of the Season, *Union Signal*, April 16, 1885, 4.

42. Sally Chapin, "To the Union Signal, En Route to Ga.," *Union Signal*, February 19, 1885, 9; *Union Signal*, February 26, 1885, 1.

43. Hunt, *Union Signal*, November 19, 1885, 25; *Union Signal*, July 3, 1884, 12; Bessie Cushman, "Missouri Uplifted," *Union Signal*, May 7, 1885, 5; Mrs. H. E. Worthington, "News from the Field: Missouri," *Union Signal*, April 2, 1885, 11–12; "News from the Field: Missouri," *Union Signal*, July 5, 1884, 12.

44. "Scientific Temperance Instruction in Schools and Colleges," *N.W.C.T.U. Minutes*, 1886, ccvi–ccix; Hunt, *Decade*, 19–28.

45. Hunt, *Epoch*, 20–21; Clipping from *Nashville Tennessean*, Betty Mizell Donaldson Papers, Box 3, Folder 13, accession number 309, microfilm ed., reel no. 1, Tennessee State Library and Archives, Manuscript Unit, Nashville; "The New Education," *Union Signal*, April 16, 1885, 2.

46. Hunt, "Scientific Temperance," *Union Signal*, 6 August 1885, 9.

47. *Union Signal*, August 21, 1884, 8, November 6, 1884, 4, 6, and March 12, 1885, 9; Hunt, "Why I Do Not Endorse Smith's Physiologies, *Union Signal*, March 25, 1886, 8; "Temperance Text-books: Safe and Unsafe," *Union Signal*, September 10, 1885, 9.

48. "Scientific Instruction," *Union Signal*, August 21, 1884, 8; "The Battle of

the Books," *Union Signal*, December 17, 1885, 2; *Union Signal*, October 4, 1883, 2, July 10, 1884, 8–9, August 21, 1884, 6, October 16, 1884, 9, 11, September 15, 1885, 9, May 13, 1886, 16; Hunt, *Decade*, 17.

49. *Union Signal*, October 2, 1884, 11; *Union Signal*, July 10, 1884, 8–9.

50. "How Shall Temperance Teaching Be Given in Our Public Schools?" *Union Signal*, July 12, 1883, 8; Alice M. Guernsey, "Temperance in Schools," *Union Signal*, February 1, 1883, 2; Hunt, "How to Teach It," *Union Signal*, November 17, 1887, 5.

51. Frances Willard, "Annual Address to the 1884 W.C.T.U. Convention," *Union Signal*, October 30, 1884, 3; Miss Cora Thomas, "Annual Meeting of the W. C. T. U.— News from the Field: District of Columbia," *Union Signal*, October 2, 1884, 10; M. G. "How Shall We Interest the Teachers," *Union Signal*, October 4, 1885, 2.

52. Frank Waldo, "The Scientific Period of the Temperance Movement," *School Physiology Journal* 15, no.8 (April 1906): 116.

53. Cherrington, III: 1269–70; *Union Signal*, January 21, 1886, 2, and August 25, 1887, 3.

54. "A Brief History of the W.C.T.U." (Evanston, Illinois: Union Signal, 1907), 40.

55. Ibid. *Union Signal*, January 21, 1886, 2; Mrs. James Havens, "Narcotics," *N.W.C.T.U. Minutes*, 1886, lxxvii–lxxix.

56. Ibid.

57. Ibid.

58. Mrs. F. H. Ingalls, "Narcotics," *N.W.C.T.U. Minutes*, 1887, cc–cci. *Union Signal*, January 5, 1899, 10.

59. Ibid.

60. "A Brief History of the W.C.T.U.," 1907, 40.

61. Ingalls, "Narcotics," *N.W.C.T.U. Minutes*, 1887, ccii, cciii.

62. Ibid.

63. *Union Signal*, January 5, 1899, 10; *N.W.C.T.U. Minutes*, 1889, Appendix, ccxlvi–ccxlvii.

64. Foster, "Legislation," *N.W.C.T.U. Minutes*, 1886, cxiii, and "The Legislative Gains of the Season," *Union Signal*, April 16, 1885, 2, and January 5, 1899, 10; Foster, "Department of Legislation," *N.W.C.T.U. Minutes*, 1883, 124–27; L. A. Nash, "News from the Field: Oregon — Mrs. J. Ellen Foster at Corvallis," August 14, 1884, 10.

65. See, for example, *Union Signal*, June 5, 1884, 15; *Union Signal*, April, 24, 1884, 1, and May 20, 1884, 1; *Union Signal*, April 22, 1886, 13.

Chapter 5. The N.W.C.T.U. Crusaders, II

1. One of Willard's biographers wrote, "Criticism came from some of the most influential officers and most dedicated pure food, drink, and drug advocates. Judith Ellen Foster, superintendent of the Department of Legislation, with a large group of intellectual cohorts, left the W.C.T.U. in opposition to Willard's endorsement of the Prohibition Party. In public, Mary Levitt, one of Willard's closest friends and the first W.C.T.U. world missionary, found fault with Willard's behavior and in

private accused her of disloyalty and deviousness. Ida Wells, a young black teacher, journalist, and popular W.C.T.U. lecturer, criticized Willard's equivocations on racial issues. Caroline B. Buell, N.W.C.T.U. Corresponding Secretary, and Dr. Bessie Bushman of the National W.C.T.U. Hospital, spokesperson for a large dissenting Chicago clique, charged Willard of misdirecting W.C.T.U. energies. Esther Pugh, the national treasurer, and Alice Guernsey, a member of the executive committee, censured her for assuming too much power and spending too lavishly in the European style." Mary Hunt represented a wing of the W.C.T.U. that opposed endorsing the Prohibition and Fusion Parties. Bordin, *Frances Willard*, 200–13; *W.C.T.U. Reports*, 1894, 1896.

2. Bordin, *Frances Willard*, 203.

3. Bordin, *Frances Willard*, 149–50, 155; "President's Address," *N.W.C.T.U. Reports*, 1905, 108–09.

4. *N.W.C.T.U. Reports*, 1898, 198.

5. Ibid.

6. Ibid, 201.

7. Ibid. *Union Signal*, January 20, 1898, 14.

8. Purington, "Health and Heredity," *N.W.C.T.U. Reports*, 1906, 212; "The Boston Food Fair" *Club Woman*, October 1899, 87.

9. *Journal of Proceedings of the National Pure Food and Drug Congress, 1898*, (Washington, D.C., Government Printing Office, 1898).

10. Purington, "Health and Heredity," *W.C.T.U.Reports*, 1906, 212; *Journal of Proceedings of the National Pure Food and Drug Congress*, 1898; Wedderburn's role in the fight for pure food, drink, and drugs was obscured by his rivalry with Wiley and objections to his work by J. Sterling Morton, Secretary of Agriculture. Wedderburn's earliest contribution to the fight for pure food, drink, and drugs was *A Popular Treatise on the Extent and Character of Food Adulteration*, published by the U.S. Department of Agriculture as Bulletin 25 of the Division of Chemistry. This study was commissioned by the Division of Chemistry to appeal to popular opinion. It consisted of significant reports and opinions that showed state laws were not adequate to protect the consumer and honest manufacturers. The arguments bore a striking resemblance to the propaganda that the W.C.T.U. had been circulating since 1882 — that fraud was so widespread it extended to almost every article of food; that adulteration was particularly detrimental in robbing the consumer of adequate nutrition, denying the farmer his profits, encouraging foreign governments to discriminate against American products, and corrupting the morals of the people. Poisonous adulterations made food less nutritious and wholesome, impaired health, and frequently caused death. Morton discontinued publication of the bulletin and Wiley considered the Preface a compilation of "extravagant assertions," "erroneous," and "virtually worthless." See Letters, Wiley to Morton, March 28, June 22, July 10 and 31, September 7, 1893; Morton to Wiley, July 10, September 5, 1893, National Archives, RG 97.

11. Congress, Senate, "Memorial from the National Pure Food and Drug Congress," 55th Cong., 2nd sess., *S. R. 233*. For a more detailed discussion of this event, see Anderson, *Health*, 124–28.

12. *N.W.C.T.U. Reports*, 1901, 211–12.

13. Ibid., 209–12.

14. *N.W.C.T.U. Reports*, 1897, 280; *Reports*, 1898, 199–200; *Reports*, 1902, 202; *Union Signal*, September 23, 1897, 13.

15. *N.W.C.T.U. Reports*, 1901, 222; For a discussion of the extent of their

interests, see Sophie F. Grubb, "Civics: Have Women an Interest in Them?" *Union Signal*, October 7, 1897, 4.

16. *N.W.C.T.U. Reports*, 1902, 232, and *N.W.C.T.U. Reports*, 1903, 202.

17. *N.W.C.T.U. Reports*, 1895, 6, and *N.W.C.T.U. Reports*, 1898, 299.

18. *N.W.C.T.U. Reports*, 1895, 212; *N.W.C.T.U. Reports*, 1897, 288–300; *N.W.C.T.U. Reports*, 1898, 6, 213; *N.W.C.T.U. Reports*, 1900, 211–219; and *N.W.C.T.U. Reports*, 1901, 217–21.

19. Ibid; *N.W.C.T.U. Reports*, 1901, 222.

20. Ibid; Hunt, *Epoch*, 45–50,

21. *N.W.C.T.U. Reports*, 1906, 222.

22. Ibid.; Hunt, *N.W.C.T.U. Reports*, 1901, 220.

23. One of the best summaries of Mary Hannah Hanchett Hunt's later relationship with the W.C.T.U. is found in Randall C. Jimerson, Francis S. Blouin, and Charles A. Isetts, eds., *Guide to the Microfilm Edition of the Temperance and Prohibition Papers* (Ann Arbor: University of Michigan, 1977), 161–64.

24. "News of the Week — Mrs. Hunt Honored," *Union Signal*, April 2, 1903, 1.

25. Laurel G. Bowen, "Series, IX, Scientific Temperance Federation, 1881–1934," in Jimerson, Blouin, and Isetts, *Guide to the Microfilm Edition*, 161–63.

26. *N.W.C.T.U. Reports*, 1906, 222.

27. Mrs. E. B. Ingalls, "Narcotics," *N.W.C.T.U. Minutes*, 1893–1894, 312–15.

28. Ibid.

29. *N.W.C.T.U. Reports*, 1893, 433–35.

30. Ingalls, *N.W.C.T.U. Reports*, 1903, 240.

31. Ibid.

32. Ibid.

33. Ingalls, *N.W.C.T.U. Reports*, 1903, 240–41.

34. Ingalls, *N.W.C.T.U. Reports*, 1901, 253.

35. "A Brief History of the W.C.T.U.," 1907, 39–40.

36. Ibid.

37. Allen, *Alcohol*, 26, 312. 316.

38. Ibid., 24.

39. Ibid., 24–25.

40. Ibid., 24–26.

41. *N.W.C.T.U. Reports*, 1897, 280–87.

42. Ibid.

43. *N.W.C.T.U. Reports*, 1898, 202–07; *N.W.C.T.U. Reports*, 1897, 280–89.

44. Allen, *Alcohol*, Chapters 13 and 14.

45. Ibid.; *N.W.C.T.U. Reports*, 1900, 208–12.

46. Ibid.

47. Ibid.

48. Allen, *Alcohol*, ii, 300, 317–19.

49. Ibid., 26.

50. *N.W.C.T.U. Reports*, 1902, 232–33.

51. For a discussion of Foster's disaffection with the W.C.T.U., see Bordin, *Women and Temperance*, 124–25.

52. Mrs. Clinton Smith, "Mrs. Ellis in the Field," *Union Signal*, April 20, 1899, 6.

53. *Union Signal*, December 12, 1901, 5, January 2, 1902, 1, July 30, 1925, 7.

54. *Union Signal*, January 5, 1899, 10; *N.W.C.T.U. Reports*, 1905, 109.

55. Ibid. For a discussion of Margaret Ellis' accomplishments in Washington, D.C., see Ian Tyrrell, *Woman's World, Woman's Empire* (Chapel Hill and London: University of North Carolina Press, 1991), 160–61, 214–16.

56. Bordin, *Women and Temperance*, 155.

57. Ibid.; Richard W. Leeman, *"Do Everything" Reform: The Oratory of Frances E. Willard* (New York: Greenwood, 1992), 90.

58. Willard, "President's Address 1897," cited in Leeman, *Do Everything*, 189.

59. See, for example, "Advantages of a Drug-Free Lifestyle," "Stop Now Don't Get Hooked," "Choose," "Clowning Around with Drugs Is No Laughing Matter," "A Special Invitation for You," and "Presenting the Woman's Christian Temperance Union" (Evanston, Illinois: Signal Press, n.d.).

Chapter 6. The G.F.W.C. Crusaders

1. Louise B. Ernst, "Literature and Life," an address given at the Twelfth Convention of the Ohio Federation, *Club Notes for Club Women*, December 1907, 97 (hereafter cited as *Club Notes*).

2. Mildred Carlson Ahloren, "Foreword," in Wells, *Unity in Diversity* (hereafter cited as Wells), vii.

3. Wood, *The History of the General Federation of Women's Clubs* (hereafter cited as Wood), 71, 84; Helen M. Winslow, "Notes," *Club Woman*, February 1898, 1.

4. Croly, *The History of the Women's Club Movement*, (hereafter cited as Croly, *History*), ix, 112, 125, 128.

5. Karen Blair, *The Clubwoman as Feminist*, 93; Louisa B. Poppenheim, "How Shall We Use the Club," *Keystone*, October 1899, 10–11; Ernst, "Literature and Life," *Club Notes*, December 1907, 97.

6. Sarah Platt Decker, "An Address to the General Federation of Women's Clubs, July 17, 1907," *Club Notes*, August 1907, 188–93.

7. Ibid.

8. Wood, 166–67; Nonfederated clubs, which followed the Federation lead, totaled an estimated two times that number. State federations that remained outside the Federation until after 1906 worked vigorously for both state and federal food, drink, and drug regulation. The Alabama State Federation did not affiliate with the National Federation until 1907, after the pure food, drink, and drug bill became law. Virginia, Nevada, and New Mexico State Federations joined the national organization later. A majority of clubwomen in these states felt they could accomplish more effective work on their own and preferred to work independently. In minor respects they were right. Pure food committees, such as the one in the Alabama Federation functioned effectively in both educational and legislative capacities, and were more sensitive to opinion at the local and state level. They were able to benefit from the Federation movement, and to adapt its methods without subscribing to all of its policies. As one of their critics observed, unfederated clubs were able to feed off the federation without paying the tab. "Alabama in the General Federation," *Federation Bulletin*, November 1907, 54–55.

9. Karen Blair has discussed this aspect of club life in greater detail, Blair, 57–77; Poppenheim, "How Shall We Use the Club," *Keystone*, October 1899, 10–11.

10. Wells, 61; Wood, 21; Mrs. C. J. McClung "Club Government — Methods," *Club Woman*, February 1898, 140–41.

11. Eva Perry Moore, "Forward," in Wood, iv.

12. "Our Patent Politics," *Union Signal*, October 28, 1897, 8. Baker, "Domestication of Politics," 639–41.

13. Ibid.

14. Mrs. D. H. Kornhauser, "Cause of Increase of Snobbishness," *Club Notes*, April 1908, 55–56.

15. Mrs. E. E. Trayer, "Is a Caste Spirit Developing in America?" *Club Notes*, April 1908, 57.

16. Wood, 183; Isabell Churchill, "President's Annual Message: Colorado Federation of Women's Clubs," *Business Woman's Magazine* 5, no. 4 (November 1905): 398. For an example of an outline of study suggested by the Committee of Household Economics, see *Club Notes*, April 1907, 45.

17. "In the Interest Of Righteousness," *Club Woman*, October 1899, 23.

18. Marian A. McBride, "Domestic Science and the Home," *Club Woman*, February 1903, 221.

19. McBride, "Domestic Science and the Home," *Club Woman*, November 1902, 104–05, and December 1902, 148–49.

20. Ibid., 220.

21. Clara P. Bourland, "The Relation of the Woman's Club to Civic Life," *Club Woman*, April 1898, 5.

22. Ibid.

23. Georgie A. Bacon, "Report of the Civil Service Reform Committee of the General Federation," *Federation Bulletin*, June 1904, 189–91.

24. "Nebraska," *Club Woman*, December 1902, 131; "The Work of Women's Clubs," *Federation Bulletin*, January 1904, 42; "Work in the State Federations. Idaho," *Federation Bulletin*, 182.

25. *Club Woman*, April 1902, 266; Mrs. Frederick Hanger, "Objectionable Advertising," *Club Woman*, September 1902, 7.

26. *Club Woman*, December 1902, 126; Wells, 63.

27. Wells, 166; Mrs. Arthur Courtenay Neville, "Interesting Exhibit at the Louisiana Purchase Exposition for the Student of Household Economics," *Club Woman*, May 1904, 78.

28. Wood 183; Georgie A. Bacon, "The Business Sessions of the Biennial," *Federation Bulletin*, June 1904, 187.

29. Wood, 186, 188–91; Mary E. Craigie, "Splendid Work of Colorado Women," May 1907, newspaper clipping in Conine Collection, Special Collections, Denver Public Library (hereafter cited as Conine Collection).

30. Wood, 212; Wells, 65–72.

31. Ibid.; Dimies T. S. Denison, "The President of the General Federation," *Federation Bulletin*, November 1904, 40–41.

32. Ibid.; Wood, 190.

33. Conine Collection.

34. Wood, 191.

35. Ibid.; Wood 244–45, 248.

36. Ibid.

37. Wells, 72–76; Wood, 148, 191, 244–45.

38. Wood, 195; Letters received, Mil–Mis, Miller to Wiley, March 27, 1905, National Archives, RG 97, Box 62 (hereafter cited as National Archives, RG 97).

39. *Club Notes*, April 1907, 29.

40. See Elizabeth Foster, "Pure Food," Massachusetts State Federation, *Federation Bulletin*, November 1905, 84–85; Foster, "Pure Food in the Senate," *Federation Bulletin*, December 1904, 69.

41. Ibid.

42. Ibid.

43. Foster, "Pure Food," *Federation Bulletin*, November 1905, 84.

44. National Archives, RG 97, Foster to Wiley, November 17, 1904.

45. "Report of the Pure Food Committee," *Club Notes*, October 1907, 38–40.

46. Craigie, clipping in Conine Collection; *Business Woman's Magazine* 5, no. 4 (November 1905): 399; McBride, "Domestic Science," *Club Woman*, 220.

47. James, James, and Boyer, *Notable Women*, 2: 360–61.

48. Ibid. Looking through Lakey's correspondence with Wiley and her public support of him, some researchers have attributed her loyalty to Wiley, despite his coolness, to a somewhat amusing example of the unrelenting pursuit of an eligible Washington bachelor by a New Jersey spinster. Despite its marginal relevance to the pure food and drug crusade, but in light of her motives, perhaps not so irrelevant after all. Such a lampoon is too much an example of unwarranted historical stereotype to ignore. Wiley's voluminous public and private papers suggest intimate relationships with other women, one of whom was particularly persistent, but they reveal no personal relationships between Lakey and Wiley. It may be that Lakey harbored romantic aspirations toward Wiley, but I found no evidence to indicate that either Lakey or Wiley considered their acquaintance anything more than intense involvement in the pure food, drink, and drug cause. Anderson, *Health*, 169–70

49. Library of Congress, Harvey W. Wiley Collection, letters, Wiley to Lakey, July 11, November 24, December 2, 1903; Lakey to Wiley, November 22, 1903, May 6, June 2, July 8, 1904.

50. National Archives, RG 97, Miller to Wiley, January 7, 1905.

51. Emily Lee Sherwood, "The National Congress of Mothers, Held at the Baptist Church, Washington, D.C., February 16–18, 1899," *Union Signal*, March 2, 1899, 2.

52. Montgomery Mother's Circle, *Minute Books*, Alabama Historical Society, Montgomery, Alabama.

53. *New York Times*, Sunday, December 3, 1905, 5.

54. Ibid.

55. Ibid.

56. Ibid.

57. Duffy, II: 107, and Duffy, II: 258, citing *Ordinances, Resolutions, etc., Passed by the Common Council*, 1907, X: 125–26, 258. The milk depots, originated by Nathan Strauss, the National Consumers' League, and other charitable organizations in 1893 to provide free or low cost milk to needy infants and children, previously were funded very inadequately and sporadically by a few philanthropic agencies and individuals.

58. "The Women's Educational and Industrial Union," *Federation Bulletin*, December 1903, 28–29; "A Case of Overcrowding," *Federation Bulletin*, November 1904, 45.

59. Alice S. Harris "North-West District," *Club Notes*, November 1907, 82–84.

60. Ibid.

61. R. J. DeVore, "South-West District," *Club Notes*, November 1907, 90.

Chapter 7. The National Consumers' League Crusaders

1. "Scope and Content Note," Introduction to the Records of the National Consumers' League, Manuscript Division, Library of Congress, 3; Florence Kelley, "The Consumers' League" *Keystone*, October 1900, 10.

2. *Consumers' Reports*, 1903, 6–7.

3. Ibid.

4. Ibid.

5. Ibid.

6. Wood, *The History of the Federation* (hereafter cited as Wood), 325.

7. Cited in Blair, *The Clubwoman as Feminist*, 33.

8. Wood, p. 325; Sarah Platt Decker, "A Message for Massachusetts Club Women," Address at the Presidents' Breakfast in Boston, October 1, 1904, *Federation Bulletin*, November 1904, 42–43, and Address at the Federation Day exercise at the Amphitheater, Chautauqua, New York, July 17, 1907; Sarah B. Visanska, "The American Woman of Today," *Keystone*, March 1900, 9.

9. Editorial, *Federation Bulletin*, October 1904, 1–2; Mary E. Calkins, "The Consumers' League and the State Federation," *Federation Bulletin*, November 1904, 43–44.

10. *Consumers' Reports*, 1903, 16.

11. Wood, 139.

12. *Consumers' Reports*, 1905, n.p.

13. *Consumers' Reports*, 1906, 50–80; *Keystone*, July 1905, 8; Incoming letters "L," Lakey to Wiley, March 9, April 14 and 26, May 11, 12, 16, June 26, October 21, 1905; Lakey to Bigelow, August 22, 1905; Letters received, Mil–Mis, Helen Guthrie Miller to Wiley, March 27, 1905, National Archives, RG 97.

14. *Consumer's Reports*, 1906, 50–80, and *Consumers' Reports*, 1907, 46–48. See also, letterheads on correspondence, Incoming letters, Lakey to Wiley, 1906–1908, National Archives, RG 97.

15. Wood, 164; *Union Signal*, February 23, 1899, 2, and March 2, 1899, 2.

16. Ibid.; *Union Signal*, July 31, 1884, 1, August 28, 1884, 10, and June 3, 1886, 2.

17. *Union Signal*, February 23, 1899, 2, and March 2, 1899, 2; Croly, *History*, 410.

18. Wood, 189.

19. "Trusts," *Union Signal*, April 13, 1899, 9.

20. Missouri Federation of Women's Clubs, *Minutes*, 1899–1902, Western Historical Manuscripts, Ellis Library, University of Missouri, Columbia, 82. Alice Lakey, "The Pure Food Investigation Committee," *Consumers' Reports*, 1906, 51.

21. Ibid.

22. Ibid.

23. Ibid.

24. *Consumers' Reports*, 1905, n.p.

25. "Waging War on Poor Food," *Elizabeth Daily Journal*, Elizabeth, New Jersey, January 11, 1906, clipping in letters received, National Archives, RG 97.

26. Ibid.

27. Ibid.

28. Ibid.

29. Ibid.
30. Ibid.
31. *Consumers' Reports*, 1906, 50–51.
32. Wiley to Lakey, January 17, 1906, Outgoing letters, National Archives, RG 97, Book 175, 66–67.
33. Bigelow to Lakey, August 18 and 29, 1905, Outgoing letters, Bureau of Chemistry, National Archives, RG 97.
34. "Mr. Roosevelt's Views on 'Patent Medicine,'" *Ladies' Home Journal*, April 1906, 21.
35. *Consumers' Reports*, 1906, 51; Wilson to Roosevelt, November 2, 1905, Records of the Office of the Secretary of Agriculture, National Archives, RG 97, Bureau of Chemistry Bulletin 99, 77–78, and *Journal of Tenth Annual Convention of the National Association of State Food and Dairy Commissioners*, 1906 (New York, 1907), 44–46, both cited in Anderson, *Health*, 173. *Federation Bulletin*, December 1905, 146–47.
36. Ibid.
37. Ibid.
38. Ibid.; Wiley, *Crime*, 53–55; Letters, Wilson to Roosevelt, November 2, 1905, National Archives, RG 97; *Congressional Record*, 59th Cong., 1st sess., 1906, *Consumers' League Reports*, 1906, 51; Sullivan, II: 530–34; The Memorial was signed by J. B. Nobel, President Interstate Pure Food Commission, Connecticut; Horace Ankeney, Food Commissioner, Ohio, Executive Committee, Interstate Pure Food Commission; T. K. Bruner, Secretary, Board of Agriculture, North Carolina; Alice Lakey, Pure Food Committee, Federation Women's Clubs and National Consumers' League; Mrs. F. V. Covill, Twentieth Century Club; E. F. Ladd, Food Commissioner, North Dakota; M. A. Scovell, Director, Kentucky Experimental Station; R. M. Allen, Secretary and Executive Officer, Food Division, Kentucky Experimental Station, Secretary, Interstate Pure Food Commission. *Federation Bulletin*, December 1905, 146, 148.
39. *Consumers' Reports*, 1906, 50–52; Incoming letters, "L," "One Woman's Campaign For a Pure Food Bill," clipping from the *New York Press*, Sunday morning, February 4, 1906, attached to Lakey to Wiley, October 9, 1905, and, "Miss Lakey's Itinerary," clipping from the *Cranford (New Jersey) Examiner* loose in the file, National Archives, RG 97.
40. Mary Sherman, "Manufacture of Foods in Tenements," *Consumers' Reports*, 1906, 35–49.
41. Ibid.
42. Ibid.
43. Ibid.
44. Ibid.
45. Ibid.
46. Ibid.
47. George W. Goler, "Milk Statistics," *Consumers' Reports*, 1905, 38–43.
48. Ibid.
49. Duffy II: 133
50. Ibid.
51. Ibid., 134–35, 254–55.
52. Ibid., 34–35; *Consumers' Reports*, 1906, 50–52.
53. Ibid.

54. Letter, Henry Beach Needham to Robert M. Allen, February 4, 1907, National Archives, RG 97, General Correspondence, Box 55, 2303.

55. Duffy I: 34–35. *Consumers' Reports*, 1906, 50–52.

Chapter 8. The Southern Crusaders

1. Donaldson Papers, Special Collections, University of Tennessee, Nashville.

2. Louisa B. Poppenheim, "Southern Club Women and What They are Doing," *Federation Bulletin*, May 1905, 254–56.

3. Ibid.

4. Ibid.

5. Mrs. A. E. Smith, "Woman's Part in Civil Service Reform," *Keystone*, August 1900, 11, 12.

6. Poppenheim, "Southern Club Women," *Federation Bulletin*, May 1905, 254–56.

7. Ibid.

8. Lucy Bramlett Patterson, "The Benefits of Getting Together", Annual Report of the President of the North Carolina Federation of Women's Clubs, delivered at Concord, October 14, 1903, *Keystone*, November 1903, 11; Rebecca Felton Papers, Box 1, Ms. 82, f. 11, letters, Special Collections, University of Georgia, Athens.

9. Congress, Senate, Committee on Manufactures, *Hearings on the Bill (S. 198) for Preventing the Adulterations, Misbrandings, and Imitation of Food, Beverages, Candies, Drugs, Condiments in the District of Columbia and the Territories, and for Regulating Interstate Traffic Therein, and for Other Purposes, and the Bill (H.R. 6295) for Preventing the Adulteration or Misbranding of Foods or Drugs, and for Regulating Traffic Therein, and for Other Purposes*, 57th Cong., 1st sess., January 6, 1904, statement of Warwick Massey Hough, 38–53.

10. Young, *Toadstool Millionaires*, 98–99; Stewart H. Holbrook, *The Golden Age of Quackery* (New York: Macmillan, 1959), 103–10.

11. Sally F. Chapin, "Alabama Again," *Union Signal*, August 2, 1883, 5.

12. Ida Marshall Lining, "What the South Needs," *Keystone*, February 1904, 9.

13. Poppenheim, "Southern Club Women," *Federation Bulletin*, May 1905, 254–56.

14. Congress, House, Congressman Adamson speaking against the Pure Food Bill, *Congressional Record*, 59th Cong., 1st sess., 1906, 8955.

15. Ibid; Congress, Senate, *Cong.Rec.*, 59th Cong., 1st sess., 1906, 896, 2720–21.

16. Ibid., 9062–66.

17. Cartwright, *Dark Paradise*, 36–42, 240, and fn. 5–7.

18. *Southern Woman's Magazine*, May 1904, 39–40, January 1905, 28, February 1905, 2, March 1905, 41, Publication Announcement, April 1905, n.p., June 1905, 3.

19. *Keystone*, December 1904, 7, March 1901, 2. For example of proprietary advertisements, see November 1899, 16, ad for Norman's Cordial, and June 1900, 4, for Hall and Cheney advertisement.

20. Donaldson Papers, University of Tennessee.

21. *Keystone*, May 1905, 4–5, June 1905, 7, October 1905, 3, and April 1906, 7.

22. Ibid.

23. Clippings, Atlanta Women's Club Collection, University of Georgia, Athens. The series ran in issues of *Keystone* from May 1904–June 1906.

24. *Mobile Daily Register*, January 28, 1906, 4.

25. Ibid.

26. Ibid., June 9, 1906, 1.

27. Bessie V. Bushman, M.D., "Health," *N.W.C.T.U. Minutes*, 1886, Appendix, lvi.

28. *Union Signal*, January 25, 1888, 10, and February 22, 1888, 4; *N.W.C.T.U. Minutes and Reports*, 1882–1906.

29. Scott, *Invisible*, 216. *Union Signal*, February 22, 1883, 40.

30. Bordin, *Frances Willard*, 115; Scott, *Invisible*, 345; Richard W. Leeman, "*Do Everything" Reform*, 16.

31. Bordin, *Frances Willard*, 114–15.

32. Ibid. 115; Willard, *Women and Temperance*, 35; Georgia Hulse McLeod, Report of Superintendent of Department of Southern Work, *N.W.C.T.U. Minutes*, 1882, Appendix, lv–lvii.

33. Bordin, *Frances Willard*, 114, from Sally Chapin, Letter to the Editor, *Our Union*, 1881; Georgia Hulse McLeod, "A Look at the Harvest Fields," *Union Signal*, May 3, 1893.

34. Presidential Address, *N.W.C.T.U. Minutes*, 1881, lxxv.

35. Bordin, *Frances Willard*, 114.

36. *N.W.C.T.U. Minutes*, 1881, 22–27, 49.

37. Ibid.

38. Ibid.

39. *Union Signal*, January 25, 1882, 10.

40. Ellen C. Bryce, "Alabama," *Union Signal*, April 30, 1885, 2; *Union Signal*, July 12, 1885, 4.

41. Sally F. Chapin, "Alabama Again," *Union Signal*, August 2, 1883, 5.

42. Sally F. Chapin, "Novel Experiences, Hard Work and Rare Enjoyment," *Union Signal*, May 9, 1883, 4–5.

43. *Union Signal*, July 12, 1883, 4.

44. Sally Chapin, correspondence, "Mrs. Chapin in Georgia," *Union Signal*, May 22, 1884, 4.

45. Ibid.

46. Ibid.

47. Chapin, "Novel Experiences," *Union Signal*, May 9, 1883, 4–5.

48. Mrs. Walter Gwynn, "News from the Field: Southern Gleanings—Florida, *Union Signal*, September 4, 1884, 10.

49. Helen H. Rothrock, "News from the Field: Alabama," *Union Signal*, October 2, 1884, 10.

50. Ibid.

51. "News from the Field: Miss Kimball's Impressions and Experiences," *Union Signal*, May 17, 1883, 12.

52. "News From the Field: Virginia, Second Annual Convention of the W.C.T.U.," *Union Signal*, October 2, 1884, 10.

53. Hunt, *Epoch*, 18–22.

54. Caroline E. Merrick, "Women and Temperance, Annual Address of Mrs. Judge Merrick Before the Louisiana W.C.T.U.," *Union Signal*, April 17, 1884, 11.

55. Hunt, *Epoch*, 18–20.

56. Ibid.

57. Ibid.; Sally F. Chapin, "Louisiana Second Annual Convention," *Union Signal*, April 3, 1884, 5, 12; Mary R. Goodale, "News from the Field: Louisiana," *Union Signal*, August 14, 1884, 11.

58. Hunt, *Epoch*, 18–20.

59. Ibid. The bill passed with only four opposing votes in the House and none in the Senate.

60. Ibid, 20–21.

61. Ibid.

62. Ibid.

63. Ibid.

64. *Richmond Times*, December 16, 1884, cited in Suzanne Lebsock, *Virginia Women, 1600–1945* (Richmond: Virginia State Library, 1987), 108.

65. Florida, Report of State Convention, *Union Signal*, April 17, 1884, 11; Hunt, *Decade*, 67–71; "Southern Awakenings," *Union Signal*, June 4, 1885, 3; "News From the Field: South Carolina," *Union Signal*, May 22, 1884, 10; H. B. K, "Notes of Work," *Union Signal*, April 8, 1886, 11; *N.W.C.T.U. Minutes*, 1886, Appendix, ccxix, ccxxii, ccxiii.

66. Hunt, *Decade*, 68.

67. Georgia Hulse McLeod, "The Eastern South," *Union Signal*, May 21, 1885, 3; Mrs. S. W. Tudor, "The Victory in Maryland," *Union Signal*, April 22, 1886, 9; *Union Signal*, June 24, 1886, 1. The opium law imposed a penalty, for establishing or keeping an opium den, of imprisonment in jail not exceeding one year, and fine not exceeding $500 ; for enticing or persuading any person to visit such a place the penalty was the same.

68. Sally F. Chapin, "A Word from Mrs. Chapin, *Union Signal*, June 4, 1885, 9.

69. Missouri H. Stokes, "Georgia's Temperance Status: The Local Option Bill Passed — Physiological Instruction Defeated," *Union Signal*, October 22, 1885, 9.

70. Ibid.

71. *N.W.C.T.U. Minutes*, 1886, Appendix, ccxx.

Chapter 9. Pure Food, Drink, and Drug Protagonists

1. Croly, *History*, 375.

2. Starr, *Social Transformation*, 91.

3. Hunt, *Epoch*, 7.

4. Croly, *History*, 590; "Annual Address of Frances E. Willard," at the Tenth Annual Meeting at Detroit, Michigan, October 31 to November 4, 1883, *Union Signal*, November 8, 1883, 2.

5. Martha N. Hathaway, "News from the Field: Southern California," *Union Signal*, March 19, 1885, 11.

6. Hunt, *Epoch*, 7.

7. Frances E. Willard, "Narcissa Edith White, of Pennsylvania," *Union Signal*, December 10, 1885, 4–5.

8. Belle P. Roberts, "Mrs. Clara Hoffman," *Union Signal*, June 2, 1887, 10.

9. James, James, and Boyer, *Notable Women*, 3: 171–72; Jeannette Grimme, "Clara Cleghorn Hoffman," in Mary K. Dains, ed., *Show Me Missouri Women: Selected Biographies* (Kirksville, Missouri: Thomas Jefferson University Press, 1989).

10. Elizabeth C. McCrimmon, "Dr. Martha Hughes Cannon: First Woman State Senator in America," Utah State Historical Society, Salt Lake City, Utah.

11. "Brief History Notes Contributions to Utah," and Julie A. Dockstader, "Pioneer Woman Remembered for Achievements as Doctor, Senator," (*Salt Lake City*) *Church News*, August 26, 1995, 4; David Clifton, "Utah Left Stamp on Females, Do Same for Mail," *Salt Lake Tribune*, Wednesday, May 19, 1993, 1.

12. M. Bard Shipp, "External Sources of Infection," and "Habitual Use of Drugs," *Salt Lake Sanitarian*, September 1889, 162–63, "Narcotics," October 1889, 164, "Adulteration of Foods and Drugs," November 1889, 38.

13. Jemima Helen Campbell, "Phoebe Ann Campbell," unpublished manuscript in the possession of author.

14. *Union Signal*, June 18, 1903. 4.

15. Dr. Dora Green Wilson, Report of the Anti-Narcotics Department, *Proceedings of the 24th Annual Convention of the Missouri W.C.T.U.*, held at Charleston, Missouri, October 1–8, 1906, Missouri State Historical Society, Columbia, 103.

16. Lucius M. S. Zeuch, ed., *History of Medical Practice in Illinois* (Chicago: The Book Press, 1927), 63–66; Croly, *History*, 402.

17. Harvey W. Wiley, Typescript of an article for *Good Housekeeping*, Anna Kelton Wiley Papers, Box 84, Manuscript Division, Library of Congress; Wiley, *Autobiography*, 13–62.

18. Ibid., Wiley, Typescript.

19. Ibid.

20. *N.W.C.T.U. Reports*, 1898, 201.

21. Extract from a letter written by Miss Epsie Patterson to the Mississippi Federation of Women's Clubs, "Official Club News," *Keystone*, October 1905, 5.

22. For a discussion of the background and work of nurses among all classes of people and their interest in social reform, see Susan Armeny, "Resolute Enthusiasts: The Effort to Professionalize American Nursing, 1880–1915," Ph.D. dissertation, University of Missouri, 1983.

23. Zeuch, *History of Medical Practice in Illinois*, 373–79; James, James, and Boyer, *Notable Women*, 3: 171–72.

24. Allen, *Alcohol*, 41–44; "The Family Physician," *Union Signal*, February 3, 1887, 2; Mary Ellen West, "Illinois: Hygiene and Heredity — State Normal Institute at Lake Bluff," *Union Signal*, August 28, 1884, 18; Zeuch, *History of Medical Practice in Illinois*, 609.

25. Editorial, *Keystone*, September, 1903, 3.

26. Editorial, *Keystone*, February, 1903, 3; Another account is found in Duffy, II: 254.

27. Armeny, *Resolute Enthusiasts*, 44, 66–67, 75–76.

28. *Consumers' Reports*, 1905, 43.

29. Ibid.

30. Ibid.

31. C. P. Ravenel, "90th Anniversary of the Ladies' Benevolent Society," *Keystone*, February 1903, 5; "The Visiting Nurse," Superintendent's Annual Report at

the Ninety-fourth Annual Meeting of the Ladies' Benevolent Society of Charleston, S.C., held January 16, 1907, *Keystone*, August 1903, 3.

32. Ibid.; Editorial, *Keystone*, September 1903, 3.

33. For a discussion of the visiting nurse program, see Susan Armeny, "Resolute Enthusiasts," 529–617.

34. Ellen H. Richards, "Legislation on Food Adulteration," *Science*, August 22, 1890, 101–04, and "Domestic Science," *Club Woman*, March 1899, 195.

35. Adade Mitchell Wheeler and Marlene Stein Wortman, *The Roads They Made: Women in Illinois History* (Chicago: Charles H. Kerr, 1977), 94.

36. Ibid.

37. Minutes of the Hypatia Club, Wichita City Library, Wichita, Kansas.

38. *Federation Bulletin*, December 1904, 68.

39. Mary E. McDowell, "The Chief Hindrance to Juvenile Work," *Union Signal*, January 6, 1887, 7–8; for a life sketch of Mary McDowell, see James, James, and Boyer, *Notable Women*, II: 462–64; *Chicago Daily Tribune*, February 18, 1906, cited in Anderson, *Health*, 179.

40. *Keystone*, February 1900, 3.

41. *Federation Bulletin*, October 1904, 1–2; Letter, Mary Alden Ward to Alice Lakey, May 10, 1905, in "L," Bureau of Chemistry Papers, National Archives, RG 97; *Club Woman*, June 1900, 98.

42. *Club Notes*, July 1907, 147.

43. "About Women," *Union Signal*, March 9, 1899, 2; *Keystone*, July 1905, 8; Willard, *Women and Temperance*, 147–53; Anderson, *Health*, 239.

Chapter 10. Breakthrough: Partners in the Crusade

1. "Medical Temperance," *Union Signal*, May 31, 1906, 8.

2. *Popular Science*, June 1883, May 1891, April 1896, August 1897; Allen, *Alcohol*, 26; Edward William Bok, *The Americanization of Edward Bok*, 28th ed. (New York: Charles Scribner's Sons, 1923), 1, 8 (hereafter cited as Bok, *Americanization*).

3. Bok, *Americanization*, 15–77, 104.

4. Ibid., 158, 166.

5. Ibid., 163, 168, 297–308; Edward Bok, "Why Patent Medicines are Dangerous," *Ladies' Home Journal*, January 1906, 18; Grover Cleveland, "Woman's Mission and Woman's Clubs," *Ladies' Home Journal*, May 1905, 3–4.

6. Martha M. Allen, "The Department of Medical Temperance and its Part in 'Patent' Medicine Agitation," *Union Signal*, May 24, 1906, 3; Martha M. Allen, "Non-Alcoholic Medicines," *N.W.C.T.U. Reports*, 1903, 203–04.

7. Ibid.; Allen, "Agitation," *Union Signal*, May 24, 1906, 3.

8. Ibid.; Bok, *Americanization*, 341–44; Maud Banfield, "Patent Medicines," *Ladies' Home Journal*, May 1903, 26; Edward Bok, "A Few Words to the W.C.T.U.," *Ladies' Home Journal*, September 1904, 16.

9. Bok, *Americanization*, 342; Bok, "The Patent-Medicine Curse," *Ladies' Home Journal*, May 1904, 18, and "Doctor Pierce's Favorite Prescription, A Retraction," *Ladies' Home Journal*, July 1904, 18.

10. Ibid.

11. Bok, "How the Private Confidences of Women Are Laughed At," *Ladies' Home Journal*, November 1904, 18.

12. Bok, *Americanization*, 342–43; Allen, "Agitation," *Union Signal*, May 24, 1906, 3, and "Concerning Fake Testimonials," *Union Signal*, September 27, 1906, 3–4; Mark Sullivan, "The Inside Story of a Sham," *Ladies' Home Journal*, January 1906, 14, "How the Game of Free Medical Advice Is Worked," 18, and "Did Mr. Bok Tell the Truth?" 23.

13. Bok, *Americanization*, 343, 344; Sullivan's article in *Collier's* was published in November 4, 1905, and is reprinted in Arthur and Lila Weinberg, *Muckrakers*, 179–94.

14. Allen, "Agitation," *Union Signal*, May 24, 1906, 3; The series appeared in *Collier's* from October 7, 1905 through February 17, 1906, and a second series ran from July 14 through September 22, 1906; Samuel Hopkins Adams, *The Great American Fraud* (Chicago: Press of the American Medical Association, 1906).

15. Samuel Hopkins Adams, "The Scavengers," *Collier's*, January 13, 1906, 18–20.

16. *Collier's*, March 10, 1906, 8, and March 24, 1906, 22; Stewart H. Holbrook *The Golden Age of Quackery* (New York: Macmillan, 1959), 26–27.

17. Ibid.

18. Margaret E. Sangster, "The Mother's Temper," *Woman's Home Companion*, August 1903, 27; Henry Irving Dodge, "The Truth About Food-Adulteration," *Woman's Home Companion*, March 1905, 6–7, 48; Mary Taylor-Ross, "In Case of Accident,"*Woman's Home Companion*, August 1905, 46.

19. J. M. Taylor, "Drug Abuses, Their Effects on the People," *Popular Science Monthly* 70 (May 1907): 459–63 and H. C. Wood, "Facts About Nostrums," *Popular Science Monthly* 68 (June 1905): 531–56; "Patent Medicine Crusade," *Nation* 81 (November 9, 1905): 376; *Outlook* 82 (April 7, 1906): 778–79.

20. *N.W.C.T.U. Reports*, 1905, 229.

21. See, for example, *New York Times*, 1903: 20 February, 16, 22 February, 24, 23 February, 6, 27 February, 8, 8 March, 15, 22 March, 29, 29 April 2; 1904:23 June, 8; 1906: 22 June, 1, 23 June, 8, 24 June, 6.

22. *New York Times*, June 8, 1905, 8.

23. Anderson, *Health*, 98–116.

24. Robert Crunden, *Ministers of Reform*, 183–88.

25. Department of Agriculture, Bureau of Chemistry, Bulletin 84, *Influence of Food Preservatives and Artificial Colors on the Digestion and Health, Part I* (Washington: 1904–08), 7–31; Wiley, *Crime*, 57–77; Dodge, "The Truth About Food-Adulteration," *Woman's Home Companion*, March 1905, 6–7, 48.

26. *Washington Post*, November 21, December 16, 21, 23, 25, 26, and 30, 1902, January 7, 11, and October 13, 1903.

27. Scott C. Bone to Wiley, December 24, 1902, Wiley Papers, Library of Congress.

28. Congress, Senate, "Adulteration of Food Products," *S. R. 141*, 56th Cong., 2nd sess.; *Journal of Proceedings of the Eighth Annual Convention and International Pure Food Congress of the National Association of State Dairy and Food Commissioners*, 1904, 148–49.

29. Letters, Kebler to Wiley, June 30, 1903, Item 600, Book 117, Bureau of Chemistry, National Archives, RG 97; Letters, Wiley to Kebler, January 23, 1903, to Sullivan, March 16, 1905, National Archives, RG 97; Wiley, "Federal Control of Drugs" and "The Bureau of Chemistry and Medical Science," Manuscripts of Addresses, Wiley Papers, Library of Congress.

30. Anderson, *Health*, 145, 147, 165, 195–96.

31. Letters, Wiley to Heyburn, December 20, 1904, January 8, 1905, National Archives, RG 97.

32. Letters, Wiley to Heyburn, August 12, 1904, National Archives, RG 97.

33. Ibid. "With the State Press," *Union Signal*, April 26, 1906, 12.

34. Incoming letters, Lakey to Wiley, July 8, 1904; Outgoing letters, Wiley to Lakey, 27 January 1904, National Archives, RG 97.

35. Wiley, *Autobiography*, 200–01; Incoming letters, Lakey to Wiley, November 10, and December 31, 1905, National Archives, RG 97; Anderson, *Health*, 195–96.

36. Wiley Papers, General Correspondence, Box 61, Manuscript Division, Library of Congress.

37. *Weldon Brinton Heyburn, Memorial Addresses Delivered in the Senate and the House of Representatives of the United States, Sixty-second Congress, third session, February 23, 1913, and March 1, 1913* (Washington, D.C., Congress Joint Committee on Printing, 1914), 37, 54–55.

38. Ibid., 62–63; Judith Nielsen, "Biographical Sketch" University of Idaho, Moscow, Idaho, Special Collections, Group 6, Box 2, Folder 6, W. B. Heyburn Collection, 2.

39. *Heyburn, Memorial Addresses in Congress*, 66–72, 87.

40. Rufus George Cook, "A Study of the Political Career of Brinton Heyburn," Master's thesis, 1964, 97–99.

41. *Heyburn, Memorial Addresses in Congress*, 94.

42. Quoted in Allen, *Alcohol*, 334.

43. "Work of the State Federations: Idaho," *Federation Bulletin*, June 1904, 182.

44. Congress, Senate Hearings, *Cong. Rec.*, 1904, 88, 112.

45. Ibid., 100, 113.

46. Cook, "A Study of the Political Career of Brinton Heyburn," xii.

47. Congress, House Committee on Interstate and Foreign Commerce, *Hearings ... on the Pure Food Bills*, 56th Cong., 1st sess., (Washington, D.C.: Government Printing Office, 1902), 112–13, 117–18.

48. Congress, Senate, *Final Report of the Louisiana Exposition Commission*, Document No. 202, 59th Cong., 1st sess., February 8, 1906, (Washington, D.C.: Government Printing Office, 1906), 12, 13, 428.

49. Letters received, R. M. Allen to Wiley, April 18, 1904, National Archives, RG 97.

50. Ibid.; Letters, R. M. Allen to Wiley, July 15, July 22, July 27, August 1, and September 23, 1904, and Lakey to Wiley, October 21, 1905, National Archives, RG 97; *Journal of Proceedings of the Eighth Annual Convention and International Pure Food Congress of the National Association of State Dairy and Food Commissioners*, 1904, 148–49.

51. Ibid., 64, 148–49, 189–206, 263–90, 298–67.

52. Mrs. Arthur Courtenay Neville, "Interesting Exhibit at the Louisiana Purchase Exposition for the Student of Household Economics," *Club Woman*, May 1904, 76–77; Letters, R. M. Allen to Wiley, February 23, and December 5, 1904, National Archives, RG 97.

53. Sullivan, II: 523–25.

54. Letters, R. M. Allen to Mark Sullivan, 1927, cited in Ibid.

55. Letters, R. M. Allen to Wiley, December 5, 1904, National Archives, RG 97.

56. *Senate Reports*, 1904, 16.
57. Congress, Senate Hearings, *Cong. Rec.*, 1904, 7.
58. Ibid., 8.
59. Ibid., 8–9.
60. Ibid.
61. Ibid., 119–21, 139.
62. Ibid.
63. Ibid., 119–21; Letters, Wiley to Heyburn, January 17, 1906, National Archives, RG 97; Congress, Senate, *Cong. Rec.*, 59th Cong., 1st sess., 1906, 896, 2720–21.
64. Statement of Warwick Massey Hough, Congress, Senate Hearings, 1904, 38–53.
65. Quoted in Lakey, "The Club Woman's Duty," *Federation Bulletin*, October 1905, 8.
66. Ibid.
67. See Congress, Senate Hearings, *Cong. Rec.*, 1904, 78–101.
68. *National Druggist* 36 (1906): 210, 372.
69. Henry Wayland Hill, ed., *Municipality of Buffalo, New York: A History, 1720–1923*, Vol. 3 (New York and Chicago: Lewis Historical, 1923), 145–50; for an example, see advertisement in *Union Signal*, April 9, 1905, 23.
70. Hill, *Municipality of Buffalo*, 145–50.
71. Ibid.
72. Ibid.
73. Congress, Senate Hearings, *Cong. Rec.*, 1904, 88–112.
74. *H. R. 1319*, 57th Cong., 1st sess., 1904, 6.
75. Views of Mr. Adamson, *H. R. 1319*, 57th Cong., 1st sess., 1904, 7.
76. The Views of Mr. Corliss, *H. R. 1319*, 57th Cong., 1st sess., 1904, 8.
77. *N.W.C.T.U. Reports*, 1903, 202.
78. *N.W.C.T.U. Reports*, 1905, 299.

Chapter 11. Io Triomphe!

1. Editorial, *Union Signal*, July 1906, 1.
2. In 1848 Congress enacted a bill to prevent the importation of adulterated drugs, and in 1883 passed a similar law applying to tea. After England, Germany, and Sweden passed food and drugs acts in the 1870s, federal legislators proposed several general bills, none of which emerged from committee; Anderson, *Health*, 69, 70. Wiley, "Food Adulteration and Its Legal Remedies," Manuscripts of addresses, Wiley Papers, Library of Congress. For a list of the most important pure food bills, see RG 97, Box 16, National Archives.
3. "List of Pure Food Bills," Bureau of Chemistry Papers, Box 16, National Archives; Congress, House, "Adulteration of Food," *H. R. 1880*, 49th Cong., 1st sess.; Congress, House, "Adulterated Articles of Food, Drink, and Drugs," *H. R. 3341*, 50th Cong., 1st sess.; Congress, Senate, *S. R. No. 1366*, 51st Cong., 1st sess. A good analysis of the early bills is found in Anderson, *Health*, 123–134.
4. "List of Pure Food Bills," Bureau of Chemistry Papers, Box 16, National Archives, RG 97; Congress, House, *Hearings Before the Committee on Interstate and Foreign Commerce on Pure Food Bills …* (Washington, D.C.: Government Print-

ing Office, 1904), 3, 42; Purington, "Domestic Science," *N.W.C.T.U. Reports*, 1903, 202; Newspaper clipping accompanying letter, Lakey to Wiley, July 5, 1904, in Incoming letters, Bureau of Chemistry, National Archives, RG 97. *Cong. Rec.*, 57th Cong., 2nd sess., 1904, House, 445–58, and Senate, 1724–29, 2647, 2964–67.

5. Letters, R. M. Allen to Wiley, April 18, 1904, National Archives, RG 97.

6. Senate, *Cong. Rec.*, 58th Cong., 3rd session, 1905, 126–29, 195–90, 3843–55.

7. William Randolph Hearst, "The Kind of Law That Cannot Be Passed," *New York Evening Journal*, January 9, 1906, Editorial page.

8. Ibid.; Helen Miller, "Pure Food, What the Federation is Doing," *Federation Bulletin*, June 7, 1905,

9. Letters received, Helen Miller to Wiley, January 7, 1905, Box 62, National Archives, RG 97.

10. Ibid.; *Chicago Daily Tribune*, February 18, 1906; *Some Forms of Food Adulteration and Simple Methods for Their Detection*, Bureau of Chemistry, Bulletin 100, (Washington, D.C.: Government Printing Office, 1906).

11. Ibid., 894–95.

12. Senate, *Cong. Rec.*, 59th Cong., 1st sess., 1906, 894–98, 1216–21.

13. *Chicago Tribune*, February 21 and 22, 1906; Beveridge cited in Sullivan, II: 533–34; Senate, *Cong. Rec.*, 59th Cong., 1st sess., January 18, 1906, 1216–19.

14. Sullivan, II: 531–32; Senate, *Cong. Rec.*, 58th Cong., 1st sess., December 13, 1905.

15. Senate, *Cong. Rec.*, 59th Cong., 1st sess., 1923, 2652–53.

16. Ibid., 1923.

17. Ibid., 1129–1135. Sullivan, II: 531–32. Senate, *Cong. Rec.*, 59th Cong., 1st sess., 1906, 2652.

18. Wiley, *Crime*, 52–53; Edward Lowry, "The Senate Plot Against Pure Food," *World's Work* 10 (May 1905): 6215–17; Letters, Wiley to A. P. Gardner, January 26, 1906, National Archives, RG 97; Senate, *Cong. Rec.*, 59th Cong., 1st sess., 1906, 2644, 2647–62, 2724–28, 2771–73.

19. "Pure Food Bill Passed By the Senate, 63 to 4," *New York Times*, February 22, 1905, 5.

20. Letters, Lakey to Wiley, February 26, 1906, and Miller to Wiley, March 9, 1906, National Archives, RG 97.

21. Sullivan, II: 534; Letters, Lakey to Bigelow, May 15, 1906, and May 18, 1906, National Archives, RG 97.

22. *Federation Bulletin*, June 1906, 435–58.

23. Ibid., 445; Wood, *History of the General Federation of Women's Clubs*, 216.

24. Ibid., March 1906, 285–86, and June 1906, 450, 453; Wood, 210–11; *Federation Bulletin*, June 1906, 446.

25. Ibid.

26. *Federation Bulletin*, June 1906, 438.

27. *New York Times*, June 4, 1906, 9.

28. Ibid., June 5, 1906, 1, and June 8, 1906, 3.

29. Upton Sinclair, "What Life Means to Me," *Cosmopolitan*, October 1906, cited in Weinberg, *Muckrakers*, 205–06; Sullivan, II: 471–83.

30. Ibid.; Mary E. McDowell Manuscript, cited in Allen F. Davis, *Spearheads of Reform* (New York: Oxford University Press, 1967), 33, 112–22; "Women and the Packing House," *Woman's Standard*, July 1906, n.p.

31. Ibid., Sullivan, II: 535–36.

32. *New York Times*, June 5, 1906, 1–2.

33. Ibid.

34. Ibid.

35. Ibid., June 6, 1906, 8.

36. Editorial, "Filth and Impudence," *New York Times*, June 6, 1906, 8.

37. "Stockyard Improvements," *New York Times*, June 6, 1906, 2.

38. Ibid.; "State Commissioner's Order," *New York Times*, June 6, 1906, 2.

39. "Physicians and Pure Food," *Federation Bulletin*, June 1906, 476–77.

40. "Pure Food Bill Stirs the House to Interest," *New York Times*, June 22, 1906, 1–2.

41. Ibid.

42. Congress, House, *Cong. Rec.*, 59th Cong., 3rd sess., June 22, 1906, 8978–79, June 23 and 24, 1906, 8889–8909, 8955–94, 9001–02, 9052–67.

43. Ibid., 8982.

44. *New York Times*, June 24, 1906, 6; House, *Cong. Rec.*, 59th Cong., 2nd sess., 1906, 9067–76.

45. "Pure Food Bill," 59th Cong., 1st sess, *H. R. 5056*; *Cong. Rec.*, 59th Cong., 1st sess., 1906, 9379–81, 9496–97, 9655, 9737–40; *Cong. Rec.*, 59th Cong., 2nd sess., June 28, 1906, 9496; *New York Times*, June 30, 1906, 2.

46. *New York Times*, February 22, 1906, 5; *Heyburn, Memorial Addresses in Congress*, 13.

47. Anderson, *Health*, 190.

48. *Heyburn, Memorial Addresses in Congress*, 13, 54, 67.

49. Margaret Dye Ellis, "Patent Medicine Interests Suffer Defeat," *Union Signal*, July 5, 1906, 28.

50. *N.W.C.T.U. Reports*, 1906, 114.

51. Elizabeth Foster, "Pure Food," *Federation Bulletin*, July 1907, 30.

52. Dr. Dora Green Wilson, Report of the Anti-Narcotics Department, Proceedings of the 24th Annual Convention of the Missouri W.C.T.U., held at Charleston, Missouri, October 1–8, 1906, Missouri State Historical Society, Columbia.

53. Annie Laws, "The President's Address to the Twelfth Convention of the Ohio State Federation of Women's Clubs," *Club Notes*, November 1907, 67, 72–73.

54. Mrs. J. Sydney Robbins, "Editorial," Alabama State Federation of Women's Clubs Page, *Mobile Daily Register*, June 24, 1906, in custody of the State Department of Archives and History, Montgomery, Alabama, Florence Kelley, "8th Annual Report of the Secretary to the Council," *Consumers' Reports*, 1902, 2, 14; Anna Kelton Wiley, "Let's Keep the Food Law Pure," *Club Woman*, Baltimore, Maryland, February, 1931, n.p.; Anna Kelton Wiley Papers, Box 182, Manuscript Division, Library of Congress, Washington, D.C.

55. Allen, *Alcohol*, 27.

56. Editorial, *Union Signal*, July 1906, 1; *Federation Bulletin*, April 1906, 333–34, and May 1906, 430; heading above the advertising pages, *Club Notes*, April 1907.

57. Letters sent, Harvey W. Wiley, to Mrs. Walter McNab Miller, March 13, 1906, Letterpress Book 180, National Archives, RG 97, 39–40; "Men's Opinions," *Federation Bulletin*, May 1906, 430; Wiley, *Crime*, 52; "Editorial," *Federation Bulletin* December 1911, 133.

58. "Men's Opinions," *Federation Bulletin*, May 1906, 430.

59. Ibid.; Letters, McCumber to Lakey, February 23, 1906, National Archives, RG 97.

60. Ibid. Outgoing letters, Heyburn to Lakey, February 23, and March 10, 1906, National Archives, RG 97.

61. Editorial, (*New York City*) *Sun*, cited by Alice Lakey in the *Federation Bulletin*, October 1906, 20; Editorial, "Good Food Assurance," *Good Housekeeping*, January 1907, 60, Library of Congress.

62. L. D. Gibbs, "Woman's Capture of Congress," *Good Housekeeping*, January 1907, 36–38, Library of Congress.

63. Ibid.

64. Ibid.

65. Wiley, *Crimes*, 53.

66. Gibbs, 36–38.

67. Extract from a Washington, D.C., newspaper, 1906, cited in Wood, 206.

68. Alsberg, in Ravenel, 216; Sullivan, II: 483.

Chapter 12. "The Augean Stables Are Still Unclean

1. R. J. DeVore, "Report from the South-West District," *Club Notes*, November 1907, 89; In Greek mythology, the Augean Stables referred to the stables of Augeas, one of the argonauts, which contained 3,000 oxen and was uncleaned for 30 years; eventually cleaned by Hercules in one day by diverting the river Alpheus though them, *Webster's New Century Dictionary* (New York: Standard Reference Works, 1956).

2. See *Consumers' Reports*, 1907 and *N.W.C.T.U. Reports*, 1907; *Club Notes*, October 1907, 38.

3. "Objects of the Food Committee's work for the Coming Year," attached to letter, Lakey to Wiley, March 14, 1907, National Archives, RG 97, Box 40, 3450; Lakey, "Report of the Pure Food Committee," *Consumers' Reports*, 1907, 48.

4. Letter, Lakey to Wiley, March 14, 1907, National Archives, RG 97, Box 40, General Correspondence, 3450 (filed under A. Lakey). Purington, "Health and Heredity. What Next?" *N.W.C.T.U. Reports*, 1906, 214.

5. Incoming letters, Lakey to Wiley, November 12, 1906, National Archives, RG 97; "Dealers Laugh at Pure Food Regulations," clipping from the *New York World*, January 21, 1907, attached to Incoming letter, Keenan to Keebler, March 25, 1907, Bureau of Chemistry, National Archives, RG 97, Box 30, 1680.

6. For examples of inquiries, see Letters received, Rosina Lothringer to Wiley, February 4, 1907, Bureau of Chemistry, National Archives, RG 97, Box 56, 7293; O. E. Barker to Wilson, August 13, 1907, Box 93, 15804; J. V. Maucher to Wilson, January 7, 1907, Box 30, 1530; Irene P. Maufret to Wilson, January 19, 1907, Box 30; for discussions of unpreparedness, see inserts accompanying Thomas J. Keenan to Lyman Keebler, March 25, 1907, Box 30, 1680.

7. Ibid.; *New York Times*, February 9, 1911, 6

8. Purington, "Health and Heredity," *N.W.C.T.U. Reports*, 1906, 215, and *N.W.C.T.U. Reports*, 1908, 239.

9. Lakey, "Food Law Wanted," *Newark Evening News*, March 12, 1907, clipping attached to letter, Lakey to Wiley, March 14, 1907, copy of a circular sent to women's organizations by Lakey, March 8, 1907, Wiley to Lakey, March 15, 1907, and March 21, 1907, and Lakey to Wiley, September 4, 1907, all in National

Archives, RG 97, Box 40, 3450; "Report of the Pure Food Committee," *Federation Bulletin*, June 1907, 354–55; Lakey, "Report of the Food Committee," *Consumers' Reports*, 1909, 56.

10. "Clean Meat and Pure Milk are Vital Public Needs," *Cranford Chronicle*, June 6, 1907, transcript of article attached to letter, Lakey to Wiley, September 4, 1907, National Archives, RG 97, Box 40, 3450; Lakey, "Report of the Pure Food Committee," *Consumers' Reports*, 1909, 56; "Report of the Pure Food Committee," *Federation Bulletin*, June 1907, 354–55.

11. Ibid.; Lakey, "Report of the Pure Food Committee," *Consumers' Reports*, 1909, 53, 57.

12. *Consumers' Reports*, 1907, 47, and 1909, 58; Mary Ritter Beard, *Woman's Work in Municipalities* (New York: D. Appleton, 1915), 75; Lakey, "Report of the Pure Food Committee," *Consumers' Reports*, 1910, 50.

13. Beard, *Woman's Work*, 71–73.

14. Lakey, "Report of the Pure Food Committee," *Consumers' Reports*, 1909, 53–54.

15. Ibid.

16. Helen McNab Miller, "A Study of the Milk Supply," *Federation Bulletin*, April 1907, 261–63.

17. Helen McNab Miller, "Report of the Pure Food Committee," *Club Notes*, October 1907, 38–39.

18. *Club Notes*, March 1907, 8; Margaret Dye Ellis, "Our Washington Letter," *Union Signal*, February 1, 1912, 2; *Consumers' Reports*, 1907, 47.

19. Ibid.

20. Eliza Ingalls, "Anti-Narcotics," *N.W.C.T.U. Reports*, 1911, 274; Martha M. Allen, "Medical Temperance," *N.W.C.T.U. Reports*, 1910, 217.

21. Incoming letters, Lakey to Wiley, March 14, 1907, National Archives, RG 97.

22. Purington, "Health and Heredity," *N.W.C.T.U. Reports*, 1908, 239; Letter, Lakey to Wilson, February 23, 1907, and Wiley to Lakey, February 26, 1907, March 22, 1907, and December 30, 1907, Lakey to Wiley, March 20, 1907, December 18, 1907, G. E. Parish to Lakey, April 27, 1907, National Archives, RG 97, Box 40, 3450.

23. *Consumers' Reports*, 1907–1909.

24. Allen "Medical Temperance," *N.W.C.T.U. Reports*, 1906, 215–19.

25. Margaret Dye Ellis, "Our Washington Letter," *Union Signal*, July 11, 1912, 2.

26. *Consumers' Reports*, 1907, 47, and *Consumers' Reports*, 1909, 58. Allen, "Medical Temperance," *N.W.C.T.U. Reports*, 1915, 181. "Dealers Laugh at Pure Food Regulations," *New York World*, January 21, 1907.

27. Purington, "Health and Heredity," *N.W.C.T.U. Reports*, 1909, 239, and *N.W.C.T.U. Reports*, 1908, 214.

28. Sara Phillips Thomas, "Convention of American Society for the Study of Alcohol and Other Narcotics, *Union Signal*, December 26, 1912, 11; "Progress in Pharmacy," and Charles H. LaWall, "The Food and Drugs Act in Its Relation to Public Health," *American Journal of Pharmacy*, March 1907, 107, 130–32.

29. "The Century of the Child," *Union Signal*, July 18, 1912, 1–2.

30. *Mobile Daily Register* 86, no. 149 (July 8, 1906), Sec. 2, Sunday supplement, 1, State Department of Archives and History, Montgomery, Alabama.

31. Purington, "Health and Heredity," *N.W.C.T.U. Reports*, 1906, 212.

32. Robert Cumming Wilson, *Drugs and Pharmacy in the Life of Georgia, 1733–1959* (Atlanta: Foote and Davis, 1959), 153–54, 161.

33. Editorial, *Federation Bulletin*, December 1911, 133.

34. Alsberg, in Ravenel, 210.

35. Letters, Adams to Wiley, March 26, 1907, and Wiley to Adams, April 1, 1907, General Correspondence, National Archives, RG 97.

36. Letter, Wiley to Lakey, November 4, 1907, National Archives, RG 97, Box 50, 3450.

37. Alsberg, in Ravenel, 219.

38. "Dealers Laugh at Pure Food Regulations," *New York World*, January 21, 1907.

39. Allen, *Alcohol*, 27, and "The Pure Food Law and Proprietary Medicines," *Union Signal*, August 23, 1906, 4.

40. *Club Notes*, March 1907, 2.

41. Ibid.; Letter, Lakey to Bigelow, February 23, 1907, and loose circular signed by John Martin and Alice Lakey, dated April 1907, National Archives, RG 97, Box 40, 3450; *Consumers' Reports*, 1907, 53–60; Letters, R. M. Allen to Needham, January 31, 1907, National Archives, RG 97; "Joker in Food Law: People's Lobby Denounces Tawney's Amendment," *Washington Herald*, February 4, 1907, clipping in National Archives, RG 97, Box 55.

42. Anna Kelton Wiley Papers, Library of Congress, 29.

43. Wiley, *Crime*, 108–13; Lakey, *Consumers' Reports*, 1909, 56, and *Consumers' Reports*, 1910, 47–48.

44. Ibid.

45. Lakey, "Report of the Pure Food Committee," *Consumers' Reports*, 1911, 45, and *Consumer's Reports*, 1912, 34–35.

46. Lakey, "Report of the Pure Food Committee," *Consumers' Reports*, 1910, 45.

47. James C. Munch and James C. Munch, Jr., "Notices of Judgment: The First Thousand," *Food, Drug and Cosmetic Law Journal* 10 (April 1955): 219–42.

48. Lakey, "Report of the Pure Food Committee," *Consumers' Reports*, 1909, 55.

49. *U.S. v. Johnson*, 221, U.S. 488 (1911), cited in Temin, *Taking Your Medicine*, 32–33.

50. Temin, 33–34; 37 Stat. 416 (1912).

51. Margaret Dye Ellis, "Our Washington Letter," *Union Signal*, January 30, 1913, 2.

52. 38 Stat. 785 (1914); Young, *Medical Messiahs*, 44–45; Eliza B. Ingalls, "Anti-Narcotics," *N.W.C.T.U. Reports*, 1915, 231–32.

53. Wells, *Unity*, 458–64.

54. Quoted in Ibid., 459–60.

55. Ibid.

56. *Club Notes*, March 1907, 8; Helen McNab Miller to Carolyn Lucille Meyer, July 19, 1933, Kalispell, Montana, Western Historical Manuscript Collection, Ellis Library, University of Missouri, Columbia.

57. Francis Waite Leiter, "Health," *N.W.C.T.U. Reports*, 1914, 152.

58. See *N.W.C.T.U. Reports*, 1913–1915.

59. See *Consumers' Reports*, 1909–1912.

60. *Consumers' League Reports*, 1907, 46–47, and 1909, 54; Alice Lakey, "Food from the Consumers' Point of View," *Federation Bulletin*, December 1906, 89; James, James, and Boyer, *Notable Women*, 360.

61. Wiley, *Crime*, 263–64.

62. Lakey, "Report of the Pure Food Committee," *Consumers' Reports*, 1909, 55.

63. Lakey, "Report of the Pure Food Committee," *Consumers' Reports*, 1911, 35; Margaret Dye Ellis, "Our Washington Letter," *Union Signal*, March 28, 1912, 3.

64. Lakey, "Report of the Pure Food Committee," *Consumers' Reports*, 1912, 35–36; Purington, "Health and Heredity," *Union Signal*, February 1, 1912, 10.

65. Harvey W. Wiley Papers, 95690, Manuscript Division, Library of Congress, 2–3. For Roosevelt's stand on pure food, drink, and drug regulation, see Wiley, *Crimes*, 263–74. Purington, "Health and Heredity," *N.W.C.T.U. Reports*, 1912, 204.

66. *Heyburn, Memorial Addresses in Congress*, 62nd Cong., 3rd sess., 1914, 11–12, 56, 63–65, 105.

67. Paula Baker, "Domestication of Politics," 620; Wells, *Unity*, 202; *Woman's Standard*, Waterloo, Iowa, July 1906, n.p.

68. *Annual Report of the Woman's Christian Temperance Union of Virginia* (Winchester: 1888), 11, quoted in Lebsock, *Virginia Women 1600–1945, "A Share of the Honor"* (Richmond: Virginia State Library, 1987), fn., 108; Sally F. Chapin, "Response to Addresses of Welcome on Behalf of the South," *N.W.C.T.U. Reports*, 1881, "The Alabama Convention," correspondence, *Union Signal*, December 3, 1885, 8, and "Lessons From the South," *Union Signal*, July 31, 1884, 5.

69. "Suffrage Not Ripe: Federation Will Get It Later," excerpt from the *St. Paul Pioneer-Press*, reprinted in the *Woman's Standard*, Waterloo, Iowa, July 1906, n.p.; *Keystone*, October 1905, 11.

70. "Hobble the Pure Food Law: Special Interests Do as They Please, Consumers' League Is Told," *New York Times*, February 9, 1911, 6.

71. "Why She Wanted to Vote," *Woman's Standard*, March 1906, 1, and Anna H. Shaw, "The Relation of the Home to the Ballot," 4, in the same issue.

72. *New York Times*, September 3, 1911, 6.

73. *Mobile Daily Register*, July 1, 1906, Sect. 2, 4, clippings, Atlanta Women's Club Collection, Folder 4, Manuscript 353.

74. Mary L. Driggs, "News from the Field: Arkansas–Report of State Convention," *Union Signal*, June 5, 1884, 10; Clippings from *The Atlanta Constitution*, Special Collections, University of Georgia, Athens.

75. "Why She Wanted to Vote," *Woman's Standard*, March 1906, 1; Jane Addams, "The Larger Aspects of the Woman's Movement," *Annals of the American Academy of Political and Social Science,* 56 (November 1914): 1–8.

76. See Young, *Medical Messiahs*, 42–43, for a discussion of the Elixir of Sulfanilamide disaster; Helen B. Taussig, "The Thalidomide Syndrome," *Scientific American* 207 (August 1962): 29–35; Morton Mintz, "'Heroine' of FDA Keeps Bad Drug Off Market," *Washington Post*, July 15, 1962, A1; Ralph Nader, "We're Still in the Jungle," *New Republic*, July 15, 1967, 11, and "Watch That Hamburger," *New Republic*, August 19, 1967; Nick Kotz, "Meat Inspection: The New Jungle," *Nation*, September 18, 1967, 45.

Conclusion

1. Taken from an address to the Ohio Federation of Women's Clubs by Alice S. Harris, "North-West District," *Club Notes*, November 1907, 87.

2. Edward Hallett Carr, *What Is History: The George Macaulay Trevelyn Lectures Delivered at the University of Cambridge*, January–March 1961 (New York: Vintage, 1961), 178–79.

3. Quoted in Stephan Thernstrom, *Poverty and Progress: Social Mobility in a Nineteenth Century City* (Cambridge and London: Harvard University Press, 1964), 1.

4. Scott, *Invisible*, 152.

5. Baker, "Domestication," in Gordon, *Women, the State, and Welfare*, 666; Blair, *The Clubwoman as Feminist*, 5, 71.

6. Otto Nathan and Heinz Nordon, eds., *Einstein of Peace* (New York: Avenel Books, 1981), 161.

7. For Unger's comments see Irwin Unger, *These United States: The Questions of Our Past*, 3rd ed., Vol. 2 (Englewood Cliffs, New Jersey: Prentice-Hall, 1986), 595.

8. Ibid.

9. Sullivan, I: 1–2.

Selected Sources

Manuscripts and Papers

Armstrong, Mary C. "History of the Iowa Federation of Women's Clubs, 1893–1968." Iowa Historical Society, Des Moines, Iowa.

Axtell, Gertrude. "The Pleiades Club, History and Accomplishments." Special Collections, MG 25, Box 1, f. 10, 11. University of Idaho, Moscow, Idaho.

Cannon, Martha. Hughes Papers. Utah Historical Society, Salt Lake City, Utah.

Conine, Martha A. Bushell. Papers, 1896–1910. Microfilm ed., 1976. Western History, Denver Public Library, Denver, Colorado.

Donaldson, Betty Mizell. Papers, 1887–1938. Microfilm ed. Manuscript and Records Section, Tennessee State Library and Archives, Nashville, Tennessee.

Felton, Rebecca. Papers. Special Collections, University of Georgia, Athens, Georgia.

Fulmer, Elton. Letters, 1906–1907. Washington State Chemist's Records. Special Collections, Washington State University, Pullman, Washington.

Heyburn, Weldon Brinton. Papers. Special Collections, University of Idaho, Moscow, Idaho.

Lease, Mary Elizabeth. Biographical Material. Women's Club Records. Wichita City Library, Wichita, Kansas.

Smith, Addison Taylor. Collection. Manuscript 22. Manuscripts and Archives Collections. Idaho Historical Society, Boise, Idaho.

Temperance and Prohibition Papers. Jointly held by Ohio Historical Society and Michigan Historical Collections. Microfilm edition. University of Ohio, Columbus, Ohio.

United States Department of Agriculture. Bureau of Chemistry Papers. National Archives, RG 97, Washington, D.C.

Woman's Christian Temperance Union Papers. Frances Willard Memorial Library, Evanston, Illinois.

Wiley, Anna Kelton. Papers. Manuscripts Division, Library of Congress, Washington, D.C.

Wiley, Harvey Washington. Papers. Manuscripts Division, Library of Congress, Washington, D.C.

Articles

"Laws Regulating the Practice of Medicine in the Various States and Territories of the United States." *American Journal of the American Medical Association* 37 (November 16, 1901): 1304–18.

Zimmerman, Jonathan. "The 'Queen of the Lobby': Mary Hunt, Scientific Temperance, and the Dilemma of Democratic Education in America, 1879–1906." *History of Education Quarterly* 32, no. 1 (Spring 1992): 1–30.

Journals, Magazines, and Newspapers

American Journal of Pharmacy. 1905–1907. Microfilm ed. Ellis Library, University of Missouri, Columbia, Missouri.

The Atlanta Constitution. Clippings, 1905–1907. Atlanta Historical Society, Atlanta, Georgia.

Business Woman's Magazine. 1904–1907. Louise Lee Hardin, ed. Microfilm ed. Denver Public Library, Denver, Colorado.

Club Notes for Club Women. March 1907–August 1908. Louise Graham, ed. Oberlin College. Oberlin, Ohio.

Club Woman. 1897–1904. Helen M. Winslow, ed. Boston, Massachusetts. Periodicals Division, Library of Congress. Washington, D.C.

The Club Woman's Weekly. 1907–1908. New York City, New York. Periodicals Division, Library of Congress. Washington, D.C.

Colorado W.C.T.U. Messenger. 1898–1911. Highlands, Colorado. Laura A. Perry, ed. Special Collections, University of Colorado, Boulder, Colorado.

General Federation Bulletin. 1907–1911. Boston, Massachusetts. Mary Alden Ward and Helen A. Winslow, editors and publishers. Microfilmed by Research Publications, Inc. Oberlin College Library, Oberlin, Ohio.

Good Housekeeping. January 1907. Springfield, Massachusetts. Phelps Publishing Co., and Periodicals Division, Library of Congress, Washington, D.C.

The Keystone. 1899–1913. Charleston, South Carolina. Ida Marshall Lining, Mary Poppenheim, and Louisa Poppenheim, eds. Microfilm ed. Filmed by Greenwood Press at the Periodicals Division, Library of Congress, Washington, D.C.

Ladies' Home Journal. 1903–1907. Edward Bok, ed. The Curtis Publishing Co., Philadelphia, Pennsylvania, and Periodicals Division, Library of Congress, Washington, D.C.

Mobile Daily Register. 1906. Mobile, Alabama. On file at the State Department of Archives and History, Montgomery, Alabama.

New York Times. January–June, 1906. Microfilm Edition. Film Collection, Ellis Library, University of Missouri.

Our Messenger. 1904–1906. Downs, Kansas. Kansas State Historical Society, Topeka, Kansas.

The Salt Lake Sanitarian. 1888. Salt Lake City, Utah. M. Bard Shipp, M.D., publisher and editor. Utah Historical Society, Salt Lake City, Utah.

School Physiology Journal. 1897–1907. Boston, Massachusetts. Mary H. Hunt, editor and publisher. Willard Memorial Library, Evanston, Illinois.

Southern Woman's Magazine. February 1904–August 1905. Maria Goodwin Stewart, ed. Atlanta, Georgia. Microfilm edition. Filmed by Research Publications at the Periodicals Division, Library of Congress, Washington, D.C.

Union Signal. 1892–1914. Evanston, Illinois. Various editors. Published by the National Woman's Christian Temperance Union. Willard Memorial Library, Evanston, Illinois.

Utah Historical Quarterly. Winter 1970 and Summer 1976. Utah State Historical Society, Salt Lake City, Utah.

Woman's Exponent. May 1905–December 1906. Salt Lake City, Utah. Emmeline B. Bells, editor and publisher. Special Collections, Brigham Young University, Provo, Utah.

Woman's Home Companion. March 1905–March 1906. Arthur T. Vance, ed. The Crowell Publishing Co. New York City, Chicago, and Springfield, Ohio.

Woman's Standard. 1906. Waterloo, Iowa. Iowa State Historical Society, Des Moines, Iowa.

Minutes and Reports

Atlanta Women's Club Collection. Special Collections, University of Georgia, Athens, Georgia.

Colorado W.C.T.U. Papers. Western Collections. Norlan Library, University of Colorado, Boulder, Colorado.

Woman's Columbian Club. Minutes. 1982–1908. Manuscript 356. Idaho Historical Society, Boise, Idaho.

Missouri Federation of Women's Clubs. Minutes. 1896–1906. Special Collections, Missouri State Historical Society, Columbia, Missouri.

Montgomery Mother's Circle. Minutes. 1900–1913. Alabama Department of Archives and History, Manuscript Division, Ms. II-10-42, Montgomery, Alabama.

National Consumers' League. *Consumers' Reports.* Records. 1903–1909. Microfilm. Manuscripts Division, Library of Congress, Washington, D.C.

National Woman's Christian Temperance Union Annual Meetings, Minutes, 1881–1894. Chicago: Woman's Temperance Publishing Association, 1881–1894.

National Woman's Christian Temperance Union Annual Meetings, Reports, 1895–1914. Chicago: Woman's Temperance Publishing Association, 1805–1914.

Shakespeare Club of Clinton, Missouri. Minutes. Vol. III. Joint Collection. Western Historical Manuscript Collection, Ellis Library, University of Missouri, Columbia, and Manuscripts, Missouri State Historical Society, Columbia, Missouri.

Published Works

Addams, Jane. *Democracy and Social Ethics.* New York: Macmillan, 1902.

Allen, Martha M. *Alcohol a Dangerous and Unnecessary Medicine, How and Why: What Medical Writers Say.* Marcellus, New York: The Department of Medical Temperance of the National Woman's Christian Temperance Union, 1900.

American Medical Association. Council on Pharmacy and Chemistry. *Nostrums and Quackery*. Chicago: American Medical Association, 1912.

Anderson, Oscar E., Jr. *The Health of a Nation: Harvey W. Wiley and the Fight for Pure Food*. Chicago: University of Chicago Press, 1958.

Beard, Mary Ritter. *Woman's Work in Municipalities*. New York: D. Appleton, 1915.

Bender, George A. *Great Moments in Pharmacy*. Detroit: Northwood Institute Press, 1966.

Berg, Barbara J. *The Remembered Gate: Origins of American Feminism: The Woman and the City, 1800–1860*. New York: Oxford University Press, 1978.

Blair, Karen J. *The Clubwoman as Feminist: True Womanhood Redefined, 1868–1914*. New York: Holmes and Meier, 1980.

Bok, Edward William. *The Americanization of Edward Bok*. 28th ed. New York: Charles Scribner's Sons, 1923.

Bordin, Ruth. *Frances Willard: A Biography*. Chapel Hill and London: University of North Carolina Press, 1986.

_____. *Women and Temperance: The Quest for Power and Liberty, 1873–1900*. Philadelphia: Temple University Press, 1981.

Brieger, Gert H., ed. *Medical America in the Nineteenth Century: Readings from the Literature*. Baltimore: Johns Hopkins Press, 1972.

Carson, Gerald. *One for a Man, Two for a Horse*. New York: Doubleday, 1960.

Chapin, Clara C., ed. *Thumb Nail Sketches of White Ribbon Women*. Chicago: Woman's Temperance Publishing Association, 1895.

Cherrington, Ernest Hurst, ed. *Standard Encyclopedia of the Alcohol Problem*. 3 vols. Westerville, Ohio: privately published, 1928.

Croly, Jane Cunningham. *The History of the Woman's Club Movement in America*. New York: Henry G. Allen, 1898.

Crunden, Robert. *Ministers of Reform: The Progressives' Achievement in American Civilization, 1889–1920*. New York: Basic Books, 1982.

Dowling, Henry F. *Medicine for Man: The Development, Regulation, and Use of Prescription Drugs*. New York: Knopf, 1970.

Duffy, John. *A History of Public Health in New York City, 1625–1866*. New York: Russell Sage Foundation, 1968.

_____. *A History of Public Health in New York City, 1866–1966*. New York: Russell Sage Foundation, 1974.

Engel, Leonard. *Medicine Makers of Kalamazoo*. New York: McGraw Hill, 1961.

Epstein, Barbara Leslie. *The Politics of Domesticity: Women, Evangelism, and Temperance in Nineteenth-Century America*. Middletown, Connecticut: Wesleyan University Press, 1981.

Fishbein, Morris L. *A History of the American Medical Association, 1847–1947*. Philadelphia: W. B. Saunders, 1947.

Flexner, Abraham. *Medical Education in the United States and Canada; A Report to the Carnegie Foundation for the Advancement of Teaching*. New York: Arno Press and The New York Times, 1972.

Flexner, Eleanor. *Century of Struggle: The Woman's Rights Movement in the United States*. New York: Atheneum, 1970.

Goodman, Louis S., and Alfred Gilman, ed. *The Pharmacological Basis of Therapeutics*. New York: McMillan, 1975.

Gordon, Linda, ed. *Women, the State, and Welfare.* Madison: University of Wisconsin Press, 1990.

Harrison, John M., and Harry H. Stein, eds. *Muckraking: Past Present and Future.* University Park and London: Pennsylvania State University Press, 1973.

Hays, Samuel P. *The Response to Industrialism, 1885–1914.* Chicago: University of Chicago Press, 1957.

Hechtlinger, Adelaide. *The Great Patent Medicine Era.* New York: Grosset and Dunlap, 1970.

Hofstadter, Richard. *Age of Reform: From Bryan to F.D.R.* Paperback ed. New York: Vintage, 1955.

Holbrook, Stewart H. *The Golden Age of Quackery.* New York: Macmillan, 1959.

Hunt, Mary H. *An Epoch of the Nineteenth Century: An Outline of the Work for Scientific Temperance Education in the Public Schools of the United States.* Boston: P. H. Foster, 1897.

_____. *A History of the First Decade of the Department of Scientific Temperance Instruction in Schools and Colleges, of the Woman's Christian Temperance Union.* 2nd ed. Boston: Washington Press, 1891.

James, Edward T., Janet Wilson James, and Paul S. Boyer. *Notable American Women, 1607–1950: A Biographical Dictionary.* 3 vols. Cambridge: Harvard University Press, 1971.

Jimerson, Randall C., Francis S. Blouin, and Charles A. Isetts, eds. *Guide to the Microfilm Edition of the Temperance and Prohibition Papers.* Ann Arbor: University of Michigan, 1977.

Katz, Esther, and Anita Rapone, eds. *Women's Experience in America: An Historical Anthology.* New Brunswick, New Jersey: Transaction, 1980.

Kett, Joseph F. *The Formation of the American Medical Profession: The Role of Institutions, 1780–1860.* New Haven: Yale University Press, 1968.

Kolko, Gabriel. *The Triumph of Conservatism: A Reinterpretation of American History, 1900–1916.* New York: Macmillan, 1963.

Lebsock, Suzanne. *Virginia Women, 1600–1945: "A Share of Honour."* Richmond: Virginia State Library, 1987.

Leeman, Richard W. *"Do Everything" Reform: The Oratory of Frances E. Willard.* New York: Greenwood, 1992.

Lender, Mark Edward. *Dictionary of American Temperance Biography: From Temperance Reform to Alcohol Research, the 1600s to the 1980s.* Westport, Connecticut: Greenwood, 1984.

Lenz, Elinor, and Barbara Myerhoff. *The Feminization of America: How Women's Values Are Changing Our Public and Private Lives.* Los Angeles: Jeremy P. Tarcher, 1985.

Martin, Theodora Penny. *The Sound of Our Own Voices: Women's Study Clubs, 1860–1910.* Boston: Beacon, 1987.

Muncy, Robyn. *Creating a Female Dominion in American Reform, 1890–1935.* New York: Oxford University Press, 1991.

National Woman's Christian Temperance Union. *A Brief History of the Woman's Christian Temperance Union.* 2nd ed. Evanston, Illinois: The Union Signal, 1907.

Ravenel, Mazyck P., ed. *A Half Century of Public Health.* New York: American Public Health Association, 1921.

Roosevelt, Theodore. *Realizable Ideals: Earl Lecture of Pacific Theological Seminary*

Delivered at Berkeley, California, in 1911. Essay Index Reprint Series. Freeport, New York: Books for Libraries, 1969. First published 1911.

Ross, Edward Alsworth. *Sin and Society: An Analysis of Latter Day Sin and Society.* New York: Harper and Row, 1973. Reprint of Houghton, Mifflin, 1907.

Rothstein, William G. *American Physicians in the Nineteenth Century: From Sects to Science.* Baltimore: Johns Hopkins University Press, 1972.

Scott, Anne Firor. *The Southern Lady: From Pedestal to Politics, 1830–1930.* Chicago: University of Chicago Press, 1970.

_____. *Making the Invisible Woman Visible.* Urbana and Chicago: University of Illinois Press, 1984.

Sinclair, Upton. *The Jungle.* New York: Doubleday, Page, 1906.

Smith, Page. *America Enters the World: A People's History of the Progressive Era and World War I.* New York: McGraw Hill, 1985.

_____. *The Rise of Industrial America: A People's History of the Post-Reconstruction Era.* New York: McGraw Hill, 1984.

Starr, Paul. *The Social Transformation of American Medicine.* New York: Basic, 1982.

Steele, Joel Dorman. *Hygienic Physiology, with a Special Reference to the use of Alcoholic Drinks and Narcotics.* New York and Chicago: A. S. Barnes, 1884.

Sullivan, Mark. *Our Times: The United States, 1900–1925.* Vol. II. America Finding Herself Series. New York: Charles Scribner's Sons, 1927.

Temin, Peter. *Taking Your Medicine: Drug Regulation in the United States.* Cambridge: Harvard University Press, 1980.

Thelen, David P. *The New Citizenship: Origins of Progressivism in Wisconsin, 1885–1900.* Columbia: University of Missouri Press, 1972.

_____. *Paths of Resistance: Tradition and Dignity in Industrializing Missouri.* New York and Oxford: Oxford University Press, 1986.

Tralalay, Paul, ed., *Drugs in Our Society.* Baltimore: Johns Hopkins University Press, 1964.

Tyrrell, Ian. *Woman's World, Woman's Empire: The Woman's Christian Temperance Union in International Perspective, 1880–1930.* Chapel Hill and London: University of North Carolina Press, 1991.

U.S. Congress. House. Committee on Interstate and Foreign Commerce. 1904. *Hearings on the Pure Food Bills H.R. 5077 and 6295 for Preventing the Adulteration, Misbranding, and Imitation of Foods, Beverages, Candies, Drugs, and Condiments in the District of Columbia and the Territories, and for Regulating Interstate Traffic Therein, and for Other Purposes.* 57th Cong., 1st sess., January 5, 1904.

U.S. Congress. House and Senate. Entries relating to the Pure Food, Drink, and Drug Bill. 56th–59th Congresses. *Congressional Record* (1903–1906). Vols. 36–40.

U.S. Congress. Senate. Committee on Manufactures. 1904. *Hearings on the Bill (S. 198) For Preventing the Adulteration, Misbranding, and Imitation of Foods, Drugs, and Condiments in the District of Columbia and the Territories, and for Regulating Interstate Traffic Therein, and for Other Purposes, and the Bill (H.R. 6295) for Preventing the Adulteration or Misbranding of Foods or Drugs, and for Regulating Traffic Therein, and for Other Purposes.* 57th Cong., 1st sess., January 6, 1904.

U. S. Congress. Senate. Committee on Manufacturers. 1900. *Adulteration of Food*

Products. Report (516) submitted by William E. Mason. 56th Cong., 1st sess., 1900.

Weinberg, Arthur, and Lila Weinberg, eds. *The Muckrakers: The Era in Journalism That Moved America to Reform — The Most Significant Magazine Articles of 1902–1912*. Paperback edition. New York: G.P. Putnam's Sons, 1964. Originally published, New York: Simon and Schuster, 1961.

Wells, Mildred White, ed., *Unity in Diversity: The History of the General Federation of Women's Clubs*. Washington, D.C.: General Federation of Women's Clubs, 1953.

Wheeler, Adade Mitchell, and Marlene Stein Wortman. *The Roads They Made: Women in Illinois History*. Chicago: Charles H. Kerr, 1977.

Wiebe, Robert H. *The Search for Order, 1877–1920*. New York: Hill and Wang, 1967.

Wiley, Harvey W. *Harvey W. Wiley: An Autobiography*. Indianapolis: Bobbs-Merrill, 1930.

_____. *Foods and Their Adulteration: Origin, Manufacture, and Composition of Food Products; Infants' and Invalids' Foods; Detection of Common Adulterations, and Food Standards*. 2nd ed. Philadelphia: P. Blakiston's Son, 1911.

_____. *The History of a Crime Against the Food Law: The Amazing Story of the National Food and Drugs Law Intended to Protect the Health of the People Perverted to Protect Adulteration of Foods and Drugs*. Washington, D.C.: Privately published by Harvey W. Wiley, M.D., 1929.

Willard, Frances E. *Woman and Temperance: or, The Work and Workers of the Woman's Christian Temperance Union*. 3rd ed. Hartford, Connecticut: Park, 1883.

_____. *Glimpses of Fifty Years: The Autobiography of an American Woman*. Chicago: Woman's Christian Temperance Union Publishing Association, 1889.

Wilson, Robert Cumming. *Drugs and Pharmacy in the Life of Georgia, 1733–1959*. Atlanta: Foot and Davis, 1959.

Wood, Mary I. *The History of the General Federation of Women's Clubs for the First Twenty-two Years of Its Organization*. New York: History Department of the General Federation of Women's Clubs, 1912.

Young, James Harvey. *The Toadstool Millionaires: A Social History of Patent Medicines in America Before Federal Regulation*. Princeton: Princeton University Press, 1961.

_____. *The Medical Messiahs: A Social History of Health Quackery in Twentieth-Century America*. Princeton: Princeton University Press, 1967.

Zeuch, Lucius M. S., ed. *History of Medical Practice in Illinois*. Chicagp: The Book Press, 1927.

Unpublished Dissertations and Theses

Armeny, Susan. "Resolute Enthusiasts: The Effort To Professionalize American Nursing, 1880–1915." Ph.D. dissertation. Columbia: University of Missouri, 1983.

Cook, Rufus George. "A Study of the Political Career of Weldon Brinton Heyburn Through His First Term in the United States Senate, 1852–1909." Master's thesis. Moscow, Idaho: University of Idaho, 1964.

Eickhoff, Harold Walter. "The Organization and Regulation of Medicine in Missouri, 1883–1901." Ph.D. dissertation. Columbia: University of Missouri, 1964.

Meyer, Carolyn Lucile. "The Inception of Pure Food and Drugs Legislation in Missouri." Unpublished master's thesis. Columbia: University of Missouri, 1933.

Index